D0161538

DOSTOEVSKY

The adventurer
In humanity has not conceived of a race
Completely physical in a physical world.

Wallace Stevens, *L'Esthétique du Mal*.

DOSTOEVSKY

The Seeds of Revolt

1821-1849

JOSEPH FRANK

PRINCETON UNIVERSITY

PRESS

To my wife Guiguite,
  Enfin!—
and my daughters Claudine and Isabelle,
who grew up with "Dostoevsky."

CONTENTS

vii

CONTENTS

LIST OF ILLUSTRATIONS

PREFACE

The present volume is the first of a series devoted to the life and works of Dostoevsky. As presently planned, it will be composed of four volumes, dealing, in chronological sequence, each with another period of Dostoevsky's life. A complete version of the entire work already exists in draft, and I hope to be able to publish the remainder—other obligations permitting—within a reasonable number of years.

The entire project originated about twenty years ago, when I was invited to give a series of lectures by the Christian Gauss Seminars at Princeton University. The Seminars were then under the chairmanship of E.B.O. Borgerhoff, soon to become a dear friend, and whose rare combination of debonair charm and scholarly seriousness still remains alive in the memory of those who knew him well. At that time I was very much interested in the new Existentialist literature making such a splash in the immediate postwar period, and I chose as my subject the topic, "Existential Themes in Modern Literature." To provide some historical background, I began with an analysis of Dostoevsky's *Notes from Underground* as a precursor of the mood and the themes that one found in French Existentialism. My interpretation of that work derived from the writings of Leo Shestov and Nikolay Berdyaev, and I stressed the irrationalism and amoralism of the underground man as he tragically and defiantly asserted the freedom of his personality in the face of the laws of nature, whatever the cost to himself and to others.

Even as I was expounding this view, though, I had the uneasy feeling that it was far from adequate. What it accentuated in the work was unquestionably there; but so was much else to which an Existentialist reading offered no clue whatever. When I began to write up my lectures, I decided to study *Notes from Underground* more thoroughly, and to investigate the social-cultural background that so obviously served as Dostoevsky's point of departure. This led me to read whatever I could find about the period in the languages at my disposal, and finally, when the limitations of such sources became apparent, to learn Russian. As time went by, I realized that my interest in Existentialism had greatly diminished, while my fascination with Dostoevsky and Russian culture of the nineteenth century continued to grow by leaps and bounds. I abandoned the idea of writing up my lectures and decided instead to write a book on Dostoevsky.

This was the far-away and almost accidental origin of the present book and its successors—though I had no intention of writing a work on any such scale when I started out.

The intrinsic interest of the material, however, led me on further and further. And I gradually realized that, if I were to do justice to my vision of Dostoevsky, it would be necessary to present him in the context of a massive reconstruction of the social-cultural life of his period. For this vision may be summed up, briefly, by saying that I see Dostoevsky's work as a brilliant artistic synthesis of the major issues of his time, a personal utterance, to be sure, but one, more than most, oriented by concerns outside himself. It is not simply—as we too often tend to think in the West—the passionately febrile expression of an unbalanced but extraordinarily gifted temperament. Indeed, one way of defining Dostoevsky's genius is to locate it in his ability to fuse his private dilemmas with those raging in the society of which he was a part.

My interest in Dostoevsky's personal life is therefore strictly limited, and anyone who seeks a conventional biography in the following pages will be sorely disappointed. Numerous works of this kind already exist, and I never had any intention of adding still another to their number. I sketch in the background of the events of Dostoevsky's private existence, but I deal at length only with those aspects of his quotidian experience which seem to me to have some critical relevance—only with those that help to cast some light on his books. My work is thus not a biography, or if so, only in a special sense—for I do not go from the life to the work, but rather the other way round. My purpose is to interpret Dostoevsky's art, and this purpose commands my choice of detail and my perspective. It has always seemed to me paradoxical that what is of greatest interest about the life of an artist—indeed, the only reason we are concerned with him at all, i.e., his works—are ordinarily scanted in the usual biography in favor of personal anecdote and the details of private life. Such a narrative may contribute to the study of human character, or to the social history of the period it depicts, but it usually leaves art in the background; or at best, treats it only as ancillary and as an adjunct to more fundamental life-experiences. I have adopted the opposite procedure of making Dostoevsky the man an adjunct to his artistic concerns and their products—a procedure which seems to me to correspond more accurately to the actual hierarchy of values in the life of any creative personality.

This does not mean that I see any unbridgeable gap between art and "life"; but this latter word can be taken on the level of *l'homme moyen sensuel*, or on that of an artist who lives equally at the level of mind, spirit, and consciousness. For this reason, rather than devoting space to the routine incidents of Dostoevsky's day-to-day existence, I dwell much more on the social-cultural milieu in which he lived. It is from this milieu that he derived the ideas and values through which he assimilated whatever life-experiences came his way, and was enabled to transform them into the themes and technique of his art. I shall try to show that an exploration of his life from this point of view, on the plane of what Hegel would call the "objective spirit" of Dostoevsky's time, can lead to, if not a totally different, then a far better understanding of the significance of his achievement. This is of course not a new approach to Dostoevsky, particularly in the Russian criticism of the last half-century, and I am conscious of a considerable obligation to such predecessors as Leonid Grossman, N. F. Belchikov, A. S. Dolinin, and V. L. Komarovich. I have tried to build on the foundations they have laid, and to put to good use a freedom of interpretation they were not always able to enjoy.

During the twenty or so years I have thought about this book—though only able to work on it intermittently because of the demands of a teaching career largely devoted to other subjects—I have of course accumulated a great many debts of gratitude towards those who have encouraged me to persist in what, all too often, seemed a quixotic undertaking. Several of those to whom I feel most grateful are now, alas, deceased: R. P. Blackmur, Alexandre Koyré, Erich Kahler, H. B. Parkes. Their active concern for my progress was a potent stimulus in moments of discouragement, and I shall never forget an approving letter from the first at a dark moment, a smiling remark from the second that opened a whole new horizon on an important problem, an enthusiastic telephone call from the third after reading a chapter. The fourth was a teacher and inspiration of my youth who became a companion in maturity, and I should have liked to present him with a copy of this volume that he never doubted would get written.

Others who have helped me greatly over the years are Allen Tate, Francis Fergusson, and Harry Levin, to all of whom I am indebted both intellectually and personally, and on whose friendship I could always rely. John McCormick, Lionel Abel, Ralph Manheim, Charles Foster, Jackson Matthews, Theodore Weiss, Eugene Goodheart, and David Goldstein are other friends associated with the present work, and from whose presence I have derived cheer, sustenance, and ideas. M. and Mme Georges Ambrosino of Paris invariably asked about my "Dostoevski" whenever I turned up, and Mme Ambrosino translated several chapters of an early draft into French; the publication of these sections in *Critique* was the result of their efforts. I am immensely grateful for their help, offered with such warm spontaneity, and I cherish the recollection of discussions about Dostoevsky in the *cercle* that gathered around them every Saturday evening to read a philosophical text. Pierre Andler is another French friend who kindly translated articles and reviews connected with my Dostoevsky researches for *Le Contrat Social*, and exhibited a lively appreciation of their contents.

It is rare when experts in one field welcome the efforts of an unlicensed intruder into their domain. Not a professional Slavist myself, I am all the more happy to record the welcome I have received from various members of the academic community of Slavists in the United States. They kindly overlooked the deficiencies of my preparation, and were more than willing to give my ideas a hearing. Their advice has constantly served to guide my own researches, and their knowledge has always been at my disposal to supplement the gaps of my own. I am particularly grateful to Rufus Mathewson for many years of close friendship and conversations in Grimaud, Paris, New York, and London, and to Robert L. Jackson, Robert Belknap, Donald Fanger, my colleague Clarence Brown, Victor Weintraub, René Wellek, and Victor Ehrlich for their support and stimulation. It was also my good fortune to have encountered Father George Florovsky at Princeton, and to imbibe, from this greatest of living Russian cultural historians, some sense of the tradition descending from Dostoevsky of which he is one of the last representatives.

Richard Ellmann selflessly took time out from his own work to read the first several chapters of the final draft, and to suggest many corrections and improvements which have been incorporated into the text. Paul Zweig read an earlier version of the same material, and his perceptive criticisms led to a complete recasting of the original; Robert Belknap read the same manuscript, and made many helpful comments. Rufus Mathewson, Harry Levin, Francis Fergusson, and S. Frederick Starr read the final draft, and gave me the benefit of their observations. My heartfelt thanks to them all.

Over the years I have received much support from various foundations and academic institutions. I should like to thank the Guggenheim Foundation, the Bollingen Foundation, and the American Council of Learned Societies for grants-in-aid. The University of Minnesota, Rutgers University, Harvard University, and Princeton University were all kind enough to supply funds for research and editorial expenses. My work was also much facilitated by the cooperation of librarians in these universities, and, in France, at the École des

Langues Orientales, the reading room of the Institut des Études Slaves, and the Bibliothèque de la Sorbonne.

My typist, Mrs. Helen Wright, patiently untangled all my errors, and cheered me greatly by finding the text itself to be absorbing. Gaylord Brynolfson took the laborious task of compiling the index off my shoulders and corrected many textual oversights. The title of the present volume was supplied by my oldest daughter, Claudine, in the course of a long automobile trip between Marbella and Santander. My mother-in-law, Mrs. Paulette Straus, eagerly fulfilled a long-awaited opportunity to help with the proofreading. My copy editor, Polly Hanford, was a patient and skillful guide through the intricacies of preparing the book for the press.

My wife, French by birth and a mathematician by profession, carefully scrutinized each draft as it came into being, and held me to the highest standards of conceptual rigor as well as lucidity and felicity of expression. Whatever of such qualities this book may possess is as much her work as my own; and her faith in the value of what I had undertaken, as the years went by and the end never seemed to be in sight, is really responsible for the project having been brought even as far as the publication of this first volume.

Joseph Frank

Paris, February, 1976

TRANSLITERATION

The problem of transliteration is always a difficult one, and I have opted for the simplest solution. For all Russian words, names or otherwise, I use System I in the transliteration chart contained in J. Thomas Shaw, *The Transliteration of Modern Russian for English Language Publications* (Madison, Milwaukee, and London, 1967), 8-9. I have, however, occasionally inserted a "y" to indicate a soft sound where this would not be the natural pronunciation of the transliterated word in English, even though System I does not pay any attention to this feature of Russian. And I have always used English forms, rather than transliteration, where such exist and have become customary (Alexander rather than Aleksandr, for example).

Citations to Dostoevsky's texts in Russian are made in two editions. The *Arabic* numerals refer to the volumes of the new Soviet edition now in the course of publication: F. M. Dostoevsky, *Polnoe Sobranie Sochinenii* (Leningrad, 1972–); 13 volumes of this planned 30-volume publication have so far been published as this work goes to press. For material not yet in this edition, I have used *Roman* numerals to refer to the best previous Soviet edition: F. M. Dostoevsky, *Polnoe Sobranie Khudozhestvennikh Proizvedenii*, ed. B. Tomashevsky and K. Khalabaev, 13 vols. (Leningrad, 1926-1930).

For my quotations from Dostoevsky's short stories and novels, I have used the translations of Constance Garnett because she takes fewer liberties with the literal meaning than more recent translators. However, I have not hesitated to alter her version where this seemed indicated. If no source is given for a translation, I have made it myself.

PART I

Moscow

I see in criticism a fervent effort to bring out the full power of the chosen work. It is just the opposite, then, to what Sainte-Beuve does when he takes us from the work to the author and then sprays him with a shower of anecdotes. Criticism is not biography, nor is it justified as an independent labor unless its purpose is to complete the work. This means first of all that the critic is expected to provide in his work all the sentimental and ideological aids which will enable the ordinary reader to receive the most intense and clearest possible impression of the book.

José Ortega y Gasset, *Meditations on Quixote*

CHAPTER 1

Prelude

The last years of the reign of Alexander I were a troubled, uncertain, and gloomy time in Russian history. Alexander had come to the throne as the result of a palace revolution against his father, Paul I, whose increasingly erratic and insensate rule led his entourage to suspect madness. The coup was carried out with at least the implicit consent of Alexander, whose accession to power, after his father's murder, at first aroused great hopes of liberal reform in the small, enlightened segment of Russian society. Alexander's tutor, carefully selected by his grandmother Catherine the Great, had been a Swiss of advanced liberal views named La Harpe. This partisan of the Enlightenment imbued his royal pupil with republican and even democratic ideas; and during the first years of his reign, Alexander surrounded himself with a band of young aristocrats sharing his progressive persuasions. A good deal of work was done preparing plans for major social reforms, such as the abolition of serfdom and the granting of personal civil rights to all members of the population. Alexander's attention, however, was soon diverted from internal affairs by the great drama then proceeding on the European stage—the rise of Napoleon as a world-conqueror. Allied at first with Napoleon, and then becoming his implacable foe, Alexander I led his people in the great national upsurge that resulted in the defeat of the Grand Army and its hitherto invincible leader.

The triumph over Napoleon brought Russian armies to the shores of the Atlantic, and exposed both officers and men (the majority of the troops were peasant serfs) to prolonged contact with the relative freedom and amenities of life in Western Europe. It was expected that, in reward for the loyalty of his people, Alexander would make some spectacular gesture consonant with his earlier intentions and institute the social reforms that had been put aside to meet the menace of Napoleon. But the passage of time, and the epochal events he had lived through, had not left Alexander unchanged. More and more he had come under the influence of the religious mysticism and irrationalism so prevalent in the immediate post-Napoleonic era. Instead of reforms, the period between 1820 and 1825 saw an intensification of reaction and the repression of any overt manifestation of liberal ideas and tendencies in Russia.

Meanwhile, secret societies had begun to form among the most brilliant and cultivated cadres of the Russian officers' corps. These societies, grouping the scions of some of the most important aristocratic families, sprang from impatience with Alexander's dilatoriness and a desire to transform Russia on the model of Western liberal and democratic ideas. Some of the societies were moderate in their aims, others more radical; but all were discontent with Alexander's evident abandonment of his earlier hopes and ambitions as a social reformer. Alexander died unexpectedly in November 1825; and the societies seized the opportunity a month later, at the time of the coronation of Nicholas I, to launch a pitifully abortive eight-hour uprising known to history as the Decembrist insurrection. An apocryphal story about this event has it that the mutinous troops, told to shout for "Constantine and *konstitutsia*" (Constantine, the older brother of Nicholas, had renounced the throne and had a reputation as a liberal), believed that the second noun, whose gender in Russian is feminine, referred to Constantine's wife. Whether true or only a witticism, the story highlights the isolation of the aristocratic rebels; and their revolution was crushed with a few whiffs of grapeshot by the new Tsar, who condemned five of the ringleaders to be hanged and thirty-one to be exiled to Siberia for life. Nicholas thus provided the nascent Russian intelligentsia with its first candidates for the new martyrology that would soon replace the saints of the Orthodox Church.

Feodor Mikhailovich Dostoevsky was born in Moscow on October 3, 1821, just a few years before this crucial event in Russian history; and he was, of course, too young at the time to have had any awareness of the ill-fated uprising and its tragic aftermath. But these events, nonetheless, were destined to be interwoven with his life in the most intimate fashion. The world in which Dostoevsky grew up lived in the shadow of the Decembrist insurrection, and suffered from the harsh police-state atmosphere instituted by Nicholas I to ensure that nothing similar could occur again. Later, himself an exile in Siberia, Dostoevsky would meet the wives and families of the surviving Decembrists, who had dedicated themselves to alleviating the lot of the newly arrived "unfortunates." These women had voluntarily followed their husbands to Siberia; and their selfless devotion, as well as their unceasing efforts to soften the blows of fate for a new generation of political exiles, served him as a living refutation of all theories denying the existence of free will and the possibility of moral heroism and self-sacrifice.

Most important of all, the Decembrist insurrection marked the opening skirmish in the long and deadly duel between the Russian intelligentsia and the supreme autocratic power that shaped the course of Russian history and Russian culture in Dostoevsky's lifetime. And it was out of the inner moral and spiritual crises of this intelligentsia —out of their self-alienation, and their desperate search for new values on which to found their lives—that the child born in Moscow at the conclusion of the reign of Alexander I would one day produce his great novels.

CHAPTER 2

The Family

Of all the great Russian writers of the first part of the nineteenth century—Pushkin, Lermontov, Gogol, Herzen, Turgenev, Tolstoy, Nekrasov—Dostoevsky was the only one who did not come from a family belonging to the landed gentry. This is a fact of great importance, and influenced the view he took of his own position as a writer. Comparing himself with his great rival Tolstoy, as he did very frequently in later life, Dostoevsky defined the latter's work as being that of a "historian," not a novelist. For, in his view, Tolstoy depicted the life "which existed in the tranquil and stable, long-established Moscow landowners' family of the middle-upper stratum." Such a life, with its settled traditions of culture and fixed moral-social norms, had become in the nineteenth century only that of a small "minority" of Russians; it was "the life of the exceptions." The life of the majority, on the other hand, was rather one of confusion and moral chaos, of a social order in continual flux, of the incessant destruction of all the traditions of the past. Dostoevsky felt that his own work was an attempt to grapple with the chaos of the present, while Tolstoy's *Childhood, Boyhood, Youth* and *War and Peace* (it was these that he specifically had in mind) were pious efforts to enshrine for posterity the beauty of a gentry-life already vanishing and doomed to extinction. (Even in *Anna Karenina*, where Tolstoy does depict some of the moral instability that began to undermine the gentry in mid-century —an instability whose consequences can be seen in the plays of Chekhov—he still portrays gentry-life with more sympathy than Dostoevsky could ever feel.)[1]

Such a self-definition, made at a late stage of Dostoevsky's career, of course represents the distillation of many years of reflection on his literary position. But it also throws a sharp light back on Dostoevsky's own past, and helps us to see that his earliest years were spent in an atmosphere which prepared him to become the chronicler of the moral consequences of flux and change, and of the breakup of the traditional forms of Russian life. This does not mean, as too many biographers have tried to make us believe, that there was any "moral chaos" in Dostoevsky's life as a child similar to what we find in his novels.

6

1. Dr. M. A. Dostoevsky

2. Mme M. F. Dostoevsky

The assumption that he must have suffered himself all the abuses and indignities that he heaps on his various child-characters—particularly on the young hero of *A Raw Youth*—goes back to the long-discredited positivist postulate that literature can only be a literal slice of the writer's own life. But if it is illegitimate to identify Dostoevsky's life and work in this photographic fashion, a less mechanical version of such a relation should not be excluded; and the lack, during his early years, of a unified social tradition in which he could feel at home unquestionably shaped his imaginative vision. Dostoevsky's family background is marked by the clash of the old and the new in Russian life to which he was so unusually sensitive and attentive later; and we can also discern a rankling uncertainty about status that helps to explain his acute understanding for the psychological scars inflicted by social inequality.

Originally, on his father's side, the Dostoevskys had been a family belonging to the Lithuanian nobility, whose name comes from a small village (Dostoevo, in the district of Pinsk) awarded to an ancestor in the sixteenth century. From that time on, the Dostoevsky name frequently appears in the annals of the troubled border provinces of Southwest Russia. The region was one of continual strife between conflicting nationalities and creeds (Russian Orthodoxy and Polish Catholicism); and branches of the Dostoevsky family fought on both sides. The Orthodox Dostoevskys, however, falling on hard times, sank into the lowly class of the non-monastic clergy. Dostoevsky's paternal great-grandfather was a Uniat archpriest in the Ukrainian town of Bratslava; his grandfather was a priest of the same persuasion; and this is where his father was born. The Uniat denomination was a compromise worked out by the Jesuits as a means of proselytizing among the predominantly Orthodox peasantry of the region: Uniats continued to celebrate the Orthodox rites, but accepted the supreme authority of the Pope. Dostoevsky's horrified fascination with the Jesuits, whom he believed capable of any villainy to win power over men's souls, may perhaps first have been stimulated by some remark about the creed of his forebears.

Since the non-monastic clergy in Russia form a caste rather than a profession or a calling, Dostoevsky's father was naturally destined to follow the same career as *his* father. But, after graduating from a seminary at the age of fifteen, he slipped away from home, made his way to Moscow, and there succeeded in gaining admittance to the Imperial Medical-Surgical Academy in 1809. Assigned to service in a Moscow hospital during the campaign of 1812, he continued to serve in various posts as a military doctor until 1821, when he ac-

cepted a position at the Mariinsky Hospital for the Poor located on
what was then the outskirts of Moscow. His official advancement in
the service of the state was steady, if by no means spectacular; and in
April 1828, being awarded the order of St. Anna third class "for especially zealous service,"[2] he was promoted to the rank of collegiate
assessor. This entitled him to the legal status of noble in the official
Russian class system; and he hastened to establish his claim to its
privileges. On June 28, 1828, he inscribed his own name and that of
his two sons, Mikhail and Feodor (aged eight and seven years old,
respectively) on the rolls of the hereditary nobility of Moscow.

Dr. Dostoevsky had thus succeeded, with a good deal of determina-
tion and tenacity, in pulling himself up by his bootstraps, and rising from the despised priestly class to that of civil servant, member
of a learned profession, and nobleman. It is clear from the memoirs
of Dostoevsky's younger brother Andrey—our only reliable source
for these early years—that the children had been informed about the
family's ancient patent of nobility, and looked on their father's recent
elevation only as a just restoration of their rightful rank. Andrey remarks jocularly that their father had not pressed his claim to nobility
earlier because gathering together the necessary documents would
have been too expensive.[3] The Dostoevskys, it seems evident, thought
of themselves as belonging to the old gentry-aristocracy rather than
to the new service nobility created by Peter the Great—the class to
which, in fact, their father had just acceded. But their actual place
in society was in flagrant contradiction with this flattering self-image.

Medicine was an honorable but not very honorific profession in
Russia; and Dr. Dostoevsky's salary, which he was forced to supplement with private practice, was barely enough for his needs. The
Dostoevskys lived in a small, cramped apartment on the hospital
grounds, and living space was always a problem. Mikhail and Feodor
slept in a windowless compartment separated by a partition from the
antechamber; the oldest girl Varvara slept on a couch in the living
room; the younger children spent the nights in the bedroom of the
parents. It is true, as Andrey notes enviously, that his family had a
staff of six servants (a coachman, a so-called lackey, a cook, a housemaid, a laundress, and a *nyanya* or governess for the children); but
this should not be taken as an indication of affluence. From Andrey's
comment on the "lackey," who was really a *dvornik* or janitor, we see
how eager the Dostoevskys were to keep up appearances and conform
to the gentry style of life. His job was to supply the stoves with wood
in winter and to bring water for tea from a fountain two versts dis-
tant from the hospital; but when Marya Feodorovna went to town on

foot, he put on a livery and a three-cornered hat and walked proudly behind his mistress. When she used the coach without the doctor, the livery appeared again and the "lackey" stood impressively on the back footboard. "This was the unbreakable rule of Moscow etiquette in those days,"[4] Andrey remarks wryly. Dostoevsky certainly remembered this rule, and his parents' adherence to its prescripts, when Mr. Golyadkin in *The Double* hires a carriage and a livery for his barefoot servant Petrushka in order to increase his social standing in the eyes of the world.

The Dostoevskys thus aspired to live in a style really above their actual means, and their pretensions to gentry-status were wistfully incongruous with their true position in society. Dostoevsky would one day compare Alexander Herzen, born (even if out of wedlock) into the very highest stratum of the ruling class, with the critic Vissarion Belinsky, who was "not a *gentilhomme* at all! Oh no! (God knows from whom he descended! His father, it seems, was a military surgeon)."[5] So, of course, was Dostoevsky's; and the remark indicates what he must have learned to perceive as the reality of his family's situation. Despite their legal right to be considered nobility, Dr. Dostoevsky and his offspring would never enjoy the consideration to which they felt entitled by right of descent from noble forebears. Dostoevsky would later depict this old aristocracy in his works either satirically, or, in the single case of Prince Myshkin, in terms of a moral "ideal" not yet embodied in Russian social reality. In *A Raw Youth*, he throws out the suggestion of a "democratic" aristocracy of merit, which would be "an assembly of the best people in the true and literal sense, not in the sense in which it was said of the privileged class in the past" (8:186). Like his father, Dostoevsky always continued to value "aristocratic" status; but he dreamed of an aristocracy freed from all those features of snobbery, wealth, and class pride which had effectively excluded the Dostoevskys from regaining their place in the ranks of the gentry.

2

While stationed at a Moscow Hospital in 1819, the thirty-year-old Dr. Dostoevsky must have mentioned to a colleague that he was seeking a suitable bride. For he was then introduced to the family of Feodor Timofeevich Nechaev, a well-to-do Moscow merchant with an attractive, nineteen-year-old daughter, Marya Feodorovna. Marriages in those days, especially in the merchant class, were not left to chance or inclination. Dr. Dostoevsky, after being approved by the parents, was probably allowed to catch a glimpse of his future bride in church, and then invited to meet her after he agreed to a betrothal; the introduction to the girl was the sign of consent, and the future bride had nothing to say about the matter. In 1840 Dostoevsky's sister Varvara, a year younger than himself, was married off in exactly the same way by his mother's family. Both Dr. Dostoevsky and his new in-laws were similar in having risen from lowly origins to a higher position on the Russian social scale, and the latter boasted of a tradition both of cultivation and civic spirit: Dostoevsky's mother was very far from being the uncouth daughter of a typical merchant house. It is not surprising that her family and Dr. Dostoevsky should each have found the other very suitable; and relations between them were at first very cordial. Strains soon appeared, however, which, without leading to an open break, made the atmosphere between the two families tense and edgy.

The Nechaev family were very proud of a maternal ancestor, Mikhail Feodorovich Kotelnitsky, who had been educated enough to work as proofreader in a Moscow publishing house specializing in religious literature, and who, Andrey says, "was in close touch with all the writers of that time" (the end of the eighteenth century).[6] Andrey claims that Kotelnitsky belonged to a noble lineage; but if so, it was one that had not yet adopted European dress or manners. His portrait shows him in Russian costume and with a very long beard, which was worn only by the clergy, merchants, religious dissenters (these last two groups were often the same), and peasants. His son, Marya Feodorovna's uncle, studied medicine and eventually became a professor on the Medical Faculty of the University of Moscow. This learned great-uncle, seen only on festive occasions, is evoked very vividly by Andrey, and he must have seemed less strange to the Dostoevsky children—more like their own father—than other members of their mother's family. Each year during Easter week he took the brood of young male Dostoevskys to visit the street fair—the tumblers, the jugglers, the Petrouchkas, the dancing bears—set up in the field facing his small wooden house.

Looming much larger on the Dostoevsky horizon, however, were other members of Mme Dostoevsky's family, all still firmly anchored in their merchant background. Each week their maternal grandfather came to dinner on Thursday, and the children eagerly awaited his visit because he always brought them some candy. He was invariably clad in the same tawny, old-fashioned frock coat, with a medal dangling from the buttonhole on a ribbon of the Order of St. Anna. The inscription it bore was: "Not of us, Not for us, but in Thy Name!";[7] and this decoration became the symbol of a family tradition linking the Dostoevsky offspring with the heroic past of their country.

Their mother often told the children about the invasion of Moscow in 1812, when her family had evacuated the city a day or so before the arrival of Napoleon and his troops. As they were crossing a river in their carriage, an accident occurred and they were almost drowned; but though their lives were spared, the family fortune was destroyed. Their grandfather had been carrying his entire capital on his person in paper currency, and the bills were rendered worthless by their immersion. Nonetheless, on his return, he insisted on paying all his creditors down to the last ruble. No doubt it was this story which first brought the awesome and threatening name of Napoleon to Dostoevsky's awareness; but one wonders how much he could have admired the image of his grandfather's commercial probity. To a young boy whose imagination was being fed, as we shall soon see, on the more glamorous events of Karamzin's history of Russia and on the aristocratic personages of the Romantic historical novel both Russian and European, such a family tradition would probably not have proved very attractive. Dr. Dostoevsky was not raising his sons—the two older ones in particular, who were more strongly under his influence than the younger children—to take a place, however honorable, in the merchant milieu where such a story had been cherished and preserved.

The older sister of Dostoevsky's mother, Alexandra Feodorovna, had married into a family very much like her own. Her husband, A. M. Kumanin, was of merchant origin but had risen to fill various official functions; two of his brothers had served as Mayors of Moscow. The Kumanins were among those merchant families whose wealth allowed them to compete with the gentry in the opulence of their way of life; and Andrey gives a revealing picture of the arrival of his aunt to visit his mother and of the impression it made on the children. "From time to time, about twice a month, the modest . . . street resounded with the cry of the postilion, 'Slow down!, Slow down!, Slow down!,' . . . and into the courtyard of the Mariinsky Hospital drove a two-seater coach with a team of four horses and a lackey on the rear footboard, which stopped before the entrance of our apartment."[8] The Kumanins, as we see, were not averse to displaying their wealth; and they lived in a luxurious and spacious house with two lackeys always in attendance at the front door (which was used, however, only on the occasion of a formal visit). But the external trappings of gentry-life, so far as one can judge, had little effect on their mentality or habits. Andrey remembers his Kumanin uncle, who regularly dropped in to call on his mother, always taking as refreshment only a glass of water with a few lumps of sugar, and carefully eating these with a spoon as they dissolved. Such an image well conveys some of the Old Russian quality that still clung to the manners of the Kumanins.

At first, relations between the two families went very smoothly, and Dr. Dostoevsky was the family physician of his in-laws. But then, for some unknown reason, the two men quarreled. They did not speak to each other until the death of their common father-in-law, who insisted on a reconciliation at his deathbed. A formal truce, effected in accordance with his last wish, remained purely external. The old cordiality was never reestablished, and visits were exchanged between the men only at times when propriety required a show of family solidarity. One suspects that the proud and touchy Dr. Dostoevsky, who probably felt superior to his brother-in-law both by birth and education, took offense at some remark made by his wealthier relation. In any case, he later had to swallow his pride and appeal to him for financial succor on several occasions—which certainly did not help to improve his emotional equilibrium.

Dostoevsky's own attitude to his Kumanin relatives, whom he always regarded as vulgarians concerned only with money, no doubt continues to reflect a view he had originally picked up from his father. In a letter to Mikhail just after hearing of his father's death, Dostoevsky tells him "to spit on those insignificant little souls"[9] (meaning their Moscow relatives) who were incapable of understanding higher things; but then he sat down to write a flowery letter full of apologies for never corresponding with them at all after having left Moscow and gone to study in Petersburg. Andrey speaks of the Kumanins very warmly, and they behaved, according to their lights, in a generous and praiseworthy fashion: they looked after the younger Dostoevsky orphans as if they had been their own children. But though Dostoevsky too later appealed to them for aid at critical moments in his life, he never referred to them in private without a tinge of contempt. One of the reasons may be that the injustice of social inequality first appeared to him as an awareness of the disproportionate wealth of the spiritually inferior Kumanins compared to the modest resources of his own family. No wonder he would later be able to identify so closely with characters who suffer, not so much from actual poverty, as from the humiliation of their lowly status vis-à-vis the wealthy and the powerful!

Dostoevsky spent the first thirteen years of his life entirely at home, beginning to attend school only in 1835. What do we know about his mother and father, and of the family life they created?

Dostoevsky always spoke of his mother with great warmth and affection; and the picture that emerges from the memoir material shows her to have been a very engaging and attractive person. Marya Feodorovna, as we have already remarked, was unusually cultivated for a daughter of the merchant class, and like her husband—we shall give more details in chaper 5—had assimilated a good bit of the culture of the gentry. A pastel portrait of her at the age of twenty-three, painted by a relative, shows a round, pert face, broad cheekbones, a warm and sympathetic glance, and a winsome, friendly smile much less formal than the frilly lace collar of her party gown. In a letter, she describes her character as being one of "natural gaiety";[10] and this inborn sunniness, though sorely tried by the strains of domestic life, shines through everything that we know about her.

If the Dostoevsky household, during the years of Feodor's childhood, was filled with the pleasant sounds of friendly social life, it was because Marya Feodorovna was so well liked by the other wives in the hospital society of which the Dostoevskys were a part. Andrey lists those who regularly came for a cup of coffee in the morning to chat about the price of food, the latest fashions, and the availability of materials needed for their dressmaking. Every Sunday, too, the children looked forward to the impromptu guitar concert that their mother gave with their uncle, her younger brother, who was also an accomplished performer (Dostoevsky inherited this taste for music from his mother, and remained an ardent concertgoer all his life). This much-appreciated diversion ended in 1834, when the young man was discovered to have been carrying on an affair with a pretty Dostoevsky housemaid. Reprimanded by his sister, he responded with a coarse epithet; and Dr. Dostoevsky slapped him in the face. Uncle Mikhail Feodorovich never set foot in the Dostoevsky house again, and the incident, of course, did not improve relations between Dr. Dostoevsky and his Moscow in-laws. After that time, it was only on the rare occasions when the parents went out in the evening that the children had some musical entertainment. Marya Feodorovna always told the servants to amuse them, and they came in from the kitchen to sing and dance.

Marya Feodorovna was not only a warm, loving, and cheerful mother but also a vigorous and efficient manager of the affairs of the family. Three years after Dr. Dostoevsky became a nobleman, he used his newly acquired right to own land to purchase a small estate about 150 versts from Moscow called Darovoe; the purchase was made in the name of his wife, which probably indicates that the funds came from her family. A year later, as the result of a quarrel with a neighbor over land demarcation, the Dostoevskys hastened to acquire an adjacent piece of property—the hamlet of Cheremoshnia—whose purchase caused them to go heavily into debt. No doubt the acquisition of a landed estate with peasant serfs seemed to make good business sense to the doctor; and it was a place where his family could spend the summer in the open air. But in the back of his mind there was probably also the desire to give some concrete social embodiment to his dream of becoming a member of the landed gentry. It was Marya Feodorovna, however, who went to the country every spring to supervise the work; the doctor himself could get away from his practice only on flying visits.

Located on poor farming land, which did not even furnish enough fodder for the livestock, the Dostoevsky estate yielded only a miserable existence to its peasant population; but as long as Marya Feodorovna was in charge, things did not go too badly. During the first summer, she managed, by a system of canals, to bring water into the village from a nearby spring to feed a large pond, which she then stocked with fish sent from Moscow by her husband. The peasants could water their livestock more easily, the children could amuse themselves by fishing, and the food supply was augmented. She was also a humane and kindhearted proprietor, who distributed grain for sowing to the poorest peasants in early spring when they had none of their own, even though this was considered to encourage laziness and to be bad estate-management. The discipline she enforced was the very opposite of harsh or rigorous, and Dr. Dostoevsky reprimands her several times in his letters for not being more severe. Almost a hundred years later (1925), the legend of her leniency and compassion still persisted among the descendants of the peasants of Darovoe.[11] It was no doubt from Marya Feodorovna that Dostoevsky first learned to feel that sympathy for the unfortunate and deprived that became so important for his work.

Dostoevsky's father, Mikhail Andreevich, forms a strong contrast in character to his wife. His portrait shows him to have been handsome in a rugged roughhewn way, though with coarse and heavy features. His dress uniform, with its high, stiff, gilded collar, gives an air of rigidity to the set of his head barely offset by the faintest of smiles; and the rigidity was much more typical of the man than was

15

the trace of affability. Since so much legend has accumulated around the figure of Mikhail Andreevich, it is difficult to obtain any image of him that seems reasonably balanced. A good deal of harm has been done by the casual comparison suggested by Dostoevsky's daughter Lyubov between her paternal grandfather and Feodor Pavlovich Karamazov. "I have always thought," she writes, "that Dostoevsky had his father in mind when he created the type of old Karamazov."[12] It is true that, a few sentences later, she qualifies this identification: "It must be understood that this likeness between my grandfather and the old Karamazov is merely supposition on my part, for which there is no documentary evidence." But this proviso is rarely cited, and has not prevented commentators—chief among them Sigmund Freud—from enthusiastically accepting the identification of Dr. Dostoevsky with his son's fascinatingly repulsive fictional creation. It has thus become customary to exaggerate and distort whatever facts are available about Dr. Dostoevsky so as to depict him in conformity with his presumed *alter ego*. Dr. Dostoevsky was a man who had many faults; but it must be stated very emphatically that he did not in the least resemble the cynical and dissolute patriarch of the Karamazov family. He was a hard-working medical practitioner, whose ability was so appreciated by his superiors that, when he decided to retire, he was offered a substantial promotion to change his mind (which makes very dubious the oft-repeated assertion that he was a pronounced alcoholic); he was also a faithful husband, a responsible father, and a believing Christian. These qualities did not make him either a lovable or an appealing human being; but his virtues were as important as his defects in determining the environment in which Dostoevsky grew up.

Dr. Dostoevsky, in the first place, suffered from some sort of nervous affliction that strongly affected his character and disposition. Bad weather always brought on severe headaches and resulted in moods of gloom and melancholy; the return of good weather relieved his condition and brightened his outlook. Whether this neurasthenia was a symptom of a mild form of epilepsy it is impossible to say; but Dostoevsky later traced the incidence of his own epileptic attacks to such climatic changes. If Dr. Dostoevsky was, as even Andrey Dostoevsky is forced to concede, "very exacting and impatient, and, most of all, very irritable,"[13] this can be attributed to the extreme and unremitting state of nervous tension induced by his illness. Dostoevsky, who inherited this aspect of his father's character, constantly complained in later life about his own inability to master his nerves, and was also given to uncontrollable explosions of temper.

16

Dr. Dostoevsky was thus a naggingly unhappy man, whose depressive tendencies colored every aspect of his life. They made him suspicious and mistrustful, and unable to find satisfaction in either his career or his family. He suspected the household servants of cheating, and watched over them with a cranky surveillance characteristic of his attitude toward the world in general. He believed that he was being unfairly treated in the service, and that his superiors were reaping the benefits of his unrewarded labors in the hospital. Even if both these conjectures may have had some basis in fact, he brooded over them in a manner quite out of proportion to their real importance. His relations with the Kumanins were also a continual source of vexation because, not being a strong and inwardly secure personality, his pride only had the effect of filling him with an impotent bitterness at his feelings of inferiority. He remarks in one letter that he dislikes going to visit his daughter Varvara, then living with the Kumanins, because he felt that his presence there "bored" his relatives.[14] This acute social sensitivity is another trait transmitted from father to son; many Dostoevsky characters will be tormented by the unflattering image of themselves that they see reflected in the eyes of others.

What sustained Mikhail Andreevich in the midst of his woes—what enabled him, all things considered, to lead a normal and reasonably successful life—was, first and foremost, the unstinting and limitless devotion of his wife. But in his very darkest moments, when no earthly succor seemed available, he took refuge in the conviction of his own virtue and rectitude, and in the belief that God was on his side against a hostile or indifferent world. "In Moscow," he writes to his wife on returning from the country, "I found waiting for me only trouble and vexation; and I sit brooding with my head in my hands and grieve, there is no place to lay my head, not to mention anyone with whom I can share my sorrow; but God will judge them because of my misery."[15] This astonishing conviction that he was one of God's elect, this unshakable self-assurance that he was among the chosen, constituted the very core of Dr. Dostoevsky's being. It was this which made him so self-righteous and pharisaical, so intolerant of the smallest fault, so persuaded that only perfect obedience from his family to all his wishes could compensate for all his toil and labor on their behalf. If Dostoevsky later found such sanctimonious virtue intolerable, and stressed the importance of love and forgiveness for sinners rather than harsh condemnation of their shortcomings, it is no doubt because he had suffered from his father's intractable code of morality as a boy, and had inwardly been grateful to his mother's milder and more generous version of the obligations of the Christian faith.

One should avoid, however, painting the picture of Dr. Dostoevsky with too black a palette. For while he may have made his family pay a heavy psychic price for his virtues, these virtues did exist as a fact of their daily lives. Dr. Dostoevsky was, as we shall soon see in more detail, an extremely conscientious father, who devoted an unusual amount of his time personally to educating his children. Nor, so far as his family was concerned, was he a harsh or cruel man in any brutal physical sense. In the early nineteenth century, corporal punishment was accepted as an indispensable means of instilling discipline; and in Russia the flogging and beating of both children and the lower classes was accepted as a matter of course. Dr. Dostoevsky, however, never struck any of his children, despite his irritability and his temper; the only punishment they had to fear was a verbal rebuke —sometimes severe, it is true, but all the same milder than a blow. It was to avoid having his children beaten that, though he could scarcely afford to do so, Dr. Dostoevsky sent them all to private schools rather than to public institutions. And even after his two older sons had gone away to study at military schools, Dr. Dostoevsky still continued to worry about them and to bombard them—as well as others, when his sons neglected to write—with inquiries about their welfare.

If we disregard Dr. Dostoevsky's personality and look only at the way he fulfilled his paternal responsibilities, we can understand a remark that Dostoevsky made sometime in the late 1870s, when he was most concerned about the breakup of the Russian family that he believed he could discern taking place all around him. Evidently recalling his own family life as the very *opposite* of the "accidental families" of the present, Dostoevsky said to his brother Andrey that their parents had been "outstanding people." If they had been alive in the present rather than the beginning of the century, they would still, he maintained, merit the same designation. "And such family men, such fathers . . . we ourselves are quite incapable of being, brother!"[16] he added. Such words represent only one aspect of Dostoevsky's relation to his father; but they are a tribute which, to an impartial observer, is not unwarranted by the facts.

4

Despite the diversity of their characters, there is every reason to believe that Dr. Dostoevsky and his wife were a devoted and loving couple. Their twenty years of marriage produced a family of eight children (one twin daughter died a few days after birth); and nobody reading their letters without *parti pris* can doubt that they were deeply attached to each other. "Good-bye, my soul, my little dove, my happiness, joy of my life, I kiss you until I'm out of breath. Kiss the children for me."[17] So writes Dr. Dostoevsky to Marya Feodorovna after fourteen years of marriage; and while some allowance must be made for the florid rhetoric of the time, these words seem far in excess of what convention might require. Marya Feodorovna is equally lavish with her endearments. "Make the trip here soon, my sweetheart," she writes from Darovoe, "come my angel, my only wish is to have you visit me, you know that it's the greatest holiday for me, the greatest pleasure in my life is when you're with me."[18]

"As far back as I can recall," Dostoevsky remarked in 1873, "I remember the love shown me by my parents."[19] Dostoevsky's works are so full of poor, unhappy, abandoned and brutalized children that there has been an inevitable tendency to identify his own childhood with such experiences, despite his explicit disclaimer. The letters of his parents, however, leave no doubt that his recollections were not gilded in any way. They reflect the image of a close-knit and united family, where concern for the children was in the foreground of the parents' preoccupation. V. S. Nechaeva—the Soviet Russian scholar who has studied Dostoevsky's family life with the most sobriety, and edited and published the letters of his parents—comments that "there would seem to be no doubt of the genuine devotion of Mikhail Andreevich Dostoevsky to his family, his love for his wife, and the care for his children that fills all his letters. It would be strange to see in the expression of these feelings any design or falsity—the letters, in fact, express with total sincerity the fundamental significance and content of the interests of Mikhail Andreevich."[20] The same is true even more strongly of the letters of his wife, which add warmth and tenderness to Dr. Dostoevsky's rigorous sense of parental obligation.

Nonetheless, the letters also reveal a secret tragedy that undermined what seems to have been this exemplary marriage. Dr. Dostoevsky's emotional insecurity was so great, his suspicion and mistrust of the world sometimes reached such a pathological pitch, that he became intensely jealous of his wife and suspected her of infidelity. One such incident occurred in 1835, when he learned, apparently to his surprise, that she was pregnant with the child who became Dostoevsky's youngest sister Alexandra. Andrey recalls seeing his mother, at this time, break into hysterical weeping after having communicated some information to his father by which he was surprised and vexed. The scene, he explains, was probably caused by the announcement of his mother's pregnancy; but he assumes that his father's displeasure was only at the prospect of an unwanted new addition to the family.

The letters indicate, however, that Dr. Dostoevsky was tormented by doubts about his wife's faithfulness, although he made no direct accusations. Schooled by long experience, Marya Feodorovna was able to read his state of mind through the distraught tone of his letters and his deep mood of depression. "My friend," she writes, "thinking all this over, I wonder whether you are not tortured by that unjust suspicion, so deadly for us both, that I have been unfaithful to you."[21]

Her denial of any wrongdoing is written with an eloquence and expressiveness that even her second son might have envied; if literary talent can be inherited, we need look no further to see from whom Dostoevsky acquired his own. "I swear," she writes, ". . . that my present pregnancy is the seventh and strongest bond of our mutual love, on my side a love that is pure, sacred, chaste and passionate, unaltered from the day of our marriage." There is also a fine sense of dignity in her explanation that she has never before deigned to reaffirm her marriage oath "because I was ashamed to lower myself by swearing to my faithfulness during our sixteen years of marriage."[22] Dr. Dostoevsky nonetheless remained adamant in his dark imaginings, and even accused her of deliberately delaying her departure from the country, so as to avoid returning to Moscow, until it was too late to make the journey without risking a miscarriage. In reply, she writes sadly that "time and years flow by, creases and bitterness spread over the face; natural gaiety of character is turned into sorrowful melancholy, and that's my fate, that's the reward for my chaste, passionate love; and if I were not strengthened by the purity of my conscience and my hope in Providence, the end of my days would be pitiful indeed."[23]

One could easily imagine the life of the Dostoevsky family being torn apart and subject to constant emotional upheaval because of recurring episodes of this kind. But, so far as can be judged, nothing dramatic seems to have occurred. It is striking that, in the very letters we have been citing, the current of ordinary life flows on as placidly as before. Information about the affairs of the estate are exchanged, and the older boys in Moscow append the usual loving postscript to their mother; there is no break in the family routine whatever, and both partners, in the midst of recriminations, continue to assure the other of their undying love and devotion. Indeed, it is difficult to estimate just how serious a disturbance such episodes were; in this instance the crisis seems to have been quickly surmounted. Dr. Dostoevsky went to the country in July to assist at the delivery of Alexandra, and then, on returning in August, writes affectionately to his wife: "Believe me, reading your letter, I tearfully thanked God first of all, and you secondly, my dear. . . . I kiss your hand a million million times, and pray to God that you remain in good health for our happiness."[24] Not a word recalls the tensions of the previous month; Marya Feodorovna's soothing and loving presence seems to have worked wonders. We should therefore be very cautious in attempting to gauge the normal atmosphere of Dostoevsky's family life only from the handful of letters in our possession, which represent those periods when the lonely and brooding Mikhail Andreevich was apt to be at his worst.

Moreover, from everything we know about the character of the couple, it is very unlikely that the hidden strains of their married life would erupt in any unseemly fashion. If Andrey, after sixty years, remembered so vividly the one incident of his mother's sobbing, it was because displays of such extreme emotion between the parents were probably quite rare. Nothing was more important for the Dostoevskys than to present an image of well-bred propriety and gentry-refinement to the world; it is impossible to imagine them in their cramped apartment, with a household staff in the kitchen and neighboring hospital families all around, indulging in the violent quarrels and scandalous outbursts that Dostoevsky later so often depicted in his novels. If Dr. Dostoevsky's relations with his wife became tense, he probably alternated between a grim and ominously-laden silence and endless censoriousness about the minutiae of daily life. His reluctance to speak out openly in the instance of Alexandra may be taken as typical; and when Marya Feodorovna herself stated the issue bluntly, he rebuked her for writing to him so directly and possibly revealing their family secret to prying eyes. The impulse to cover and conceal is manifest, and was certainly operative in his personal behavior as well. It is therefore probable that the household in which Dostoevsky grew up was characterized far more by order, regularity, and routine, and by a deceptively calm surface of domestic tranquillity, than by the familial chaos that so preoccupied him half a century later.

But even though it is illegitimate, in my view, to make any simple-minded equation between Dostoevsky's portrayal of family life and his own childhood, the two cannot of course be separated entirely. We can hardly doubt that the gifted and perceptive little boy would become aware of the stresses underlying the sedate routine of his early years, and that he learned to feel it as beset with hidden tensions and antagonisms—as constantly subject to extreme fluctuations in emotional distance between intimacy and withdrawal. Family life for Dostoevsky would never be serene and untroubled, never something taken for granted and accepted simply as a *donnée*; it would always

21

be a battleground and a struggle of wills, just as he had first learned to sense it from the secret life of his parents. And for a boy and youth destined to become famous for his understanding of the intricacies of human psychology, it was excellent training to have been reared in a household where the significance of behavior was kept hidden from view, and where his curiosity was stimulated to intuit and unravel its concealed meanings. One may perhaps see here the origin of Dostoevsky's profound sense for the *mystery* of personality, and his tendency to explore it, as it were, from the outside in, always moving from the exterior to deeper and deeper subterranean levels that are only gradually brought to light. Possibly his preference for revealing character by sudden outbursts of self-confession may go back to the strong impression left by his father's occasional eruptions, which came as an unexpected disclosure of what had been seething and simmering in the depths. But it is time now to cut speculation short, and to turn to what can be established about Dostoevsky as a child.

CHAPTER 3

Childhood, Boyhood, Youth

Feodor Mikhailovich was the second child and second son of the Dostoevsky family. We may assume that he was swaddled, like all Russian children, and we know that he was suckled by a wet nurse. Only the eldest son Mikhail was breast-fed by Marya Feodorovna; the other children were all given to peasant wet nurses hired for the occasion because their mother developed some chest complaint that may have been a precursor of the tuberculosis from which she died. Andrey remarks that Mikhail was her favorite son for this reason; and he is the only child mentioned by name in her letters. One might imagine this as having stimulated a severe rivalry between Mikhail and the next in line, Feodor; but there is no evidence that any hostility existed. The reason is that, as Andrey observes, "older brother Mikhail was, even in childhood, less lively, less energetic, and less mettlesome than brother Feodor, who was a real ball of fire in everything he did, as our parents said."[1] Mikhail was more or less content to take a back seat to Feodor very early in their lives. He decorated the younger children with colors from his paintbox, for example, when they played Indians—a game invented by Feodor, and in which he was chief of the tribe—but did not participate and compete. Later he continued in much the same role, supplying his brother with funds to establish their magazine *Time* (*Vremya*) in the early 1860s, and serving as business manager while Feodor was in active editorial charge.

Life in the Dostoevsky family was carefully organized around the pattern of Dr. Dostoevsky's daily routine, which has been described by Andrey. The family awakened promptly at six in the morning, and at eight Dr. Dostoevsky went to the hospital for his morning rounds. The apartment then was tidied up so that, when he returned at nine, it had assumed its daytime order. Dr. Dostoevsky then spent the remainder of the morning visiting his private patients in Moscow, and during this period the children were put to their lessons. They learned to read almost as soon as they were out of the cradle, and were instructed either by tutors who came to the house or by their elder brothers and sisters; there was no lengthy period of respite in

23

their lives when they could simply indulge in the carefree pleasures and irresponsibilities of childhood. "Feodor Mikhailovich," writes his first biographer Orest Miller, reporting Dostoevsky's own recollections, "remembered . . . that they [the children] were strictly supervised and taught to study very early. At the age of four, he was already placed in front of a book and told insistently: 'Study!' "[2]

Dr. Dostoevsky returned about twelve, no doubt inquired about the work that had been accomplished, and lunch was served at one o'clock. Then he retired for his daily nap on the couch in the living room, and a deathly silence had to be maintained for one and a half to two hours so as not to disturb his rest. During the summer months, one of the children was regularly assigned to sit by the slumbering *paterfamilias* and wave away the flies with a branch freshly cut each day for the purpose. Andrey remembers the strain of sitting for this length of time as quietly as possible, and trying to make sure that the sleeper was not awakened. For if he were, a severe scolding would hail down on the luckless head of the sinner.

At four in the afternoon, the family gathered again for tea, and Dr. Dostoevsky returned to the hospital. The evenings were spent in the living room, usually lit by two tallow candles; wax candles were used only when guests were expected, or for some family holiday or feast day. Each evening before dinner, if Dr. Dostoevsky was not too busy with his sick lists, he read aloud to the children. At nine in the evening the family had dinner, and the children, after saying their prayers in front of the icon, then went to bed. "The day was spent in our family," Andrey comments, "according to a routine established once and for all, and repeated day after day, very monotonously."[3] Feodor was also subjected to this routine from his earliest years—one which combined the physical discomfort of crowded and gloomy quarters ("low ceilings and cramped rooms crush the mind and the spirit," Raskolnikov tells Sonya) with the psychic discomfort of an unrelaxing pressure to work under the eye of a stern paternal overseer.

To be sure, it would be inaccurate to picture Dostoevsky's childhood as having been completely deprived of normal amusements. In the depths of winter, no doubt, the children remained largely indoors; but when the weather permitted, they could use as playground the spacious, tree-shaded walks of the hospital grounds, which were also occupied by convalescent patients taking the air. There, under the watchful eye of their *nyanya*, they could romp around with playmates belonging to other families on the hospital staff. Such freedom, however, was always relative, and strict orders had been given—and were enforced—concerning their conduct in a public place. Ball-throwing of any kind was outlawed for fear of hitting the other strollers, and any noisy or rowdy behavior was strictly forbidden. It was also forbidden, no doubt for social reasons, to converse with the convalescing adults, who were all charity cases belonging to the lower classes of the city. But there is a tradition that Feodor, the future chronicler of the plight of "the insulted and injured," infringed this parental injunction and gave rein to his all-consuming curiosity and precocious sympathy for the unfortunate.

During the periods of mild weather, the Dostoevsky family also went for regular walks in the early evening to the wood that lay quite close to the hospital. Dr. Dostoevsky himself was in charge of these excursions, and the children were consequently held in with a very tight rein; any gamboling or frisking about, any display of exuberance or animal spirits, was out of the question. Moreover, Dr. Dostoevsky did not believe in allowing his children to waste their time in idleness, even on these family recreations. Andrey describes him taking the occasion to give them lessons in geometry, using the crazy-quilt pattern of the Moscow streets to illustrate the various types of angle. The importance of hard work and self-discipline was constantly drummed into their minds; and though their father did not terrorize them physically, his impatient vigilance constantly hung over their heads as a threat. It is probable that, when Dostoevsky spoke to his friend Dr. Yanovsky in the late 1840s about "the difficult and joyless circumstances of his childhood,"[4] he was thinking of "circumstances" such as those we have outlined, rather than the more sensational events conjured up in the imagination of various biographers creating their image after the example of Dostoevsky's novels.

2

One of the great question marks about Dostoevsky's childhood is whether there is any early evidence of the epilepsy from which he suffered in later life, any particular incident or conjunction of incidents that foreshadow its emotional ravages. The answer to this question can only be an unambiguous negative—there is no such evidence in the source material at our disposal. We do know, on Dostoevsky's own testimony, that he was the victim of an auditory hallucination in 1831 at the age of ten:—but that is all. Nonetheless, certain supposed "facts" have been worked into a legend about Dostoevsky's childhood that must be dealt with before we proceed any further. The source of this legend is Sigmund Freud's famous article, "Dostoevsky and Parricide"; and the prestige of Freud's name has given the "facts" that he adduces the stamp of "scientific" respectability. But these "facts" can be shown to be extremely dubious at best, and at worst simply mistakes.

The origin of the Dostoevsky "legend," as Freud constructs it, is a tantalizing footnote in the official biography (1883) by Orest Miller and Nikolay Strakhov. In the section written by Miller, he remarks that, according to one well-informed source, Dostoevsky's epilepsy had been linked with "a very particular piece of evidence about the illness of Feodor Mikhailovich which relates to his earliest youth and connects it with a tragic event in their [the Dostoevsky's] family life."[5] Freud evidently came across a translation of this footnote long before his article (which appeared in 1928), and refers to it in a letter to Stefan Zweig in 1920. "Somewhere in a biography of D.," he writes, "I was shown a passage which traced back the later affliction of the man to the boy's having been punished by his father under very serious circumstances—I vaguely remember the word 'tragic,' am I right? Out of 'discretion,' of course, the author didn't say what it was all about."[6] What Freud thinks "it was all about" may be inferred from his further remark that, for the author of *Primary Experiences* (*Erste Erlebnisse*)—a volume of short stories by Zweig all dealing with the sexual awakening of children and adolescents—the meaning of such a "childhood scene" does not have to be explained. It is clear that Freud is reading his own theories into the footnote, and has transformed its allusiveness into the image of a severe punishment for some childhood sexual offense (probably a punishment for masturbation leading to the formation of an acute castration complex).

What the footnote really means, of course, is anybody's guess; but the most plausible interpretation is that it springs from the murder of Dostoevsky's father by his peasants in the spring of 1839 (see note on pp. 86-87 for more recent findings on the supposed murder). This murder was kept a carefully guarded secret and never publicly acknowledged until 1921. However, rumors about it began to circulate shortly after Dostoevsky's death in 1881; and these rumors traced back the first appearance of his epilepsy to this "tragic event." We shall set aside, for later discussion, the question of whether there is any good reason to believe that Dostoevsky's first fit of epilepsy coincided with the reception of the news about his father's death. Here we merely wish to establish that the footnote, in all likelihood, refers to something that occurred when Dostoevsky was eighteen years old and far from being a child (although, to Orest Miller writing in 1883, what had happened more than forty years before could well have seemed to have been in Dostoevsky's "earliest youth"). Moreover, this occur-rence had nothing to do with a sexual trauma.

Freud could not have known about the murder of Dostoevsky's fa-ther in 1920; but by 1928 it was common knowledge. Indeed, he refers to it, in accordance with the family tradition, as the immediate cause of Dostoevsky's initial epileptic attack. Nonetheless, Freud seems to be unaware of the connection between the concealment of the murder and the mysterious footnote, and he continues to cling to the convic-tion formed years before that some "tragic event" had occurred in Dostoevsky's childhood. In his article, he specifically cites the foot-note as *evidence* of such a childhood trauma, and again alludes ironi-cally to the "discretion" which veils its "true" (i.e., sexual) significance from "biographers and scientific research workers."[7] It is because of this assumption that, without citing any additional material, he speaks self-confidently of Dr. Dostoevsky as having been "especially violent *in reality*" (italics added) toward Feodor, and of the boy as having developed, over and above the normal Oedipal antagonism, an intense death wish against his father. It was the inner conflict between this death wish (assimilated into an ego predisposed to bisexuality, hence to masochism) and a severe superego (incorporating all the harsh-ness and cruelty of the sadistic father) which, in Freud's view, trig-gered the first epileptic crisis when the death wish was transformed from fantasy into reality.

To confirm this diagnosis, Freud cites two "facts" supposedly re-vealing telltale symptoms of this death wish. "We have one certain starting point," he writes. "We know the meaning of the first attacks from which Dostoevsky suffered in his early years, long before the incidence of his 'epilepsy.' These attacks had the significance of death: they were heralded by a fear of death and consisted of lethargic, som-nolent states. The illness first came over him, while he was still a boy, in the form of a sudden, groundless melancholy, a feeling, as he later told his friend Solovyev, as though he were going to die on the spot. And there in fact followed a state exactly similar to real death. His brother Andrey tells us that even when he was quite young Feodor used to leave little notes about before he went to sleep saying that he was afraid he might fall into this death-like sleep during the night and therefore begged that his burial should be postponed for five days." Freud interprets these fears as an identification with the person one wishes dead, and as a "self-punishment for a death wish against a hated father."[8]

Once again, however, Freud is badly misled, partly no doubt be-cause of the inadequacy of his information, certainly by his eagerness to find biographical confirmation for his theory about the relation between Dostoevsky's epilepsy and supposed parricidal impulses. In the article by Solovyev, Dostoevsky dates the experiences he speaks of as having occurred about "two years before he went to Siberia"—hence in 1846; and this time coincides with the outbreak of a severe nervous disorder about which we are independently informed by his letters of the time.[9] Similarly, Andrey's information about the notes does not place them in childhood, as Freud imagines; there is no mention of any such documents in Andrey's memoirs, where he evokes these childhood years. Rather, he speaks of the notes in a context that unmistakably places them in the period between 1843-1849. All our information about these notes from other sources also refer to the middle or late 1840s; it is likely that they date from the onset of Dostoevsky's nervous disorder of 1846.[10] There is thus not a shred of real evidence to confirm Freud's "legend" about Dostoevsky's childhood: neither the footnote, nor Solovyev, nor Andrey Dostoevsky. Freud's article contains some shrewd and penetrating remarks about Dostoevsky's masochistic and guilt-ridden personality; but the case history he constructed in the effort to "explain" him in psychoanalytic terms is purely fictitious. (For more information, see Appendix, below.)

3

A great change occurred in the life of the Dostoevsky children when their parents acquired the small property at Darovoe in 1831. Feodor and Mikhail spent four months there with their mother every year for four years; after this time, because of their studies, they could come only for shorter stretches of a month or so. These carefree times in the country, removed from paternal scrutiny and under the mild and loving supervision of their mother, were the sunniest periods in Dostoevsky's boyhood. If he later told his second wife that he had had a "happy and placid childhood."[11] it was undoubtedly of these months in the country that he was thinking, free from the menace of paternal disapproval and of all the oppressive confinement of life in the city. Evocations of a happy childhood are exceedingly rare in Dostoevsky's novels, and the one or two that exist are set either in a village (*Poor Folk*), or on a country estate (*A Little Hero,. The Village of Stepanchikovo*); no pleasant memories were linked in his sensibility with life in the city. "Not only that first voyage to the village," Andrey writes, "but all the following trips there always filled me with some kind of ecstatic excitement."[12] No doubt the high-spirited and impressionable Feodor experienced the same sensation even more intensely as the carriage to Darovoe pulled away every spring with bells tinkling on the horses' harness, and as the at first unfamiliar (and then beloved) rural sights began to unroll before his eyes.

It is revelatory that Andrey remembers the environs of Darovoe as having been "very pleasant and picturesque."[13] V. S. Nechaeva, more impartially, describes the landscape surrounding the village as being "dull and monotonous";[14] but no doubt Andrey's reaction represents the joyous response of the children to the broad expanse of field and the limitless possibilities of freedom embodied in the unbroken horizon stretching as far as the eye could see. The Dostoevsky family lived in a small, three-room cottage with a thatched roof and sheltered by a grove of ancient linden trees. Nearby was a birchwood called Brykovo (the name was later used in *The Devils* for the wood in which Stavrogin fights a duel), and it was called "Fedya's wood" by the family because Feodor spent so much time roaming in its depths. Many years later, he was to evoke these boyhood rambles in fervent words: "And in all my life nothing have I loved as much as the forest, with its mushrooms and wild berries, its insects and birds and little hedgehogs [in *The Idiot*, it might be recalled, Aglaya sends a hedgehog to Prince Myshkin as a token of reconciliation] and squirrels; its damp odor of dead leaves, which I adored."[15]

These sojourns in the country also offered Dostoevsky his first opportunity to become acquainted with the Russian peasantry at close

3. Dostoevsky's country cottage in Darovoe

quarters (previously he had known only the house-serfs of his family, who had adapted themselves to city life and acquired the manners and habits of servants). Marya Feodorovna was, as we have said, an efficient and kindhearted proprietor, and the Dostoevskys lived in close and friendly contact with the rest of the village. The children were allowed to roam freely without any supervision, and to enlist the aid of serf-children in their games. It is true, as Andrey admits a bit shamefacedly, that the Dostoevsky offspring did not fail to assert their social superiority, and used the serf-children as helpers and assistants (for example, to bait the fishing lines with which they tried their luck in the pond). But they were not cut off from them by any insurmountable class barrier, as would have been the case on a larger and wealthier property.

The children were also allowed to mingle freely with the older peasants in the fields, and even to assist them—playfully, of course—in their work. Feodor once ran back two versts to the village, according to Andrey, to bring water to a peasant mother at work in the field who wished to give her baby a drink. One of Dostoevsky's earliest letters—a postscript added to a letter of his father's—reveals the close attention he paid to the work on the estate. "Come home to us, dearest Maminka," he writes at thirteen, "the rest of the grain won't take long and, I think, you have gathered in a bit of the buckwheat already."[16] This untroubled boyhood relation with the peasants certainly contributed to shape Dostoevsky's later social ideas; one may say that he aimed to bring about, on a national scale, the same harmonious unity between the educated classes and the peasantry that he remembered having known as a child. And while he does not portray the Russian peasant at all, except in *The House of the Dead*, these childhood summers—in the opinion of a shrewd observer who knew Dostoevsky personally (Count Peter Semenov)—brought him "closer to the peasantry, their way of life, and the entire moral physiognomy of the Russian people," than most scions of the landed gentry "whose parents purposely kept them from any association with the peasants."[17]*

Andrey's account of his brother at Darovoe gives us the first glimpse

---

* Semenov's assertion about the usual conventions of gentry-life may be documented with a quotation from the memoirs of Tolstoy's second son, Ilya, born in 1866. "The world was divided into two parts," he writes: "one composed of ourselves and the other of everyone else. We were special people and the others were not our equals. . . . It was mostly *maman*, of course, who was guilty of entertaining such notions, but *papa*, too, jealously guarded us from association with the village children. He was responsible to a considerable degree for the groundless arrogance and self-esteem that such an upbringing inculcated into us, and from which I found it so hard to free myself." Cited in Edward Crankshaw, *Tolstoy: The Making of a Novelist* (New York, 1974), 253.

of certain traits of Dostoevsky's character. It is not only that he manifests his leadership and asserts his superiority to the more passive Mikhail; we can also note a need to test himself, and to titillate his nerves and sensibility by taking risks. The country around Darovoe was crisscrossed with numerous ravines—the remains of an old river-bed—that provided a haunt for snakes and occasionally for wandering wolves. The children were warned to avoid them by their mother, but this did not stop Feodor from plunging into "Fedya's wood" with a delicious shudder of fear. He confided his sensations on doing so to a passage in the original version of *Poor Folk*, later eliminated in revision. "I remember that at the back of our garden was a wood, thick, verdant, shadowy, sprawling, richly overgrown with foliage. . . . This wood was my favorite place to walk, but I was afraid to go into it very far . . . it seems as if someone is calling there, as if someone is beckoning there . . . where the smooth stumps of trees are scattered about more blackly and thickly, *where the ravines begin*. . . . (Italics added.) It becomes painful and terrifying, all around nothing but a dead silence; the heart shivers with some sort of obscure feeling, and you continue, you continue farther, carefully. . . . How sharply etched in my memory is that wood, those stealthy walks, and those feelings—a strange mixture of pleasure, childish curiosity and terror . . ." (1: 443).

There is another incident recounted by Andrey that must have also given Feodor a special *frisson*, and that seems symbolic and premonitory. Just behind the linden grove was a cemetery; on its edge a weather-beaten old chapel decorated with icons. The chapel was never locked; and one day, on a walk with the housemaid Vera—the same "lively and sprightly person"[18] who caused the quarrel between Dr. Dostoevsky and Uncle Mikhail Feodorovich—the children entered the chapel, took down the icons, and organized a mock religious procession in the fields complete with songs and prayers, and with Vera in the lead. This shocking sacrilege was repeated two or three times; but news of it reached the ears of Marya Feodorovna, who put a stop to such goings-on and gave the children a severe scolding. One wonders whether Vera was as responsible for the whole affair as Andrey pretends, and whether the restless and inventive Feodor, who had thought up all the other games, might not also have taken the initiative in inventing this one too. He was always to remain both fascinated and horrified by the temptation of sacrilege, and all of his great novels deal with the theme in one form or another. In *The Brothers Karamazov*, Smerdyakov as a child is described as having secretly hung cats, and then burying them with a mock religious ceremony.

Dostoevsky never forgot his summers in Darovoe, and in 1877, shortly after returning there to visit for the first time since his childhood, wrote of "that tiny and unimportant spot [which] left a very deep and strong impression on me for the remainder of my life."[19] Names of places, and of people that he knew there, constantly turn up in his work (we have already mentioned Brykovo), most abundantly in *The Brothers Karamazov* which he was beginning to think of at the time of his belated return to the scenes of his youth. The name of Cheremoshnia is used for the property to which old Karamazov sends his son Ivan to conclude the sale of some woodland. Grigory Vasiliev was the name of the rather incompetent peasant overseer in Darovoe, and it is also the name of old Karamazov's pious and stubborn servant. The village harbored a *durochka*, a female simpleton or half-wit named Agrafena, who lived out of doors for most of the year and, in the dead of winter, was forcibly taken in and sheltered by one peasant family or another. She is clearly the prototype of Lizaveta Smerdyakova, and suffered the same unhappy fate: despite her infirmity, she became pregnant and gave birth to a child who died shortly after birth. Andrey describes her as continually muttering something disconnected and incomprehensible about her dead child in the cemetery, exactly like another Dostoevskian *durochka*, Marya Lebyadkina in *The Devils*.

Other echoes of these years can be found in Dostoevsky's portrait of the peasant Marey, which will be discussed further on, and perhaps too in the famous dream-sequence during the preliminary interrogation of Dimitry Karamazov. A fire broke out in Darovoe in the spring of 1833, and most of the village was destroyed; the children's arrival there that year presented them with an image of desolation. "The whole estate," writes Andrey, "looked like a desert, with charred posts sticking up here and there."[20] Dostoevsky probably drew on such impressions for Dimitry's dream-image: "Not far off was a village, he could see the black huts, and half the huts were burnt down, there were only the charred beams sticking up. And as they drove in, there were peasant women drawn up along the road, a lot of women, a whole row, all thin and wan, with their faces a sort of brownish color, especially one at the edge, a tall, bony woman, who looked forty, but might have been only twenty, with a long, thin face. And in her, arms was a little baby crying. And her breasts seemed so dried up that there was not a drop of milk in them. And the child cried and cried, and held out its little bare arms, with its little fists blue from cold" (x: 178). The immense pity that fills Dimitry at this poignant spectacle of suffering indicates that he has already entered on the path to his moral conversion. Andrey does not mention a similar gathering, but it is not unlikely that such a congregation assembled at the outskirts of the village to plead for help from the masters in time of trouble. Each family was given fifty rubles as a loan (a considerable sum in those days) to help in the work of reconstruction, and it is doubtful whether it was ever repaid.

4
———

In 1833, Mikhail and Feodor left home for the first time to go to a day school; a year later they were sent to Chermak's, the best boarding school in Moscow. Dostoevsky later gave the boarding school depicted in *A Raw Youth* a slight variation of the name of the day school (Touchard for Souchard). The narrator of the novel, Arkady Dolgoruky, is the illegitimate son of a gentry father of the highest social rank and of a peasant mother. The school is the place where Arkady first becomes aware of the shame of his birth, and of the fact that he has no right to claim the consideration due his father's family. For here he is publicly humiliated, separated from the other "respectable" children, beaten on the average of once a month, and of course properly despised by his schoolfellows. Most of this comes much more from the pages of Dickens than from real life; it is absurd to imagine that the sons of Dr. Dostoevsky went through anything remotely resembling the treatment that Arkady received. But such scenes may, all the same, contain a core of personal experience. Souchard's school was Dostoevsky's first real contact with the outside world, the first time he had stepped beyond the protective confines of the family circle. It may also have been the moment when he began to assess the illusoriness of his own family claim to hereditary rank.

The preparation for boarding school, in any case, was tied up with a particularly trying experience for the two older boys. All the teaching at Souchard's day school was done by members of the family, none of whom had a knowledge of Latin. But mastery of that tongue was required at Chermak's, and Dr. Dostoevsky himself decided to fill in the deficiency. These lessons provide Andrey with the most graphic illustration of his father's hair-trigger temper. "At the slightest error of [my] brothers, father always became angry, flew into a passion, called them sluggards and fools; in the most extreme, though rarer, instances, he even broke off the lesson without finishing it, which was considered worse than any punishment."[21] Normally, when instruction was given at home, the children sat at table with their tutors; but Dr. Dostoevsky required his sons to stand stiffly at attention throughout the Latin drill. From this we may conclude that he had already decided to enroll them in some kind of military establishment, and was trying to accustom them to the rigors of martial discipline. No doubt, as Andrey remarks, his "brothers were very much afraid of these lessons,"[22] but the fear was also probably mingled with a sense of their father's deep concern for their future.

The transition from home to school, and particularly to boarding school, came as a rude shock to Feodor. Despite his father's flare-ups, home was still a comfortable and familiar place, and his mother a perpetual source of solace and consolation. By contrast, the new world of the school was unfamiliar and frightening. We can use the words of the heroine of *Poor Folk* to evoke what were probably the reactions of her creator. "How sad I was at first with strangers. . . . It was so stern, so exacting! The fixed hours for everything, the meals in common, the tedious teachers—all that at first fretted and harassed me. . . . I would sit over my French translation or vocabularies, not daring to move and dreaming all the while of our little home, of father, of mother, of our old nurse, of nurse's stories . . ." (I: 28). Such feelings and details have the ring of biographical truth. Another reminiscence of this initiation may be contained in the image of Alyosha Karamazov surrounded by his schoolmates, who "forcibly held his hands from his ears, and shouted obscenities into them . . ." (IX: 23). The Dostoevsky children had lived in a peasant village and were certainly familiar with the facts of life; but they had been carefully shielded from a knowledge of vice and perversity. Andrey, who first went to another boarding school in Moscow (Kister's) before entering Chermak's, remembers his own introduction to such matters by his schoolfellows with distaste. "There was no nastiness, no abominable vice, which was not taught to the innocent youngsters who had just left the paternal home."[23]

There is only one independent account that allows us to catch a glimpse of Dostoevsky in his school years. This is provided by a slightly younger playmate from the hospital garden, who turned up at Chermak's. "On the first day I arrived," he writes, "I gave way to a surge of childish despair on finding myself torn away from the family, surrounded by strange faces, and, as a newcomer, exposed to their taunts. During the recreation period, I heard a familiar voice among those of the children milling about me. It was that of Feodor Mikhailovich Dostoevsky, who, on seeing me, came up at once, chased away the mocking scamps, and began to console me—which he soon succeeded in doing completely and successfully. He often visited me after that in class, guided me in my work, and lightened my sadness by his exciting stories during the recreation period."[24]

This pattern of behavior illustrates two aspects of Dostoevsky's character that remain constant: his staunch independence, and his willingness to intervene personally against a situation that offended his moral instincts. He refused to bait a helpless newcomer, even though this was the savage ritual prevailing in that schoolboy milieu; and he was not afraid to spring to the defense of the helpless and persecuted. His skill in telling exciting stories is also worthy of notice. Dostoevsky's independence and self-assertiveness was exhibited, not only in relation to his schoolmates, but apparently to his father as well. Andrey tells us that Feodor was sometimes so unrestrained in maintaining his own point of view that Dr. Dostoevsky would say, with the wisdom of experience: "Really, Fedya, control yourself, you'll get into trouble . . . and end up under the red cap,"[25] i.e., wearing the headgear of the convict regiments of the Russian Army. Dostoevsky did, as a matter of fact, serve in such a regiment after his release from prison camp in 1854.

5

The routine of these years of schooling was as invariable as those of early childhood. Every weekend the older boys returned home, and once again a passage from *Poor Folk* may help to evoke the joyous and exuberant atmosphere of these reunions. "I would arrive home gay and happy, would kiss everyone as though I had been away for ten years. There would be explanations, talk; descriptions would begin" (1: 28). Andrey too remembers the "genuine pleasure" he felt each Saturday, "after the week-long confinement in a boarding school I disliked, at spending a day and a half in our blessed family circle. . . ."[26] On such days the midday meal lasted much longer, and the boys, full of the events of the week, hastened to convey all their impressions and reactions to their parents. Once the first excitement of reunion was over, however, there was little else to do except read, and supervise the assignments handed out the week before to their younger brothers and sisters. Visits were still restricted to the immediate family; callers their own age were few and far between; nor were the older boys ever allowed to go out unaccompanied or given any pocket money. Such restraints, however, were merely the custom of the times and the society. Tolstoy also was not allowed out alone, and made his first excursion in Moscow on the sly, at the age of sixteen, borrowing some cash from the servants in order to finance his adventure.

There is only one friend whose name is mentioned by Andrey as having come to visit Mikhail and Feodor, and who, as we know, made a strong impression on the latter. This was Vanya Umnov, the son of a friend of the family, who was somewhat older than the two Dostoevsky boys, and went to the Russian equivalent of a public high school. Umnov also had literary interests, and must have impressed the Dostoevskys with his superior knowledge of what was going on in the world. He lent them a manuscript copy of a work that had been prohibited by the censor, Voekov's *The Madhouse*—a long satirical poem, in the style of Pope's *Dunciad*, directed against the then-reigning luminaries of Russian literature and society. The Dostoevsky brothers learned a good many of its stinging epigrammatic characterizations by heart, and then recited some of them for the benefit of their father. Dr. Dostoevsky, disliking the irreverence of the verses, at first thought the poem only a schoolboy prank; but when persuaded that it came from the pen of a well-known writer, he declared it "unseemly" because it "contained impertinent references to highly placed personages and important writers, and particularly to Zhukovsky" (his own favorite poet).[27] Nonetheless, Mikhail and Feodor kept on reciting passages from the poem so often, and with such obvious delight, that Andrey could still remember some of them at the end of the century. It is clear that Feodor did not share his father's veneration for constituted authority, and enjoyed seeing it mocked and ridiculed.

Many years later, the name of Vanya Umnov turns up in Dostoevsky's notes for the *Life of a Great Sinner*, along with a good many other details and references to these years of Dostoevsky's youth. All these details, however, are used only to particularize the background of Dostoevsky's intended character, who is engaged, even as a young boy, in the wildest and most extreme adventures, and who cannot by any stretch of the imagination be taken as Dostoevsky's image of what his own life was like at the time. The references to Umnov nonetheless convey the competitiveness that Dostoevsky probably began to feel toward the more sophisticated and slightly older boy. For example: "Umnov, knows Gogol by heart."[28] Dostoevsky substitutes Gogol for Voekov, and for another minor writer they heard about through Umnov (Yershov), for greater symbolic-historical effectiveness. Another note stresses the rivalry between the youthful "great sinner" and Umnov. "He meets Umnov who proves to him that he knows more than he does. Upon his return home, he tells the Lame Girl that Umnov is a fool who knows nothing; he gives the Lame Girl a beating, and from here on seeks Umnov's company."[29] The second sentence transposes into a violent dramatic action—an action appropriate to the intended character—Dostoevsky's envy of Umnov and his struggle against admitting the latter's superiority. We shall soon see Dostoevsky engaged in the same struggle against the entire generation of his literary rivals in Petersburg.

The last years of Dostoevsky's life in Moscow were darkened by his mother's illness, which took a sharp turn for the worse in the fall of 1836. It became clear that Marya Feodorovna was losing strength very rapidly; soon it became impossible for her even to comb her long and luxuriant hair, which then had to be clipped short. Medical consultations were held every day by the doctor and his colleagues, including the chief of staff, and the visits of relatives succeeded each other in a never-ending and exhausting file. "This was the bitterest time in the childhood period of our lives," writes Andrey. "And no wonder! We were about to lose our mother any minute. . . . Father was totally destroyed."[30] Just before the end, Marya Feodorovna regained consciousness, called for the icon of the Savior, and then blessed her children and her husband. "It was a moving scene and we all wept," Andrey recalls.[31] No doubt Feodor, who was later to include so many similar deathbed scenes in his works, also remembered his mother's pious and all-forgiving demise very vividly.

But it was not only the impending crisis in his family life that troubled Feodor during his last two years at home; he also knew that he was destined for a career repugnant to his deepest inclinations. Dr. Dostoevsky had decided that his two elder sons were to be military engineers, and in the fall of 1836 submitted a request through his hospital superior for their admission to the Academy of Engineers in St. Petersburg at government expense. Neither Mikhail nor Feodor had the slightest desire to become engineers; both were dreaming of literary fame and fortune; but once their father's request was granted, the die was cast. No doubt this decision stirred up a good deal of resentment and hostility, particularly in the fiery Feodor; but this was blunted by the lesson so often hammered home to the Dostoevsky children by their father. "He often repeated that he was a poor man," Andrey observes, "that his children, especially the younger ones, had to be ready to make their own way, that they would remain impoverished at his death, etc. All this painted a gloomy picture!" The post of military engineer offered solid financial advantages—especially to those who did not scruple to participate in a little graft on the side—and Dr. Dostoevsky no doubt believed he was doing the best he possibly could for his offspring. Feodor was thus compelled by necessity to envisage a future that went deeply against the grain of his temperament and interests, and violated the hopes and aspirations that he nourished in private.

6
———

What little we know of Dostoevsky in these years makes it likely that he began to chafe very early under the restricting atmosphere of his home life, and the necessity of knuckling under to a rigidly inflexible and emotionally unstable father who tended to identify his own wishes with the sacred dictates of God Himself. Such feelings of disaffection, however, were certainly counterbalanced both by the natural inclination to accept and revere paternal authority, and, as Feodor grew older, by his growing awareness of Dr. Dostoevsky's genuine dedication to the welfare of his family. For while the burdens that Dr. Dostoevsky imposed on his children were heavy indeed, their future, as they well knew, was at the center of his preoccupations; nor did he ever allow them to forget that his laborious life was devoted to their interests. Moreover, the adolescent Dostoevsky, endowed with the psychological insight he was soon to display in his works, probably could sense his father's anxieties behind the stiff and official authoritarian façade.

Dostoevsky's only direct utterance about his father while the latter was still alive is made in a letter to Mikhail; and its mixture of pity with some impatience reveals Dostoevsky's ambivalence. "I feel sorry for our poor father," he writes. "A strange character! Oh, how much unhappiness he has had to bear! I could weep from bitterness that there is nothing to console him. But, do you know, Papa doesn't know the world at all. He has lived in it for 50 years and retains the same ideas about people as 30 years ago. Happy ignorance! But he is very disillusioned with it. That seems our common fate."[32] This was written after the death of Marya Feodorovna had deprived Dr. Dostoevsky of his sole sustaining support in the midst of his woes; but it surely represents an opinion that his son had begun to form long before. Twenty years later—giving some advice to his friend Baron Vrangel, who was then having difficulties with *his* father—Dostoevsky imagines the senior Vrangel (whom he had never met) as "a strange blend of the gloomiest suspicion, morbid sensitivity, and generosity." He assures Vrangel that "I have known exactly such a relationship as yours with him. He is to be pitied, too, as you know better than I."[33] Dostoevsky advises his much younger friend that the only way to avoid unbearable friction is by parting; and this may cast some light on the apparent passivity with which he accepted his father's decision to consign him to the Academy of Engineers.

If we are to seek for some image of Dostoevsky's father in his works, it is useless to go to the creations of his maturity; whatever father figures we find there are too much intertwined with later experiences and ideological motifs to have any biographical value. But the picture given of Varvara's father in *Poor Folk* comes straight from Dostoevsky's still-fresh memories of his youth, and is steeped in the details of his daily life. "I tried my very utmost to learn and please father. I saw he was spending his last farthing on me and God knows what straits he was in. Every day he grew more gloomy, more ill-humored, more angry. . . . Father would begin saying that I was no joy, no comfort to them; that they were depriving themselves of everything for my sake and I could not speak French yet; in fact all his failures, all his misfortunes were vented on me and mother. . . . I was to blame for everything, I was responsible for everything! And this was not because father did not love me; he was devoted to mother and me, but it was just his character" (1: 29). It is very likely that Dostoevsky had heard just such reproaches on numerous occasions, and had tried to excuse them in his heart in the same way. And we see that he depicts his father, not as a brutal and heartless despot, but as a harassed and finally pitiable figure driven to desperation by the difficulties of his situation.

Some of the traits of Dr. Dostoevsky, drawn this time with a satirical rather than a pathetic pen, can also be found in the first version of another early work, *Netotchka Nezvanova*. A character named Feodor Ferapontovich, a minor civil service official, feels that his merits are unrecognized by society and constantly reproaches his children for ingratitude. "Turning to his little children, he would ask them in a threatening and reproachful voice: 'What have they done for all the kindness he had shown them? Have they recompensed him, by assiduous study and impeccable pronunciation of French, for all his sleepless nights, all his labors, all his blood, for anything? for anything?' In other words, Feodor Ferapontovich, giving free rein to his self-indulgence, would begin to wreak on his family the incomprehensible indifference of people and society to his familial and civic good works, and every evening turned his house into a little hell" (2: 444). At the same time, he is shown to have taken in the orphaned son of a relative, and the narrator assures us "that this man is not at all evil, only funny and amusing to an advanced degree" (*ibid.*). Moreover, the qualities in his character held up to ridicule are attributed to some sort of hidden suffering: "whether from the fact that he had been hurt, or cut down by somebody, some kind of secret enemy who constantly insulted his self-respect," etc. (*ibid.*). One can imagine the young Dostoevsky speculating in much the same way about the sources of his father's more galling peculiarities.

Certain traits of Dostoevsky's character may plausibly be attributed to the effects of his relationship with his father. All the people who had any prolonged personal contact with Dostoevsky remark on the secretiveness and evasiveness of his personality; he was not someone who opened himself easily or willingly to others. There is scarcely a memoir about him that does not comment on this lack of expansiveness; and such memoirs, as a result, actually tell us very little of crucial importance. One suspects that this elusiveness may well have developed from the need to dissimulate as a means of coping with his father's combination of capriciousness and severity. The pathological shyness from which Dostoevsky suffered all his life can possibly also be attributed to the same cause—an unwillingness to expose himself, a fear of being rebuffed and emotionally abused that had become second nature.

Most important of all, as Freud noted, is that Dostoevsky internalized as a child a highly developed sense of guilt. But Freud's explanation of this guilt in terms of the usual Oedipal sexual rivalry over the mother is too universal and hypothetical to be very useful. It is more helpful, at this stage of Dostoevsky's life, to view his guilt feelings in the light of the paternal insistence on scholastic achievement as a moral obligation, and as the only defense against grinding poverty and loss of status. The importance given to this aspect of life in the family is well illustrated by a little ceremony that took place every year on Dr. Dostoevsky's name day, and which later turns up in *The Village of Stepanchikovo* performed for the benefit of Colonel Rostanev, a father of ideal kindness and goodness.

The two older boys and eventually the oldest girl (whether in unison or separately is not clear) prepared a morning greeting for their father on that joyous occasion. This meant memorizing a French poem, carefully copying it on fine paper, presenting it to their father when he appeared, and then reciting it by heart—with as good an accent as they could muster—while he followed with the written text. "Father was very touched," Andrey says, "and warmly kissed the purveyor of greetings";[34] clearly the most welcome present he could receive was this evidence of their progress in learning French. Dostoevsky's genius first reveals itself by the creation of characters desperately eager to satisfy their bureaucratic superiors in some routine clerical task (not so far removed from schoolwork, after all); consumed with guilt at their velleities of rebellion; and oppressed by their sense of social inferiority. No wonder! All through his childhood, Dostoevsky had been placed psychically in exactly the same position by his father, and by the obvious social situation of his family.

The ambivalence of Dostoevsky's emotions about his father was also, unquestionably, of the greatest significance for his future. No doubt it was in the fluctuations of his own psyche between resentment and filial piety that he first glimpsed the psychological paradoxes whose exploration became the hallmark of his genius. And one can locate the emotive roots of his Christian ideal in the evident desire of the young Dostoevsky to resolve this ambivalence by an act of self-transcendence, a sacrifice of the ego through identification with the other (in this case, his father). Whether one calls such a sacrifice moral masochism like Freud or, more traditionally, moral self-conquest, the fact remains that Dostoevsky as a boy and youth was not only hostile and inimical to his father but also struggled to understand and to forgive him. This struggle then became fused with the Christian images and ideals which, as we shall see in the next chapter, he was taught from the very first moment that he awoke consciously to life. All of Dostoevsky's later values can thus be seen as deriving from the synthesis of this early psychic need with the religious superstructure that gave it a universal and cosmic import, and elevated it to the stature of the fulfillment of man's destiny on earth.

CHAPTER 4

The Religious Background

Dostoevsky's contemporary, Alexander Herzen—whose memoirs, *My Past and Thoughts*, is both a great work of art and an indispensable sourcebook for Russian culture of the nineteenth century—remarks that "nowhere does religion play so modest a role in education as in Russia."[1] Herzen was, of course, talking about the education of the children of the landed or service aristocracy, whose parents had been raised for several generations on the culture of the French Enlightenment and for whom Voltaire had been a kind of patron saint. By the beginning of the nineteenth century, such parents had long since ceased to be concerned about Orthodox Christianity, even though they continued to baptize their children in the state religion and to structure their lives in accordance with its rituals. The war years and the post-Napoleonic period, in Russia as elsewhere, was marked by a wave of emotionalism and a revival of religion. But in Russia this stimulated the growth of Freemasonry and various revivalist sects (Pierre Bezhukov in *War and Peace*, it will be recalled, typically joins a Masonic lodge for spiritual solace) rather than any massive return to the official faith. Most upper-class Russians would have shared the attitude exemplified in Herzen's anecdote about his host at a dinner party who, when asked whether he was serving Lenten dishes out of personal conviction, replied that it was "simply and solely for the sake of the servants."[2]

Parents with such ideas would scarcely consider it indispensable to provide their offspring with any kind of formal religious education. Herzen read the New Testament as a boy in German because of his Lutheran mother, and was taken by her to the Protestant church in Moscow once a month as an outing; but it was only at fifteen (after he had read Voltaire, as he remarks) that "my father brought in a priest to give religious instruction so far as this was necessary for entrance to the University."[3] Tolstoy, though raised largely by devout female relatives, was also never given any religious education as a child; and the most recent student of his religious thought comments on the vagueness he displayed as a boy about the essentials of the Christian faith.[4] Turgenev's monstrous mother, whose gratuitous birchings of her son make Dr. Dostoevsky seem like an angel of sweetness and light, held the religion of the common people in such contempt that, instead of the usual prayers, she substituted each day at table the reading of a French translation of Thomas à Kempis.

Only against such a background can one appreciate the full force of Dostoevsky's quiet words: "I came from a pious Russian family. . . . In our family, we knew the Gospel almost from the cradle."[5] This is, as we know from Andrey, literally true: the children were all taught to read by their mother from a well-known eighteenth century religious primer, translated from the German and entitled *One Hundred and Four Sacred Stories from the Old and New Testaments.* (Father Zosima, incidentally, was also taught to read from the same book, and we know that Dostoevsky found a copy in a second-hand bookstore and treasured it as a memento.) Coarse lithographs accompanying the text depicted various episodes from the Scriptures— the creation of the world, Adam and Eve in Paradise, the Flood, the raising of Lazarus, the rebellion of Job the just man against God, etc. The very first impressions that awakened the consciousness of the child were those embodying the teachings of the Christian faith; and the world thereafter for Dostoevsky would always remain transfigured by the glow of this supernatural illumination. Dostoevsky was to say later that the problem of the existence of God had tormented him all his life; but this only confirms that it was always emotionally impossible for him ever to accept a world that had no relation to a God of any kind.*

This saturation of the imagination of the child with religious images and feelings no doubt helps to explain what Dostoevsky recalled as his very earliest memories. One was the flight of a dove across the cupola of a small village church where he had been taken by his mother—an incident he used many years later in *A Raw Youth.* Doves in Russia were revered as symbols of the Holy Ghost, and it was forbidden to kill them; perhaps his mother told him that the

---

* Some evocative words in a biography of Cardinal Newman may help to illustrate the effects of this early religious education on Dostoevsky. "It is difficult for anyone who has never experienced it to form even a remote idea of what a religious training, founded wholly and solely on a study of the Bible, really is. For a thoughtful and imaginative child it results in a kind of supernatural humanism quite unique in its character. The world, human history, the life of mankind are bathed in a light that nothing henceforth avails to dim or to extinguish. The presence of God, everywhere active, all-powerful, reigns over all things, animate and inanimate. There are those countless figures of Patriarchs, Prophets, Kings and Apostles, Saints and Sinners, or rather of sinners called to repentance, of Saints conscious of their sin, who, for such as are familiar with them, seem more real than the folk we meet every day." Louis Bouyer, *Newman,* trans. J. Lewis May (New York, 1960), 13.

bird was a messenger of God, and this served to stamp the impression on his mind. Another childhood memory was that of being called into the family living room and asked to say his prayers before the icons in the presence of admiring guests—probably his mother's family. "I put all my trust in Thee, O Lord!" the child intoned. "Mother of God, keep me and preserve me under Thy wing!" In the atmosphere of the Dostoevsky household, such a childish performance of a religious ritual was evidently a source of pride and social satisfaction.[6]

To reinforce the effect of this early religious initiation, a deacon came to the house regularly, once the children had learned to read, to continue their lessons on a more formal basis. This clergyman also taught at the neighboring Catherine Institute for Girls, a fashionable school for daughters of the aristocracy; and this meant that, unlike the majority of the Russian non-monastic clergy, he would have been both highly literate and well-mannered. He was, at any rate, a skillful and eloquent pedagogue. "He possessed an uncommon verbal gift," writes Andrey, "and the entire lesson, which in the old fashion lasted from one and a half to two hours, was spent telling stories, or, as we called it, interpreting the Scriptures. . . . I can say quite positively that he touched our youthful hearts by his lessons and stories."[7] Particularly vivid were his narratives about the Flood, and about Joseph and the miracle of the Nativity. The children also were required to study the introduction to religion composed by the Metropolitan Filaret, whose first sentence Andrey still remembers after more than half a century: "The One God, worshipped in the Holy Trinity, is eternal, that is, has no beginning nor end to his being, but always was, is, and will be. . . ."[8] This was much more philosophy, as Andrey aptly comments, than an introduction to religion for children; and one assumes that his opinion expresses that of his older brothers at the time. The attempt of theologians to rationalize the mysteries of faith, it would appear, never held any appeal to Dostoevsky from the very beginning. But what stirred his feelings to the depths was the story of the Advent as a divine-human narrative full of character and action—as an account of real people living and responding with passion and fervor to the word of God.

2

Learning his lessons was of course only one channel—and not by any means the most important—through which religious impressions flooded into Dostoevsky's sensibility as a child. Religion not only

loomed large because of its manifest status in the eyes of his parents
and relatives (as in the recollection about the prayer); it was also
involved quite naturally with the most exciting experiences of his
earliest years, the events that stood out as joyful breaks in his
monotonous and laborious routine. The name of Dostoevsky has
become so inalterably associated with that of St. Petersburg that
one tends to forget he was born in Moscow—"the city of innumerable churches, of everlasting bells, of endless processions, of palace
and church combined," the city which the peasants called "our holy
mother."[9] The beating heart of all this intense religious life was the
Kremlin; and whenever the Dostoevsky family went for an outing
in the city, they invariably directed their steps toward this sacred
spot. "Every visit to the Kremlin and the Moscow cathedrals," Dostoevsky remembered later, "was, for me, something very solemn."[10]
Time and again he wandered through its forest of bulbous cupolas;
listened to the many-tongued harmony of its bell towers; contemplated its treasured relics and richly decorated cathedrals, from
whose walls the Orthodox saints, as the much-travelled Théophile
Gautier saw them, stared down with eyes that seemed "to menace,
though their arms extended to bless."[11]

The stout walls and crenelated battlements of the Kremlin bore
mute testimony to its function as a fortress as well as a religious
sanctuary, and reminded the onlooker that it was not only a place
of sacred worship but also a monument of Russia's historical
grandeur. The God-anointed Tsars were crowned in the Cathedral
of the Assumption; another church contained the sepulchers of
all the past rulers of Russia, who, clothed in flowing white robes,
and with a halo encircling their heads, appeared on the wall above
each tomb. The Russian crown jewels, dazzling in their brilliant
profusion, provided, in the words of the Marquis de Custine, "a
history in precious stones"[12] of the prodigious rise of the Russian
Empire. In Russia, as a student of its ecclesiastical history reminds
us, "the national and religious elements have been identified far
more closely than in the West";[13] and one of the great landmarks
of this symbiosis is the Kremlin. The Russian struggle against
foreign invaders—whether pagan Tartar, Mohammedan Turk, German or Polish Catholic, or Swedish Lutheran—has always been
a struggle on behalf of the Orthodox faith. By the early nineteenth
century, the two powerful idea-feelings of religion and nationalism
had been inseparable for Russians for a thousand years. One can
well understand how they must have blended together in Dostoevsky's consciousness, during these childhood excursions, into an

inextricable mélange of ardor and devotion that he later found it impossible to disentangle.

3
―――――

Up until the age of ten, when their parents acquired their small property in the country, the Dostoevsky children left the city only once a year. Mme Dostoevsky always took the older children, accompanied by some relatives or friends, for an annual spring excursion to the monastery of the Trinity and St. Sergey about sixty miles from Moscow. This journey required several days by carriage (an exciting enough event for the children even by itself), and terminated in a vast, fortress-like beehive of churches, monasteries, and hostelries which, over the centuries, had clustered round the spot where St. Sergey had first constructed a hut in the northern forests.

A famous hermit and ascetic, St. Sergey had retired to the forest in the fourteenth century to lead a life of prayer and privation. But he became the patron saint of Moscow when, after blessing the armies of Prince Dimitry, and sending two of his priestly followers to accompany the troops, they inflicted a crushing defeat on the hitherto invincible Tartar hordes. Since that time, the name of St. Sergey had become "at least as dear to every Russian heart, and as familiar among Russian homes, as William Tell to a Swiss or as Joan of Arc to a Frenchman."[14] St. Sergey's humble dwelling in the woods gradually grew into one of the main focuses—more important even than the Kremlin—for the indigenous Russian amalgam of religio-patriotic sentiment. And its importance as such a symbol was reinforced in the seventeenth century, when it became the center of national resistance against the Polish invaders in the Time of Troubles.

Each year the Dostoevsky children visited this vast religious caravansery, swarming both with lowly peasant pilgrims in bark shoes and elegant visitors in glittering uniforms and gowns in the very latest French mode. Each visit, as Andrey Dostoevsky recalls, constituted an "epoch" in the lives of all the children;[15] for his brother Feodor they were an unforgettable experience. When, in 1870, he first conceived the idea of setting a novel in a monastery, he wrote to a friend: "I am an expert in this world, and I have known the Russian monastery from childhood."[16] One of the most famous stories in the canonical life of St. Sergey is that of the bear, who emerged from the woods one day to come face-to-face with the saint. Subdued by the sanctity of the holy man, the animal peacefully accepted some of the bread and water which was St. Sergey's only nourishment, and then returned regularly each day to share this frugal meal. This touching friendship between the brute beast and the Russian saint is depicted among the frescoes on the entrance tower to the monastery; and Dostoevsky as a child must have seen it there many times. When Father Zossima, in his days as a wandering priest, preaches to a young peasant lad about the innocence and sinlessness of animals and of all of nature, it is the story of St. Sergey and his bear that he uses to point the moral.

Some of the other impressions that Dostoevsky may have retained from these visits can be visualized with the aid of Gautier's *Voyage en Russie*. The center of devotion was the reliquary of St. Sergey, whose gilded silver tomb reposed under a massive silver canopy supported by four columns of the same precious metal. "Around this mass of silversmith's work, shimmering with light, *muzhiks*, pilgrims, the faithful of all kinds, lost in ecstatic admiration, prayed, crossed themselves, and performed all the devotions of the Russian faith. It made up a picture worthy of Rembrandt. The glittering tomb threw patches of light on the kneeling peasants, making a forehead glow, a beard sparkle, a profile stand out sharply, while the lower portions of the body remained bathed in shadow and lost in the coarse thickness of the garments. There were superb heads to be seen, illuminated with fervor and faith."[17] It may have been here that Dostoevsky witnessed for the first time the therapeutic healing of possessed and hysterical peasant women that he describes in *The Brothers Karamazov*. It was certainly of St. Sergey that Dostoevsky was thinking when Father Zosima proclaims: "Of old, leaders of the people came from among us, and why should they not again?" (IX: 310).

4

<hr>

One can gauge from such details how completely Dostoevsky's childhood immersed him in the spiritual and cultural atmosphere of Old Russian piety, and brought him emotively close to the beliefs and feelings of the illiterate peasantry still untouched by secular Western culture. For the Russian upper class, of course, religion and the people were inseparable, and it was by frequenting the servants' quarters that the offspring of the aristocracy first made some acquaintance with the sources of their native culture and the deep religious roots of Russian folk-feeling. The role that Pushkin assigned to his old nurse as a transmitter of folk-tradition has immortalized this crucial encounter in the lives of so

many educated Russians. Dostoevsky also went through a similar
archetypal initiation; but for him the contrast between his home
and family environment and that of the servants and the peasants
was much less accentuated. One can scarcely imagine him hiding
in a closet, like the young Tolstoy, to watch the exciting and unfamiliar spectacle of the saintly fool (*yurodivi*) who lived in the
Tolstoy household saying his nightly prayers amidst sobs and exclamations. There was nothing exotic about the people and their faith
to Dostoevsky as a child, and both entered his world in a much more
natural and easygoing fashion.

One of the recurring events that the Dostoevsky children looked
forward to with the greatest eagerness was the visit of the wet
nurses who had been employed to suckle them in infancy. These
peasant women lived in villages close to Moscow, and once a year,
during the winter lull in peasant life, they came to pay a ceremonial
call on the family and spend two or three days as guests. Such
visits always gave rise to an orgy of storytelling in the late afternoon,
after the children had done their lessons and it was too cold to go
out of doors. Andrey remembered these stories as being a mixture
of fairytales and Russian folk-legends; but his four-year-older brother
Feodor recalled another type of story, perhaps told by a different
storyteller before Andrey was even out of the cradle.

"Who has read the *Acta Martyrum*?" Dostoevsky asks the readers
of his *Diary of a Writer*. "Somebody in a monastery; among laymen
—some professor as a matter of duty, or some odd fellow who fasts
and attends vespers. . . . And now, would you believe that in the
whole of Russia the knowledge of the *Acta Martyrum* is extremely
widely diffused—of course, not of the book *in toto*, but of its spirit,
at least. Why so? Because there are a great many tellers—men and
women—of the lives of the saints. . . . In childhood I heard these
narratives myself, before I even learned to read."[18] These stories of
the lives of the saints were no doubt steeped in the special spirit
of Russian kenoticism—the glorification of passive, completely non-
heroic and non-resisting suffering, the suffering of the despised and
humiliated Christ—which is so remarkable a feature of the Russian
religious tradition.[19] Even a skeptical foreign observer like the French
liberal Leroy-Beaulieu, who had vast personal acquaintance with Russian life and culture, was still struck toward the end of the nineteenth
century by the admiration of the Russian common people for "the
spirit of asceticism and renunciation, the love of poverty, the craving
for self-sacrifice and self-mortification."[20] It was impressions such as
these, garnered in earliest childhood from the lips of humble peasant

storytellers, which nourished Dostoevsky's unshakable conviction that the soul of the Russian peasant was imbued with the Christian ethos of love and self-sacrifice.

5

Two important incidents that Dostoevsky never forgot vividly etched on his boyish imagination examples of what he came to regard as this ethos in action. One involved the chief housekeeper and *nyanya*, Alyona Frolovna, whose personage loomed very large in the lives of all the children—not only because she was, as Andrey tells us, unusually tall and corpulent, but also because she was a commanding presence as a personality. Alyona was not a serf but a free Moscow townswoman, and she was very proud that her status raised her a cut above "the lowest." But her attitudes and cast of mind were much the same, and she brought with her the pagan superstitions and the ritual formalism that the Russian lower classes blended so naturally with their Christianity. Alyona was charged with teaching the children to behave properly and to learn table manners; and she informed them solemnly that it would be a deadly sin to eat any food without first having taken a bite of bread, "for so God had ordained!" Suffering from frequent nightmares, she always attributed her outcries, which woke the entire family, to the nocturnal visits of the *domovo*—the Russian house-demon or hobgoblin—who had been strangling her with his claws. Alyona had never been married, and called herself a "bride of Christ" (the phrase made a great impression on the children); her sister—a nun living in a cloister near Petersburg—came to visit her once a year, and always spent the day with the Dostoevsky family.[21]

The figure of Alyona was thus surrounded for the children with a certain nimbus of the sacred; and this must have made the incident on which Dostoevsky reports even more symbolically striking. It occurred shortly after the Dostoevskys had purchased their country property, and was only the first of the misfortunes destined to become linked with this unhappy spot for the family. During the spring of 1833, the news arrived unexpectedly of the fire we have already mentioned; most of the peasant huts had been destroyed, and the loss, as well as the cost of replacement, was a staggering financial blow for the hard-pressed family. While they were still reeling under the shock of the news, Alyona's response was to offer the savings being accumulated for her old age: "Suddenly, she whispered to mother: 'If you should need money, take mine; I have no use for it; I don't

49

need it. . . . ' "[22] This impulsive gesture remained in the memory of the twelve-year-old Feodor as typical of the capacity of the Russian people, in moments of moral stress, to live up to the Christian ideals they nominally revered, but which, in the ordinary course of daily life, they so often violated and betrayed.

Another incident of the same kind, also described in the *Diary of a Writer*, again served to fix in Dostoevsky's sensibility an image of the Russian people that nothing afterwards would really change. One day, during the course of his beloved excursions in the forest, he was the victim of an auditory hallucination—the one and only sign of a nervous disorder that we know about from his boyhood. Believing that he had heard the cry: "A wolf is on the loose!", and seized by panic, he bolted from the wood and ran up to a *muzhik* plowing in a field. This was one of the peasants of the village, Marey by name, "almost fifty years old, stocky, pretty tall, with many gray hairs in his bushy flaxen beard." Marey comforted the frightened child with a smile (Dostoevsky calls it "motherly"), stroked his cheek with an earth-blackened hand, and sent him home with the assurance that he would keep the boy in sight. " 'Now, Christ be with you, now, go!'—and he made the sign of the cross over me, and crossed himself as well."[23] Dostoevsky never forgot the tenderness and loving kindness of the peasant serf toward the helpless and frightened son of the masters who held him in bondage. Many years later, the image of Marey rose up before him again in Siberia and helped him inwardly to accept his Russian fellow convicts, despite all their quarrelsomeness and brutality, because he was convinced that the feelings of a Marey were still alive in their souls and could be reawakened.

6

Dostoevsky's family, rooted in its clerical and merchant origins, had remained relatively untouched by the skepticism and religious incredulity so prevalent among the Russian gentry. But if we are truly to understand the strength of the early influences shaping Dostoevsky's mentality, something more must be said about the spiritual climate prevailing in the home and about the personal piety of his parents. For it is important to realize that, as a child, he never felt any separation between the sacred and the profane, between the ordinary and the miraculous; religion was never for him a matter only of particular ritual occasions or periodic festivities. The texture of his everyday life was controlled by much the same supernatural forces which, in a more naively superstitious form, also dominated the mentality of the Russian common people.

To begin with, Dostoevsky's family were scrupulously faithful about fulfilling all the customary obligations of the Orthodox Church. "Our parents were very religious, especially our mother," writes Andrey. "Every Sunday and every religious holiday we unfailingly went to church for mass and, the evening before, to vespers."[24] More important was that the entire mental world of the parents was religiously oriented, and that God permeated every aspect of the young Dostoevsky's quotidian existence—much as He would have done centuries earlier in an English Puritan or German Pietist household. Andrey Dostoevsky tells us that, after the conclusion of the purchase of their estate, his parents immediately went off to utter a prayer of thanksgiving at the chapel of the Iversky Madonna—the most revered icon in Moscow, which the people, in 1812, had wished to carry into battle against the French. The same reflex occurred when the family suddenly heard the news of the fire on their country estate. "I remember that my parents fell on their knees before the icons in the living room," writes Andrey, "and then left to pray to the Iversky Madonna."[25]

One has only to glance at the letters of Dostoevsky's parents to be struck by this piously devout aspect of their mentality, and to observe them speaking of God with the same combination of sentimental unction and intense practicality that is so striking— and now seems so strange—in Defoe's novels, or in the sermons of English Puritan divines. For all his medical degree and scientific education, Dr. Dostoevsky never lost the clerical stamp of his early training, and the style of his letters is full of Church Slavonic expressions that reveal his thorough acquaintance with ecclesiastical literature. "How great is the divine mercy!" he writes to his oldest son Mikhail. "How unworthy are we to give thanks to the great and bountiful God for His inexpressible mercy to us! How unjustly have we grumbled, yes, let this serve as an admonitory example for the remainder of our lives, since the All-Highest sent us this transitory trial for our own good and our own welfare!"[26] The occasion for this edifying outburst was the acceptance of Mikhail (who had been refused admittance to the Academy of Military Engineers in 1837) into another school of the same kind.

The letters of Dostoevsky's mother are more personally expressive in tone, and influenced by the late eighteenth century sentimental novel rather than by the lives of the saints. But here too the intermingling of the sublime and the trivial, the religious and the mun-

danely practical, is very much in evidence. "I thank you, my most beloved friend, for your message," Mme Dostoevsky writes her husband
from the country; "I revived completely after receiving your letter,
my dear friend, and have given thanks to God a hundredfold that He
was gracious enough to hear my prayers and brought you safely to
Moscow. Do not grumble against God, my friend, do not grieve for me.
You know that we were punished by Him; but also granted His grace.
With complete steadfastness and faith, let us rely on His sacred
providence and He will not withhold His mercy from us."[27] What misfortune Mme Dostoevsky refers to here is unknown; perhaps it was
connected with the death of her father, which had occurred just a few
months earlier. In any case, the remainder of the letter is taken up
with a lawsuit in which the Dostoevskys had just become involved
concerning Darovoe, and with other purely business matters relating
to the crops and the peasants.

It may be taken for granted that the children were continually being admonished and instructed in much the same style. And for the
most gifted of them all, young Feodor, this habit of mind began to
stir reflections very early on the most profound and insoluble of religious enigmas—the enigma of God's relation to man, and the existence of evil, pain, and suffering in a world where the will of a beneficent God presumably prevails. Such reflections would surely have
been stimulated by the continual discomfiture with life that his father
never hesitated to voice, and which, from time to time, take on a truly
Job-like note. "True," he writes his wife, "I will not hide from you that
there are sometimes minutes in which I anger my Creator by grum-
bling against the briefness of the days given me by my lot in life; but
do not think anything of it; it will pass."[28] It is improbable that Dr.
Dostoevsky, like the father of Kierkegaard, ever rose in revolt against
God and cursed him because of the harshness of his fate; but the
temptation to do so was continually there, and, given his explosive
irritability, would scarcely have been concealed.

Many years later, when Dostoevsky was reading the Book of Job
once again—as he had done so many times before—he wrote his wife
that it put him into such a state of "unhealthy rapture" that he almost
cried. "It's a strange thing, Anya, this book is one of the first in my
life which made an impression on me; I was then still almost a
child."[29] There is an allusion to this revelatory experience of the young
boy in *The Brothers Karamazov*, where Father Zosima recalls being
struck by a reading of the Book of Job at the age of eight, and feeling
that "for the first time in my life I consciously received the seed of
God's word in my heart" (IX: 287). This seed was one day to flower

into the magnificent growth of Ivan Karamazov's passionate protest against God's injustice and the Legend of the Grand Inquisitor; but it also grew into Alyosha's submission to the awesomeness of the infinite before which Job too had once bowed his head, and into Zosima's teaching of the necessity for an ultimate faith in the goodness of God's mysterious wisdom. It is Dostoevsky's genius as a writer to have been able to feel (and to express) both these extremes of rejection and acceptance; it is simply not true, as Leo Shestov has argued with such influential eloquence, that only the negative pole represents the "real" or the "genuine" Dostoevsky.[30] Moreover, while the tension of this polarity may have developed out of the ambivalence of Dostoevsky's psychodynamic relation with his father, what is more important is to see how early it was transposed and projected into the religious symbolism of the eternal problem of theodicy.

CHAPTER 5

The Cultural Background

Even though, compared to his contemporaries, Dostoevsky received an unusually thorough religious education, his spiritual nourishment as a boy was not derived exclusively from this one source. It is by no means true to say, as E. J. Simmons has done, that Dostoevsky's education was "pitifully inadequate" compared to that of gentry-children like Herzen, Turgenev, or Tolstoy because "the actual books assigned in the formal instruction which his father procured for him seem to have been mostly religious."[1] Such a judgment reflects the uncommon stress laid on religion in Dostoevsky's upbringing; but it also caters to a prejudice which is inclined to trace the so-called negligences of Dostoevsky's style—his supposed lack of artistic "finish"—to an insufficient early training of his taste. Actually, a closer look will show that Dostoevsky's literary and cultural education was by no means neglected or inferior.

Dr. Dostoevsky knew very well that the open sesame to any sort of advancement in Russian society for his sons was a knowledge of French; and a language tutor named Souchard (whose day school they later attended) was engaged simultaneously with the deacon who gave them religious instruction. Like his clerical counterpart, Souchard also taught at the Catherine Institute; and he was probably more qualified than the usual ragtag and bobtail of foreigners employed in Russia to initiate the young into the mysteries of the major European tongues. Moreover, so far as one can judge, the study of both religion and French were nicely (even if perhaps accidentally) adjusted to each other. The only text we know assigned by Monsieur Souchard was Voltaire's *La Henriade*—a heroic epic (notorious as the last of its kind) filled with the religious orthodoxy appropriate to the theme. Portions of this work were recited for the edification of Dr. Dostoevsky on one of the name-day celebrations already described.* Souchard, in addition, was so ardent a Russian patriot

---

* As a sample, we may cite the concluding words about Henri IV. "Il avoue, avec foi, que la religion / Est au-dessus de l'homme et confond la raison." "He confesses, with faith, that religion / Is far above man and perplexes his reason." *Oeuvres complètes de Voltaire* (Paris, 1819), 8: 297.

that he asked for (and received) special permission from Nicholas I to russify his name. Such a personage was not likely to imbue his pupils, as did so many of the tutors of aristocratic families, with dangerously subversive notions whether in religion or in politics. Herzen, for example, was told by *his* French tutor that Louis XVI had been rightfully executed as a traitor to France.

2

The secular education of the Dostoevsky children was also carried on by the parents themselves in nightly reading sessions. One should not, of course, overestimate the importance of such exceedingly early ideological and artistic stimulation; but it is striking all the same to see by how many threads it is tied to the maturer Dostoevsky. He remembered in 1863 how "I used to spend the long winter evenings before going to bed listening (for I could not yet read), agape with ecstasy and terror, as my parents read aloud to me from the novels of Ann Radcliffe. Then I would rave deliriously about them in my sleep" (5: 46). This was the unforgettable fashion in which he first became acquainted with the novelistic mode that transformed the art of narrative at the end of the eighteenth century, and whose technique was then used by Scott and Balzac for more elevated artistic purposes. The main structural features of this technique are a plot based on mystery and suspense; characters who always find themselves in situations of extreme psychological and erotic tension; incidents of murder and mayhem of various sorts; and an atmosphere calculated to impart a shiver of the demonic or supernatural. Dostoevsky would later take over such features of the Gothic technique and carry them to a peak of perfection that has never been surpassed.

Dr. Dostoevsky, when he could find time in the evenings (and he seems to have done so more often than not), also offered his children more serious provender. What he read them was Karamzin's *History of the Russian State*, the first work to disinter the Russian past from dusty monkish chronicles and poetic legend, and to present it as a national epic appealing to a wide circle of cultivated readers: Karamzin, as Pushkin remarked, discovered the Russian past as Columbus had discovered America. Writing in the great eighteenth century tradition of admiration for enlightened despotism, Karamzin stressed the importance of the autocratic power in maintaining Russian unity and preserving national independence once the Tartar yoke had been thrown off. Andrey tells us that Karamzin was his brother

Feodor's bedside book, a work he read and reread continuously. Dostoevsky's later support of the enlightened Tsarism of Alexander II certainly drew on such long-standing immersion in Karamzin's historical vision for some of its sustenance.

"I grew up on Karamzin,"[2] Dostoevsky wrote appositely in 1870, when this pillar of Russian letters was under attack as a political reactionary. The same could be said for Dostoevsky's whole generation, though the average acquaintance with Karamzin's works would scarcely have been so early or so intimate. Second in importance only to his *History* was the famous *Letters of a Russian Traveller*—a brilliant account of his *Wanderjahre* in Switzerland, Germany, France, and England; this book too was read aloud and discussed in the Dostoevsky family circle. By any standard, Karamzin's work is one of the best personal accounts of late eighteenth century European civilization ever written; and it provided several generations of Russian readers with a splendid panorama of the mythical European world that they tried so desperately to emulate from afar. The impression they derived from the book, however, could not help but be rather mixed. Karamzin was filled with a naïve admiration for everything he saw, and was eager to spur his country on to join in the march of European progress; but he also communicated a sense of foreboding.

The early stages of the French Revolution coincided with his first visit to France; and while, like so many others, the Masonic liberal Karamzin greeted the revolution with some of the same feelings as Wordsworth ("But Europe at that time was thrilled with joy, / France standing on the top of golden hours"),[3] like Wordsworth its later phases also filled him with dismay and disillusion. By the time he came to publish his *Letters*, he warned his countrymen against following the European path insofar as this had led to subversion and social chaos. Karamzin's *Letters* thus helped to propagate the idea, so important for Russian thought in the nineteenth century, that Europe was a doomed and dying civilization. When Ivan Karamazov intones his litany over the vanished splendors of the European cultural "graveyard," he is only echoing sentiments that Dostoevsky had picked up long ago in Karamzin's pages.

The influence of Karamzin's *Letters* on Dostoevsky has never been explored in detail, but it is certainly more important than this neglect implies. Early in the book, for example, Karamzin drops in to pay a call on Kant, the sage of Königsberg, who received his uninvited young Russian visitor very hospitably. And the philosopher could not resist the chance to expound for his benefit, in a form suitable for unsophisticated ears, the two main ideas of the *Critique of Practical Reason* published just the year before. Kant explains that the consciousness of good and evil is innate to mankind, written indelibly into the human heart. Earthly life, however, reveals a glaring contradiction: the virtuous in this world, those who choose to live by the good and obey the moral law, are not always the ones who prosper and receive their just reward. But if, as we must assume, the Eternal Creative Mind is rational and beneficent, then we must also assume that this contradiction will not be left unresolved. Hence we postulate the existence of an immortal life after physical death in which the good receive their reward, even though this postulate can never be *proven* by human reason. Dostoevsky thus first came across these two ideas —that moral consciousness (conscience) is an ineradicable part of human nature, and that immortality is a necessary condition of any world order claiming to make moral sense—when he read Karamzin as a boy; and what he acquired subsequently only built on this foundation.* It is also amusing to note that most of the French tags that turn up in his pages (*l'homme de la nature et de la vérité*, etc.) can all be found in Karamzin's *Letters*, and that the book contains an account of two heroic, star-crossed lovers, Teresa and Faldoni, whose names Dostoevsky will use in *Poor Folk*.

Dostoevsky did not learn only from Karamzin's *History* and *Letters*; he was also, as a child, introduced to his short stories, written in a

---

* Karamzin's interview with Kant is so interesting, and so little known, that I cannot resist quoting the crucial passage. "Activity is man's lot," Kant said. "He can never be completely content with that which he has, but is always striving to obtain something more. Death surprises us on the road toward something we still desire. Give a man everything he desires and yet at that very moment he will feel that this *everything* is not *everything*. Failing to see the aim or purpose of our striving in this life, we assume there is a future where the knot must be untied. This thought is all the more attractive to man, since here there is no balance between joy and sorrow, between pleasure and pain. I take comfort in the fact that I am already sixty and that soon I shall reach the end of my life, for I hope to begin another, a better one.

"When I consider the joys I have known, I now feel no pleasure, but when I remember those occasions when I acted in conformity with the moral law inscribed in my heart, I am gladdened. I speak of the moral law. We might call it conscience, a sense of good and evil—but it exists. I lied. No one knows of my lie, yet I feel ashamed. When we speak of the future life, probability is not certainty; but when we have weighed everything, reason bids us believe in it. And suppose we were to see it with our own eyes, as it were? If we were much taken with it, we would no longer be able to interest ourselves in the present life, but would be in a continuous state of languor. And, in the opposite case, we would not be able to comfort ourselves by saying, midst the trials and tribulations of the present life, 'Perhaps it will be better there!' But when we speak of destiny, of a future life, and so on, we presume the existence of an Eternal Creative Reason which created everything for some purpose and everything good. What? How? But here even the wisest man admits his ignorance. Here reason extinguishes her lamp and we are left in darkness. Only fancy can wander in this darkness and create fictions." N. M. Karamzin, *Letters of a Russian Traveller, 1789-1790*, trans. and abridged by Florence Jonas (New York, 1957), 40-41.

pathetic-pastoral vein influenced by Sterne, Gessner, and Florian. The most famous and popular of these is called *Poor Liza*, and this title is echoed in that of Dostoevsky's first novel, *Poor Folk*. Karamzin's sentimental idyll laments tearfully over the sad fate of a beauteous and virtuous peasant maiden, seduced and betrayed by a well-meaning but weak-willed young aristocrat; and while Karamzin's treatment of this motif cannot be considered "realistic" by any stretch of the imagination, he is nonetheless the first major Russian writer to broach a subject reflecting some of the existing social tensions of Russian life. Moreover, his parenthetical remark that "peasant women also know how to love" created a sensation by daring to affirm a common humanity between the peasant-serf and the aristocrat. Timid and affected though it may be, Karamzin's humanitarianism was still a direct precursor of the "philanthropic" social realism of the Natural School of the 1840s; and this is the tradition of Russian literature in which Dostoevsky will begin his career.

3

Many other Russian works, as we know from Andrey, were also read in the family circle. He mentions a biography of the great Russian humanist Lomonosov, who was both poet and scientist, and a whole series of fairly recent historical novels by Russian imitators of Walter Scott (Zagoskin, Lazhechnikov, Masalsky). Such authors reveal the interest of the senior Dostoevskys in the newest literary products of Romantic nationalism. The parents also introduced the children to the work of their favorite poet, Zhukovsky, who was strongly influenced by the English "graveyard school" of Gray and Young and by the ballad-poetry of the German Romantics. No doubt Zhukovsky appealed to the elder Dostoevskys because of his melancholy disenchantment with earthly life and his nostalgia for a realm of bliss beyond the grave. Dostoevsky also became familiar with the poetry of Derzhavin—the only Russian poet of the eighteenth century with any genuine inspiration—whose famous ode to God, written in the tradition of philosophical Deism, powerfully evokes the immensity of the universe and the immeasurable majesty of God's creative power. It must certainly have made a great impression on the young sensibility so responsive to the Book of Job.

All these details, taken from the memoirs of Andrey Dostoevsky, would hardly seem very unusual in a Western European household of the same period. But, for a Russian child of the time, it was by no means the rule to have received so careful a cultural initiation, and in particular one imbued so strongly with the achievements of Russian literature. Despite his study of French, it was Russian culture that loomed largest on Dostoevsky's horizon as a child and overshadowed all the others. Here too, as in the case of his religious education, the contrast with the majority of his contemporaries is very marked.

Unlike Dr. Dostoevsky, Russian parents of the upper class for the most part took very little personal interest in the education of their children; they turned them over to foreign tutors and governesses as soon as they were out of swaddling bands to acquire the requisite polish of European manners. As a result, while the young Russian nobleman more often than not would be "at home in the literature and history of Western Europe," he was apt to be "quite ignorant of Russian letters and the past of his own homeland."[4] Herzen's first reading experiences, for example, were provided by his father's extensive library of eighteenth century French literature; he does not mention a single Russian book in *My Past and Thoughts* among those he best loved as a child. Tolstoy immortalized his good-hearted German tutor Feodor Ivanovich in *Childhood*, and he also learned French from his aunt; but while he could recite some poems of Pushkin at the age of eight, he had stumbled on them himself and never received any tutoring in Russian literature or history before going to school a year later. Turgenev too had French and German tutors, but only learned to read and write in Russian from his father's serf-valet; it was at the age of eight, after surreptitiously breaking into a locked room containing a moldering library, that the first Russian book he ever read (Kheraskov's hoary old epic, *Rossiad*) came into his hands.* Dostoevsky was thus taught at a much earlier age to identify himself emotionally with Russia and its past, and to take pride in the attainments of the new Russian culture being created in emulation of that of Western Europe.

4

Just when Dr. Dostoevsky decided that his two elder sons should embark on a career of military engineering is impossible to say; but the type of education he gave them encouraged a taste for the humanities rather than for the sciences or mathematics. No doubt the

---

* This type of Russian upper-class education, with its neglect of the native language, continued well into the twentieth century. "During one of [my father's] short stays with us in the country that summer" writes Vladimir Nabokov, "he ascertained, with patriotic dismay, that my brother and I could read and write English but not Russian (except KAKAO and MAMA). It was decided that the village schoolmaster should come every afternoon to give us lessons and take us for walks." This was in 1905. Vladimir Nabokov, *Speak, Memory!* (New York, 1968), 20.

readings in the family circle were designed to stimulate and benefit the children and to turn them into God-fearing and loyal citizens of the Tsar. Dr. Dostoevsky did not foresee that it would inspire in both Mikhail and Feodor a love for literature that rapidly became all-exclusive, and which, as they matured, turned into dreams of pursuing literary careers. Such dreams were unquestionably stimulated by two decisive literary encounters whose echoes were later to make themselves heard in unmistakable fashion. In both cases the work or works concerned either directly deal with—or were understood by the youthful Dostoevsky to deal with—the theme of a threat to the sanctity of family bonds and the moral and social importance of preserving them intact.

One memorable revelation was a performance of Schiller's *The Robbers*, to which Dr. Dostoevsky took his wife and older sons in 1831. Theatergoing was a luxury that the Dostoevskys could not ordinarily afford (at least with the children in tow), and Andrey notes only one such enjoyable occasion—the performance of a light comedy called *Jacko, or the Brazilian Ape*, whose high point was the acrobatics of the actor playing the ape. During the season of 1830-1831, however, the Moscow theater staged a series of Schiller plays with the famous actor Mochalov in the main roles; and Dr. Dostoevsky felt that this great cultural event was too important to be missed. His second son remembered the evening all his life, and referred to it in a letter shortly before his death. "I can justly say," he writes, "that the tremendous impression I carried away from it then acted very richly on my spiritual side."[5]

This, presumably, was Dostoevsky's first encounter with the work of the German poet whose role in Russian culture of the early nineteenth century was perhaps more important than that of any other foreign writer.[6] Dostoevsky had very good reason to say, as he did in 1861: "Yes, Schiller really became part of the flesh and blood of Russian society. . . . We were raised on his works, he became part of us, and affected our development in many ways." (XIII: 107) Fifteen years later, in the *Diary of a Writer*, he remarks that even though Schiller, *l'ami de l'humanité*, was made an honorary French citizen by the Constitutional Convention of 1793, he "was much more national and more akin to the barbarous Russians than to France," and that "he soaked into the Russian soul, left an impression on it, and almost marked an epoch in the history of our development."[7] There can be no doubt that, beginning in 1831, Schiller did soak into the soul of Dostoevsky. It is true that some characters of the post-Siberian Dostoevsky often jeeringly use the name of Schiller, and the epithet of "Schillerism," as tags for an impossibly sentimental view of human nature; but this does not indicate any change in Dostoevsky's own admiration for Schiller's work, or in his conviction that Schiller's ideals were noble and inspiring. During the last years of his life, he tried to read *The Robbers* to his own children; but, alas, it simply put them to sleep.

What can we imagine to have been the "tremendous impression" that Dostoevsky first derived from Schiller's violent *Sturm-und-Drang* theatrics? For one thing, there is Karl Moor's stormy revolt against divine and human fatherhood, his Robin Hood attempt to rectify the injustices of his society by himself becoming a criminal and a murderer, or at least the leader of murderers. For another, he would have been shocked by the blasphemy and parricidal villainy of Franz Moor, who uses the cynical doctrines of eighteenth century materialism to justify his crimes. This was probably Dostoevsky's first encounter with such ideas, which resemble those he was later to attack in the 1860s when they resuscitated in the guise of Russian Nihilism. Franz Moor's terror of Hell and eternal damnation, despite his professed atheism, provided a fearful illustration of how impossible it was to eradicate that spark of conscience from the human breast about which, as the youthful Dostoevsky may have recalled, Kant had also spoken. And when Karl Moor, abandoning his life as a marauder, finally surrenders voluntarily to a clergyman who represents the law of God on earth, he acknowledges the existence of a moral power stronger than his own individual will—a power to whom alone is reserved the task of meting out Divine justice. These themes of Schiller remained with Dostoevsky all his life; and when he came to write his own version of *The Robbers* in *The Brothers Karamazov*, the abundance of Schillerian references and quotations indicates to what extent Dostoevsky could still express his own deepest values in Schillerian terms.

Another writer who bemused Dostoevsky's boyhood, and to whom he later also attributed an important influence on his spiritual development, was Walter Scott. During one of the summers at Darovoe, at the age of twelve, Dostoevsky gobbled up all the novels of Scott; Andrey depicts him as always carrying around a copy of *Quentin Durward* or *Waverley* while at home. The Dostoevskys had their own set of the works of "the Scottish enchanter" (Pushkin) in a translation that was heavy and old-fashioned; but even so the books were eagerly read and reread by the children. In the same letter that speaks of Schiller, Dostoevsky urges his correspondent to encourage his adolescent daughter to read Scott, adding that "as a result of this reading I carried with me into life so many beautiful and lofty impressions that, surely, they provided my soul with great strength in the fight against seductive, passionate, and corrupting impressions."[8]

Once again it is difficult to be certain what these "beautiful and lofty impressions" were. But some indication is given in a passage (subsequently deleted) from the magazine text of *Netotchka Nezvanova* (1849). The poor young orphan girl Netotchka arrives to live in an aristocratic household after suffering a terrible childhood of poverty and psychic torment; and she finds consolation in her discovery of Scott's novels. "The feeling for the family portrayed so poetically in the novels of Scott, and developed through all his books with such love, forced itself into my soul deliciously and powerfully as an answer to my memories and sufferings. This feeling for the family was the ideal in whose name Scott created his novels, a feeling to which they gave an exalted historical meaning, and which they depicted as the condition for the preservation of mankind" (2: 450-451).

Such ideas about Scott could of course scarcely have been formulated by Dostoevsky at the age of twelve; but there is no reason to doubt that he felt something like the emotion they record. Perhaps this aspect of Scott struck him so forcibly because, as in the case of Netotchka, it provided emotional compensation for some of the lacks in his own family life. Perhaps, too, just as Schiller had done, it showed him the importance of preserving the unity of the family at whatever cost, and thus helped him to accept his own situation with a little more equanimity. It is also interesting to observe that the budding consciousness of the youthful Dostoevsky may have sensed the "feeling for the family" in Scott to have "an exalted historical meaning"— probably an allusion to Scott's Toryism, and his glorification of patriarchal relations between ruler and ruled as the surest anchor of social stability. If so, this is exactly the relation between the Tsar-Father and his "children"—his subjects—that Dostoevsky will later convince himself existed in Russia, and which served as a bulwark, in his view, against the disintegrating individualism of European society. At the time the passage about Scott was written, just before Dostoevsky's arrest as a political conspirator, he of course had quite different notions; but the ideal that he had picked up from Scott of a social order based on a "feeling for the family" clearly attracted him very powerfully all the same. Later on, he too came to believe that the protection of this "feeling" was a necessary "condition for the preservation of mankind." And if *The Brothers Karamazov*, after *King Lear*, is the greatest work ever written to illustrate the moral horrors that ensue when family bonds disintegrate, it is partly because Dostoevsky had been mulling over this theme all his life.

The years of Dostoevsky's adolescence were a period of intense literary and intellectual assimilation, and thanks to Andrey's information we can document the wide range of his brother's tastes and interests. Feodor became thoroughly familiar with all the styles and forms of Russian prose, beginning with Karamzin and the historical novel and ranging through such works as Begichev's family-chronicle novel *The Kholmsky Family* (which, in its idealization of the life of the landed gentry, is a precursor of *War and Peace*), and Dahl's colloquial sketches of peasant life that foreshadow Turgenev. Among Russian novels, two were his particular favorites: Narezhny's *Bursak* (a picaresque tale in the tradition of *Gil Blas*, with some scenes of seminary life in the Ukraine that influenced Gogol); and *Serdtse i Dumka* (*Heart and Head*) by one of the most original novelists of the 1830s, Alexander Veltman, who here uses the motif of the double for comic and satiric purposes.

Dr. Dostoevsky was a subscriber to the successful new periodical, *The Library for Reading*, edited by that eccentric figure, the Russified Pole Osip Senkovsky. A professor of Near Eastern languages at the University of St. Petersburg, and a linguist of extraordinary gifts, Senkovsky was also an influential editor, critic, and madcap parodist writing under the name of Baron Brambeus. Even though a fierce opponent of the new Romanticism, particularly of the French variety, Senkovsky was a shrewd enough editor to translate some of the early works of Balzac and George Sand (in truncated versions to be sure), and to give them a good deal of critical attention. One of his favorite targets for attack was the historical novel ("the fruit of the seductive fornication of history and imagination"),[9] and Dostoevsky later recalled that the spate of such novels had once "provided pleasant food for the wit of Baron Brambeus" (3: 12). It was probably in the pages of the *Library for Reading* that Dostoevsky first became aware of such writers as Victor Hugo, Balzac, and George Sand, who were soon to play so important a part in his spiritual and literary evolution.

At the same time, Dostoevsky was also receiving his first important exposure to German Idealist and Romantic ideas in the classroom. His professor of literature during his senior year was I. I. Davydov, one of the small group of academics responsible for propagating Schelling's ideas in Russia, who thoroughly indoctrinated Dostoevsky with the whole tradition of German Romantic Idealist art and esthetics that dominated Russian culture in the 1830s. What affected him most profoundly was Schelling's view of art as an organ of metaphysical cognition—indeed, as *the* vehicle through which the mysteries of the highest transcendental truths are revealed to mankind. The entire generation of the 1840s, as a matter of fact, became imbued with this belief in the exalted metaphysical mission of art; and no one was to defend it in the future with more passion and brilliance than Dostoevsky. As we shall see, Dostoevsky was also influenced by Schelling's view that the highest truths were closed to discursive reason but accessible to apprehension by a superior faculty of "intellectual intuition," as well as by his Idealist conception of nature as dynamic rather than static and mechanical—or, in other words, as exhibiting a spiritual meaning and purpose. Such ideas must have seemed to the young Dostoevsky a welcome confirmation, offered by the most up-to-date science and philosophy, of the religious convictions he had been taught as a child and had always accepted.

6

Of even greater importance for Dostoevsky than all the influences we have mentioned so far, however, was that of Alexander Pushkin. Some of Pushkin's prose was read in the family circle (perhaps his *Tales of Belkin* and *History of the Pugachev Uprising*, both published in 1834), but his reputation was as yet by no means established; and the juvenile enthusiasm of both Mikhail and Feodor for his work gives evidence of their serious literary propensities. There was, it would appear, a friendly family dispute between the generations about the comparative merits of Zhukovsky and Pushkin, and a competition was organized to settle the issue. Mikhail memorized Zhukovsky's *Count Hapsburg*; Feodor was assigned Pushkin's *The Death of Oleg*; both were recited for the parental jury—who declared Zhukovsky the winner hands down, though without at all convincing their offspring. Marya Feodorovna often asked her elder sons to recite the two poems, and listening to them was one of the last pleasures she enjoyed on her deathbed. Some of Pushkin's greatest works appeared during Dostoevsky's adolescence (*The Queen of Spades, Songs of the Western Slavs, The Covetous Knight, The Bronze Horseman, Egyptian Nights*), and though greeted tepidly by the critics were avidly read by the young Feodor.

Dostoevsky's devotion to Pushkin, and his admiration for his writings, was unquestionably one of the decisive formative experiences of his life. How intimately he identified with the great creator of modern Russian literature may be judged from his reaction on hearing of Pushkin's death in February 1837: he told the family that, if he were not already wearing mourning for his mother, he would have wished to do so for Pushkin. For all its extravagance, there is something impulsively right in this youthful desire; if it was his mother who had given birth to him in the flesh, it was Pushkin who had given birth to him in the world of the spirit. Pushkin dominates Dostoevsky's literary life from beginning to end, and the great writer he defended against his father in his youth is also the one to whom he devoted his last public utterance. In the famous speech that he gave at the dedication of a Pushkin monument in 1880—a speech that caused a national sensation—Dostoevsky celebrated Pushkin's supreme importance for Russian culture, and interpreted his work as the first (and still unsurpassed) utterance of Russia's deepest moral-national values. Pushkin's work, in any case, did provide the foundations and define the horizon of Dostoevsky's own creative universe. To be sure, Pushkin's serene and classical art—so attractive in its capacity to suggest profundity without portentousness, and relying on elegant linguistic precision to obtain its effects—is light-years removed from Dostoevsky's frenzied world of violent emotion and tortured souls; but Dostoevsky's work is one continuous, sustained dialogue with Pushkin all the same.

This is true, of course, in the simplest and most literal sense: Dostoevsky read and reread Pushkin, meditated unceasingly on his works, and bequeathed to posterity a series of inspired readings of them that have permanently affected Russian criticism. Even more, Dostoevsky's own writings are impossible to imagine without taking Pushkin into account as a predecessor. Leonid Grossman has well said that "both the negative and the positive creations of Pushkin were equally close and equally dear to him [Dostoevsky]. His greatest figures are linked to Pushkin's heroes, and often are manifestly deepenings of the original Pushkinian sketches that lift them to the level of tragic intensity."[10] This is particularly true of Dostoevsky's post-Siberian period, where his characters rise to genuinely tragic heights; but it is no less applicable to his works of the 1840s, even though here he reduces and contracts (rather than expands or deepens) certain Pushkinian motifs. The terrified clerks of the early stories could not have existed without *The Bronze Horseman* and *The Station Master*; Raskolnikov re-creates the murderous folly of Pushkin's Hermann in *The Queen of Spades*, who is equally obsessed by an *idée fixe* and equally ready to murder to obtain wealth and power; Stavrogin transforms the charming ne'er-do-well Eugene Onegin into a terrifying demonic force. The theme of impostership— so brilliantly dramatized in *Boris Godunov*, and so fateful and omnipresent in Russian history—also haunts Dostoevsky's pages from first to last, beginning with *The Double*, taken up again in *The Devils*, and culminating majestically with the Legend of the Grand Inquisitor.

D. V. Grigorovich, who later became a novelist of note, was for a time a fellow student with Dostoevsky at the Academy of Military Engineers. And he remembers being quite impressed not only by Dostoevsky's thorough knowledge of Pushkin's works, but also by the fact that only he, among all the other students, really took Pushkin's death to heart. This is a valuable confirmation of what we learn from Andrey; and it enables us to fix an illuminating image of Dostoevsky at this time of his life. What already distinguishes him from his fellows is the depth of his involvement with literature; it is clear that he was living emotionally in a world quite different from most of his comrades, whose heads were filled with quite other and more immediately practical concerns. At the age of sixteen, it is the disastrous fate of his literary idol, as well as all that Pushkin's death implied for Russian culture, which already involves Dostoevsky's deepest feelings. And if we are ever to understand him properly, we should do well to keep in mind this precocious capacity to pour the full intensity of his private emotions into what was, essentially, a matter of cultural and national concern.

PART II

St. Petersburg

CHAPTER 6

The Academy of Engineers

The death of Marya Feodorovna snapped the strongest emotional thread tying the young Dostoevsky to Moscow; but he could scarcely have felt any eagerness to begin his career in the Academy of Engineers. The inner conflict between his desire to leave, and the bleakness of the prospect ahead, probably accounts for the persistence of the mysterious illness that struck him down just before departure. Without any apparent cause, he lost his voice and seemed to have contracted some throat or chest ailment whose diagnosis was uncertain. Nothing would cure his malady, and the impending trip to St. Petersburg had to be postponed and wait on his recovery. Finally, Dr. Dostoevsky was advised to begin the journey and trust to the revivifying effects of travel and change of scenery to act favorably on the patient. Andrey remarks that his brother's voice, after that time, always retained a curious throaty quality which never appeared quite normal.

The advice given Dr. Dostoevsky turned out to be well founded, and Feodor's illness passed away once the gates of Moscow were left behind. And no wonder! What Russian youth would not have felt a surge of strength and excitement at the prospect of going to St. Petersburg for the first time? Dostoevsky may already have read those marvelous lines from the prologue to *The Bronze Horseman*, published shortly after Pushkin's death, in which he celebrates the panorama of Peter's majestic creation. "And that young city, of northern lands the beauty and the marvel, from dank of forests, damp of bogs, rose up in all its grandeur and its pride; where once the Finnish fisher, Nature's sullen stepchild, had all alone beside low-lying shores let down his ragged nets, today by bustling docks, crowd, strong and shapely, bulks of tower and palace; ships swarm from all earth's ends to that rich port; Neva has clothed herself in stone; bridges have spanned her waters; her isles with groves dark-green are covered over; and now before the younger capital, old Moscow dims—as, before the new Tsarina, the widow of the purple."[1] For all young Russians, the journey from Moscow to St. Petersburg was a symbol of entrance into the modern world, the journey from past to present, from the city of monasteries and religious processions to that of severe government buildings and monstrous military parades, the journey to the spot where Peter the Great had broken "a window through to Europe." It was also, for Mikhail and Feodor Dostoevsky, the journey from boyhood to manhood, the end of the secure and protected family world they had known and the beginning of the insecurities of independence.

Many years later, Dostoevsky wrote an account of this journey in The *Diary of a Writer* which evokes the state of mind in which both boys approached this new era in their lives. It is clear that, so far as Feodor was concerned, he was already oppressed by the dilemma that poisoned his life up to his retirement from the Army in 1844. Both he and his brother, he tells us, had their heads stuffed full of the mathematics that were necessary for their entrance examination into the Academy; but both were secretly harboring literary ambitions and even actively engaged in composition. "We dreamt only of poetry and poets. My brother wrote verses, at least three poems a day even on the road, and I spent all my time composing in my head a novel of Venetian life."[2] The two young men planned, on their arrival in Petersburg, immediately to visit the site of the duel in which Pushkin had been killed four months earlier and then "to see the room in which his soul expired"[3] (we do not know whether this intention was ever carried out). Both were possessed by a mood of vague yearning and expectancy to which the mature Dostoevsky gives both a moral and a cultural significance. "My brother and I were then longing for a new life, we dreamt about something enormous, about everything 'beautiful and sublime'; such touching words then were still fresh, and uttered without irony."[4] With this Schillerian tag, the two brothers are placed within that atmosphere of morally exalted Romantic fervor so characteristic of the Russian culture of the 1830s.

It is against the background of this lofty moral idealism that one must gauge the shock of what then occurred. At a posting-station along the road, the Dostoevskys went to take some refreshments at an inn. Looking through the window, they saw the whirlwind arrival of a government courier wearing the imposing and elaborate full uniform of the time crowned by the white, yellow, and green plumes of a three-cornered hat waving in the wind. The courier, a powerful and red-faced man, rushed into the station (to drink a glass of vodka, according to the Dostoevskys' coachman), emerged again rapidly, and leaped into a new troika. No sooner was he installed than he rose to his feet and began to beat the driver, a young peasant lad, on the back of the neck with his fist. The horses lurched forward as the

4. A government courier on a mission

driver frantically whipped them up, and the troika vanished from sight with the courier's fist moving mechanically up and down in relentless rhythm as the whip rose and fell in a corresponding tempo.* At the end of this account Dostoevsky imagines the young peasant, on returning to his village, being ridiculed because of his sore neck, and then beating his wife to revenge his own humiliation. "This sickening picture," he says, "remained in my memory all my life."[5]

These words appeared in *The Diary of a Writer* in 1876; and one might well suspect that Dostoevsky was perhaps recalling this incident for the public occasion and exaggerating its importance. But in the notebooks for *Crime and Punishment*, talking solely to himself, he jots down: "My first personal insult, the horse, the courier."[6] This confirms the primacy of the experience for Dostoevsky, and the formative role that he assigns it in his own self-development. For the courier became nothing less than a symbol for the brutal, oppressive government that he served—a government whose domination over an

---

* Incidents of this kind were very common in Dostoevsky's time. The Marquis de Custine, in his *La Russie en 1839*, describes a similar scene. "A little further on I saw a mounted courier, a *feldjaeger* or some other infamous employee of the government, get out of his carriage, run up to one of the two polite coachmen and strike him brutally with his whip, with a stick, and with his fists. . . ." Cited in George F. Kennan, *The Marquis de Custine and His Russia in 1839* (Princeton, N.J., 1971), 28.

enslaved peasantry by naked force incited all the violence and harshness of peasant life. "Never was I able to forget the courier, and much that was shameful and cruel in the Russian people I was then inclined for a long while, as it were involuntarily, to explain in an obviously much too one-sided fashion."[7] With these guarded phrases, Dostoevsky is telling his readers that, in his youth, he had explained the vices of the Russian peasantry solely in social-political terms, solely as a result of the clenched fist crashing down on the back of their necks; and he was convinced that these vices would vanish once the fist had been stayed.

Dostoevsky here is giving us an extremely valuable clue to the motivation of his radicalism in the 1840s, when nothing would obsess him more passionately than the issue of serfdom. "This little scene appeared to me, so to speak, as an emblem, as something very graphically demonstrating the link between cause and effect. Here every blow dealt to the animal leaped out of each blow dealt at the man. At the end of the 1840s, in the epoch of my most unrestrained and fervent dreams, it suddenly occurred to me that, if ever I were to found a philanthropic society, I would without fail engrave this courier's troika on the seal of the society as its emblem and sign."[8] In the late 1840s, the word "philanthropic" in Russian was synonymous with radical or Socialist; and Dostoevsky did more than "dream" of founding such a society: he belonged to a secret group in 1849 dedicated to stirring up revolutionary opposition to peasant enslavement.

These passages, moreover, not only tell us a good deal about the Dostoevsky of the late 1840s; they also bring us a bit closer to the youth of sixteen just about to take his first independent steps in the world. They indicate, for one thing, that Dostoevsky up to that time must have led a fairly sheltered life: he would scarcely have been so affected by the behavior of the courier if he had been hardened to such mistreatment of the common people in his immediate surroundings. He had, after all, grown up in a society built on serfdom; he had read *Poor Liza* (not to mention much else) a long while before; certainly, by the age of sixteen, he must have become aware of the iniquity of turning human beings into chattel. To have remembered the incident at the posting-station all his life as "my first personal insult" would thus indicate that his knowledge had so far remained bookish. It is probable that he had never witnessed any corporal maltreatment of serfs with his own eyes; it seems certain that he had never observed such unimpassioned, systematic, and methodical brutality exercised on a perfectly blameless victim. The "official" nature of the inhumanity in this instance perhaps lit up in a flash, for the first time, the presumptive social source of the evil. And once again it is necessary to note, just as we did with the news of Pushkin's death, the capacity of his sensibility to be stirred at its deepest levels by a public and social matter in which, strictly speaking, he was not personally involved at all.

Why so little attention has been paid to this traumatic episode, called to our attention by Dostoevsky himself, is one of the minor mysteries of the study of his work. Or rather, it is a testimony to the power of critical clichés, which persist in seeing the early Dostoevsky as a "Romantic" (which he was) and in viewing the Romanticism of the early nineteenth century as a totally solipsistic and introspective movement turning its back on the turbulent social-political problems of "real life" (which it was not). The governments of the time had quite a different opinion, as Benedetto Croce has well pointed out. "The suffering of the world, the mystery of the universe, the impulse toward the sublime in love and heroism, the grief and despair over a dreamt-of but unattainable beatitude, the Hamlet-like visits to cemeteries, the romantic pallor, romantic beards, and romantic haircuts—all these and similar things gave evidence of restive spirits. It was expected and feared that they would join conspiratorial sects and rise with arms in their hands the moment they had the chance."[9] The young Dostoevsky was unquestionably a Romantic; but this does not mean, as even one of the very best of his biographers has asserted, that "the impressions which [he] gleaned from literature were far more important to him than those offered by life."[10] On the contrary, the two reinforced and strengthened each other and cannot legitimately be separated: Dostoevsky would not have been so overcome by the beating of the peasant coachman if he had not read Karamzin and Pushkin, and had not already made his own some of Schiller's moral ideal of "the beautiful and sublime."

2

This shocking episode with the coachman was Dostoevsky's introduction to the reality of the world of St. Petersburg, and to all the sordid underside of the resplendent façade of the government in whose service he was about to enter. During the next few years, he would have ample opportunity to enlarge and enrich his awareness of this aspect of Russian life. Indeed, his very first contact with officialdom brought him face-to-face with the hidden corruption that ran through all the institutions of Russian society.

On arriving in St. Petersburg, Dr. Dostoevsky deposited his sons in a preparatory school run by a retired officer of the Academy—a school whose pupils were known always "to do very well" on the entrance examinations. Here the young Dostoevskys studied throughout the succeeding months until the beginning of 1838. Even this important patronage, however, did not prove enough to guarantee success. Mikhail was finally refused on grounds of "ill health"; Feodor, though passing brilliantly, did not receive one of the limited number of vacancies available for entrance without payment of the admission fee. This had been promised originally when Dr. Dostoevsky had made application for his sons; but such places, it turned out, were reserved for those students able to make "gifts" to the examiners. "What rottenness!" Dostoevsky indignantly writes his father. "This completely floored me. We, who struggle for every last ruble, have to pay, while others—the sons of rich fathers—are accepted without fee. God be with them!"[11] Luckily, the Kumanins came to the rescue and offered to supply the required amount. Mikhail was finally admitted to another school of Army Engineers, and, after a few months in Petersburg, was transferred to Revel in the Baltic provinces.

From a purely worldly point of view, Dr. Dostoevsky had chosen very well for his sons. The Academy of Military Engineers was considered the finest establishment of its kind in Russia in the 1830s, and places in it were particularly sought because it was known to enjoy the patronage of Nicholas I. Comfortably housed in the imposing Mikhailovsky palace, which had been originally built in a massive, pseudo-Gothic style for Paul I, and then redone in the 1820s to conform more to Neo-Classic taste, it was here that Paul had been murdered in the palace conspiracy that raised Alexander I to the throne. The bedroom of the slain Emperor had been converted into a religious chapel, as if in expiation for the act of parricide; and the memory of this deed, so frequent in the annals of the Russian ruling house, was still alive for those who inhabited the palace that Paul had built as a retreat. A bit later, under Alexander, its already sinister reputation was increased because it housed the apartment of the notorious Mme Tatarinova, the head of a religious sect which included people in the highest circles of the court. Here they gathered to sing, do round dances, and celebrate the other rites of their ecstatic cult, which drew inspiration from the heretical peasant sects of the flagellants (*khlysty*) and the castrates (*skoptsy*). Stories about these unseemly proceedings were told by one of the older noncommissioned officers, who had been stationed in the Academy since the days when the group had been tolerated. These narratives made a great impres-

5. The Academy of Engineers

6. Interior of the Academy: A dormitory

sion on Dostoevsky, and are probably the beginning of his fascination with the underground religious doctrines of the Russian sects.*

Dostoevsky's life in the Academy was one long torture, and he always looked back on the decision to send him there as a woeful mistake. "We were taken, my brother and I, to Petersburg and to the Academy of Engineers," he wrote late in life, "and thus our future was spoiled. In my opinion, it was an error."[12] The error consisted not only in overlooking the real bent of his interests, but also of placing him in a milieu dominated by physical violence, military harshness, and iron discipline, rather than by the relaxed democratic camaraderie that Herzen depicts as reigning among his fellow students at the University of Moscow during the same years. In the very first letter to his father after being admitted to the Academy, Dostoevsky writes: "I can't say anything good about my comrades";[13] and the same judgment is repeated exactly twenty years later. "What examples I saw before me!" Dostoevsky reminisces. "I saw children of thirteen already reckoning out their entire lives: where they could attain to what rank, what is more profitable, how to rake in cash (I was in the Engineers), and what was the fastest way to get a cushy, independent command!"[14]

For the young man from Moscow, whose head was filled with thoughts of "the beautiful and sublime," the moral mediocrity of his comrades came as a withering disillusionment. And if he had been outraged and insulted by the incident of the government courier, one can well imagine his horror at the savagery of the upper classes of the Academy toward the lower, and toward all those to whom they stood in a position of authority. The memoirs of D. V. Grigorovich give a searing picture of this feature of Academy life; and even at a distance of sixty years, the evocation of such memories still brought back to him "a painful feeling."[15] Merciless hazing and tormenting of the lowerclassmen was one of the privileges enjoyed by the older students, who made ample use of their prerogatives. The authorities closed their eyes to this cruel sport so long as external discipline was maintained; and any protest or resistance could bring on a mass beating that frequently landed the offender in the hospital. "Everything that was just, but oppressed and looked down upon," writes the underground man of his schoolfellows, "they laughed at heartlessly

---

* Dostoevsky did not forget Mme Tatarinova and her sect, and refers to them years later in the context of a discussion of new forms of the same religious unrest. "Even the Templars were persecuted for whirling and prophesying; and the Quakers whirl and prophesy; and the Delphic oracle in antiquity whirled and prophesied; and they whirled and prophesied at the home of Tatarinova. . . ." DW (January 1877), 569.

and shamefully. They took rank for intelligence; even at sixteen they were already talking about a snug berth" (5: 139). This passage corresponds to everything we know about the Academy and Dostoevsky's opinions of his fellow students.

On finding himself thrown into this totally uncongenial milieu, Dostoevsky's first reaction was to feel himself a complete stranger and an outcast. Using the language of the Romantic literature that he was then absorbing, he writes to Mikhail just six months after his admission: "I do not know whether my melancholy thoughts will ever cease. Only one condition is given to the lot of man: the atmosphere of his soul is composed of the union of heaven and earth; what an unnatural child man is; the law of spiritual nature is broken. . . . It seems to me that our world is the purgatory of heavenly spirits darkened by sinful thoughts. It seems to me that the world has taken on a negative meaning, and that from a high, refined spirituality there has emerged a satire. If into this picture stumbles a person clashing with the effect and the idea of the whole, in a word, a totally foreign presence . . . what happens? The picture is spoiled and can no longer exist!"[16] Dostoevsky manifestly casts himself in the role of such a "foreign presence" in the world of the Academy, and, as we shall see in a moment, he did everything he could to change the picture of life that he found there. But the purely biographical origin of such a response should not cause us to overlook its larger significance. For it shows that Dostoevsky was already beginning to think of human life as an eternal struggle between the material and the spiritual in man's nature; and he would always continue to regard the world as a "purgatory," whose trials and tribulations serve the supreme purpose of moral purification.

3
—————

That Dostoevsky was indeed a "foreign presence" in the Academy is amply confirmed by the recollections of all the various people who knew him during these years. A younger fellow student whom he befriended, and who later became a noted artist, gives this picture: "His uniform hung awkwardly, and his knapsack, shako, rifle—all those looked like some sort of fetters that he was obliged to wear temporarily and which weighed him down."[17] Grigorovich tells us that Dostoevsky "already then exhibited traits of unsociability, stayed to one side, did not participate in diversions, sat and buried himself in books, and sought a place to be alone."[18] A. I. Savelyev, a young officer then on duty in the Academy, remarks that "he was so unlike the rest of his comrades in all his actions, inclinations, and habits, so original and out of the ordinary, that at first all this seemed strange, unnatural, mysterious, and aroused anxiety and perplexity; but then, when it did nobody any harm, the commanding officers and his comrades stopped paying attention to these eccentricities."[19]

Savelyev's memories are particularly valuable because, in addition to such confirming generalities, they also contain more specific information about Dostoevsky's ideas and attitudes. Of special interest is the observation that "he was very religious, and zealously performed all the obligations of the Orthodox Christian faith. He could be seen with the Bible, Zschokke's *Die Stunden der Andacht*, etc. After the lectures on religion by Father Poluektov, Feodor Mikhailovich would continue in conversation with him for a long while. All this struck his comrades so much that they dubbed him the monk Photius."[20] The work referred to by the German-Swiss pastor Heinrich Zschokke, best known as a writer of popular adventure novels, is a famous collection of devotional essays widely read in the late eighteenth and early nineteenth century. A Freemason and a partisan of the French Revolution, Zschokke preached a sentimental version of Christianity entirely free of dogmatic content and with a strong emphasis on the necessity of giving Christian love a social application. Dostoevsky would have been familiar with such views from his reading of Karamzin, and, there can be no doubt, sympathized with them thoroughly. Nor did he content himself only with harboring such social-Christian ideas in secrecy and solitude; he tried quite courageously to put them into practice by opposing some of the abuses of Academy life.

Dostoevsky was of course revolted at the inhuman treatment of the lowerclassmen (the "hazel hens," as they were called) by the senior students; and, along with one of his few friends (Ivan Berezhetsky), he did what he could to protect them. Savelyev recalls that Dostoevsky and Berezhetsky stood out from the run of students by their "particularly evident spiritual qualities, for example, their compassion for the poor, weak, and unprotected." They "employed every means to stop this customary violence [hazing], just as they tried to protect the watchmen and all those who looked after the services of the school."[21] Physical maltreatment of the teachers of foreign languages, especially Germans, was also a favorite indoor sport at the Academy; and this too Dostoevsky fought against as much as possible, though not always with success.

During the summer months, when the students camped in a small village near the summer palace of the royal family at Peterhof, the two friends were horrified at the poverty and destitution of the peasants in the region. They accordingly took the lead in organizing a collection among their comrades, and distributed the funds they gathered to those who most needed assistance. As a final trait, Savelyev remarks on Dostoevsky's burning indignation at the corruption in the Army from which he had suffered himself. He had an accurate and detailed knowledge of specific cases, probably picked up from stories and rumors circulating in the military milieu. It would mean nothing to cite the examples that Savelyev gives; but they included a number of high-ranking officers of aristocratic lineage whom Dostoevsky did not hesitate for a moment to criticize in conversation, and who were later demoted or imprisoned for exactly the peculations that he alleged.

From Savelyev's account, one gathers that Dostoevsky was, if not popular with his comrades in the Academy, at least respected by them for his staunchness of character and refusal to compromise with his moral convictions. "They quickly came to like him," Savelyev writes, perhaps exaggerating somewhat, "and often followed his advice or opinion."[22] He was, at any rate, the editor of, and no doubt the chief contributor to, the lithographed student newspaper called (rather oddly) the *Revelsky Snyatok**—which would indicate a certain amount of public authority and acceptance. And, even though known as a solitary, he did have a small circle of like-minded friends, some of whom were destined to play an important role in his life.

With D. V. Grigorovich he shared a passionate interest in literature and the arts; with A. N. Beketov, who was to become the center of a "progressive" circle in the 1840s, a deep social concern and moral passion; Ivan Berezhetsky, who vanishes from sight except for this brief moment of his friendship with Dostoevsky, may have attracted him by a certain intellectual pretentiousness and the airs of a dandy that he affected. Berezhetsky was rather ostentatiously wealthy, always dressed foppishly, and wore a watch and a diamond ring; Dostoevsky certainly envied him his affluence, and probably also admired his mixture of humanitarianism and haughty elegance. It is Berezhetsky who is mentioned in all the memoirs as Dostoevsky's closest friend in the Academy. Savelyev pictures them strolling through the ample rooms of the palace and talking of contemporary poetry (Zhukovsky, Pushkin, Vyazemsky), while the rest of the student body were at the regular Tuesday evening dance class or engaged in outdoor sports. Another memoirist depicts them arguing

* *Snyatok* is the name of a small fish, a smelt.

loudly about Schiller, with Dostoevsky running after Berezhetsky in the corridors to drive home the final word.

In his study of Dostoevsky's character, Freud has referred to "the latent homosexuality" that he believes is revealed by "the important part played by male friendships in his [Dostoevsky's] life."[23] There can be no question that his friendship with Berezhetsky was very important. Writing to Mikhail at the beginning of 1840, Feodor says that, in the preceding year, he had had a friend for whom he had felt "the love of a brother"; "I had a companion at my side, the one creature I loved in that way." This could only have been Berezhetsky, with whom, as we know, he communed over the works of Schiller. "You wrote to me, brother, that I had not read Schiller. You are mistaken, brother. I learned Schiller by heart, talked him, dreamed him; . . . Reading Schiller with him, I verified in him the noble, fiery Don Carlos and Marquis Posa and Mortimer. That friendship brought me so much sorrow and joy! . . . but the name of Schiller has become near and dear to me, a kind of magic sound, evoking so many reveries; they are bitter, brother. . . ."[24]

To express such sentiments about a male friendship may now seem very suspect, and there is no reason to deny that an element of latent sexuality may have been among its components. But the temperature of such relations in early nineteenth century Russia was extremely high; and a passionate male attachment under the magical aegis of Schiller was a fairly common occurrence in the 1830s.* What it represented, in this instance, may be deduced from the names of the Schillerian characters whom Dostoevsky believed he saw embodied in his friend. Don Carlos, the heir to the Spanish throne at the height of Spanish power, and his childhood playmate the Marquis Posa, are both engaged in a plot to give freedom of thought and religion to the suffering people of the Netherlands groaning under

---

* As only one example, Alexander Herzen's *Memoirs of a Young Man* (1840) describes his friendship with Nikolay Ogarev with exactly the same throb of emotion. "By some incomprehensible force we gravitated toward each other; I had a presentiment of him as a brother, a close kinsman of my soul, and he felt the same about me. . . . we were in love *à la lettre*, and we fell more and more in love with every day." Schiller was their ideal, and "we appropriated to ourselves the characters of all his heroes. Life opened out before us triumphantly, majestically; we sincerely vowed to sacrifice our lives for the good of mankind," etc. *My Past and Thoughts* (New York, 1968), 4: 1823. (See Ch. 4, n. 1 for full citation.)

Another instance of such a friendship, of similar importance for Russian culture, was that between V. G. Belinsky and Nikolay Stankevich. "References to Belinsky in Stankevich's letters to others," writes Edward J. Brown, "betray a special warmth of feeling, an unashamed love, which is difficult to imagine in our day, when the romantic exaltation of friendship is so far out of fashion." *Stankevich and His Moscow Circle 1830-1840* (Stanford, Calif., 1966), 88.

Spanish oppression. The Grand Inquisitor in *Don Carlos*, who appears in the last act as the awesome incarnation of a total tyranny over the human spirit, certainly contributed to Dostoevsky's famous Legend of the Grand Inquisitor thirty years later. Mortimer is a young English nobleman in *Maria Stuart*, who leads an unsuccessful plot to free the beauteous, sinful but repentant Mary from imprisonment and finally execution at the hands of the cold and vengeful Queen Elizabeth of England. All three characters are young men inspired by high idealism, by love, or by friendship to serve the great social causes of freedom and justice.

Why the recollection of his friendship with Berezhetsky should have been "bitter" to Dostoevsky we do not know; some rift had obviously occurred. Here again the lucubrations of the underground man may help to fill us in. "Once, indeed, I did have a friend. But I was already a tyrant at heart; I wanted to exercise unbounded sway over him; I tried to instill into him a contempt for his surroundings; I required of him a disdainful and complete break with those surroundings. . . . But when he devoted himself to me entirely I began to hate him immediately and repulsed him—as though all I needed him for was to win a victory over him, to subjugate him and nothing else" (5: 140). If this passage has any autobiographical validity, it would represent Dostoevsky's mature self-judgment on the perversities of his own character—perversities that we shall soon have ample occasion to see him exhibiting all too publicly. This makes it very likely that he displayed similar traits in his relation to Berezhetsky, which are of course exaggerated and magnified by the underground man. The difficulties of Dostoevsky's position in the Academy no doubt led him to place too great an emotional burden on Berezhetsky, to impose such great demands on his sympathy and patience that they finally became intolerable. One may perhaps date the beginning of Dostoevsky's critical attitude toward "Schillerism" as a mode of behavior from such an experience.

4

The most important event occurring in Dostoevsky's life during his years at the Academy was the death (or, to be more accurate, the murder) of his father; and no part of his biography has attracted more attention and speculation, or been given greater importance in determining the course of his future. For this reason, it is well to remember that, at the time of the murder, Dostoevsky had not laid eyes on his father for two years. After depositing his sons in

St. Petersburg, Dr. Dostoevsky returned to Moscow and never saw them again. For reasons of health (his application for retirement complains of rheumatic attacks and failing eyesight), he resigned his post and went to live in Darovoe. Deprived of the support of Marya Feodorovna, and of his one or two friends on the hospital staff, he went to pieces morally in the loneliness and solitude of the provinces. Alyona Frolovna, who continued in her post as housekeeper, heard him carrying on long conversations with his dead wife as if she were present; and it was at this time that he took to drinking heavily. One of the two young village girls who had served the Dostoevskys as housemaids in Moscow, the high-spirited daughter of a Darovoe peasant named Katerina, became his mistress and bore him an illegitimate child in 1838. All of the stories used by biographers to link Dr. Dostoevsky with Feodor Karamazov refer to these last two years of his life between 1837 and 1839, though whether Feodor Dostoevsky had any knowledge of what was happening to his father at the time is highly unlikely—one cannot imagine from where he could have obtained the information. After the murder, to be sure, he must have been given word-of-mouth reports of his father's decline; but it is erroneous to imply that he was an eyewitness to any behavior comparable to what he depicted more than forty years later.

Freud has built an elaborate construction on Dostoevsky's presumptive reaction to the news of the murder, which, according to psychoanalytic theory, fulfilled the parricidal impulses that he had been harboring (but suppressing) all along. Overcome with guilt on hearing the news, which objectified his most secret and most unbearable wishes, he punished himself by means of his first true epileptic seizure. For the moment, let us try to remove the question of Dostoevsky's guilt feelings from the realm of psychoanalytic speculation, and examine instead the available evidence concerning his relations with his father in the two years preceding the latter's terrible demise. There are, as we shall see, good reasons to accept Freud's *aperçu* that Dostoevsky felt implicated in the murder and emotionally assumed a large share of the guilt; but these reasons are quite other than the ones that Freud alleges.

From the very beginning of their stay in Petersburg, the problems involved in launching his two sons properly on their future careers were a constant source of anxiety for Dr. Dostoevsky. Nothing seemed to go as had been planned, and unanticipated expenses kept mounting. There is a good deal of discussion in the correspondence about three hundred rubles that Dr. Dostoevsky had paid, in addition to the regular fee of the preparatory school, so that his sons could receive supplementary instruction in artillery and fortifications —only to learn from them finally that "the three hundred rubles were not at all necessary for [Kostomarov]."[25] The news of Mikhail's rejection by the Academy was a great blow, and so was Feodor's failure to obtain free admission. Dr. Dostoevsky's letters are full of concern and trepidation; but though his own financial resources were being strained to the utmost, he tried as best he could to meet the demands of his sons. A joint letter from them in December 1837 thanks him for the receipt of seventy rubles, which they say is more than sufficient to satisfy their needs. "We have just received your letter, and along with it seventy rubles, money soaked in the sweat of toil and your own deprivation. Oh, how that makes it precious to us now! We thank you, thank you from the bottom of our heart, which is fully aware of everything you are doing for us."[26] This is the somewhat *exalté* style—an imitation of the tone of their parents' letters—in which both Mikhail and Feodor write to their father. But both were aware that their sentiments were fully justified by the objective situation, and there is no reason to consider them hypocritical.

Dr. Dostoevsky's chagrins were by no means finished even after his sons had settled into the harness of their respective establishments. Feodor, for reasons that still remain obscure, failed to be promoted during his first year of study; and on receiving the letter announcing the unhappy news, Dr. Dostoevsky suffered a partial stroke that required the local doctor to bleed him as a remedy. Dostoevsky explained the setback, in letters both to his father and Mikhail, as the result of the enmity of some professors (he mentions only one, the professor of algebra, to Mikhail); and he lists his course grades, which are excellent, as proof of the injustice. Recently, however, it has been discovered that he neglected to list his grade in military drill, which was abysmally low and may have been the real cause of his failure. The uncertainty in the story about his professors, and his convenient failure to mention the telltale grade, makes this assumption quite plausible. But since he knew that favoritism was rife in the Academy, he may very well have believed that his deficiencies in drill alone would not have been enough to cancel out all his other work. Whatever the explanation, there is no doubt that the whole affair left him with a very bad conscience so far as his father was concerned. And when he tells Mikhail that "I would regret nothing if the tears of our poor father did not burn my soul,"[27] at least the last part of this utterance may be taken at face value.

This episode is not the only aspect of Dostoevsky's life at this time that may have given him a bad conscience. It is quite likely that he also felt troubled and uneasy at the reiterated demands he made on his father, despite everything he knew of the family's straitened circumstances, for extra money. These requests were all couched in terms of necessity; but their real source was Dostoevsky's desire not to cut too sorry a figure among his more affluent comrades who came from wealthier families. Dostoevsky may have held most of his fellow students in contempt, but he obviously could not endure the idea of being considered by them both personally odd *and* socially inferior; and the struggle to maintain his social status and self-esteem is quite naïvely evident in his letters. He writes his father in June 1838 that all of his money had been spent, explaining that, for the May parade of the Academy before the royal family, he had bought himself a new shako. "Absolutely all my new comrades acquired their own shakos; and my government issue might have caught the eye of the Tsar."[28] Since, a bit earlier, he notes proudly that 140,000 troops had participated in the spectacle, this eventuality hardly seems a likelihood; nor is it self-evident that Nicholas would have been displeased by the sight of a regulation shako.

The same pattern appears in his requests to his father for additional funds to tide him over the summer months when the students pitched camp at Peterhof. "Out in camp," he writes, "the most awful necessities arise, and without money there you're in trouble."[29] What these "awful necessities" are he does not say; but in a later letter he lists a sum for having his boots cleaned as an unavoidable camp expense. The next spring he asks for money so that he can buy an extra pair of boots besides those issued, order his own tea in addition to the regular ration, and acquire a locker for his books. In justifying this request, he explains to his father that he is merely conforming to the "rules" of his present society. "Why be an exception?" he asks, revealing his own dilemma. "Such exceptions are sometimes exposed to the most awful unpleasantnesses."[30] The "rules" he talks about, however, were purely self-imposed, or rather imposed by the need to maintain a becoming social position in the eyes of his comrades. This is confirmed by the memoirs of Count Peter Semenov, whose comments on Dostoevsky are always very much to the point (Semenov later became a noted explorer, geographer, and natural scientist, who also assembled one of the finest collections in Europe of Dutch art of the seventeenth century and wrote a major work on the subject). It so happened that Semenov shared the same bivouac at Peterhof with Dostoevsky, though the two had not yet met at the time. "I lived in the same camp with him, in the same linen tents . . . and I got along without my own tea (we received some in the morning and the evening), without any more boots than I was issued, and without a trunk for my books, though I read as much as F. M. Dostoevsky. As a result, all this was not actual need but simply a desire not to be different from other comrades who had their own tea and boots and trunk."[31]

So far as one can judge, Dostoevsky never wrote home for funds without eventually receiving the sum requested. In March 1839, he wrote that he was fifty rubles in debt (without explaining why or for what), and asked for ten rubles in addition to pay summer expenses at camp. In answer, he received bills that could be exchanged for ninety-four rubles. Two months later he made the additional request for his tea, his boots, and his trunk; and this drew a response in which Dr. Dostoevsky paints a somber picture of the economic state of affairs at Darovoe—a picture fully in accord with the known facts. He reminds his son that, for the last several years, there had been poor harvests, and Dr. Dostoevsky predicts that this year will bring on total ruin. Even the previous year, he says, things had been so bad that the straw roofs of the peasant huts had been used for fodder; "but that was nothing compared to the present distress. From the beginning of spring not a drop of water, not even dew. Heat and terrible winds have ruined everything. What threatens is not only ruin but total starvation. After this can you continue to grumble at your father for not sending you money?"[32] All the same, the amount Dostoevsky had asked for was dispatched with the warning to use it sparingly.

This letter was written on May 27, 1839; Dr. Dostoevsky was murdered sometime in early June, perhaps a week or two later; his despairing communication to his son was, literally, his last testament, and Dostoevsky must have received it almost simultaneously with the news of his father's death.

5

It is not necessary to inquire here into the conflicting versions that have been given of the murder. Whether it was a spontaneous outburst of rage or carefully concerted in advance; whether the cause was the unbearable exactions and severity of Dr. Dostoevsky—who made the hapless peasants pay dearly for his own grief and desolation—or whether there was an element of revenge because of his affair with Katerina; whether his fate was sealed by the notable restiveness of the peasants in that region during 1839 because of the burning drought and the miserable crops—none of these questions can really be answered conclusively. What is important is that the murder took place, and that most of the male population of the village was involved. Death apparently came by suffocation, and no marks of foul play were visible on the body.* Dr. Dostoevsky was reported to have died of an apoplectic stroke; and though the truth was known throughout the district, the family decided to let the matter rest. The Kumanins had no great love for the irascible doctor in any case; the murder would have been almost impossible to prove; and, even if proved, it would have meant the exile of almost all the male serfs and the effective destruction of the children's patrimony. Andrey Dostoevsky surmises that his two older brothers knew the truth almost from the very start; he learned about it only indirectly, being too young at the time to be told.†

* One of the rumors about the murder, which continues to be propagated, is that Dr. Dostoevsky was sexually assaulted or mutilated. Henri Troyat writes that one of the murderers "squeezed his [the victim's] genitals with all his might"; Marthe Robert, more recently, speaks confidently of "the castration that accompanied the crime." Henri Troyat, *Dostoievski* (Paris, 1960), 52; Marthe Robert, "L'Inconscient, creuset de l'oeuvre," in the collective volume, *Dostoievski* (Paris, 1971), 148.

The only reliable information about the murder—and it is still second-hand—comes from two sources: the memoirs of Andrey Dostoevsky, and word-of-mouth accounts gathered from descendants of Darovoe peasants by V. S. Nechaeva and others, which are summarized in her book. Such testimony is of course hearsay at a distance of almost a hundred years, and hearsay embellished with all the earthy motifs of the peasant oral tradition. There is an obscure phrase in *one* of the Nechaeva stories that can be interpreted to mean approximately what Troyat reports as a fact. There is nothing about castration anywhere. *DVS*, 1: 89; Nechaeva, *V Seme i Usadbe Dostoevskikh*, 54. (See Ch. 2, n. 4 for full citation.)

† As the present volume goes to press, some important new material has come to light that casts considerable doubt on whether the death of Dr. Dostoevsky was a murder at all. According to the account given by Andrey, the presumed murder was hushed up, and the cause of death given as an apoplectic stroke, because the peasants succeeded in bribing the local authorities with a considerable sum of money. Where the impoverished peasants managed to raise the large amount required is a mystery which Andrey mentions without clarifying; but he accepts as fact that the necessary funds were found. A week after the event, with Dr. Dostoevsky already in his grave, his mother-in-law arrived to gather up the younger children and look after other affairs. She was told by some neighbors—a retired Major Khotyaitsev and his wife—that the death had not been natural but a murder; they advised her to let the matter rest so as to guard the interests of the family. This was the version of Dr. Dostoevsky's end that she brought back to Moscow, and which was accepted by the family.

A recent investigator, who has gone back to inspect the records of the district in which the Dostoevsky property was located, has come up with quite a different picture of events. In the first place, Dr. Dostoevsky's corpse, far from having been hustled unceremoniously out of the way, was examined independently by two local doctors, both of whom concurred on the cause of death as being apoplexy. Secondly, a rumor about a possible murder was first brought to the attention of the authorities by another neighbor, A. I. Leybrekht, who attributed the rumor, however, to Khotyaitsev. The provincial court took the matter under investigation, questioned the Major, and, when he denied having said anything, arranged for a confrontation between the two men. Khotyaitsev persisted in his denial; and Leybrekht then revealed that the former had *asked* him specifically to alert the authorities to the possibility of murder. Khotyaitsev, it is necessary to know, was involved in a lawsuit against the Dostoevskys over some issue of

From all this, one can well surmise that Dostoevsky may have been overwhelmed by a shock of guilt and remorse on hearing of his father's death and learning its true cause. The uneasiness he had felt all through this period—an uneasiness caused both by his failure to gain promotion, and by the awareness that he was exploiting his father's meager resources to appease his craving for social status—could have suddenly exploded in a frenzy of self-accusation. If his father had been mistreating the peasants abominably, was not he really to blame? Was it not to satisfy his purely fanciful "needs" that his father had come to his horrible end? After all, he had been familiar with the peasants at Darovoe since childhood. He knew they were not monsters and criminals; on the contrary, he above all was aware that, for all their uncouthness, they were capable of great kindness and the most humane, Christian feelings. Would they have murdered their master without the most extreme provocation? The guilt feelings he had always harbored toward his father even as a little boy must now have swelled to a piercing pitch of self-accusation because of his own possible share in having brought on the family tragedy.

If we assume that the turmoil of Dostoevsky's psyche can be described in some such terms, then we can come much closer than Freud to providing a *specific* explanation for Dostoevsky's behavior in the 1840s and for the character of his work. Freud's observation

---

land-demarcation, and was a much wealthier landowner with five hundred souls. If some of the Dostoevsky peasants had been deported to Siberia as murderers, he could have snapped up the adjacent property for a song. This may explain why he wished to spread the rumor of murder, but at the same time appear to be a friend of the family concerned over their interests.

The matter continued to be investigated for over a year by various provincial legal bodies. Questions were sent to Moscow to Dr. Dostoevsky's relatives, and to the children's *nyanya*, Alyona Frolovna, who had been in Darovoe at the time of death. Several peasants considered to be among the murderers (according to the usual version) were called in for interrogation; but no evidence of foul play was discovered. It should be remembered that any kind of justifiable "suspicion" would have been enough to condemn the peasants to exile, and that the murder of a landowner was a crime that the government would have been eager to punish very harshly.

In the light of these new facts, the usual depiction of how Dr. Dostoevsky died becomes very dubious indeed. The entire story about the murder originated with Khotyaitsev, who had reasons of self-interest for wishing it to be accepted; there is no other evidence besides his own by anyone who could have had personal knowledge. It is also difficult to believe that *all* those concerned with the case, including the two doctors, could have been bribed, if only because the sum required would have been truly enormous. None of this further investigation was apparently known to Dr. Dostoevsky's surviving children; and the story told to their grandmother by Khotyaitsev, entering into the family tradition, was given credence by Dostoevsky himself with incalculable consequences for his moral and emotional equilibrium. *DVS* I: 89-90; G. Fedorov, "K biografii F. M. Dostoevskogo," *Literaturnaya Gazeta*, No. 25 (June 18, 1975), 7.

about Dostoevsky's "sympathy by identification" with criminals in his major novels does not apply at all to his writings in the 1840s; nor does Freud give any reason why the Oedipal revolt against the father should have assumed the *particular* humanitarian form of joining a conspiracy to spread propaganda against serfdom. But if the guilt that Dostoevsky felt for the murder of his father is of the kind suggested here, nothing would have been more natural than for him to try to relieve it by projecting it externally in social terms.

The sensitive humanitarian, the devotee of "the beautiful and sublime," had already been shocked at the beating of a peasant coachman. How much more would he have been overwhelmed by the scenes at Darovoe that his tortured imagination conjured up—scenes for which he could not avoid assuming some of the responsibility? And thus his sense of guilt became transformed into the burning hatred of serfdom that he manifested—a hatred so great that, as we shall see, he could not bear to hear its abuses described without a reaction of intense emotional agitation. The existence of serfdom had now become literally unbearable for him because he could never free himself from the sickening feeling that, in helping to foment its worst excesses, he had brought on his father's death. Only through the abolition of serfdom, only through the destruction of the monstrous system, could the trauma of his guilt be assuaged; and it was for this goal that he ultimately risked his life and was sent to Siberia.

To this extent, and for these far more self-evident reasons, one can accept Freud's view that Dostoevsky emotionally assumed a burden of parricidal guilt. But Freud's acceptance of the family tradition that the shock of the news brought on Dostoevsky's first epileptic seizure is a far more dubious matter. Freud, of course, was eager to give credence to this tradition because it supported his assumption that Dostoevsky's epilepsy was not organic but hysterical in origin. (He does not mention the fact—perhaps he was ignorant of it—that Dostoevsky's three-year-old son Aleksey died of a severe epileptic attack in 1878, which would appear to indicate some sort of hereditary origin for the affliction.) Moreover, the presumed coincidence of the first attack and the father's murder served as confirmation of Freud's belief that Dostoevsky was caught in an irreconcilable conflict between parricidal impulses and a guilty need for self-punishment. But the rumor on which he relies is formally contradicted by the letters of Dostoevsky himself in 1854, when he first mentions the disease and its symptoms; and it seems unlikely in view of all the other circumstances.

None of the people who knew Dostoevsky in the Academy, and who left memoirs, refer to any such attack. All were writing after Dostoevsky's death, when the mention of his epilepsy would not have been embarrassing and when its existence had long been public knowledge. Also, it should be remembered that Dostoevsky was then living in common quarters with a hundred other classmates, and was constantly under supervision and surveillance: an epileptic attack would have been very hard to conceal. One can only agree with E. H. Carr who, after a careful survey of all the original material, concludes: "The evidence is at best pure hearsay; it contradicts all our other information, written as well as verbal; and it is probable that a story so poorly attested would not have been taken seriously if it had not happened to fit in so well with the hypothesis of the psychoanalysts."[33] Rumors are notoriously difficult either to prove or to discredit; and no doubt a margin of uncertainty will always continue to surround this issue. But since there are other (and very convincing) reasons for believing Dostoevsky to have been overcome with feelings of guilt at the murder of his father, the question of whether the first signs of his illness appeared in the spring of 1839, or, as is much more likely, several years later, no longer has the importance for us that it did for Freud.*

6

Dostoevsky's only recorded response to the death of his father—a letter to Mikhail in mid-August 1839—makes no mention of any unusual perturbation on receipt of the news. "My dear brother! I have shed many tears over the death of father"—this is all that is said, although if he had had anything in the nature of what might have been considered a "fainting fit," there was no reason to have kept it a secret. The letter, nonetheless, is worth a little closer scrutiny than it has usually received. What seems to trouble Dostoevsky most is the fate of his younger brothers and sisters, not so much practically as morally; he finds distasteful the idea that they will be educated by the Kuma-

---

* One can still wonder why Mme Dostoevsky should have spread such a rumor if it were not true. Carr has suggested that it was put about to counter another rumor—namely, that Dostoevsky's first attack had been caused by a flogging while a convict in Siberia. The image of Dostoevsky being flogged was too demeaning for the worshipful Anna Grigoryevna to endure. For Carr's article, see note 33, Chapter 6.

Another and less complicated possibility is that it was simply the result of an error. When Dostoevsky failed to be promoted in the Academy of Engineers, we know that this failure caused his father to have a slight stroke and that Dostoevsky himself fell sick and spent some time in the hospital. This was just a year before the murder. Dostoevsky may have said something about having been sick around that time because of grief about his father, and this led to the inference about an attack of epilepsy. See Grigorovich's reference to Dostoevsky's illness in DVS, I: 129.

nins. Hence he fervently approves of Mikhail's plan—never, to be sure, put into practice—to retire to Darovoe after becoming an officer and devoting himself to their upbringing. "The harmonious organization of the soul in the midst of one's own family, the development of all tendencies on Christian principles, the pride of family virtues, the fear of sin and dishonor—this is the result of such an education. The bones of our parents then will sleep tranquilly in the moist earth."[34] This is, clearly, the kind of careful upbringing and education that he felt he had been given himself, and which he now tends to idealize under the shock of his loss. There is a total sense of identification with his father in such words, which leads to the desire to perpetuate the values of the family tradition as Dostoevsky now sees them. This may have been his first reaction—one of compensation—to the wave of guilt that swept over him, and which is possibly betrayed by the reference to the restlessness of his parents in their grave.

At the same time, the letter also expresses a certain sense of relief, as if a burden had been lifted off Dostoevsky's shoulders. It is curious to see him telling Mikhail that now, more often than in the past, he is able to look on everything that surrounds him in the Academy much more calmly. One reason for this is certainly that it was now permissible to regard the Academy as merely a way station in his life; and he speaks openly for the first time about his intention to abandon the Army. "My one goal is to be free. I am sacrificing everything for that. But often, often I think, what will freedom bring me? . . . what will I be, alone in the crowd of the unknowns?"[35] Despite such nagging fears, Dostoevsky expresses confidence in himself and the future, and the firm conviction that his "sacred hopes" will one day be realized. No doubt Dostoevsky had begun to cherish such hopes secretly a good while before; but he had never dared previously to acknowledge a defiance of his father's wishes—a defiance which could only have led to a terrible and heartbreaking clash of wills. The death of his father had cleared this major emotional obstacle from his path; and his sense of guilt was thus also accompanied by a sense of liberation.

It was, perhaps, an obscure awareness of some such feeling which now impels Dostoevsky to remark that his soul was "no longer accessible to its old stormy surges," and that it was "like the heart of a man concealing a profound enigma." Moreover, the aim of his life henceforth, he says, will be "to study 'the meaning of life and man.'" Professing a qualified satisfaction with the progress he has already made in this enterprise, he adds the revealing information that he pursues it by delving into the "characters in the writers with whom the best part of my life is spent freely and joyously." "Man is an enigma," he continues, a few sentences later. "This enigma must be solved, and if you spend all your life at it, don't say you have wasted your time; I occupy myself with this enigma because I wish to be a man."[36] These impressive words are often quoted to express Dostoevsky's sense of his own mission as a writer; and it is no coincidence that they appear in the only letter commenting on the murder of his father. For no event could have driven home to him more intimately and starkly the enigma of man and human life—the enigma of the sudden irruption of irrational, uncontrollable, and destructive forces both within the world and in the human psyche; the enigma of the incalculable moral consequences even of such venial self-indulgence as his own demands on his father. It was this enigma which, indeed, he was to spend the rest of his life trying to solve; and no one can accuse him, while doing so, of having wasted his time.

CHAPTER 7

"A Marvellous, Exalted Being"

It has become more or less accepted that Dostoevsky's education at the Academy of Engineers was sadly deficient. There is no doubt that, particularly in the more advanced classes, he did waste a good deal of time slaving away at mathematics and engineering requirements. But the Academy also entertained the laudable ambition of providing some sort of humanistic education for these future officers of the Russian Army; and at least during the first year or two his studies were not a total loss. He attended lectures on religion, history, civil architecture, Russian and French language and literature, and also lessons in German. He added a good command of this latter language to his mastery of French; and the excellent drawings and sketches in his notebooks—both of European architecture, as well as visualizations of his characters—prove that he acquired considerable skill in this branch of the fine arts. Moreover, the professors of Russian and French literature at the Academy were both conscientious pedagogues, and certainly increased Dostoevsky's systematic knowledge of their subjects.

The chair in Russian literature at the Academy was held by V. T. Plaksin, who, just a few years earlier, had published a widely used handbook on the history of Russian literature. A frequent contributor to the literary periodicals, Plaksin can be described as a moderate partisan of Romanticism. He accepted Romanticism as the art of the modern world; he believed that religion—Christianity, of course—had created modernity and Romanticism; and he stressed nationalism as inseparable from Romantic creation. Genius he defined as the capacity to uncover the mystery of what seems commonplace and even repulsive, and to lift it to the level of the refined and the beautiful. Plaksin lectured on Pushkin and Lermontov, and on the Russian folk-poet Koltsov, a cattle dealer by trade, who was one of the few Russian writers to have emerged from the people. Indeed, a good deal of attention was given to Russian folk-poetry, of which Plaksin was a connoisseur. His view that genius consisted in raising the ordinary to the more elevated led him to take a rather dim view of the early works of Gogol; and he was pilloried in the 1840s for an incautious remark in his handbook that, while Gogol was "a great artist," his writings were nonetheless "full of repellent errors."[1] Whether Dostoevsky agreed with this judgment as a student is impossible to say; but there is no evidence that he had any serious interest in Gogol before 1842.

From Plaksin, Dostoevsky could not have acquired very much more in the way of ideas about literature than he had already obtained from Davydov in Moscow; both would have taught him essentially the same German Romantic doctrines. His professor of French literature, however, Joseph Cournant, was something else entirely. High praise is given to Cournant's course in the memoirs of I. Sechenov, later the famous physiologist and teacher of Pavlov, who entered the Academy in 1843. Dostoevsky too benefited from Cournant's talents, and his letters soon become studded with references not only to Racine, Corneille, and Pascal, but also to such French Renaissance writers as Ronsard and Malherbe. More important is that Cournant included contemporary literature in his purview, and introduced his students to Balzac, Hugo, George Sand, and Eugène Sue. Writing to his father in May 1839, Dostoevsky says that it is "absolutely necessary" for him to subscribe to a French circulating library. "How many great works of genius there are—mathematical and military genius--in the French language."[2] This is another, perhaps less invidious, example of Dostoevsky's subterfuges to obtain money; but the urge to keep up with current French publications is surely a tribute to the stimulus imparted by Cournant's course.

2

Dostoevsky's studies at the Academy provided, however, only the minor part of his education. The major share was obtained in the company of a young man who had nothing to do with military engineering. This was Ivan Nikolaevich Shidlovsky, a chance acquaintance whom the Dostoevskys met on the first day of their arrival in St. Petersburg. Both Shidlovsky and the Dostoevskys had converged on the capital at the same time and met when they put up at the same hostelry. The young Shidlovsky, then only twenty-one years of age, made a great impression both on the slightly younger Dostoevsky brothers and—more surprisingly—on the usually mistrustful and cross-grained doctor. It would almost appear as if he had confided the care of his two sons to their new young friend; and it was through Shidlovsky that, in the next two years, he sometimes sent them funds and obtained information when they failed to write. In 1873, Dostoevsky told a young writer, come to gather material about him for a biographical article: "Mention Shidlovsky . . . without fail, it makes no difference that nobody knows him and that he did not leave any literary name. . . . he was a very important person for me then, and he deserves not to have his name sink into oblivion."[3]

Who is this friend to whom Dostoevsky acknowledged owing so much? Ivan Shidlovsky, when Dostoevsky first met him, had come to Petersburg to take up a post in the Ministry of Finance, and to become part of that swarming world of Russian bureaucracy soon to be depicted in Dostoevsky's works. Like the Dostoevsky brothers, however, his heart was in literature and not in service to the state. Tall and striking in appearance, eloquent and loquacious, Shidlovsky impressed everybody by the depth of his culture and the passion of his perorations on lofty topics—perorations that he was always able to top off with an apt quotation from Pushkin. Naturally, he wrote poetry himself, and he soon succeeded, not only in breaking into print, but also in gaining entrée into the outer fringes of the literary life of the capital. Shortly after arriving he called on N. A. Polevoy, the defender of French Romanticism, whose own magazine had been closed in 1839 because of what Pushkin called its "Jacobin" tendencies, and who had joined the staff of another publication. One can well imagine the tremendous effect that Shidlovsky must have made on the two budding authors, and the aureole that soon surrounded him in their bedazzled eyes. Not his least importance for Dostoevsky was that Shidlovsky was the first person to take his literary aspirations seriously, and to encourage them with example, precept and counsel.

Whenever Dostoevsky could get away from the Academy for a free moment, he would spend it with Shidlovsky; and when his friend left Petersburg for good, probably sometime in late 1839, he was disconsolate. "My friendship with Shidlovsky gave me so many hours of a better life," he writes Mikhail. "I often sat together with him for whole evenings talking of God knows what! Oh, what a pure and candid soul!"[4] These conversations were very far from being idle social chatter, or limited even to an exchange on more intimate personal matters. They were, rather, dialogues about the great writers whom Dostoevsky was now reading under Shidlovsky's tutelage. Evoking their last evening together before Shidlovsky's departure, Dostoevsky continues: "Oh, what an evening that was! We recalled our winter days, when we spoke of Homer, Shakespeare, Schiller, Hoffmann, those about whom we had talked so much, whom we had read so much!"[5] Shidlovsky was thus Dostoevsky's literary guide and mentor in this very impressionable period of his life; and it was largely through his eyes that Dostoevsky now began to view the great Romantic culture-heroes whose very names filled him with awe.

3

What little information we have about Shidlovsky shows him to have been a typical Russian Romantic of the 1830s, consumed, as they all were, with unappeasable desires that could not be satisfied within the bounds of earthly life and torn by tempestuous passions. His few extant poems are all expressions of this Romantic malaise, which leads him to melancholy questionings about the meaning of human existence. No answer is ever given to these inquiries; but Shidlovsky is consoled by the belief that there is a God who sometimes vouchsafes his presence in nature, and holds out hope of solace to unhappy humans. Indeed, the stars become for him, as they were to be for Alyosha Karamazov, the visible signals guiding mankind on its painful path to God ("The stars guiding my way / He kindles clearly there in the blue").[6] One of his best images compares a shooting star to a tear of God, come to light up for an instant the darkness of terrestrial life. Dostoevsky was a great admirer of these poems, and could hardly wait to read them. "Ah, soon, soon, I shall read the new poems of Ivan Nikolaevich," he writes Mikhail in the fall of 1838. "What poetry! What inspired ideas!"[7] Posterity has been much less kind to these products of Shidlovsky's inspiration; the one Russian critic to discuss them at all remarks on their "rhetorical inflation," and their reliance on "the formulas of passion and feeling" of the period.[8]

Besides the seven poems of Shidlovsky that have been unearthed and published, there is only one other document giving us any first-hand impression of his personality. This is a long letter that he wrote to Mikhail in February 1839, at a time when his friendship with Feodor was flourishing, and when, it can be assumed, the latter was intimately familiar with every tremor of Shidlovsky's psyche. The letter is a long, rambling communication, leaping waywardly from one topic to another and giving a vivid impression of Shidlovsky's many-sided and unbuttoned personality. The range of literary reference is wide, and illustrates the depth and seriousness of his concern with the day-to-day life of the Russian cultural scene; but there is nothing pompous or pretentious about him, nothing stiff or formally pedagogic. On the contrary, he writes equally freely and casually about his urge to go off on a drinking spree with Mikhail (apparently one of his favorite companions for such an escapade), and his flirtations with the wives of friends who aspire to be immortalized in his verse. Shidlovsky, evidently, was one of those "broad" Russian natures, oscillating between the most contradictory moral impulses, that Dostoevsky later so often portrayed. No doubt his complete freedom from any kind of stuffiness constituted one source of the magnetism he exercised on his younger friends. But Shidlovsky's ebullience did not prevent him—either then or later—from plunging into one severe spiritual crisis after another brought on by his torn and divided personality.

Probably as the result of an unhappy love affair, he tells Mikhail that his heart, just before Christmas, "had been overcome by the decision to dissolve the shackles of existence, to escape from this captivity; and the watery bed, the bed of my darling Fontanka [a canal], tempted me as passionately as the bridal bed does the new bride."[9] Shidlovsky tried to fight off this temptation to suicide by increased fervency in prayer; but to no avail. However, on Christmas itself, the miracle occurred: "some sort of wonderful illumination shone before my eyes; tears gushed forth passionately—and I believed." Now, he realizes that "life is an unbroken chain of God's kindnesses"; to take one's life means "to renounce some of the charity of God," and to display ingratitude to the divine power Who "with all His Mercy spends Himself for each of my moments."[10] Suicide is permissible, he says, only to those like Werther and Chatterton, who have turned away from life entirely and whom life itself has rejected. But, Shidlovsky continues, this is not at all his own situation: he feels obligated (presumably to God) for the hours in which he writes poetry, for beef, and for wine—and, who knows, perhaps the laurels of poetic fame will also someday be his! Such sudden and unexpected shifts of mood were unquestionably part of Shidlovsky's charm.

One other passage of the letter must be cited at length, as an example of the ideas that Dostoevsky was eagerly absorbing from the lips of his master. "We must believe," he writes, "that God is good, for otherwise He is not God; that the beauty of the Universe is this visible and tangible goodness, and the substantial, necessary unity of this and other truth; only then does our soul recognize all in itself, throw a web of sympathy around the boundaries of being, and in the center of the web embrace God Himself. This is the only true sign of the great poet, who is man at his highest peak; soil him with dirt, slander him, oppress him, torture him, his soul will nonetheless stand firm, true to itself, and the Angel of inspiration will guide him safely out of the dungeon of life into the world of immortality and onto the couch of all-pervading glory. Polevoy once beautifully said to me that one must look on man as a means for the manifestation of the sublime in mankind; but the body, a clay vessel, sooner or later is shattered, and all our past vices and occasional virtues vanish without a trace."[11] This is a fine example both of the Romantic egoism and of the urge for pantheistic self-obliteration that had been stimulated by the influence of Schelling and was so widespread in the 1830s. Just a few years earlier (1833), in his famous *Literary Reveries*, the young critic V. G. Belinsky—soon to become the most important cultural force of his time—had written that man's "infinite, supreme felicity consists in the dissolution of [the] *Self* in the feeling of love" for all of God's creation.[12]

4

How thoroughly Dostoevsky assimilated the values of this Romantic phase of Russian culture may be judged from what he writes to Mikhail, approximately a year later, in a letter describing Shidlovsky in the throes of his earlier crisis. "One had only to look at him to see what he was: a martyr! He had become thin; his cheeks sunken; his sparkling eyes dry and burning; the moral beauty of his face heightened as the physical declined. He was suffering, cruelly suffering. My God, how he loved the young girl (Marie, I believe). She had married someone else. Without this love he would not have been this priest of poetry, pure, noble, disinterested. . . . Sometimes on winter evenings (just about a year ago) while going to his modest lodgings, I could not help recalling the sad winter of Onegin in Petersburg (eighth chapter). But the person in front of me was not a cold creature, a dreamer despite himself; he was a marvellous, exalted being, the true sketch of man as Shakespeare and Schiller have shown him; but he was just then on the point of falling into the dark madness of Byronic characters."[13] This last phrase probably alludes to Shidlovsky's struggle against the temptation of suicide.

Dostoevsky's wide-eyed hero worship is touchingly naive in its expression; but it is much more than merely another case-book illustration of adolescent inflammability whose effects were not likely to be very long-lasting. For what Dostoevsky saw confronting him in Shidlovsky was the living embodiment of the great Romantic conflict between man and his destiny by which his imagination had now become ignited. Shidlovsky brought him face-to-face with "the true sketch of man" as "a marvellous, exalted being," just as Dostoevsky had learned to apprehend him in Shakespeare and Schiller; no classroom lectures and no poring over texts could have conveyed with such vital immediacy the heights and depths of the Romantic experience. And the influence of Shidlovsky naturally contributed to strengthen Dostoevsky's own commitment to the Romantic values that his friend and mentor was exemplifying so dramatically. The supreme nobility of a hopeless (and disinterested *because* hopeless) passion; the spiritual value of suffering for an unattainable ideal; the role of the poet as self-sacrificing "priest" of this Romantic dispensation, proclaiming his faith, and his love of God, in the midst of his travails—all this Dostoevsky now accepts as the very acme of sublimity. Indeed, Shidlovsky is presented in such terms so as to glorify and justify him against some accusation or expression of disapproval made by Mikhail in an earlier letter that has been lost.

M. H. Abrams, with his usual authority, has recently sharpened our awareness of the extent to which the "characteristic concepts and patterns of Romantic philosophy and literature are a displaced and reconstituted theology"[14] and represent a return to Christian fashions of feeling. "A conspicuous Romantic tendency, after the rationalism and decorum of the Enlightenment," he writes, "was a reversion to the stark drama and suprarational mysteries of the Christian story and doctrines and to the violent conflicts and abrupt reversals of the Christian inner life, turning on extremes of destruction and creation, hell and heaven, exile and reunion, death and rebirth, dejection and joy, paradise lost and paradise regained."[15] The Romantic values that Dostoevsky assimilated from Shidlovsky were thus a recasting, in early nineteenth century terms, of the same religious agitations and questionings that had stirred him profoundly as a little boy in the Book of Job. And here we can locate an even deeper reason, besides the ones already mentioned, for the importance that Dostoevsky assigned to Shidlovsky in his life: Shidlovsky's primary role was to have aided Dostoevsky in making the transition between his childhood faith and its sophisticated modern equivalents. No wonder Dostoevsky was everlastingly grateful to the man who had performed this crucial task.

In addition, Shidlovsky offered him a compelling example, by his own continued adherence to Orthodox forms of worship, of how the two could be combined. This meant that Dostoevsky did not have to suffer any wrenching shock, any agonizing reevaluation of his old beliefs, in adapting himself to the new world of Romantic culture that he was so eager to assimilate. For the young Dostoevsky who had been dubbed "the monk Photius" by his comrades, and was probably ridiculed because of his religiosity, Shidlovsky's friendship supplied a major prop in supporting his self-esteem. Nor should one underestimate the future influence of Shidlovsky's living demonstration that intense religious commitment could be combined with a frank confession of the torments of doubt; genuine faith for Dostoevsky would never afterwards be confused with a tranquil acceptance of dogma. Dostoevsky, it is true, soon left this Romantic phase behind, and often later parodied and satirized various types of Romantic egoism. But the Romantic dissatisfaction with the limits of earthly life and, in particular, its positive valuation of moral suffering, always remained a permanent feature of his own world view.*

5

Shidlovsky left Petersburg sometime in late 1839 (the date is uncertain), and retired to his family estate in the province of Kharkov—never to return, and never, so far as we know, to see the Dostoevsky brothers again. He worked for a while on a history of the Russian church, and continued to write poetry; but the inner conflicts evident during his Petersburg years continued to plague him, and after a certain time he went to pieces. He oscillated between bouts of heavy drinking with the officers of his brother's regiment and renewed accesses of religious fervor. For a brief period he entered a monastery and lived as a novice; but he was excluded when his presence there led to a notable increase in the consumption of strong drink among the other monks. Later, he would occasionally don the garb of a religious pilgrim and, still an irresistible spellbinder, preach to the common people at wayside taverns in his district. An eyewitness describes him, on one such occasion, reducing the men to silent reverence and the women to tears, and gratefully accepting the glass of vodka traditionally offered to the preacher of God's word by the peasants.

Dostoevsky, we know, was eager to keep in touch with Shidlovsky, and tells Mikhail in 1846 that he has just received a visit from the brother of their friend. At this time he obtained his address (lost sometime in the interim) and letters were probably exchanged; but none have come to light so far. The fragment of a recently published letter, written by Shidlovsky to Dostoevsky after Mikhail's death in 1864, indicates that he had been in correspondence with Mikhail

---

* H. G. Schenck has perceptively remarked that "seen against the background of the secularization of our culture in the Modern Age, it would appear that the renewed emphasis on suffering [is] a characteristically Romantic trait. In marked opposition to the optimism of the Enlightenment, the Romantics can be said to have rediscovered the inevitability of human suffering." *The Mind of the European Romantics* (New York, 1969), 100.

intermittently but had lost contact with Feodor. A pathetic and nostalgic document, the letter shows Shidlovsky's awareness of the failure of his own life compared to that of his two younger friends and erstwhile admirers. He pleadingly begs Dostoevsky to take the time to send him a joint photograph as a very great favor, because "it is impossible for you not to be convinced of my love for the both of you."[16] Shidlovsky died in 1872, and it was a few months later that Dostoevsky, speaking to Vsevolod Solovyev of his erstwhile inspirer, paid a grateful tribute to his memory.

CHAPTER 8

The Two Romanticisms

Russian culture in the mid-1830s was in a period of transition between the predominant influence of German Romantic literature and Idealist philosophy on the one hand, and the beginning of a turn toward that of French social Romanticism (which included a good deal of what came to be called Realism or, in Russia, Naturalism) on the other. The generation of the 1820s had grown up in a time of great political turmoil, and took a strong interest in social and political matters. As every reader of *Eugene Onegin* will recall, the St. Petersburg dandy of the time considered an acquaintance with the doctrines of Adam Smith an indispensable part of his mental wardrobe.* The shock administered to Russian society by the Decembrist uprising and its sternly repressive aftermath, however, turned the thoughts of the next generation into other channels. The seeds of German Romantic influence had already been well planted before 1825; and they blossomed luxuriously in the sternly non-political hothouse climate fostered by Nicholas I.

As a result, all concern with the practical and empirical affairs of man and society were now scornfully rejected as unworthy of the true dignity of the human spirit. Only by striving to unriddle the secrets of the Absolute could man remain faithful to the high calling revealed to him by his own self-consciousness; and these secrets could be divined in the great artistic creations of the ages of religious faith, or in the metaphysical intuitions of the great philosophers. Art and Idealist metaphysics thus replaced all other areas of life as the focus of cultural interest. Only one publication—N. A. Polevoy's *The Moscow Telegraph*—stood out against this current, and strove, particularly after the revolution of 1830, to put in a good word for the strong social and Socialist orientation of much of the new French literature. But Polevoy's own work as a novelist reveals the hybrid amalgam of influences so typical of the mid-1830s. His best narra-

---

* "From Adam Smith he sought his training/ And was no mean economist;/ That is, he could present the gist/ Of how states prosper and stay healthy/ Without the benefit of gold,/ The secret being that, all told, the *basic staples* make them wealthy./ His father failed to understand,/ And mortgaged the ancestral land" (1.7). I use the translation by Walter Arndt (New York, 1963).

tives, published under the collective title *Dreams and Life* (1834), depict the archetypal Romantic Idealist collision between an impossibly high-principled young artist or "dreamer" and harsh reality. It is true, as Soviet critics like to point out, that his artist-heroes are all from the lower class and have to fight against social prejudice; but even they concede that his main emphasis is on the eternal disparity between the dreams of imagination and the limits of the real. Dostoevsky came to intellectual maturity during the mid-1830s, and he was profoundly affected by the disparate mixture of cultural tendencies prevalent in these years.

2

Dostoevsky's portrait of Shidlovsky is only one of the numerous passages in his letters where we can observe him busily assimilating the tenets of what may be called metaphysical Romanticism, with its strong emphasis on man's relation to a world of supernatural or transcendental forces. During the summer of 1838, as Dostoevsky proudly informs Mikhail, he read "all of Hoffmann in Russian and in German (*Kater Murr* has not been translated)," as well as "the *Faust* of Goethe and his shorter poems" and a new romantic tragedy by Polevoy entitled *Ugolino*.[1] This was exactly the moment when Belinsky was telling his friends that Hoffmann was as great a genius as Shakespeare, and when, as P. V. Annenkov recalled, "the fantastic world of Hoffmann's stories seemed . . . a particle of revelation or disclosure of the omnific Absolute Idea."[2] It is again indicative of this period of cultural fluctuation that even Alexander Herzen, who had already come under the influence of Saint-Simonism, should have made his début as a writer in 1837 with a celebration of Hoffmann's genius. Dostoevsky was thus very much in step with the time in his reading, and catching up rapidly with the latest taste.

Traces of this immersion in Hoffmann can be found in the same letter. "I have a plan: to become mad," he tells Mikhail. "Let people get angry, let them cure me, bring back my sanity."[3] No doubt Dostoevsky dreamed of this subtle form of revenge on his uncongenial classmates and surroundings; and he speaks of Hoffmann more explicitly in another remark. "If you have read all of Hoffmann you certainly remember the character of Alban. How do you like him? It is terrible to see a man who, not knowing what to do, plays with a toy which is—God!"[4] Alban is a character in Hoffmann's *Der Magnetiseur*, whose occult powers lead him into the Satanic ambition to rival God by gaining control over nature. Dostoevsky refers to him as "playing with God" because, in German Romantic thought, God is omnipresent in nature as a vital force, and whoever toys with nature is impinging on God's domain. Even at this early date, as we see, Dostoevsky exhibits a horrified fascination with the theme of man's sacrilegious aspiration to dethrone God and substitute himself in God's place; and he was very soon to encounter a much more powerful and influential effort of the same kind in the doctrines of the Young Hegelians.

There has been a good deal of discussion about Hoffmann's influence on Dostoevsky; but the German writer's effect on Russian literature was so all-pervasive that it is difficult to isolate Dostoevsky's particular debt to him with any precision. Dostoevsky had already read both Pushkin (*The Queen of Spades* is distinctly Hoffmannesque) as well as Veltman, with his use of the double as a structural device; and the early stories of Gogol also are very much influenced by Hoffmann. Nonetheless, Dostoevsky probably learned a good deal at first hand from Hoffmann's genius for depicting pathological emotional states and subconscious criminal impulses, as well as for creating a unique poetic atmosphere—a blend of the realistically trivial with a richly imaginative and fantastic dream world. Many years later, in comparing Hoffmann with Poe, Dostoevsky expressed a preference for the German over what he considered the too practical and too down-to-earth American. Poe, he said, confined his fantasy only to the framework of his stories; once given the situation, everything else is presented with startling exactitude and verisimilitude. Hoffmann, on the other hand, "personifies the forces of nature in images," allows the supernatural to intrude overtly, and "even sometimes seeks his ideal outside the confines of the earthly." This, in Dostoevsky's view, makes Hoffmann "immeasurably superior to Poe as a poet" (XIII: 524). Despite this preference, Dostoevsky's own work is closer to Poe than to Hoffmann: he too has an uncanny ability to visualize and dramatize the extraordinary within the conventions of realism, and without any supernatural intrusion.

Earlier, we noted Dostoevsky's tendency, whenever he wishes to describe his inner life, to employ the categories of Romantic metaphysics—for example, his remark about being a "foreign presence" in the Academy, and of the world as a "purgatory of celestial spirits" (a phrase with a very Schillerian ring). As the same letter continues, his mood of depression is replaced by one of stormy rebellion: "But just to see the harsh covering under which the universe languishes, to know that one explosion of the will is enough to shatter it and to fuse with the eternal, to know and to remain like the lowliest of mortals . . . that's terrible! How cowardly man is! Hamlet! Hamlet! When I recall those raging, savage speeches, in which sound the groans of a lifeless world, neither a sad murmur nor reproach plucks at my breast. . . . My soul is so crushed by sorrow, that one is afraid to understand it for fear of being torn apart."[5] Hamlet's failure to shatter the universe and "fuse with the eternal" here becomes a sign of man's degradation: humanity is not strong enough to live up to its own exalted self-awareness. Dostoevsky's accusation of "cowardice" leveled against Hamlet will one day be repeated in Raskolnikov's frenzied self-accusations because of his inability to be a "Napoleon," and inwardly remaining only one of "the lowliest of mortals." Nor would Dostoevsky forget the idea of suicide—of an "explosion of the will"—as a supreme gesture of metaphysical defiance when he comes to create the character of Kirillov in *The Devils*.

Time and again, in leafing through Dostoevsky's letters, one finds examples of how well-schooled he had become in this Romantic proclivity for casting his personal problems into cosmic and world-embracing terms. After expressing his outrage at failing to be promoted, for example, Dostoevsky goes off on the following flight: "Brother, it is sad to live without hope. . . . I look ahead and the future terrifies me. . . . I am moving in a kind of cold polar atmosphere where no ray of sunlight has ever penetrated. . . . It is long since I experienced any flash of inspiration . . . but I am often in a state like that of the Prisoner of Chillon, you remember, after the death of his brothers in the dungeon. . . . The heavenly bird of poetry does not wing toward me, nor warm my numbed spirit . . . the marvellous arabesques I used to create have lost all their gilding . . . either my heart has grown hard or . . . I dare not continue. . . ."[6] Dostoevsky's disappointment is thus translated, with a little help from Byron, into the metaphysical link between the artist and his muse, who comes from some supernatural source to provide inspiration and comfort—like Shidlovsky's tear of God—and to warm the heart and soul of the poet chilled by the iciness of life.

A passage in another letter is particularly important as the first indication of Dostoevsky's acceptance of a philosophical irrationalism, whose roots are to be found in the widespread vogue of Schelling in Russia. Mikhail had written to his brother—in what connection is not clear—that "to *know* more, one must *feel* less." Feodor's answer is a vehement assertion to the contrary. "What do you mean by the word *to know*?" he asks belligerently. "To know nature, the soul, god, love. . . . These are known by the heart, not the mind." Dostoevsky argues that thought cannot unriddle the mystery of creation because "mind is a material faculty," and as such is not in touch with transcendental truth. "Mind is an instrument, a machine, moved by the fire of the soul." It is the soul (Dostoevsky also uses the word "heart") which is the true medium for attaining the highest knowledge, for "if the goal of knowledge is love and nature, this opens up a clear field for *the heart*." Poetry is thus just as much a medium of knowledge as philosophy (Mikhail had probably argued the contrary) because "the poet, in the transport of inspiration, unriddles God."[7]

If, along with these quotations, we recall Dostoevsky's absorption of the works of Schiller in communion with Berezhetsky, we can see how strongly he came under the influence of metaphysical Romanticism. And—from the prefigurations of important motifs of the later Dostoevsky that we have noted in passing—it is clear how deep and long-lasting this influence was to remain. This does not mean, to be sure, that such Romantic intimations contain the "sources" of any of Dostoevsky's great creations. It will require his long years of hardship and suffering, and the extraordinary experiences he was forced to undergo, before Dostoevsky would be able to metamorphose the youthfully gimcrack Romantic stereotypes of his letters into the life-tempered genuineness of his tragic art. Nonetheless, metaphysical Romanticism retained its significance for Dostoevsky because it was never spiritually rejected or overcome as a whole. It opened his sensibility to the early nineteenth century forms in which man struggled to express his age-old religious questionings; and it provided some of the paradigms through which he would ultimately affirm his own genius.

3

Equally important in its effect on Dostoevsky, however, was the competing literary current of French social Romanticism. There is, it must be admitted, a certain artificiality in separating off these two Romanticisms too sharply one from the other. How, for example, is one to dissociate the metaphysical from the social in such a writer as Schiller? Auerbach has said of one of Schiller's plays, *Louise Millerin*, that it is "a dagger thrust to the heart of absolutism";[8] and the same phrase can well be applied to them all. Another German critic has written that "what Schiller furthered in his creations from *The Robbers* to *Don Carlos* was . . . what the French Revolution translated into fact."[9] The inflammatory effect of Schiller on the birth of more than one revolutionary vocation in Russia is well-known; and if Dostoevsky and Berezhetsky took on themselves the chivalric task of protecting the weak and helpless in the Academy, one may be sure that their reading of Schiller had contributed to arouse their social conscience. All this being true, however, a distinction can still usefully be drawn between those influences that taught Dostoevsky to view human life primarily in some absolute or transcendental perspective, and those which sharpened his awareness of the concrete social issues of his contemporary world.

Such issues were being posed most luridly in the new French literature which Dostoevsky had been encouraged to read by Cournant's course. Shidlovsky's guidance probably helped in this direction too, though we have no evidence in his work of any specifically social orientation. However, referring to *The Moscow Telegraph* in his letter to Mikhail, he says: "Happy is the man who has saved it like the holy of holies in his library. I am indebted to it for my very soul."[10] And Shidlovsky's friendship with Polevoy brought Dostoevsky, even if at one remove, into the orbit of the chief critical advocate of the political liberalism and moral humanitarianism of the French Romantic school. It is thus by no means accidental that, in the same letter in which he speaks of having read Hoffmann and Goethe, Dostoevsky also boasts to Mikhail of having gotten through "almost all of Balzac" and all of Hugo except *Cromwell* and *Hernani*.[11]

The impact of Balzac on Dostoevsky was nothing short of a revelation. "Balzac is great," he writes enthusiastically. "His characters are the creations of universal mind! Not the spirit of a time but the struggle of thousands of years have prepared such a result in the soul of man."[12] This is Dostoevsky's first ecstatic response to a writer who, as Leonid Grossman has said, played Virgil to his Dante. No predecessor in the European novel was more important for Dostoevsky than Balzac, and such works as *Eugénie Grandet* and *Le Père Goriot* were to serve as trail-blazers clearing the path for his own productions.

It was Balzac who took over the historical novel of Scott and used it for the treatment of contemporary social life, substituting the deceptive calm of the French provinces and the glittering kaleidoscope of Paris for Scott's Highland glens and medieval or Near Eastern pageantry. It was Balzac who first spoke of Scott as having taught him that the modern novel was "un drame dialogué";* and no one would develop the form in this direction more brilliantly than Dosto-

---

* The remark is made in *Illusions perdues*, where the aspiring young writer, Lucien de Rubempré, is told: "Vous serez tout neuf en adaptant à l'histoire de France la forme du drame dialogué de l'Écossais." Honoré de Balzac, *La Comédie humaine*, ed. Marcel Bouteron (Paris, 1947), 4: 649.

evsky. Only Balzac, of all of Dostoevsky's contemporaries, can compare with him in uniting a visionary social observation of astonishing exactitude with inner dramas of the soul that span the entire range of moral experience from the Satanic to the divine.

Balzac's artistic importance for Dostoevsky is well known and has been amply explored,[13] but no attention at all has been paid to the contribution that the French novelist undoubtedly made to Dostoevsky's social-political education. Friedrich Engels, at the very end of his life, praised Balzac for having given, in *La Comédie humaine*, "an excellent realistic history of French 'society,' which describes in the manner of a chronicle, and almost year for year between 1816 and 1846, the continually increasing attacks of the rising bourgeoisie against the aristocratic society resurrected after 1815, and which, so far as possible, had raised again the banner of *la vieille politesse française*. He describes how the last survivors of this society, which for him is exemplary, went down to defeat before the onslaught of the vulgar, wealthy upstarts or were completely corrupted by them. . . ." And from this series of novels, Engels affirms, he learned more "even in economic details (for example, the redistribution of royal and personal property after the Revolution) than from all the professional historians, economists, and statisticians of the period taken together."[14] Marx too was a great admirer of Balzac, and saw in the mysterious and all-powerful figure of Gobseck, the immensely wealthy moneylender, a symbol of the hidden power of capital that had now taken over control of the destiny of mankind.

For Balzac, modern French society was nothing but the battleground of a ruthless struggle for power between the old aristocracy of birth and breeding and the new freebooters of high finance. In this conflict to the death, all the time-honored moral foundations of the human community were being destroyed. "The Golden Calf," as Harry Levin writes, "[had] indeed usurped the altar and the throne,"[15] and Europe was doomed because it could no longer muster any higher values to oppose to the unrestricted reign of material interests. This vision of European society, blocked out in Balzac's monumental proportions, forms part of the background for Dostoevsky's later vision of the West. If Karamzin had given him a sense that Europe was moribund, it was Balzac who probably first persuaded him that it was totally in thrall to Baal, the flesh-god of materialism, and that it could not escape the catastrophe of a bloody class struggle (a conviction shared, after all, by his fellow—Balzacians Marx and Engels). But Balzac's work also gave the young Dostoevsky what may have been his first glimpse of the doctrines of the Saint-Simonian school (these are discussed, ironically but not hostilely, in *L'Illustre Gaudissart*), who opposed the inhumanity of early capitalism and preached a "New Christianity" interpreting Jesus as the prophet of a "religion of equality."

4

Great as was Dostoevsky's admiration for Balzac, it was rivaled, if not surpassed, by his worship of Victor Hugo. Just two months after first mentioning having read him, he felt qualified to reject a criticism of Hugo printed in Polevoy's journal. "Not long ago," he writes Mikhail, "I read in *The Son of the Fatherland* an essay of the critic Nisard about Victor Hugo. Oh, how low he stands in the opinion of the French! How insignificant Nisard makes out his dramas and his novels to be. They are unjust to him, and Nisard (though an intelligent man) is talking nonsense."[16] Désiré Nisard—one of the best of the French conservative critics defending the classical tradition against the Romantics—was indeed an intelligent man, and Dostoevsky's refusal to be persuaded by his arguments is eloquent proof of his admiration for Hugo.

To judge the significance of this admiration properly, we should remember that, by this time, Hugo and his writings had become a red flag—a symbol for the great wave of social humanitarianism released by the revolution of 1830. "La charité, c'est le socialisme," wrote Lamartine in 1834,[17] indicating the Christian sources of the new social movement; and it was as an expression of such Christian sentiments that Hugo spoke of his own work:

> J'ai, dans le livre, avec le drame, en prose, en vers,
> Plaidé pour les petits et pour les misérables;
> Suppliant les heureux et les inexorables;
> J'ai réhabilité le bouffon, l'histrion,
> Tous les damnés humains, Triboulet, Marion,
> Le laquais, le forçat, et la prostituée.*[18]

Hugo's writings moved Dostoevsky so deeply precisely because of this social-Christian quality; and, more than thirty years later, he still considered them inspired by "a Christian and highly moral" idea. "It can be formulated as the regeneration of fallen mankind, crushed by the unjust weight of circumstances, the inertia of centuries and

---

* "With book and play, in prose, in verse, I have/ Taken up the cause of the weak and those in misery;/ Pleading with the happy and the pitiless;/ I have raised up the clown, the comedian,/ All human beings who are damned, Triboulet, Marion,/ The lackey, the convict, and the prostitute."

by social prejudices. This idea is that of the justification of the humiliated and of all the rejected pariahs of society" (XIII: 526).

If we are to judge by his references to it later, no creation of Hugo meant more to Dostoevsky than the grisly little novel, *Le dernier jour d'un condamné*. This book—filled, as Herzen suggestively put it, with "the strange, terrible lights and shadows of a Turner"[19]—is the imaginary diary of a condemned criminal awaiting execution for some unspecified crime. No more poignant attack has ever been written on the horror of capital punishment; and there is something truly prophetic in Dostoevsky's evident fascination with this work. For he was one day to suffer exactly the same agonies as Hugo's character, and, in reliving all his torments, to reveal how indelibly Hugo's book had bitten into his mind. On returning to prison after the mock execution in 1849, when he had believed himself to be only a moment away from death before a firing squad, his first reaction was to write a letter to his brother Mikhail. And this moving document contains the French phrase, not otherwise explained—*On voit le soleil!* These are almost the very words used by Hugo's condemned man to express his desire for life at any price, even at the price of exile and hard labor that Dostoevsky had just learned he was to be forced to pay himself. It is not surprising that, having ingested this text so thoroughly, Dostoevsky should later have drawn on it for his novels. V. V. Vinogradov has shown that certain details from *Le dernier jour d'un condamné* reappear in Raskolnikov's hallucinatory dream of murdering the old pawnbroker a second time while she laughs soundlessly in his face; and also in the nightmarish episode of Kirillov's suicide in *The Devils*.[20]

Hugo's overriding importance for Dostoevsky is strikingly exhibited by a passage in a letter to Mikhail early in 1840. Feodor, in an earlier letter, had evidently compared Homer and Victor Hugo; to which Mikhail had retorted that Homer should more properly be compared with Goethe. Feodor replies with these astonishing words: "So far as Homer and Victor Hugo are concerned, it seems that you purposely misunderstand me. Here's what I said: Homer (a legendary figure perhaps like Christ, incarnated by God and sent to us) can be paralleled only with Christ, not with Goethe. . . . You see, in *The Iliad* Homer gave the entire ancient world the organization of its spiritual and earthly life, exactly in the same sense as Christ to the new. Now do you understand me? Victor Hugo as a lyric poet, with a pure angelic character, with a childlike Christian tendency in his poetry, and no one can compare with him in this. . . . Only Homer, with the same unshakable confidence in his mission, with his childlike faith in the god of poetry whom he serves, is similar in the tendency of the source of his poetry to Victor Hugo. . . ."[21]

Quite aside from its relation to Hugo, this passage is of great interest as evidence of Dostoevsky's early acquaintance with ideas then considered quite "advanced." If he is willing to entertain the thought that Homer and Christ have both been sent by God, and that their status in relation to mankind is approximately the same, then the youthful Dostoevsky can hardly be accused of any simple-minded acceptance of conventional religious notions; his words smack much more of the Utopian Socialist doctrine of religion as "progressive revelation"[22] than of Christian orthodoxy. Moreover, it is highly significant that Victor Hugo, in the modern world, plays the same role of prophetic mouthpiece of God as is assigned to Homer in the ancient one. Dostoevsky's thought seems to be that Christ had proclaimed "the organization of . . . spiritual and earthly life" for modernity, and that Hugo, inspired by this divine source, was expressing in his poetry the true meaning of Christ's teaching. This would indicate that Dostoevsky's Christianity had already become strongly social and humanitarian, and was practically identical with what was being called "Socialism" in France.

Dostoevsky's close familiarity with the writings of the French social Romantics is also displayed by another comment in his letters. Speaking of several poems written by Mikhail, he remarks that he approves of "the idea" in one of them; but then he adds that "the spirit and the expression of the poem are strongly influenced by Barbier; among others, his verses on Napoleon were fresh in your mind."[23] This ability to recognize stylistic traits bespeaks a close acquaintance with the poetry of the now-forgotten (but then very well known) Auguste Barbier, whom Sainte-Beuve called "the only poet produced by the revolution of 1830."[24] Barbier's work had been banned in Russia because of a poem attacking the suppression of the Polish uprising; but this did not prevent him from influencing Lermontov, and, a few years later, becoming the favorite poet of the Petrashevsky circle. One progressive critic, a friend of Dostoevsky's, spoke of his work as "breathing indignation against the vices and misfortunes that now torture the poorer classes of European society and . . . weep[ing] bitter tears over those forced by need into corruption, over the sufferers in Bedlam deprived of reason by their misfortunes, over the poor workers slowly dying in the suffocating factories of England."*[25]

---

* It is possible that, in Barbier's poem about Napoleon, we have one of the sources for the association between Napoleon and "bronze" in *Crime and Punish-*

Dostoevsky's sympathy with such socially conscious protest literature probably explains his enthusiasm for De Quincey's *Confessions of an English Opium Eater*, which he warmly recommended to Grigorovich. The portrait of the kindhearted little prostitute Ann of Oxford Street, who saved De Quincey's life, anticipates the long line of such spiritually superior "fallen women" in Russian literature—the most famous of them all being, of course, Sonya Marmeladov. Grigorovich speaks of having read Lamartine's long narrative poem *Jocelyn* while at the Academy, and this "humanitarian epic" (so labeled by its author) was probably also familiar to Dostoevsky as well. During the summer of 1838, no doubt on Shidlovsky's recommendation, Dostoevsky painstakingly plowed through Polevoy's six-volume *History of the Russian People*. This was the first Russian work utilizing the doctrines of the liberal French Romantic school of historians such as Thierry and Michelet, and it stressed the importance of the spirit of the people, rather than, as did Karamzin, that of the state and of morally enlightened despots.

5

Like the other members of his generation who came to maturity in the mid-1830s, Dostoevsky always remained stamped with the complex cultural physiognomy of the time. Indeed, one of the secrets of his genius may well have been his refusal ever to decide emotively between the personal and literary tensions created by his equal devotion to the two Romanticisms. On the one hand, we see his commitment to the supernatural, other-worldly and more traditionally Christian outlook of metaphysical Romanticism—Christian at least in spirit, and even though the artist is substituted for the priest and the saint. But, on the other hand, we also have the strong tug of his feelings toward the practical application of the Christian values of pity and love—toward the "philanthropic" ground swell of the French social Romanticism flooding in ever more irresistibly after 1830. The one keeps its eyes devoutly fixed on the eternal; the other responds to the needs of the moment. The former concentrates on the inner struggle of the soul for purification; the latter combats the degrading influence of a brutalizing environment. The supreme value attributed to

ment. The statue of Napoleon here is repeatedly addressed as "ce bronze," "le bronze puissant," etc. The people first pull down the statue, but then set it up again and worship it as an idol. This is exactly what Raskolnikov says the people always do with "great criminals" like Napoleon, who is castigated in the poem as responsible for a hecatomb of French lives. Auguste Barbier, *Iambes et poèmes* (Paris, 1871), 31-42.

suffering comes into conflict with compassion for the weak and the oppressed; the need to justify God's ways to man clashes with the desire to refashion the world. Dostoevsky felt the competing pull of both these moral and religious imperatives, and the balance of their opposing pressures helps to account for the unremitting tragic impact of his best work.

CHAPTER 9

The Gogol Period: I

At the beginning of 1840, Dostoevsky was still an obscure student of military engineering with vague ambitions for a literary career but with nothing to show that such ambitions would ever be realized. By 1845, however, he was being hailed by Belinsky—the most powerful critical force in Russian literature—as the newest revelation on the Russian literary horizon. During these years, he went through a metamorphosis that set him firmly on the road he was to follow the rest of his life. "Brother," he writes Mikhail in the spring of 1845, "as regards literature *I am not as I was* two years ago. Then it was childishness, nonsense. Two years of study have brought much and taken much away."[1] What took place during these two years to bring about such a realization, and how do they contrast with the three preceding them?

If we look for some answer in the events of Dostoevsky's life, there is little we find there that seems helpful or illuminating. His studies at the Academy went forward without further incident, and he was promoted to the rank of ensign in August 1841. He continued to be assigned to the Academy so as to complete his work in the higher classes for officers; but he was now entitled to live outside the school, and he immediately availed himself of the opportunity. At first he shared an apartment with a fellow engineer named Adolph Totleben. Totleben was often visited by his older brother Edward; and this chance acquaintance later played a very important role in Dostoevsky's life. Edward Ivanovich Totleben, who supervised the fortification of Sevastopol during the Crimean War, became a national hero at that desperate moment in Russian history. In response to a letter of Dostoevsky, he used his influence at the court of Alexander II to help obtain a full pardon for him after his release from the prison camp in Siberia. Dostoevsky also shared an apartment in 1843 with a young medical student from Revel—a friend of Mikhail's—named Igor Riesenkampf.

2

Riesenkampf's reminiscences of Dostoevsky, which have only recently been published, are the chief source of information about his life at this time; and they give us our first glimpse of some of the qualities in his character that were always to make relations with him so difficult and so mutable. Mikhail Dostoevsky, Riesenkampf remarks, was a calm and equable person, who knew how to master his emotions and would betray displeasure, in some social situation, only by a slight tightening of the lips. His brother Feodor was of a much more restless and inflammable disposition, always ready to be swept away by a burst of enthusiasm or anger and quite incapable of curbing himself in moments of stress. "Feodor Mikhailovich was no less good-natured and no less courteous than his brother, but when not in a good mood he often looked at everything through dark glasses, became vexed, forgot good manners, and sometimes was carried away to the point of abusiveness and loss of self-awareness."[2] The inability to bridle his temper—a trait of character that he shared with his father—was to plague Dostoevsky all his life, and to place a very heavy burden of tolerance on his friends. In the one incident of this kind described by Riesenkampf, Dostoevsky became exasperated at a social gathering made up largely of members of the foreign colony in Petersburg, "and [he] let fly with such a philippic against foreigners that the startled Swiss took him for some sort of *enragé* and thought it best to beat a retreat."[3] Dostoevsky's xenophobia, so disagreeably vehement later, thus goes a long way back and could easily be aroused.

As Dostoevsky was to do himself in a few years, Riesenkampf attributes this extraordinary irascibility to the poor state of his friend's health. To Riesenkampf's medical eye, Dostoevsky's sallow complexion indicated some blood deficiency, and he noted, too, a tendency to chronic infection of the respiratory organs. And this was not all—for Dostoevsky was continually a prey to nervous disorders of various kinds. "He constantly complained to me that, during the night, it seemed that somebody near him was snoring; as a result he could not get to sleep and somehow felt uneasy, so that he was unable to settle down. At such times he got up and spent the rest of the night reading, or most often in working on various stories he wanted to write."[4] Such bouts of insomnia were always followed by periods of extreme irritability, when he would quarrel with everybody for little or no reason. To make matters worse, Dostoevsky was haunted, as we have noted earlier, by fears of falling into a lethargic sleep and being buried alive; to forestall such a mishap, he would leave notes asking not to be entombed before the lapse of a certain number of days. Nonetheless, according to Riesenkampf, Dostoevsky made great efforts to conceal his various discomfitures and bore them very stoically;

it was only because they lived together that Riesenkampf became aware of them at all. "In the circle of his friends he always seemed lively, untroubled, self-content."[5]

During his first several years of freedom from the Academy, Dostoevsky began to lead the life of a young man about town and to savor some of the delights of a St. Petersburg resident. He assiduously attended the plays and ballets at the Alexandrinsky theatre. He turned out when Franz Liszt and Ole Bull came to town; when the great Belgian clarinetist Joseph Blaise gave a concert; when the famed Italian tenor Rubini was performing for a Russian audience. He was, if not at the première, then at one of the very first performances of Glinka's new opera, *Ruslan and Ludmilla*. Andrey Dostoevsky—who came to live with his brother in the fall of 1841, and remained for a year—mentions occasional card parties in the flat with fellow officers, and comments that "my brother liked to play cards very much."[6] Riesenkampf also notes Dostoevsky's weakness for games of chance—a weakness that was to become pathological in the 1860s. From a remark to Mikhail on the inconvenience of living with Andrey ("Impossible to work or to amuse oneself—you understand"),[7] we surmise that, when the occasion arose, Dostoevsky did not deprive himself of the other pleasures readily available to young men in the capital.

All these amusements, of course, required a liberal supply of funds; and Dostoevsky was chronically short of cash. This was not so much poverty as a careless prodigality, combined, perhaps, with a bad social conscience. For Dostoevsky received his salary as an officer as well as a large share of the income from the family estate—which was now administered by his brother-in-law Peter Karepin, who, at the age of forty, had married Dostoevsky's seventeen-year-old sister Varvara. But he was always in debt nonetheless, and he fell into the self-defeating habit of drawing his salary in advance as well as borrowing at murderous rates of interest. The thrifty Baltic German Riesenkampf, whom Mikhail had asked to keep an eye on Dostoevsky's expenses, was appalled by his total lack of the bourgeois virtues. Not only did he spend recklessly on amusements and frivolities, but he allowed himself to be fleeced unmercifully by his soldier-servant, who supported a mistress and her entire family on the pickings garnered from Dostoevsky's expenditures.

Dostoevsky graduated from the Academy in August 1843, and was placed on duty in the drafting department of the St. Petersburg Engineering Command. Relieved of the burden of his studies, he could now devote himself to attempting to replenish his funds; and we see him becoming involved in all sorts of translation schemes from which he hopes to realize a quick profit. A year later, announcing his long-cherished plan to retire from the service, he asks Karepin for the sum of a thousand silver rubles in return for surrendering his share in the estate when it came to be divided among the heirs. Karepin refused this proposition as harmful to the interests of the rest of the family; and, feeling called upon to give the young man some fatherly advice, he urged him not to lose himself in "Shakespearean dreams."[8] This Philistine animadversion on Shakespeare threw Dostoevsky into a towering rage, and he replied with a series of bitter and insulting letters filled with resentment against the father figure who now blocked his path to freedom. Dostoevsky's demands were unquestionably inordinate under the circumstances; and he does not cut a very favorable figure when he deliberately exaggerates the extent of his need, or threatens to turn over his share of the estate to his creditors. But he no doubt believed that the younger children would be taken care of by the Kumanins in any case, and he was literally desperate to scrape together all he could so as to pay his debts before taking the plunge into independence.*

These are the major events of Dostoevsky's life during this five-year period; and what they show is that, beginning in 1843, he began seriously to try to carve out a place for himself in the St. Petersburg Grub Street. This date, as we know, marked the beginning of the major mutation in his literary ideas that extended over the next two years. Since these years coincide quite exactly with the movement of Russian literature from Romanticism to social Realism, Dostoevsky's personal development can best be understood in the context of this more general evolution.

3

Dostoevsky, it will be recalled, said that he had been composing a "Venetian" novel in his head while making the journey from Moscow to St. Petersburg. This is all that we know about any literary activity on his part until the winter of 1841. Most of his time was obviously consumed by his studies, and we have seen that he read very widely; whether he was also engaged in literary production during these Academy years we do not know. Savelyev remembers a lightly clad

---

* It is not quite clear whether Dostoevsky eventually got his thousand rubles, but it seems likely. He told the commission investigating the Petrashevsky affair that he renounced his claim to his parents' estate in 1845 in return for the immediate payment of a sum of money. N. F. Belchikov, *Dostoevsky v Protsesse Petrashevtsev*, 2d ed. (Moscow, 1971), 123.

Dostoevsky sitting at one of the window-embrasures of the Palace in the dead of winter, and, oblivious of the piercing cold, writing something in a notebook. He believed this to be a first draft of *Poor Folk*, and says that Dostoevsky confirmed this suspicion forty years later in conversation. It is, however, intrinsically implausible that Dostoevsky would have been engaged on such a work at this time. If he was really trying his hand at literary composition, it is much more likely that he was working on two specimens of historical drama about which, in later life, he preferred to forget.*

Mikhail arrived in St. Petersburg to take examinations in the winter of 1840-1841; and at a farewell party in January before his departure, Dostoevsky regaled their assembled friends with readings from his works in progress. These were, according to Riesenkampf, two plays entitled *Mary Stuart* and *Boris Godunov*—and that, unfortunately, is all that posterity knows about them. Riesenkampf also tells us that Dostoevsky continued to work on *Mary Stuart* during 1842 because of the strong impression made on him by a German actress in Schiller's play. "Dostoevsky wished to rework this tragic theme in his own way, and for this purpose painstakingly undertook the reading of history as a preparation."[9] The same is presumably true for *Boris Godunov*, although no such extensive reading was necessary for the young man who had grown up on Karamzin and mastered Polevoy.

To think of Dostoevsky initiating his literary career with Romantic tragedy, rather than with a first draft of *Poor Folk*, makes much more satisfactory historical sense. Like Stendhal and Balzac, Dostoevsky probably began with the ambition of writing for the stage for the same reasons given in their case by Victor Brombert: "The novel was simply not a road to quick or sensational success. The lure of the theater, with its promise of immediate glory, audible applause, money, and women, was far greater."[10] Moreover, tragedy was the form that enjoyed the most critical prestige at the height of the Romantic period, and it was then also being cultivated both by Shidlovsky and Mikhail. Shidlovsky's letter contains a long para-

---

* Dostoevsky's negative attitude toward these early works for the stage is well illustrated in a passage from a little-known letter of Andrey's, written after his brother's death. "As far back as 1842, much earlier than *Poor Folk*, my brother was writing a drama, *Boris Godunov*. The manuscript often lay on the table, and I—sinful fellow that I am—secretly read this work with youthful enthusiasm on more than one occasion. Later, not so very long ago, perhaps in 1875, in conversation with my brother I confessed to him that I knew of the existence of his *Boris Godunov* and had read the play. To my question: 'Has the manuscript survived, brother?' he only replied, waving his hand: 'Well, that's enough! That . . . that was childish stupidity!'" Cited in *Literaturnoe Nasledstvo*, No. 86 (Moscow, 1973), 366.

graph on Hugo's *Hernani*, which he criticizes as unconvincing because the psychology of the central character is strained and artificial; and he compares Hugo unfavorably with Shakespeare, Schiller, Goethe, and Manzoni. We know that he discussed the question of dramatic form with Dostoevsky while recasting a play of his own called *Maria Simonova*. "He revised it all winter," Dostoevsky tells Mikhail at the beginning of 1840, "and he himself called the old form monstrous."[11] Mikhail himself in a letter sketched out an idea for a drama which Dostoevsky finds "lovely." "I am especially pleased that your hero, like Faust, searching for the infinite and the unattainable, goes mad just when he finds the infinite and unattainable—when he is loved. Marvelous! I'm glad that Shakespeare has taught you something."[12] Dostoevsky was to remember this Shakespearean lesson when Nastasya Filippovna, in *The Idiot*, goes mad under similar circumstances—when she too finds "the infinite and unattainable" in Prince Myshkin's "love."

In the early 1840s, Dostoevsky's mind and imagination were filled not only with the characters of Shakespeare and Schiller but also with those of Racine and Corneille. Under the influence of the fashionable Romantic criticism of French Classicism, Mikhail had said that "neither Racine nor Corneille (?!?) are able to please us because their form is defective" (this is Dostoevsky's paraphrase of his brother's position, with indignant punctuation). Feodor springs to their defense, however, by vaunting "the burning, passionate Racine, enraptured by his ideal"; and he has special words of praise for *Phèdre*, whose struggle with her guilt-haunted conscience anticipates so many of Dostoevsky's own characters. Indeed, with his subtle analyses of the secret recesses of a moral conscience divided against itself, no earlier writer is closer to Dostoevsky's psychology than the devoutly Christian Jansenist Racine.* Corneille also arouses Dostoevsky's enthusiasm, and he remarks that "with his gigantic characters and Romantic soul he is almost Shakespeare."[13] Such comments display Dostoevsky's admirable independence of judgment, his ability to appreciate creative force wherever he finds it regardless of literary fashion. They also indicate his preoccupation with the theater at this time as a source for his own inspiration.

Dostoevsky apparently gave up the effort to complete his two plays sometime in 1842; but if we are to judge by a reference a couple of

---

* What Paul Bénichou says of Racine is equally applicable to Dostoevsky. "The equivalence of love and hate, the one incessantly born from the other . . . is at the center of the Racinian psychology of love." Paul Bénichou, *Morales du grand siècle* (Paris, 1967), 223.

years later to a work called *The Jew Yankel*, he did not cease to write for the stage. For in January 1844 he asks Mikhail for a loan and promises to repay him with the following assurance: "I swear by Olympus and by my Jew Yankel (my completed drama, and by what else? perhaps by my moustaches, which I hope will grow one day) that half of what I get . . . will be yours."[14] It is impossible to judge from this jesting promise whether the play was really completed, or whether Dostoevsky merely hoped that, like the moustaches, it too would grow. But the answer to this question is less important than what we can learn from the mere title of Dostoevsky's play, whether finished or not—or whether even started. For the Jew Yankel is a minor character in Gogol's historical novel, *Taras Bulba*, and his name indicates that Dostoevsky has shifted his literary model from Pushkin and Schiller to Gogol. Moreover, that Dostoevsky should even *think* of making such a character the central figure of a play, rather than Mary Stuart or Boris Godunov, clearly highlights the trend of the times. Tragedy in the grand Romantic style was dead, and the Gogol period of Russian literature—the period of tragicomic realism and social satire—had now begun to sweep all before it.

4

The confluence of a number of causes united, in 1843, to transform the Russian literary world. One factor was the publication in 1842 of Gogol's *Dead Souls* and of his short story, *The Overcoat*. Another was the internal evolution of the critic V. G. Belinsky, who at that time was in charge of the critical section of the *Notes of the Fatherland*. A third was that Russian journalism, just at that moment, began to catch up with the new French vogue for what came to be called in Russian "the physiological sketch" (after the French *physiologie*)—that is, local-color sketches of urban life and social types which became very popular after the revolution of 1830. The combined effect of all these events gave birth to the Natural School of Russian writers in the 1840s—a group in which, with the success of *Poor Folk*, Dostoevsky immediately took a prominent place.

Gogol, to be sure, was far from having been unknown or unappreciated before 1842, and Belinsky had hailed him in 1835 as the rising young star of Russian literature. But Belinsky was just then at the beginning of his stormy and influential career, and his panegyric in praise of Gogol was by no means accepted as gospel truth. Everybody, to be sure, had been impressed with the vigor, freshness, and originality of Gogol's work, which earned him immediate personal acceptance by such luminaries as Pushkin and Zhukovsky; but the Russian critical establishment was far from being ready to accord him the status he had been given by Belinsky as "the leader of our literature."[15] Until 1842, it was much more customary to regard him, in Polevoy's words, as "first-rate, inimitable" in his own special domain, that of "the good-natured farce, good-hearted stories about little Russia."[16] It is very likely that the Romantic Shidlovsky shared some such opinion of Gogol; and Plaksin too had rated Gogol below those writers who attempted the more ambitious and elevated forms. The view of Gogol that Dostoevsky imbibed was thus scarcely such as to encourage an attitude of deference or a desire for emulation: the great figures of the Romantic pantheon were much more glamorous, and there was no disagreement about *their* stature. Dostoevsky had read Gogol by 1840—he cites a humorous sentence from one of the stories in a letter—but there is no indication as yet of any serious literary influence.

Matters were to change very drastically two years later, largely as the result of an epoch-making shift in Belinsky's ideas. We do not know exactly when Dostoevsky first began to read Belinsky and accept him as an authority. But from everything we already have learned, it is obvious that he could only have been indifferent or hostile to what he may have seen of Belinsky's work between 1838 and 1840. For these were the years when the critic was going through his celebrated "reconciliation with reality"—an event that had disastrous consequences on the whole future course of Russian culture. Six or seven years earlier, while a student at the University of Moscow, Belinsky had written a play called *Dimitry Kalinin* inspired by *The Robbers* and containing an impassioned protest against serfdom. The influence of Idealist thought, however, turned him away from social questions to the study of art and philosophy, and to the conviction that the cultivation of the self was the only source of true enlightenment and progress. But in 1837 he fell under the influence of M. A. Bakunin, the future revolutionary anarchist—who at this point in his astonishing career was preaching an interpretation of Hegel as a doctrine of total political quietism and unquestioning acceptance of "reality." With Belinsky's usual fervid extremism (he was affectionately called "furious Vissarion" by his friends), he accepted such ideas wholeheartedly and took them to lengths that caused even Bakunin to protest.

The result was a series of articles whose general thesis is well described in the memoirs of I. I. Panaev. "Carried away by Bakunin's interpretation of Hegel's philosophy and by the well-known formula, taken from that philosophy, that 'everything real is rational'—Belinsky preached reconciliation in life and in art. He struggled to become, at any price, a conservative against his own nature, and with bitterness fought for *art for art's sake*. . . . He spoke with contempt of the French Encyclopedists of the eighteenth century, of critics who refused to recognize the theory of 'art for art's sake,' of writers who showed the necessity for social reform and strove for a new life, for a renewal of society. He spoke with particular indignation of George Sand. Art represented for him some sort of higher, isolated world, enclosed in itself, occupied only with eternal truths and not having any link with the squabbles and trifles of our life, with the world in which we actually live and with which we have to come to terms."[17] What made this phase of Belinsky's career so fateful and unfortunate for Russian culture is that it linked the dissociation of art from immediate social-political concerns with the positive advocacy of political reaction. This linkage has continued to haunt the Russian relation to art ever since, and has now been exported to the rest of the world with the spread of Marxism-Leninism.

One of the first manifestations of Belinsky's dislike of contemporary French literature was an attack, in the spring of 1839, on Polevoy, its chief critical advocate in Russia; and Shidlovsky and his young friend Feodor Dostoevsky certainly discussed this jeremiad. Polevoy was accused by Belinsky of being hopelessly out-of-date because he was still enamored of his old French favorites, and had not caught up with the supreme importance of Hegel's ideas (of course, in their Bakuninesque guise). "When Mr. Polevoy embarked on his career," Belinsky writes ironically, "the names of Hugo, Lamartine, De Vigny, and Balzac thundered and sparkled—is it surprising that even now he considers them great?"[18] Belinsky, it is manifest, was under no such illusion. For the young Dostoevsky, though, Hugo's work provided the moral foundations of the modern world; and he would have rejected Belinsky's point of view with the same decisiveness as he had rejected Nisard's. About the same time, Shidlovsky attended a benefit for Polevoy in which one of the latter's plays was produced with the famous actor Karatygin in the main role. The program also included a vaudeville skit about a young student, Vissarion Grigorovich Glupinsky (*glupy* means stupid or silly), who "explains Hegelian philosophy and objective individuality to everybody, etc."[19] The author of this work, given at only one performance, remained anonymous (but was probably Polevoy); and it indicates the opinion about Belinsky that Dostoevsky would have gathered from his own literary circle.

Belinsky moved from Moscow to Petersburg in the winter of 1839 and, partly under the stimulus of a new milieu and a new group of friends, began to change his ideas very quickly. Also, he was deeply troubled by the opposition of such Moscow luminaries as Alexander Herzen and T. N. Granovsky, whose opinions he could not help respecting, to his uncritical adulation of Russian "reality." During the winter of 1841, his new circle gathered at the home of I. I. Panaev once a week for conversation and conviviality; and here Belinsky became acquainted for the first time with the newest French thought. Panaev translated the articles of Pierre Leroux from the *Revue Indépendante*, just then beginning to appear; the conclusion of George Sand's *Spiridion* was put into Russian especially for Belinsky's benefit; Thiers' *Histoire de la Révolution en 1789* was read, as well as Louis Blanc's vehemently Socialist *Histoire des dix ans*. "His [Belinsky's] previous indignation against George Sand," Panaev writes, ". . . was replaced by the most passionate enthusiasm for her. All his previous literary authorities and idols—Goethe, Walter Scott, Schiller, Hoffmann—faded before her. . . . He would only speak of George Sand and [Pierre] Leroux."[20]

The result of all this, in little more than a year, was to transform Belinsky from his previous disdain for social-political concerns into a violent partisan of the new French social doctrines. In the fall of 1841, he writes to his friend V. P. Botkin that "the idea of Socialism" had become for him "the idea of ideas, the being of beings, the question of questions, the alpha and omega of belief and knowledge. . . . It has (for me) engulfed history and religion and philosophy."[21] It is clear that, whatever "Socialism" may mean to Belinsky, it is infinitely more than merely the adoption of a new set of social-political ideas. And when he tries to speak about it in more detail, we see that what has impressed him most is the apocalyptic and Messianic aspect of all the Utopian Socialist tenets—the idea, particularly strong in the Sand-Leroux preachments, that Socialism is the final realization on earth of the true teachings of Christ. The last chapters of *Spiridion* reveal that the unsullied doctrine of Christ, shamefully travestied by the despotic Roman Catholic Church, is the same as that proclaimed by the French Revolution. For the great Christian heretics of the past, beginning with Joachim of Flora, have always upheld the eternal evangel of liberty, equality, and fraternity, which is nothing but the modern social-political translation of the original meaning of the Christian doctrine of love.

The influence of such ideas, intermingled with other Sandian notions bearing on the relations between the sexes, is quite perceptible in Belinsky's exposition of his new credo. "And there will come a time—I fervently believe it—when no one will be burned, no one will be decapitated, when the criminal will plead for death as a mercy and salvation and death will be denied him, but life will serve as his punishment as death does now; when there will be no senseless forms and rites, no contracts and stipulations on feeling, no duty and obligation, and we shall not yield to will but to love alone; when there will be no husbands and wives, but lovers and mistresses, and when the mistress comes to the lover saying: 'I love another,' the lover will answer: 'I cannot be happy without you, I shall suffer all my life; but go to him whom you love,' and will not accept her sacrifice, should she through generosity wish to remain with him, but like God will say to her: I want blessings, not sacrifices. . . . There will be neither rich nor poor, neither kings nor subjects, there will be brethren, there will be men, and, at the word of the Apostle Paul, Christ will pass his power to the Father, and Father-Reason will hold sway once more, but this time in a new heaven and above a new world."[22] This will be the realization, as Belinsky rightly says himself, of the dream of "the Golden Age"; and this dream is what Belinsky refers to as "Socialism."

Belinsky's conversion to this kind of Socialism initiated a new phase in Russian culture of the 1840s. P. V. Annenkov, who had left Russia in the midst of Belinsky's Hegelian period, returned to Petersburg in 1843 to find, much to his surprise, that the Petersburg literati were enthralled by the very same works he had heard about in Paris. "Proudhon's book, *De la propriété*, by then almost out of date, Cabet's *Icarie*, little read in France itself except by a small circle of poor worker-dreamers, the far more widespread and popular system of Fourier—all these served as objects of study, of impassioned discussions, of questions and expectations of every sort, and understandably so. . . . Whole phalanxes of Russians . . . were overjoyed at the chance to change over from abstract, speculative thought without real content to just the same kind of abstract thought but now with a seemingly real content. . . . The books of the authors already named were in everybody's hands in those days; they were subjected to thoroughgoing study and discussion; they produced, as Schelling and Hegel had done earlier, their spokesmen, commentators, interpreters, and even, somewhat later—something which had not occurred in connection with earlier theories—their martyrs, too."[23]

6
_____

All this intellectual agitation at first went on only in the closed small circle of Belinsky's friends—the nucleus of what later came to be called his pléiade.* But this circle was composed, at the same time, of the core of the staff of *Notes of the Fatherland*; and the ideas that were stirring them soon began to find their way into its pages. There was, for example, a renewed flurry of interest in George Sand, whose novels now began to be translated almost as soon as they appeared in Paris. (Not all, to be sure; *Spiridion* was no doubt considered too dangerous even to try to get past the censorship.) Much more notice was also given to the new French literature, and attention was discreetly called to its subversive social message. Most important of all, however, was the providential publication of *Dead Souls*—a true godsend for Belinsky. For this gave him a new Russian work of major artistic stature through which he could translate his ardent social concerns into immediately relevant Russian terms.

Gogol's *Dead Souls* narrates the journey through the Russian provinces of a clever swindler, who buys up the title to serfs that have recently died but who still exist legally as names on the inventory of property. By mortgaging these titles before the inventories are revised, he can easily (and quasi-legally) make himself a tidy sum. The intrigue of the book thus deals directly with serfdom; and the very possibility that it exploits for satirical purposes stresses the transformation of human beings—"souls"—into property. Moreover, Gogol's provincial landowners are a remarkable gallery of mindless grotesques, limned by the hand of a master and totally appalling in the complacent sloth, triviality, and sordidness of their lives. Belinsky eagerly seized on the book as an exposure of the grim horrors of Russian reality, which, after his Hegelian debauch, he now found even more unbearable than ever. Naturally, one could not speak about such matters too openly in public print; but Belinsky was a master at conveying his ideas in Aesopian language, and the Russian reading public had a long experience in deciphering such codes. There was no mistaking what Belinsky meant when he called *Dead Souls* "a purely Russian and national creation, snatched from the inmost recesses of the people's life . . . pitilessly tearing the cover off

---

* In the early years of the pléiade (1840-1843), the best-known names were Panaev himself and K. D. Kavelin. Between 1843 and 1848, it blossomed out to include Nekrasov, Turgenev, Dostoevsky, Goncharov, and Saltykov-Schedrin. Ogarev and Herzen were also occasional participants when they came to Petersburg.

reality and filled with a passionate, impatient, urgent love for the fruitful core of Russian life" (read: the enslaved Russian peasant).[24]

Between 1843 and 1845, one spoke of little else in Russian literary journalism except *Dead Souls*. Belinsky engaged in indefatigable and interminable polemics both with opponents and admirers of the book—admirers who, like the Slavophils, attempted to blunt the social edge of Gogol's indictment. "It seemed as if he [Belinsky] considered it the mission of his life," P. V. Annenkov writes, "to make the content of *Dead Souls* immune to any supposition that it harbored in it anything other than a true picture, artistically, spiritually and ethnographically speaking, of the contemporary position of Russian society. . . . He tirelessly pointed out, both by word of mouth and in print, what the right attitudes toward it were, urging his auditors and readers at every opportunity to think over, but to do so seriously and sincerely, the question as to why types of such repulsiveness as were brought out in the novel made their appearance in Russia, why such incredible happenings as were related in it could come about in Russia, why such statements, opinions, views as it conveyed could exist in Russia without horrifying anyone."[25]

Belinsky's critical campaign was accompanied by general exhortations to Russian writers to follow Gogol's example. Literature, he now maintained, should turn to contemporary society for its material; and he declared George Sand the greatest of all moderns because he found in her the "vital convictions"[26] lacking in Hugo and Balzac. By 1844, in a survey of Russian literature of the previous year, Belinsky was already hailing the appearance of a new school which, though it "can barely count more than a dozen true representatives," nonetheless "is more fertile and vital than all the others" on the Russian scene. This school "deals with the most vital problems of life, destroys the old inveterate prejudices and raises its voice in indignation against the deplorable aspects of contemporary morals and manners, laying bare in all its stark and grim reality 'all that is constantly before the gaze, but which unseeing eyes heed not, all the frightful appalling mass of trivialities in which our life is steeped, all the depth of cold, disintegrated everyday characters with which our earth teems.' "*[27]

Belinsky here is talking about the young writers of the Natural School who had just begun to loom on the horizon, and whose works were being published in *Notes of the Fatherland*. This group (not yet baptized) had emerged in response to Belinsky's call for a new

---

* The phrase in single quotation marks is a citation from *Dead Souls*.

literature of social realism; but instead of taking the provincial world of *Dead Souls* as their model, its members were far more influenced by the Petersburg setting of *The Overcoat*, which coincided very opportunely with the latest foreign literary fashion. As D. V. Grigorovich recalls, "around that time (1843-1844) small volumes under the general title 'Physiology' began to show up in quantity in the shops selling foreign books; each volume contained the description of some type taken from Parisian life. . . . Imitators immediately began to appear in Russia. . . . Nekrasov, whose practical mind was always on the lookout, conceived the idea of undertaking to publish something in this line; he imagined a publication in several small volumes: *The Physiology of Petersburg.*"[28] Invited to write one of these sketches, and deciding to concentrate on the life of the Italian organ-grinders in Petersburg, Grigorovich began to haunt their performances and take notes. "I had . . . then already begun to feel an attraction for realism, the desire to depict reality as it genuinely is, as Gogol depicts it in *The Overcoat*—a story that I eagerly read through."[29] In the early autumn of 1844, running into Dostoevsky on the street haphazardly, Grigorovich dragged him home to get his opinion of this new work.

CHAPTER 10

The Gogol Period: II

By the time he chanced upon Grigorovich, Dostoevsky had already begun to go through a literary evolution similar to that of his old comrade in the Academy and of a whole generation of young men just coming to maturity. Until 1842, and despite his sympathy for the compassionate humanitarianism of the French social Romantics, it is clear that Dostoevsky was still laboring in the literary traces of the dominant taste of the 1830s. There had been, after all, no current of critical opinion in Russia indicating any other direction to follow for a young aspirant to literary fame. Belinsky's campaign on behalf of Gogol, however, and the transformation of *Notes of the Fatherland* into a Russian outpost of the French "Socialist" tendency, changed the entire picture at one stroke. And since Dostoevsky had become emotionally committed to the moral ideals of this movement a good while before Belinsky, it is not difficult to understand the alacrity with which he climbed aboard the new cultural bandwagon.

Beginning in 1843, we find the first references to his intense and enthusiastic preoccupation with Gogol. Of all Russian writers, Riesenkampf tells us, Dostoevsky "was particularly fond of reading Gogol, and loved to declaim pages of *Dead Souls* by heart."[1] Another friend, who visited Dostoevsky from time to time when he was still in the Army (hence between August 1843 and August 1844) also recalls his passion for Gogol. "In the course of our conversations, he was the first to explain to me all the great significance of the creations of Gogol, all the depths of his humor. . . . The strongest and most decisive impression was made when [he], with indescribable inspiration, revealed to me all the depth of thought in the story, *The Overcoat*. I understood everything at once, and particularly the significance of 'hidden tears through surface laughter.' "[2] If the *Jew Yankel* was finished by the latter part of January 1844, then it must have been written sometime in the autumn and winter of 1843; and it would represent Dostoevsky's first response to the changed climate of Russian literature created by the joint efforts of Gogol and Belinsky.

2

Most of the other information about Dostoevsky's literary activities concurs in depicting him as totally absorbed in the new trend. He was, for example, an assiduous reader of the French *roman-feuilleton*, which, in the early 1840s, had become a staple of French journalism and was one of the most effective means by which humanitarian and Socialist ideas were being propagated. Discovering that Eugène Sue's *Mathilde*—the first novel in which Sue shifted from naval adventures to social problems—had begun to be translated into Russian but never completed, he proposed to Mikhail in late 1843 a joint venture to translate and publish the novel themselves. Work on the book was begun, but the promised funds for publication were not forthcoming and the project had to be abandoned. Dostoevsky also read the muckraking *Les Mystères de Paris* (in which Sue popularized certain Fourierist ideas), and which, when it appeared in Russia in 1844, was greeted with an enthusiastic article by Belinsky. "The author," he wrote, "wished to present to a depraved and egoistic society worshipping the golden calf the spectacle of the sufferings of wretched people doomed to ignorance and poverty and condemned by ignorance and poverty to vice and crime."*[3] Dostoevsky was also familiar with Sue's *Le Juif errant*, on which he comments laconically in the spring of 1845: *"The Wandering Jew* isn't bad. Though Sue doesn't go very far."[4]

At the same time that he was reading Sue, Dostoevsky was also impressed, according to both Riesenkampf and Grigorovich, by Frédéric Soulié's *Les Mémoires du Diable*. Exploiting the tradition of Romantic Satanism, Soulié combined it—as Maturin had done in *Melmoth the Wanderer*—with a bitter social satire and wildly melodramatic intrigue. The aim of the book was to show that, under the Restoration and the July Monarchy, "virtue was normally persecuted and exploited, and vice, cunningly masked as virtue, was triumphant."[5] (Some reminiscences of Soulié's amiably cynical Devil may perhaps be found many years later in Ivan Karamazov's sleazy interlocutor.) Dostoevsky was also interested in Émile Souvestre, who specialized in novels with parallel plot lines contrasting the fortunes of noble, self-sacrificing characters devoted to the welfare of

---

* How seriously the book was taken as social commentary may be judged by the fact that Karl Marx, in *The Holy Family*, devoted a lengthy section to an attack on Sue's novel. He argues that the beneficent actions of Sue's aristocratic hero Prince Rodolphe of Gerolstein, who puts Fourierist ideas into practice, are insufficient to solve the problems of the working class. See Karl Marx, *Frühe Schriften*, ed. Hans-Joachim Lieber and Peter Furth (Darmstadt, 1962), 1: 727-756.

humanity with that of cold, ambitious careerists; the first invariably come to grief, while the second reach the highest rungs of the ladder in a depraved and unjust society. The *Revue Indépendante* was so impressed with Souvestre's *Mât de Cocagne* that it recommended him as a model to follow in the treatment of social themes.

It is no surprise to see Dostoevsky working, during the latter half of 1844, on a translation of George Sand's *La Dernière Aldini*: any work of Sand's was an eminently marketable commodity. *La Dernière Aldini* is one of her Venetian novels, with a high-flown love story and a totally improbable plot; but, as with most of her other works, these artistic failings are more than outweighed by the topical interest of her subject. Here she exhibits the moral superiority of a true son of the people—the offspring of humble fisher-folk in the Venetian lagoon—to the spineless and decadent aristocracy of his native country; it is little wonder that a high-spirited and willful daughter of this aristocracy, the last of the Aldini's, finds him irresistible. The book is filled with allusions to the struggle of Italy for national independence, and with flashes of the revolutionary social Christianity now making its appearance in Sand's incredibly voluminous production. "The cult of deliverance is a new cult," proclaims the hero, "liberalism is a religion which should ennoble its followers, and, like Christianity in its early days, make the slave a freeman, the freeman a saint or a martyr."[6] Dostoevsky no doubt toiled over such pages with reverence; but, having almost completed the job, he discovered to his dismay that the work had already appeared in Russian.

3

The question of George Sand's influence on Dostoevsky has never been thoroughly explored. There can be no doubt, however, that he read very widely in her numerous novels, and that, as with the entire generation of the 1840s, such works greatly enriched his acquaintance with progressive and revolutionary ideas. There is an evident allusion to this fact in the moving obituary that he wrote forty years later. George Sand, he says, was more important in Russia than Dickens or Balzac because her readers "managed to extract even from novels everything against which [they] were being guarded."[7] The great satirist Saltykov-Schedrin is even more explicit. "From the France of Saint-Simon, Cabet, Fourier, and Louis Blanc and, in particular, George Sand . . . flowed to us [in the 1840s] a faith in mankind; from there gleamed for us the certainty that the Golden Age was to be found not in the past but in the future."[8] George Sand had helped notably to inspire such a faith in Belinsky; and the novelist whom Renan once called an Aeolian harp, resounding to all the ideological currents blowing in the tempestuous 1840s, also performed the same signal service for Dostoevsky.

Whether there are any more specific connections between George Sand and Dostoevsky cannot be established with any certainty: the evidence is too scanty and almost entirely inferential. But it is very tempting to believe that Dostoevsky also read *Spiridion*, and that the book made as great an impression on him as it did on Belinsky.* There are, in any case, extremely intriguing resemblances between Sand's remarkable and little-read novel (a combination of Gothic mystery story and spiritual autobiography) and certain features in *The Brothers Karamazov*. Both are set in a monastery; both involve the transmission of an ancient and semi-heretical religious tradition; both stress that true religion should depend only on free moral choice, not on the tyranny of dogma or institutions; both contain as central characters an old and dying monk—the inheritor of this tradition, who is hated by his fellow monks—and an ardent young disciple inspired by his doctrine and his example; both dramatize the struggle between skeptical reason and true faith. In both novels, the struggle is resolved through a mystical vision that restores a selfless love for all of God's creation and revives belief in the existence of conscience and the immortality of the soul; in each, the dying guardian of the tradition sends his young follower into the world to apply the doctrine of Christian love to the ills of social life.[9] In 1876, Dostoevsky was certain that George Sand had "died a Deist with a firm belief in God and immortal life," and he points out that her Socialism, based as it was "upon the spiritual thirst of mankind for perfection and purity," coincides with Christianity in its view of human personality as morally responsible.[10] Whether or not such comments were directly inspired by recollections of *Spiridion*, they well illustrate the sort of moral-religious Christian Socialism that George Sand helped to instill in Dostoevsky himself in the early 1840s.

With the collapse of his hopes for *La Dernière Aldini*, all of Dostoevsky's plans for obtaining some extra funds by translation went glimmering. Nor was he any more successful with another project that seemed very promising at first—a complete Russian version of Schiller's plays, with Mikhail as translator and himself as editor and publisher. Mikhail did put *The Robbers* and *Don Carlos* into Russian,

* We know that Dostoevsky read *L'Uscoque*, which was published in the *Revue des Deux Mondes* in 1838. *Spiridion* began to appear in the same publication the very same year, and the eminently respectable journal was certainly available in the French library to which Dostoevsky was a subscriber.

and both were published in periodicals; but the expectation of a complete edition, with substantial profits, once again proved a will-of-the-wisp. The only enterprise of Dostoevsky's that succeeded was a translation of *Eugénie Grandet*, prompted by Balzac's triumphal presence in Petersburg in the winter of 1843. Translated over the Christmas and New Year's holidays, it was published in the *Repertoire and Pantheon* in 1844; and this was the manner in which Dostoevsky's name, prophetically linked to that of Balzac, first appeared in print. By this time he was already sharing a flat with Grigorovich, who, through his acquaintance with Nekrasov, had begun to gravitate in the orbit of the Belinsky circle.

4

The idea for *Poor Folk* was conceived in the midst of this abundance of literary activity, all prompted, in one way or another, by Dostoevsky's acute awareness of the new literary temper of the times. This awareness was not only reflected in such activities as reading and translation; it also took the form of gathering "impressions" and observations that Dostoevsky thought he could use as literary material. Riesenkampf, greatly concerned about Dostoevsky's indigence, remarks that his own medical practice also constituted a strain on Dostoevsky's resources when they shared an apartment. For the young writer exhibited a great interest in all of the patients from the lower classes who came for consultation, and was always ready to supply them with a little extra cash in return for conversation. To justify this expenditure, Dostoevsky explained: "Since I want to describe the life of poor people, I am happy at the chance to become better acquainted with the proletariat of the capital" (the new word "proletariat" was used by Dostoevsky, if we are to believe Riesenkampf). Dostoevsky also struck up an acquaintance with a down-and-out young businessman of German stock, who lived off him for a time as a sponger. This wily gentleman, who had knocked about Petersburg a good deal, was an inexhaustible source of stories that Dostoevsky noted down; and Dostoevsky tolerated him, according to Riesenkampf, because of his eagerness to obtain material that later appeared in *Poor Folk*.[11]

The first mention of the work is in a letter to Mikhail in the early fall of 1844, where Dostoevsky dwells on his dismal economic prospects. Mikhail had told him that his salvation lay in the theater; but he replies that staging a play takes time, and that he needs some revenue immediately. "I have a hope. I am finishing a novel about the size of *Eugénie Grandet*. A rather original novel. I am just re-copying it, and I should receive an answer about it by the 14th. I will give it to the *Notes of the Fatherland*. (I am satisfied with my work.) I will perhaps get 400 rubles and there you have all my hopes."[12] It is clear that Dostoevsky had destined it from the very start for the *Notes of the Fatherland*, and was writing very self-consciously to satisfy the new exigencies for Russian literature laid down by Belinsky.

Nothing else is really known about the gestation of the novel. It has been proposed that the relation of the main female character Varvara to her much older seducer, and then husband, may have been suggested by the marriage of Dostoevsky's own sister of the same name to the hated Karepin. There is no reason to deny such a possibility, any more than one would wish to deny that Dostoevsky's own misadventures with St. Petersburg moneylenders furnished him with certain details and impressions—or that the book is also filled with memories of his childhood. But to understand why all this raw material should have coalesced into the particular literary structure known as *Poor Folk*, it is necessary to pay the closest attention to an illuminating remark that he made while hard at work on the book. "You may wish to know how I occupy myself when I'm not writing," he says to Mikhail in the spring of 1845, just as he was putting the final finishing touches to his manuscript (which took longer to complete than expected). "I read. I read like a fiend, and reading has a strange effect on me. I reread some book I've read before, and it's as if new strength began to stir in me. I penetrate into everything, I understand with precision, and I myself draw from this the ability to create."[13]

If we are to seek anywhere for the "sources" of *Poor Folk*, it is thus primarily to literature that we should turn. Several scholars have argued that the nucleus of the book can be detected in Varvara's diary—as it were, the confessions, seen from the inside, of Karamzin's *Poor Liza*. And while the attempt to distinguish various strata of the novel as earlier or later seems an unnecessary expense of ingenuity, the reference in the title to Karamzin's story, as well as the style of Varvara's diary, does link her to Karamzin's bucolic sentimentalism.[14] Gogol's *The Overcoat* and Pushkin's *The Station Master* also played a role in the conception of the work, and are, as we shall see, referred to in the text. Less visible, but perhaps no less crucial, was *Eugénie Grandet*, which celebrates the simple, unassuming, unselfconscious heroism of a plain country girl who proves capable of true moral grandeur. Eugénie, stirred by the power of love, defies her despotic, inhumanly avaricious father; and, according to Balzac, this obscure family drama, even though "undignified by poison, dagger, and bloodshed," was no less cruel and fateful than that of "the princely House of Atreus."[15] Such words, as well as Balzac's example, may well have shown Dostoevsky the way to effecting a similar elevation in the human stature of his own humble protagonists.

5

One other document can also help to clarify the process of Dostoevsky's artistic maturation. This is a feuilleton that he wrote in 1861 when, turning back to look at his early work in the 1840s, he felt called upon to defend it. With some slight changes, the feuilleton reproduces the famous "vision of the Neva" that Dostoevsky first used in his short story *A Weak Heart* (1848). A later chapter will take up his use of the "vision" in his story; here we wish to see it only as part of the analysis of his own development that he offers in the feuilleton.

In general, the feuilleton provides a sketch of Dostoevsky's literary evolution from the days of his early Romanticism up to his discovery of the theme of his first novel. Writing in the first person, he places himself on the same social level and in the same surroundings as the characters of his book. This transposition is of course fictitious, but the account given of his cultural and literary formation is quite accurate. Educated, like his entire generation, on the historical novel and Romantic tragedy, he tells us that his imagination as a youth had been filled with the fantasies inspired by such reading. "Previously, in my youthful fantasy I loved to imagine myself sometimes as Pericles, sometimes as Marius, sometimes as a Christian in the time of Nero, sometimes as a knight in a tournament, sometimes as Edward Glendenning in Walter Scott's *The Monastery*, etc., etc. And what did I not live through with all my heart and soul in my impassioned and golden dreams—exactly as if from opium?" (XIII: 157).

This state of mind continued to persist even when (here is where the fiction begins) the narrator becomes a lowly government clerk in St. Petersburg and, like all the others, lodges in a poverty-stricken garret. His neighbor, another poor clerk, has a family of five daughters; and a shy flirtation develops with the eldest of the brood. They read Scott and Schiller together, and, though her name is Nadia, he calls her Amalia (after the heroine of *The Robbers*). But he pays no attention to her virginal blushes and her confusion in his presence

because "I preferred to read *Kabale und Liebe* or the stories of Hoffmann" (XIII: 158). One day she suddenly announces that she is
going to marry still another clerk—a much older man—who has just
obtained a new post; and she kisses the narrator on the brow, at parting, with a strange and twisted smile.

It is probably after this event (the time-sequence is not too clear)
that the narrator experiences his "vision." This is how he describes it:

> I remember once on a wintry January evening I was hurry-
> ing home from the Vyborg side. I was still very young then.
> When I reached the Neva, I stopped for a minute and threw a
> piercing glance along the river into the smoky, frostily dim dis-
> tance, which had suddenly turned crimson with the last purple
> of a sunset that was dying out on the hazy horizon. Night lay
> over the city, and the whole immense plain of the Neva, swollen
> with frozen snow, under the last gleam of the sun, was strewn
> with infinite myriads of sparks of spindly hoar-frost. There was
> a twenty-degree frost. . . . Frozen steam poured from tired horses,
> from running people. The taut air quivered at the slightest
> sound, and columns of smoke like giants rose from all the roofs
> on both embankments and rushed upward through the cold
> sky, twining and untwining on the way, so that it seemed new
> buildings were rising above the old ones, a new city was form-
> ing in the air. . . . It seemed, finally, that this whole world with
> all its inhabitants, strong and weak, with all their domiciles, the
> shelters of the poor or gilded mansions, resembled at this twi-
> light hour a fantastic, magic vision, a dream which would in
> its turn vanish immediately and rise up as steam toward the
> dark-blue sky. Some strange thought suddenly stirred in me. I
> shuddered, and my heart was as if flooded with a hot rush of
> blood that boiled up suddenly from the surge of a powerful but
> hitherto unknown sensation. I seemed to have understood some-
> thing in that minute which had till then only been stirring in
> me, but was still uninterpreted; it was as if my eyes had been
> opened to something new, to a completely new world, unfamiliar
> to me and known only by certain obscure rumors, by certain
> mysterious signs. I suppose that my existence began from just
> that minute . . . (*ibid.*).

No further attempt is made to explain the meaning of this "vision";
but it effects a radical transformation in the whole relation of the
narrator to reality. Earlier, he had either paid no attention to his
surroundings, or had immediately reshaped them into the conse-

crated images of his Romantic fantasy-world (*Mary Stuart* or *Boris Godunov*). Now the narrator suddenly begins to look around, and to see "some strange figures, entirely prosaic, not at all Don Carloses or Posas, just titular councillors, and yet, at the same time, fantastic titular councillors" (*ibid.*). Behind all these suddenly strange and fascinating figures, there was someone "who made faces before me, concealed behind all that fantastic crowd, and pulled some kind of strings or springs and all these puppets moved and laughed and everybody laughed!" (*ibid.*). But then the narrator catches a glimpse of another story that was no laughing matter at all—"some titular heart, honorable and pure, moral and devoted to the authorities, and together with him some young girl, humiliated and sorrowing, and all their story tore deeply at my heart" (XIII: 158-159). This story, of course, is the one that Dostoevsky tells in *Poor Folk*.

There has been a great deal of rather overheated speculation about this feuilleton, and an unfortunate tendency to take it as literal autobiography. "Up until this moment," writes K. Mochulsky, "Dostoevsky had lived in a world of romantic dreams. . . . He was blind to reality, and everything that was mysterious, fantastic, and out-of-the-ordinary would lure him into its captivating sphere," etc.[16] Even a cursory glance at Dostoevsky's letters in the early 1840s, however, is enough to show that he was very far from having been "blind to reality" (whatever that means) before his "vision." Moreover, the very text of the vision makes clear that Dostoevsky is talking about literature: the new world that swims into his ken is that of the master puppeteer Gogol, not of "life" in some elemental and naked sense. This does not mean that the "vision" may not have occurred exactly as Dostoevsky portrays it; but to speak of it as a discovery of "reality" does not advance us very far—it is much more accurate to call it a discovery of Gogol. But Gogol, as we see, is the first step; the second is the discovery of the situation of *Poor Folk* and of Dostoevsky's approach to his characters ("honorable and pure, moral and devoted to the authorities"; "humiliated and sorrowing"). Only if we can understand why the "vision" should have led from one to the other can we begin to grasp its significance for Dostoevsky.

At this point, we must turn to another variant of the "vision" used in *A Raw Youth*. "What if this [Petersburg] fog should part and float away?" writes the first-person narrator. "Would not all this rotten and slimy town go with it, rise up with the fog, and vanish like smoke, and the old Finnish marsh be left as before, and in the midst of it, perhaps, to heighten the picture, a bronze horseman on a panting, overdriven steed?" (8: 116). The image of Petersburg vanishing into the sky like smoke is thus associated with Pushkin's *The Bronze Horseman*, and, in a recent article, the Soviet Pushkinist D. D. Blagoy has pointed out some striking linguistic similarities between the "vision" and one particular episode in the poem.[17] The bronze horseman, of course, is Peter the Great as cast in the famous equestrian statue by Falconet. Pushkin's protagonist Evgeny, whose fiancée has just been swept away in the flood of 1824 evoked in the poem, shakes his fist at the statue as he passes by because Peter had implanted his city in the midst of Finnish marshes constantly exposed to the danger of inundation by the raging sea; it is Peter who is ultimately responsible for the ruin of Evgeny's life. But once the bereaved Evgeny commits his impetuous act of *lèse-majesté*, he is so terrified and guilt-stricken that he goes out of his mind, imagining that he hears the ringing hoofs of the bronze horseman pursuing him night and day; and his body is finally washed ashore on the lonely island where his beloved Parasha had once lived.

Pushkin thus dramatizes the immense power of Petersburg to crush the lives of all those lowly and helpless folk who live in the shadow of its splendors; but, even more important, he treats the fate of poor Evgeny with sympathy and compassion rather than with the ridicule that Gogol employs for similar types. After the "vision," this is exactly the attitude that Dostoevsky himself will adopt toward such characters. Pushkin, in other words, pointed the way for Dostoevsky to overcome his Romanticism without turning into a mere imitator of Gogol; the "vision" symbolizes the moment when Dostoevsky became aware of how, by following the example of Pushkin, he could join the new Gogolian trend and affirm his artistic originality at the same time. (As we shall see in a moment, this is precisely the function assigned to Pushkin's work in *Poor Folk*, though the text used is *The Station Master* rather than *The Bronze Horseman*.) If, after the "vision," Gogol's characters are seen freshly—and seen in such a way that their story "tears deeply at the heart"—it is because they are now being viewed through the prism of Pushkin. In short, the "completely new world" that the "vision" revealed to Dostoevsky was that of his own style of sentimental Naturalism, a synthesis of Gogol, Pushkin—and Dostoevsky.

CHAPTER 11

Poor Folk

No début in Russian literature has been described more vividly than that of Dostoevsky, and few, in truth, created so widespread and sensational a stir. Dostoevsky's account is well known, though he considerably exaggerates and sentimentalizes his own innocence and naiveté. "Early in the winter [of 1845], suddenly, I began to write *Poor Folk*, my first novel; before that I had never written anything. Having finished the novel, I did not know what to do with it, and to whom it should be submitted."[1] The truth, as we have seen, is a good deal different. Dostoevsky knew very well what he wished to do with his novel; and there is also some evidence contradicting the impression (given by his account, as well as that of Grigorovich) that he had not spoken of *Poor Folk* to anybody before it had been polished to his satisfaction. "Here I have begun to be pushed on all sides to give my work to the *Notes of the Fatherland*," he writes to Mikhail in March 1845.[2] Who could have been doing the pushing except Grigorovich, and why would it have been done if he had known nothing about Dostoevsky's manuscript?

There can be no doubt, however, about what occurred when the novel was ready. Grigorovich was profoundly impressed and moved by the work; he took it to Nekrasov; and both young literati shed tears over the sad plight of Dostoevsky's characters. Acting on the impulse of the moment, they rushed to Dostoevsky's apartment at four o'clock in the morning—it was a springtime St. Petersburg "white night," bright and luminous as day—to convey their emotion. The next day Nekrasov brought it to Belinsky, who greeted it with equal warmth and appreciation. P. V. Annenkov visited Belinsky while the critic was plunged in Dostoevsky's manuscript; and he has left a less well known but graphic account of Belinsky's enthusiasm at his discovery.

"On one of my visits to Belinsky, before dinnertime, when he used to rest from his morning writing, I saw him from the courtyard of his house standing at his parlor window and holding a large copy-book in his hands, his face showing all the signs of excitement. He noticed me, too, and shouted: 'Come up quickly, I have something new to tell you about.' 'You see this manuscript?' he continued, after we shook hands. 'I haven't been able to tear myself away from it for almost two days now. It's a novel by a beginner, a new talent; what this gentleman looks like and what his mental capacity is I do not know as yet, but his novel reveals such secrets of life and characters in Russia as no one before him even dreamed of. Just think of it—it's the first attempt at a social novel we've had, and done, moreover, in the way artists usually do their work; I mean, without themselves suspecting what will come out of it. The matter in it is simple: it concerns some good-hearted simpletons who assume that to love the whole world is an extraordinary pleasure and duty for every one. They cannot comprehend a thing when the wheel of life with all its rules and regulations runs over them and fractures their limbs and bones without a word. That's all there is—but what drama, what types! I forgot to tell you, the artist's name is Dostoevsky. And I'm going to give you some samples of his motifs right now.' And with extraordinary emotion Belinsky started reading the passages that struck him most, coloring them even more highly by his intonation and nervous declamation."[3]

It is somewhat difficult, more than a hundred years later, fully to share Belinsky's rapture over Dostoevsky's first novel. One reason, to be sure, is that the later works of Dostoevsky put it so much in the shade; another is that the social novel in all its varieties, especially after the vogue of late nineteenth century Naturalism, has long since ceased to hold any thematic surprises for us. *Poor Folk* is unquestionably a very talented book for a beginning writer; but Belinsky's response, aside from the well known proclivity of his excitable temperament to extreme reactions, is only explicable in terms of literary history. One must view it in the context of Belinsky's struggle against the Russian epigones of Romanticism, and his single-handed attempt to create a new movement of social Realism in Russian literature.

Before Dostoevsky, these efforts had produced a burgeoning of the physiological sketch. But while urban, lower-class Russian life had now begun to be depicted in all its forms and diversities, the emphasis was on description of externals rather than on narration, on photographic accuracy (the sketches were also called "daguerrotypes," and were accompanied by illustrations) rather than on imaginative penetration and inner identification. Dostoevsky was the first writer who, having chosen his material within the thematic range of the Natural School, had managed to produce more than a series of physiological sketches. "I am very often at Belinsky's," he writes Mikhail in the fall of 1845. "He is as well-disposed to me as one possibly could be, and seriously sees in me *a public proof* and justification of his opinions."⁴ Dostoevsky's comment hits the nail very accurately on the head. He *had* succeeded in producing the work that Belinsky had been waiting for; and the immense stir created by *Poor Folk* among contemporaries is to a large degree attributable to the controversy over the new orientation that Belinsky had given to Russian literature.

2

Poor Folk is cast in the form of an epistolary novel between two correspondents—the lowly titular councillor Makar Devushkin, a middle-aged copying-clerk employed in one of the vast offices of the St. Petersburg bureaucracy, and a young girl just barely out of her teens, Varvara Dobroselova.* Distantly related to Varvara in some obscure fashion, Devushkin is trying to protect her from the intrigues of a procuress who, in the guise of a friend of the family, has already succeeded once in selling her to a wealthy libertine. Devushkin is timidly in love with Varvara himself; but the difference in their ages makes it impossible for her to reciprocate, and her feelings do not extend beyond those of friendly affection and intense gratitude. The novel begins in spring and ends with the approach of winter (the seasons, as in other examples of the genre, parallel the curve of the action), and focus on the tiny and trivial joys and sorrows of these humble protagonists with great skill and poetic sensitivity.

Both are tender, lonely, fragile souls, whose solicitude for each other brings a ray of warmth into their otherwise bleak lives; but the innocent little idyll is soon ended by the pressure of the sordid forces against which they struggle. Devushkin reduces himself to abject poverty for the sake of Varvara, showering her with gifts of candy and fruit which he can ill afford. And he suffers agonies of humili-ation, which he tries to conceal, because of the difficulties caused by his destitution. Finally, Varvara's seducer shows up again and churl-ishly offers her marriage—not out of any feelings of remorse or attrac-tion, but solely because he wishes to engender an heir and disinherit a nephew. The hopelessness of her position, and the chance to re-establish her social situation, compel her to accept. The book ends on Devushkin's wail of anguish as Varvara vanishes forever into the

---

* Both these names have allegorical echoes. Devushkin evokes *devushka*, the word for a young girl or maiden. The incongruity of this appellation is touch-ingly humorous, and yet indicates some of the quality of Devushkin's character. Dobroselova is a combination of the Russian words for "good" and for "country village."

steppes with her callous bridegroom Bykov (whose name evokes the Russian word for a bull).

Nothing is more impressive in *Poor Folk* than the deftness with which Dostoevsky uses the epistolary form to reveal the hidden, unspoken thoughts of his characters; what one reads between the lines of their letters is more important than what appears on the surface—or rather, it is the tension between the spoken and unspoken that gives us the true access to their consciousness. Devushkin, so simple and uncomplicated at first glance, is a character constantly struggling with himself in several ways. In the first place, there is the struggle between his passion for Varvara in the full sense and his realization of its impossibility and even unsuitability. Secondly, there is the struggle to preserve his self-respect, his sense of his own human worth, in the face of the humiliations to which he is exposed both by his position and his newly felt poverty. Above all, there is his "ideological" struggle—the wrestle with the rebellious thoughts that surge up in him unexpectedly under the pressure of his emotional involvement with Varvara, and which are so much at variance with the unquestioned credo of obedience he has always accepted up to that time.

Varvara is a far less complex character, though she too is admirably caught wavering between her concern to spare Devushkin's feelings, her inability to respond to his timid advances, her distress at his impoverishment for her sake, and, at the same time, her girlishly spontaneous enjoyment of his gifts. "How many times have I told you that I need nothing, absolutely nothing; that I shall never be able to repay you for the kindnesses you have showered on me?" she writes. "And why have you sent me these flowers? . . . How charming the flowers are! Crimson, in little crosses. Where did you get such a pretty geranium?" etc. (1: 17-18).

For all her tenderness and affection for Devushkin, Varvara cannot suppress her natural and youthful pleasure at the good things of life of which she has been deprived, or which, until now, she has been offered only in exchange for the sale of her person. At the end of the book, when she appeals to Devushkin to run errands concerning her trousseau, there is even a certain thoughtless insensibility in her behavior that cannot be overlooked. A recent critic has taken her severely to task for such misconduct, and has argued that Dostoevsky wished to depict her as a shabby egotist; but this seems much too harsh a reading.[5] Dostoevsky's portrayal is all the more convincing because he does not sentimentalize Varvara excessively. Devushkin, after all, had spent his time running errands for her before, even against her protests; and, in the brief excitement of the moment, she cannot help behaving with the total self-absorption of any normal young bride preparing for the great event. Even so, she has no illusions about what awaits her as she enters into a loveless marriage with a boorish bridegroom; and her last letter is a touching expression of gratitude to her friend and benefactor.*

3

Dostoevsky surrounds this simple tale of his characters' brief encounter with a number of accessories that enlarge the story to the dimensions of a true social novel. Inserted among the earlier letters is Varvara's diary, which takes us back into her girlhood and introduces the classic contrast between the happiness and innocence of rustic childhood and the dangers and corruptions of the city. In these pages, we catch glimpses of a succession of penniless girls who have suffered the same fate as Varvara, or who, under the guise of beneficence, are being prepared for it by the sinister procuress Anna Feodorovna. This inset-diary also contains the portrait of the tubercular student Pokrovsky—Dostoevsky's first brief depiction of the new *raznochinets*† intellectual who would later evolve into Raskolnikov

---

* There is a striking comment on the character of Varvara in one of the early reviews of Dostoevsky's novel which seems to have gone unnoticed. It is all the more interesting because made by a close friend of Dostoevsky, the young critic Valerian Maikov, and probably stems from discussion with Dostoevsky himself.

Maikov remarks that readers may wonder "why the author took it into his head to depict Varvara Alekseevna sending Devushkin, with such cold despotism, to carry out her nonsensical orders to various business establishments. This trait, however, has profound meaning for a psychologist and imparts to the entire work the interest of an unusually accurate image of life. It is clear that Makar Alekseevich's love could only arouse repulsion in Varvara Alekseevna, though she stubbornly and constantly conceals this even perhaps from herself. And is there anything more burdensome on earth than concealing a dislike for a person to whom we are indebted for something, and who—God forbid!—is in love with us besides? Whoever jogs his memory a bit will surely recall that he felt the greatest antipathy, not towards enemies, but to those whom, devoted to him to the point of self-sacrifice, he could not repay with an equal depth of feeling. Varvara Alekseevna—we are firmly convinced of this—was much more weighed down by the devotion of Makar than by her crushing poverty, and she was not able—she found it impossible—to deprive herself of the right to torture him a little by treating him as a lackey the moment she felt free from the weight of his guardianship. . . . A sentimental soul, who finds the comprehension of such facts difficult to bear, can be consoled all the same because, before her voyage to the steppe, . . . Varvara Alekseevna wrote Makar Alekseevich a note in which she calls him friend and darling."

This psychology is so "Dostoevskian" that one suspects the influence of Dostoevsky's own *explication de texte*. See Valerian Maikov, *Kriticheskie Opyty* (St. Petersburg, 1891), 326. More information on Valerian Maikov will be given in Chapter 15.

† A *raznochinets* was, literally, a person without *chin*, that is, without rank or grade in government service. But the word is used more generally to mean a plebeian or commoner.

—and who, as tutor of the adolescent Varvara, stirs her first romantic feelings. Pokrovsky is the illegitimate son of Bykov by another of Anna Feodorovna's "protégées," who had been married off to a drunken ex-clerk, with the help of a liberal sum from Bykov, to save appearances. Old Pokrovsky, though a hopeless drunkard, is nonetheless consumed by admiration for his educated "son," who represents for him the glorious realm of culture and moral probity.

The sadly ineffectual efforts of old Pokrovsky to preserve his dignity, in a world that regards him with condescension and contempt, is depicted by Dostoevsky with a tragicomic pathos worthy of Dickens (Devushkin is of course engaged in the same struggle on a somewhat higher level of self-consciousness and cultural awareness). The last episode in Varvara's diary describes the broken old man following the hearse of his adored "son" to his final resting place. "The old man seemed not to feel the cold and wet and ran wailing from one side of the cart to the other, the skirts of his old coat fluttering in the wind like wings. Books were sticking out from all his pockets; in his hands was a huge volume which he held tightly. . . . The books kept falling out of his pockets into the mud. People stopped him and pointed to what he had lost, he picked them up and fell to racing after the coffin again" (1: 45). Belinsky remarked that it was impossible not to laugh at old Pokrovsky; "but if," he told his readers, "he does not touch you deeply at the same time you are

7. Old Pokrovsky running after the hearse of his son

laughing . . . do not speak of this to anyone, so that some Pokrovsky, a buffoon and a drunkard, will not have to blush for you as a human being."[6]

Another such inset-story is that of the starving clerk Gorshkov and his family, come from the provinces to clear his name of a charge of embezzlement while in government service. This is the archetypal family in the lowest depths of poverty that will appear again and again in Dostoevsky—and always characterized by the same terrible and unnatural silence, as of a suffering too deep for lamentation. There is no sound even of the children, Devushkin tells Varvara. ". . . One evening I happened to pass their door; it was unusually quiet in the house at the time; I heard a sobbing again as though they were crying so quietly, so pitifully, that it was heartrending, and the thought of those poor creatures haunted me all night so that I could not get to sleep properly" (1: 24). Devushkin, though in dire straits himself, cannot refuse to give Gorshkov twenty kopeks to buy food for his family. "I was kind to him, he's a poor, lost, scared creature; he needs a friend, so I was kind to him," he informs Varvara (1: 91). Gorshkov is another refraction of Devushkin, but in a totally pathetic tonality; he has none of the comic grotesque so strongly accented in old Pokrovsky, and still present, though considerably muted, in Devushkin himself.

All these narrative lines interweave to build up an image of the same unavailing struggle to keep afloat humanly in the face of crushing circumstances; the same treasures of sensibility, sensitivity, and moral refinement appearing in the most unlikely places—unlikely, at least, from the point of view of previous Russian literature. Everywhere poverty and humiliation, the exploitation of the weak and the helpless by the rich, powerful, and unscrupulous—all this in the midst of crowded St. Petersburg slum-life, with its nauseating odors and débris-littered dwellings. "On every landing there are boxes," Devushkin writes to Varvara, describing his quarters, "broken chairs and cupboards, rags hung out, windows broken, tubs stand about full of all sorts of dirt and litter, eggshells and the refuse of fish; there is a horrid smell . . . in fact it is not nice" (1: 22). This is an excellent instance of Dostoevsky's use of anticlimax to convey the slightly risible (but nonetheless touching and moving) quality of Devushkin as a person.

Poor Folk combined these picturesque merits of the best of the physiological sketches with a new and unerring insight into the tortures of the humiliated sensibility. "Poor people are touchy—that's in the nature of things," Devushkin explains to Varvara. "I felt that even in the past. The poor man is exacting; he takes a different view of God's world, and looks askance at every passerby and turns a troubled gaze about him and looks to every word, wondering whether people are not talking about him, whether they are saying that he is ugly, speculating about what he would feel exactly," etc. (1: 68). This "different view of God's world," the world as seen from below rather than above, constitutes the major innovation of Dostoevsky vis-à-vis Gogol, whose sympathy with his humble protagonists is never strong enough to overcome the condescension implicit in his narrative stance. The "humanism" that Belinsky hailed in Dostoevsky's work consists precisely in "having shown how much that is excellent, noble, and sacred is contained in the most limited of human natures."[7] The situations and the psychology of *Poor Folk* thus speak for themselves against class pride and class prejudice, and against the presumed superiority of the upper over the lower. But the book also contains a much more outspoken protest which, though not mentioned by Belinsky, could certainly not have left him indifferent.

4

Devushkin, as we have said, is by no means a simple character, and he undergoes a distinct evolution in the course of the book. The early letters reveal him accepting his lowly place in life without a murmur of protest, and even taking pride in performing his unassuming tasks as conscientiously as he can. "I know very well, of course, that I don't do much by copying; but all the same I am proud of working and earning my bread in the sweat of my brow. . . . My handwriting is good, distinct, and pleasant to the eye, and His Excellency is satisfied with it" (1: 47-48). Devushkin is perfectly content to be what he is and to live in the world as he finds it; what upsets him is not that he is a copying-clerk, but rather that some people think copying-clerks are ridiculous and contemptible. But this unquestioned acceptance of the rightness and justness of the social order as it exists is severely shaken by his inability to protect and provide for Varvara.

At the very lowest point of Devushkin's misery—hounded by his landlady, insulted by the boardinghouse slavies, and tormented by his tatterdermalion appearance—he loses heart entirely and takes to drink. Never had he felt so degraded and worthless; and this is the moment when a faint spark of rebellion flares even in his docile and submissive breast. Emerging onto one of the fashionable Petersburg streets, filled with luxurious shops and smartly dressed people, he is struck by the difference with the sullen and unhappy crowds of his own slum district; and he suddenly begins to wonder why he and Varvara should be condemned to poverty while others are born into the lap of luxury.

"I know, I know, my dear that it is wrong to think that, that it is free-thinking; but to speak honestly, to speak the whole truth, why is it fate, like a raven, croaks good fortune for one still unborn, while another begins life in the orphan asylum? And you know it often happens that Ivan the fool is favored by fortune" (1: 86). Fortune and merit do not coincide; nor is this revolutionary idea the full extent of Devushkin's "free-thinking." As he continues, we find him emitting the distinctively Saint-Simonian idea that the humblest worker is more entitled to respect, because more useful to society, than the wealthiest and most aristocratic social parasite. Comparing a street organ-grinder (who steps right out of Grigorovich's physiological sketch) with "a worthless profligate wretch" who ogles Varvara "from a golden eyeglass," Devushkin concludes that the organ-grinder is "more worthy of respect" because at least "he works; though in his own way, still he works" (ibid.).

All this leads Devushkin to a piercing vision of the contrasted lives of the rich and the poor—a vision which, as in one of the feuilleton-novels of Sue or Soulié, strips away the façade beyond which both classes live concealed so that one sees them simultaneously:

Now just look into it and see what is going on in those great, black, smutty buildings. . . . There, in some smoky corner, in some damp hole, which, through poverty, passes as a lodging, some workman wakes up from his sleep; and all night he has been dreaming of boots, for instance, which he had accidentally slit the day before, as though a man ought to dream of such nonsense! But he's an artisan, he's a shoemaker; it's excusable for him to think of nothing but his own occupation. His children are crying and his wife is hungry; and it's not only shoemakers who get up in the morning like that, my own—that would not matter, and would not be worth writing about, but this is the point, Varinka, close by in the same house, on a story higher or lower, a wealthy man in his gilded apartments dreams at night, it may be, of those same boots, that is, boots in a different manner, in a different sense, but still boots, for in the sense I am using the word, Varinka, everyone of us is a bit of a shoe-maker, my darling; and that would not matter, only it's a pity there is no one at that wealthy person's side, no man who would whisper in his ear: "Come, give over thinking of such things, thinking of nothing but yourself, living for nothing but yourself; your children are healthy, your wife is not begging for food. Look about you, can't you see some object more noble to worry about than your boots?" (1: 88-89).

The indifference of the rich and mighty to the misery all around them fills Devushkin with indignation—to such an extent, indeed, that he even feels for a moment that his own sense of inferiority is misplaced. "Get to the bottom of that," he says, "and then judge whether one was right to abuse oneself for no reason and to be reduced to undignified mortification" (ibid.).

This passage about "boots" clearly contains the central social theme of the book, which is Dostoevsky's variant of the same plea one finds in the French social novel of the 1830s and in Dickens—the plea addressed to the wealthy and powerful to assume some moral responsibility for their less fortunate brothers. This theme comes to a climax in the famous scene with Devushkin's Civil Service superior, when poor Devushkin, who has been careless in copying some urgently needed document, is called in for a reprimand. By this time his appearance is little better than that of a scarecrow, and his last remaining button falls off and noisily bounces along the floor as he is trying to mumble some excuse. Moved by his obvious misery, the kindhearted General privately gives Devushkin a hundred-ruble note. When the latter tries to kiss his hand in gratitude, he flushes, avoids the self-debasing gesture, and gives Devushkin an equalitarian handshake instead. "I swear that however cast down I was and afflicted in the bitterest days of our misfortune," he tells Varvara, "looking at you, at your poverty, and at myself, my degradation and my uselessness, in spite of all that, I swear that the hundred rubles is not as much to me as that His Excellency deigned to shake hands with me, a straw, a worthless drunkard" (1: 93). The General could feel not only with Devushkin's pitiful economic distress but also with his longing to preserve his self-respect: this is what saves the charitable impulse from being only still another humiliation.

Belinsky was deeply struck by this scene, and Dostoevsky reports him exclaiming over it at their first meeting: "And that torn-off button! That moment of kissing the General's hand!—why, this is no longer compassion for that unhappy man, but horror, horror! In that very gratitude is horror!"[8] It is not clear whether Belinsky is referring to the attempt to kiss the General's hand, or to Devushkin's "gratitude" for the handshake; if the latter, then he misreads Dostoevsky's meaning. For the delicacy of feeling displayed in the hand-shake, the implicit recognition of a human equality with the lowly Devushkin, is clearly intended to be seen in a favorable light. Indeed, the same symbolic point is made twice over, once before the episode with the General and once after. Devushkin resents that, before being given charity, the affairs of his destitute drinking-companion Emelyan Ilyich are investigated because this is an affront to Emelyan's dignity ("nowadays, my dear soul, benevolence is practiced in a very queer way . . ."). Similarly, when Gorshkov, after winning his law-suit, goes around muttering that his "honor" has been restored, the cynical hack-writer Ratazyaev says that, with nothing to eat, money is more important than honor. "It seemed to me," Devushkin observes, "that Gorshkov was offended . . ." (1: 69, 98).

The stress laid on this motif shows Dostoevsky's acute awareness that the spiritual is of equal importance with the material in alleviat-ing the lot of the unfortunate—even, perhaps, of greater importance, since poverty only heightens the need for self-esteem and self-respect to the point of morbidity. Indeed, the prominence of this motif in *Poor Folk* already reveals a tension in Dostoevsky's work that will have extremely important consequences later. In *Poor Folk*, this ten-sion between the spiritual and the material is still latent and in a state of equilibrium; the emphasis accorded the spiritual (or, if one prefers, the moral-psychological) dimension of human experience only heightens the pathos of the material injustices that Dostoevsky's char-acters have to suffer. But when, beginning in the early 1860s, an aggressive and blinkered materialism became the ideology of Russian radicalism, Dostoevsky broke definitively with the radicals in defense of the "spiritual" in a broad sense. This opposition between the mate-rial and the spiritual—between the satisfaction of man's material needs, and his equal inner need for dignity and self-respect—will one day, of course, culminate in the Legend of the Grand Inquisitor.

There is another aspect of the book that also gives us a glimpse into Dostoevsky's future. For it turns out that the assistance of the General, though it allows Devushkin to cope with his most pressing needs, is not really any solution to his human problem. Just after writing Varvara about his improved situation, and in a cheerful frame of mind ("it's nice to be alive, Varinka!"), Devushkin receives the news from her that Bykov is back in town and has gone to Varvara's flat in her absence (1: 96). This is the beginning of the end for Devushkin, as the book shifts from the theme of poverty to that of the impossibility of retaining Varvara. It is true that Varvara is a victim of her situation and her past; but even under the best of circumstances she could not have continued to play the role in Devushkin's life that he would have wished. That the General's charitable gesture did not solve *all* of Devushkin's problems for good has been interpreted, in recent Soviet criticism, as an indication that Dostoevsky wished to point to the necessity for a more radical change of the social order.[9] But it is much more likely that he was projecting his theme in a wider context, where the social is only one component of a still more complex human imbroglio. And the fate of Gorshkov, who dies on the very day he is fully vindicated and restored to honor and security, again illustrates Dostoevsky's awareness of human problems for which, properly speaking, there is no social solution at all.

One other motif also suggests that Dostoevsky intended a widening of the thematic horizon at this point. For while, earlier, Devushkin revolts explicitly only against the injustices of the social hierarchy, at the very end of the book there is the timid beginning of a revolt against the wisdom of God Himself. When Varvara announces her acceptance of the marriage proposal, and places her fate in God's "holy, inscrutable power," Devushkin replies: "Of course, everything is according to God's will; that is so, that certainly must be so, that is, it certainly must be God's will in this; and the Providence of the Heavenly Creator is blessed, of course, and inscrutable, and it is fate too and they are the same. . . . Only, Varinka, how can it be so soon? . . . I . . . I will be left alone" (1: 101-102). One catches here a glimpse of the future metaphysical Dostoevsky moving out beyond the confines of the question of social justice, or rather, taking it only as his point of departure.

5

The analysis of *Poor Folk* given so far remains, despite some nuances, largely within the limits of the traditional picture of Dostoevsky's early work. He was the poet of the insulted and injured, the humiliated and the oppressed—the compassionate chronicler of the lives of the St. Petersburg "poor folk" ground down by poverty and the crushing weight of an inhuman social order. This is how he was seen by Belinsky, and how he continues to be seen by the majority of his critics; nor should this human core of the book ever be overlooked or diminished in importance. But *Poor Folk*, as well as being a moving plea for social commiseration, is also a highly self-conscious and complex little creation. And if we are truly to understand the nature

of Dostoevsky's art, it is necessary to analyze it more formally in relation to the Russian literary tradition.

Poor Folk, in the first place, is cast in the form of the sentimental
epistolary novel. Swept out of fashion at the beginning of the nineteenth century by the dramatic novel of Walter Scott, its employment in the 1840s by Dostoevsky was both unexpected and somewhat
anachronistic. To be sure, the epistolary novel had by no means vanished entirely from the literary scene. George Sand's epistolary
Jacques, in a severely censored version, was appearing in the *Notes
of the Fatherland* just at the time Dostoevsky was finishing the first
draft of *Poor Folk*; and Balzac had also used the exchange-of-letters
technique for his *Mémoires des deux jeunes mariées*. Neither of these
novels, however, resembles *Poor Folk* in any other way. It is also true
that the epistolary novel is the dramatic monologue writ large, and
that Dostoevsky, with his gift for psychological dramatization, would
always continue to employ the monologue with striking effect as one
of the key narrative instruments in his repertory. But since he never
wrote another epistolary novel, his choice of the form in this case,
and the particular artistic effects that he attains through its use,
require some elucidation.

All through the eighteenth century, this type of novel had been
the form in which models of virtue and sensibility like Richardson's
Clarissa Harlowe and Rousseau's Julie, or poetic and exalted souls
like Goethe's Werther, had poured forth their lofty feelings and noble
thoughts. The epistolary novel had thus become a vehicle for high-
flown romantic sentiment, and its central characters were always
exemplary figures from the point of view of education and breeding—
even if not aristocrats in the strict sense. Indeed, the underlying social
thrust of the form was to demonstrate the moral and spiritual superiority of its largely bourgeois protagonists to the corrupt world of
class privilege in which they lived. Dostoevsky uses the form for
much the same purpose in relation to a much lower social class. But,
since the sentimental epistolary novel had traditionally become identified with highly cultivated and emotionally exalted characters, he
took a considerable artistic risk in doing so.

To portray the abortive romance of an elderly copying-clerk and a
dishonored maiden in this sentimental pattern was to violate the
hitherto accepted conventions of narrative; but, from several details,
we can see that Dostoevsky did so very self-consciously. One of the
most striking is that, in the slum boardinghouse where Devushkin
has rented a corner of the kitchen, the two servants are called Teresa

149

and Faldoni (not their real names, of course, but presumably an invention of the caustic *littérateur* Ratazyaev). Not only had Karamzin's *Letters* made these two heroic lovers famous in Russia, but their story had also furnished the subject for a French epistolary novel translated into Russian at the beginning of the century. Devushkin himself is dubbed a "Lovelace" by Ratazyaev, that is, identified with the aristocratic libertine who rapes Clarissa Harlowe and finally falls under her spell. The incongruity of these appellations illustrates the effect that Dostoevsky wishes to obtain. In the first place, by elevating his Devushkin and Varvara to the stature of epistolary protagonists, while demoting Teresa and Faldoni to the level of comic caricatures (Teresa is "a plucked, dried-up chicken"; Faldoni, "a red-haired, foul-tongued Finn, with only one eye and a snub nose"), Dostoevsky implicitly claims for his lowly characters the respect and attention hitherto accorded the much more highly placed sentimental heroes and heroines (1: 23). And by inviting the reader mentally to compare Devushkin and Lovelace, Dostoevsky exhibits the moral preeminence of the humble clerk over the brilliant but selfish and destructive aristocrat.

The originality of Dostoevsky's use of the sentimental epistolary form, as V. V. Vinogradov has remarked,[10] stands out against the background of the considerable literary tradition already existing for the portrayal of the St. Petersburg bureaucratic scribe (or *chinovnik*, as he is known in Russian). This tradition, which goes back to the 1830s, treated such a character only as material for the burlesque anecdote and satirical sketch; and one finds protests as early as 1842 against the unfair caricatures of the *chinovnik* that had become so popular a literary fashion.[11] Gogol's *The Overcoat* derives from this tradition, and keeps much of its jeering, jocular, clubroom-anecdotal tone. The narrator speaks personally to the reader, as one man of the world to another, from a point of view infinitely superior to the protagonist of the story. "He [Gogol's character] gave no thought at all to his clothes; his uniform was—well, not green but some sort of rusty muddy color. His collar was very low and narrow, so that, although his neck was not particularly long, yet, standing out of his collar, it looked as immensely long as those of the dozens of plaster kittens with nodding heads which foreigners carry about on their heads and peddle in Russia."[12]

Even though Gogol interjects a sentimental plea for pity in the midst of the burlesque anecdote, this plea is still made from a point of view outside of and superior to the character. Gogol rather awkwardly introduces a younger clerk, who one day, when Akaky is being mercilessly tormented by his office-mates, suddenly begins to feel sorry for the helpless victim and reminds the others that the almost subhuman Akaky is, after all, still their "brother." This unexpected passage clashes with the contemptuous tone and treatment accorded Akaky in the rest of the story and produces rather the effect of a tacked-on moral. Dostoevsky, on the other hand, by casting the theme of the shabby and ridiculous *chinovnik*—hitherto only a comic butt— in the form of the sentimental epistolary novel, breaks the satirical pattern and integrates his "philanthropic" theme with his form.

The same metamorphosis is carried out in Dostoevsky's conception of Devushkin's character, and in the situations he encounters. Akaky's life had been transformed by the acquisition of a new overcoat, which, for a few days, had turned him from a cipher into the sem- blance of a human being. Not an overcoat but a poor, defenseless girl gives meaning to Devushkin's hitherto empty existence; not a thing but a person, not a marvel of the tailor's craft but a human being whom he loves and cherishes. Akaky had been oblivious to the world around him, hardly existing as a consciousness except when intruded on by the grossest insults and provocations. Devushkin, on the other hand, is so excruciatingly self-conscious that the chief source of his suffering comes from the reflection of himself that he sees in the eyes of others. Incident after incident in *Poor Folk*, and innumer- able details, are taken over and re-created in this way to evoke sym- pathy and respect for Devushkin in contrast to Gogol's pitying condescension.

There has been a good deal of discussion in Russian criticism over whether, in his first work, Dostoevsky should be considered a follower or an antagonist of Gogol. Dostoevsky's contemporaries saw him pri- marily as a follower; more recent critics have focused rather on his "parodistic" transformation of Gogolian characters and motifs, which he converts from the tonality of grotesque, fantastic comedy into that of sentimental tragicomedy. These points of view, however, are not mutually exclusive, and the quarrel over them seems inspired more by disputatiousness than insight. It is clear that Dostoevsky is a fol- lower of Gogol if only because the use of Gogolian material in *Poor Folk* springs immediately to the eye; it is also clear that this material is used in quite a different way, though to speak of it as "parody" is not very satisfactory.

The term "parody"—even "serious parody," an improvement re- cently suggested by Victor Terras—does not quite cover the actual relation between Dostoevsky and Gogol, or does so only in a partial fashion. "Parody," it should be kept in mind, always implies a *reversal* of the model being parodied, and the term is therefore applicable to certain formal aspects of *Poor Folk*: Dostoevsky does reverse those *stylistic* features of *The Overcoat* that tend to ridicule Akaky Akakievich. The effect of this reversal, though, is not to *undermine* the significance of Gogol but rather to *strengthen* his overt "humanitarian" theme. Gogol's narrative technique works to create a comic distance between character and reader that defeats emotional identification; Dostoevsky counteracts the purely satirical features of the model by taking over its elements and, through his use of the sentimental epistolary form, reshaping them to accentuate Devushkin's humanity and sensibility. There is no term known to me that quite fits this process of formal parody placed in the service of thematic reinforcement. Far from being the antagonistic relation of a parodist to his model, it more resembles that of a sympathetic critic endowed with the creative ability to reshape a work so as to bring its form into harmony with its content. Both *Poor Folk* and *The Overcoat* contain the same Gogolian mixture of "laughter through tears," but in different proportions; "laughter" is uppermost for Gogol, while for Dostoevsky it is "tears" that predominate.[13]

6

Dostoevsky's novel not only contains allusions to his unprecedented revival of the sentimental epistolary form, but also incorporates hints as to the more immediate literary ancestry of the new treatment he now accords the hitherto satirized *chinovnik*. Indeed, one of the most striking features of *Poor Folk*, as A. Beletsky remarked long ago, is precisely its "literariness," the numerous references and reflections on the current literary scene that Dostoevsky manages to work into its pages.[14] Devushkin and Varvara send each other books to read, and comment on their impressions—Devushkin even dreams at one point of publishing a volume of his own poetry and becomes very self-conscious about his "style." Their remarks add up to nothing less than a self-commentary on the work provided by the author—a commentary which climaxes in Devushkin's reactions to two stories, Pushkin's *The Station Master* and Gogol's *The Overcoat*.

Varvara lends Devushkin a copy of Pushkin's *Tales of Belkin*, and the story in this volume called *The Station Master* particularly stirs him. "You know I feel exactly the same as in the book," he informs her, "and I have been at times in exactly the same positions as, for instance, Samson Vyrin, poor fellow" (1: 59). Samson Vyrin is the station master who, out of good nature and respectful docility to his betters, allows a young nobleman to seduce and run off with his beautiful daughter. The old man, unable to regain his lost child, drowns his despair in drink and dies of a broken heart. The story is told soberly and simply, with none of Gogol's ridicule or covert sneers; the figure of the heartbroken old man, helpless to assert his rights against the all-powerful nobleman, is delineated by Pushkin with genuine sympathy for his suffering. Devushkin weeps profusely over this sentimental tale, which prefigures what he foresees for Varvara and himself, and he says prophetically: "Yes, it's natural. . . . It's living! I've seen it myself; it's all about me" (*ibid.*).

Much different is his reaction to *The Overcoat*, which Varvara urges him to read (presumably finding nothing objectionable in it), though it arouses Devushkin to a violent outburst. What particularly incenses him is Gogol's supercilious depiction of Akaky Akakievich's life and character traits in a fashion that Devushkin finds personally insulting and profoundly untrue. By what right, he asks indignantly, "here under your very nose, for no apparent reason, neither with your leave nor by your leave, [does] someone make a caricature of you?" (1: 62). For Devushkin, Gogol's portrait of Akaky is nothing but a "caricature," hence fundamentally hostile; nor is he impressed by the one passage containing the plea to treat Akaky as a brother. What the author *should* have added, he asserts, is that he was "kindhearted, a good citizen, that he did not deserve such treatment from his fellow clerks, obeyed his superiors (here, he might be some kind of example), wished no one any evil, believed in God and died (if one insists that he absolutely has to die), mourned by all" (1: 62-63). Devushkin also thinks the story would be improved if it had a happy ending, and if Akaky, instead of dying, had retrieved his overcoat, received a substantial increase in salary, and thus served as an example to his insolent fellow clerks of how true virtue is rewarded.

Instead of Gogol's almost vindictive caricature, Devushkin would have liked a sentimental little tale with an edifying moral at the end; and while Dostoevsky does not, to be sure, conform to this demand of Devushkin's uncultivated taste, he does move in the direction that Devushkin desires. For he depicts the sad story of his life in the much more tenderhearted fashion of Pushkin's sentimentalism in *The Station Master*. Retaining the "naturalism" of detail and *décor* associated with the comic tradition of the portrayal of the *chinovnik*, Dostoevsky unites it with the tearful strain of Russian sentimentalism that goes back to Karamzin; and this fusion created an original artistic current within the Natural School—the current of sentimental Naturalism—which quickly found imitators and became an independent, if minor, literary movement. "Dostoevsky's novel *Poor Folk*," writes Vinogradov, "was the first act in the artistic realization of a tendency, noticeable among the ideologues of the [Natural School], in the direction of a unification of Gogolian form with sentimentalism (especially in that aspect of sentimentalism that was reborn in 'philanthropic' French literature)."[15]

Dostoevsky also carries on a running polemic throughout *Poor Folk* both with the Romantic enemies of the Natural School, and with those literary jobbers who exploited the latest fashions solely out of pecuniary motives. This is done through the character of Ratazyaev, the writer who lives in Devushkin's boardinghouse, and who not only wants to use him as literary material but also takes advantage of his wide-eyed admiration to get some copying done for nothing. Ratazyaev is the first of Dostoevsky's many unflattering portraits of the literary tribe; and it is interesting to see how early this deep-seated antipathy to his fellow writers set in. Later, when the radical journalism of the 1860s became a powerful force in Russian life, Dostoevsky's satirical thrusts against the Nihilists were usually combined with allusions to literary or publicistic activities.

Ratazyaev is a versatile hack who knocks out works in various genres, and Devushkin, terribly impressed, transcribes a few sample passages for Varvara's edification from such masterpieces as *Italian Passions* or *Yermak and Zuleika*. These give Dostoevsky the opportunity to parody romantic novels in the high-society style of Marlinsky, and to poke fun at the dime-a-dozen imitators of Scott: "Vladimir shuddered and his passion gurgled up furiously within him and his blood boiled. . . . 'I love ecstatically, furiously, madly' [he cried]. . . . 'A trivial obstacle [the husband] cannot check the all-destroying, hellish fire that harrows my exhausted breast.'" Or: "What is the poor maiden, nurtured amid the snows of Siberia in her father's *yurta* [Zuleika] to do in your cold, icy, soulless, selfish world?" Ratazyaev, though, also turns out "humorous" stories in the style of Gogol: "Ivan Prokofeyevich is a man of hasty temper, but, for all that, of rare virtues; Prokofy Ivanovich, on the other hand, is extremely fond of rarebit on toast" (1: 52-53). Ratazyaev, naturally, does not think much of *The Station Master* because now, he tells Devushkin, all that is "old-fashioned," and "books with pictures and descriptions have all come in," i.e., physiological sketches (1: 60). Just what kind of sketch Ratazyaev would write is revealed in Devushkin's horror at "Ratazyaev's disgusting design to put you and me into his writing and to describe us in a cunning satire" (1: 70).

These parodies are both amusing in themselves, and also serve by contrast to deepen and enrich the characterization of Devushkin. His admiration for such obvious trash is touching and affecting, and reveals the limits of his education (though, among the three works of literature that he tells Varvara he has read, one turns out to be a treatise on moral philosophy by the early Russian Schellingian, A. Galich). It also serves as background, however, to heighten the moral elevation of his own life. For Devushkin is *in fact* living the life of love, and is *really* engaged in the struggle against "a cold, icy, soulless, selfish world" which these bombastic exaggerations merely counterfeit. Dostoevsky thus uses the implicit relation of his form to the literary tradition, the direct comment of his characters, and satirical parody, to endow his pathetic-sentimental story with an "ideological" dimension that defines his strikingly independent position among the social-literary currents of the 1840s.

7

It should be clear by this time that *Poor Folk* is very far from being merely an unconstrained and artless outburst of sympathy, or a reflection of Dostoevsky's somber experiences among the *bas fonds* of St. Petersburg slum life. Rather, it is unmistakably an intricate and carefully elaborated little work of art that already reveals a good many facets of Dostoevsky's highly sophisticated talent. This does not mean that the sympathy was lacking or the observation nonexistent. The moving authenticity of *Poor Folk* tells us quite the opposite in every line; but we must always remember that Dostoevsky's perceptions are oriented by his artistic intentions, and that these are shaped by his relation to the literary and cultural values of his period. No approach to Dostoevsky can be truly satisfactory if it is unable to encompass *both* these facets of his work, and to clarify how they interact with each other.

Mikhail Bakhtin, in his influential book on Dostoevsky, has made some striking comments on the polyvalent nature of Dostoevsky's style, which in his view is always oriented in relation to a possible interlocutor. By this, Bakhtin means that the utterances of Dostoevsky's narrators and characters are never simply univocal descriptive reports or monologic utterances expressing the point of view of one or another character; their words always contain implicit or overt references to a network of other possible responses and points of view. Dostoevsky's language, Bakhtin argues, is always "dialogic" in this sense, even when no actual dialogue is taking place; and he illustrates his contention with a wealth of perceptive detail.[16] To be sure, he draws certain extreme conclusions from this insight which in my opinion—and in that of numerous other critics—are quite untenable;* but his analysis of the "dialogic" nature of Dostoevsky's language is not affected by his other theories. Indeed, this insight can be usefully extended, from my point of view, to characterize much more than Dostoevsky's verbal art. For it is not only Dostoevsky's use of his medium that is "dialogic"—the same idea can be applied to the nature of his creative experience as a whole. Dostoevsky was pre-eminently a *"dialogic" personality*, who lived intensely in the stream of Russian social-cultural life and projected himself passionately into the issues raised by the Russian world of his time. Just as we have seen to be true for *Poor Folk*, his works will always continue to be responses to questions posed by the Russian literary tradition, and by the wracking conflicts and debates dominating the social-cultural climate at the moment of their conception.

* Bakhtin claims that Dostoevsky invented a wholly new kind of "'polyphonic novel," unlike anything written in the form earlier, which gives each character complete autonomy and makes it impossible (as well as aesthetically undesirable) to establish any unifying perspective that may be considered Dostoevsky's own. A good, non-political criticism of this thesis, which makes the essential points, can be found in G. M. Fridlender, *Realizm Dostoevskogo* (Moscow-Leningrad, 1964), 188-191.

PART III

In The Limelight

CHAPTER 12

Belinsky and His Pléiade

Belinsky's excitement over the manuscript of *Poor Folk* quickly made Dostoevsky's name a byword among his circle, and the fame of the new young author spread throughout the literary community. I. I. Panaev, who paid Dostoevsky the compliment of immediately beginning to imitate his manner, wrote several years later: "We carried him [Dostoevsky] in our arms through the streets of the city, and, exhibiting him to the public, cried: 'Here is a little genius just born, and whose works in time will kill off all the rest of literature past and present. Bow down! Bow down!' We trumpeted his name everywhere, in the streets and in the salons."[1] The ironic tone of this passage reflects the later attitude of the Belinsky pléiade to Dostoevsky; but it confirms the enormous acclaim that he received. *Poor Folk* did not appear in the *Notes of the Fatherland* but, in January 1846, was published in the *Petersburg Almanac*, a collection of new writing edited by Nekrasov to represent the work of the Natural School. The renown of *Poor Folk*, however, had been established long before, and Dostoevsky had already written three months earlier: "As for *Poor Folk*, half of Petersburg is talking about it. Grigorovich alone is worth his weight in gold. He says to me himself: 'Je suis votre claqueur-chauffeur.' "[2]

With his usual impetuosity and wholeheartedness, Belinsky immediately adopted the young author as an intimate and spoke of him to others with unconstrained affection; Turgenev describes his attitude as being positively paternal. " 'Yes,' he [Belinsky] used to say proudly, as though he had himself been responsible for some terrific achievement, 'yes, my dear fellow, let me tell you it may be a tiny bird,' and he would put his hand about a foot from the floor to show how tiny it was, 'but it's got sharp claws.' Imagine my surprise when I met Mr. Dostoevsky a little later and saw before me a man of more than medium height, taller than Belinsky himself at any rate. But in his access of paternal tenderness to a newly discovered talent, Belinsky treated him like a son, just as if he were his own 'little boy.' "[3] "Belinsky could not be more fond of me," Feodor told Mikhail happily in the winter of 1845.[4]

Dostoevsky thus became for a season—an all too brief season—the literary lion of cultivated Petersburg society; and the newfound glory of his position, the flattering adulation he received on all sides, would have succeeded in turning the head even of a much better balanced personality. In Dostoevsky's case, it opened the floodgates of a boundless vanity which, up to this point, he had kept tightly closed. His letters are now filled with a manic exuberance and self-glorification quite comprehensible under the circumstances, but also exhibiting a dangerous lack of self-control. "Well, brother, I think that my fame will never be greater than it is now," he tells Mikhail. "Everywhere an unbelievable esteem, a passionate curiosity about me. . . . Everybody considers me some sort of prodigy. I can't even open my mouth without it being repeated in all quarters that Dostoevsky said this or Dostoevsky thinks of doing that. . . . Really, brother, if I began to recount all my successes, there would not be enough paper for them. . . . I tell you quite frankly that I am now almost drunk with my own glory."[5]

In addition to Dostoevsky's unbridled conceit, the same letter also reveals an unpleasantly vindictive streak—no doubt stemming from resentments that had been accumulating ever since, at the Academy, Dostoevsky had become acutely aware of his social inferiority to his wealthier comrades. He reports to Mikhail that two aristocratic *littérateurs*, Count Odoevsky and Count Sollogub, have been asking about him (the epigraph to *Poor Folk* is taken from a story of Odoevsky's), and that A. A. Kraevsky, the powerful proprietor of *Notes of the Fatherland*, had bluntly told Sollogub: "Dostoevsky will not honor you with the pleasure of his company." "This is really so: and now this petty little aristocrat has mounted his high horse and thinks he will crush me with the magnificence of his condescension."[6] Face-to-face with Sollogub, though, who called on him unexpectedly one day, Dostoevsky was nervous, confused, and frightened; and he attended at least one fashionable reception at the home of the hospitable Count.

More important for Dostoevsky than such casual acquaintance with celebrity-hunters was his acceptance into the charmed inner circle of the Belinsky pléiade. He immediately became involved in the burgeoning literary activities that were an offshoot of the group, and was invited by the indefatigably resourceful Nekrasov to join the staff of a new biweekly humorous publication *The Jester* (*Zuboskal*) that he planned to publish. The account that Feodor gives Mikhail of this project in the fall of 1845 reflects the campaign then being carried on by Belinsky against the Slavophils.

"The contributors for the 1st issue will include Nekrasov: 'On Several (recently occurring, of course) Petersburg Nastinesses.' (2). The future novel of *Eugène Sue: Seven Deadly Sins* (the whole novel in 3 pages). A survey of all the magazines. The lectures of Shevyrev about the harmony of Pushkin's verses, demonstrated by the fact that when he was in the Coliseum, and read them to the two ladies in his party, *all the frogs and lizards in the Coliseum crawled out to listen.* (Shevyrev gave that one in Moscow University.) Then the next meeting of the Slavophils, where it will be triumphantly proved that Adam was a Slav and lived in Russia, and on this occasion will be shown all the extraordinary importance and usefulness of the solution of this great social question for the prosperity and advantage of the Russian nation . . . . Grigorovich will write the *History of the Week*, and include some of his observations. I will write: *The Notes of a lackey about his master*, etc."[7]

Dostoevsky himself wrote the announcement of the imminent appearance of the new journal, and it was inserted in the *Notes of the Fatherland*. "The announcement created quite a fuss," he tells Mikhail jubilantly; "for it's the first time such ease and such humor has been shown in this kind of thing. I was reminded of the 1st feuilleton of Lucien de Rubempré."[8] This allusion to Balzac's hero illustrates to what extent Dostoevsky's imagination had become inflamed by his still-fresh triumph; it is regrettable that Lucien's sudden change of fortune in *Illusions perdues* did not make him somewhat more cautious. Dostoevsky's feuilleton did create a considerable fuss, but not quite of the kind he had expected; according to Grigorovich, the publication was banned because of some careless phrases in the announcement. Dostoevsky, it must be admitted, gives cause for suspicion when he places himself in the wary attitude of a prospective reader and writes that *The Jester* "may be even an unseemly pretext for something, may be even some kind of free-thinking . . .–hm! may be, even very much may be–as the present tendency goes, particularly may be" (XIII: 4). This was truly to play with fire; and the prospective publication was consumed in the flames. Some of the material prepared for *The Jester* was then used in a collection edited by Nekrasov called *April First*. Dostoevsky collaborated with Grigorovich and Nekrasov on a humorous sketch in this volume entitled–quite aptly, so far as Dostoevsky was concerned–"How Dangerous to Indulge in Vainglorious Dreams!"

3

At first everything went perfectly for Dostoevsky with the pléiade—or so at least it seemed to the eager young initiate, who, if he was not in any literal sense the "dreamer" he later made himself out to be, had yet lived a solitary life lacking any true intimacy except with Shidlovsky and with his brother Mikhail. "Recently the poet Turgenev came back from Paris (you must have heard)," he tells Mikhail, "and he attached himself to me at first sight with such devotion that Belinsky explains it by saying he has fallen in love with me! And what a man, brother! I have all but fallen in love with him myself. A poet, an aristocrat, talented, handsome, rich, intelligent, well-educated, and twenty-five years old. And, to conclude, a noble character, infinitely direct and open, formed in a good school. Read his story *Andrey Kolosov* in the *Notes of the Fatherland*. It's the man himself, though he was not thinking of self-portrayal."[9] There is a good deal of vanity in this passage, but also a touching innocence and an obvious need for genuine friendship—a need that caused him to mistake Turgenev's well known but casual affability for a sincere inclination.

The above passage was written the day after Dostoevsky had paid his first visit to the salon of the Panaevs, which had become the favorite rendezvous for Belinsky and his group. Weak-willed, good-natured, dissipated, with a knack for writing amusing satirical sketches of fashionable Petersburg life, the amiable Panaev was everybody's friend. His wife Avdotya was not only a famous beauty but the most notable bluestocking of her time, who also achieved some notoriety as a novelist. Already, or soon to become, Nekrasov's mistress (he lived with the Panaevs in a peaceful *ménage à trois* for ten years), she was at the center of mid-nineteenth century Russian literary life, and her *Memoirs* give one of the best behind-the-scenes portraits of the period. "Dostoevsky visited us for the first time in the evening with Nekrasov and Grigorovich," she writes, "who had just begun their literary careers. It was evident, from only one glance at Dostoevsky, that he was a terribly nervous and impressionable person. He was slender, short, fair-haired, with a sickly complexion; his small gray eyes darted somewhat uneasily from object to object, and his colorless lips were nervously contorted. He already knew almost all of our guests, but, clearly, he was disconcerted and did not take part in the general conversation. Everyone tried to involve him, so as to overcome his shyness, and to make him feel that he was a member of the circle."[10]

Once Dostoevsky's original diffidence had worn off his manner changed completely, and he began to display in public the same uncontrollable vanity so noticeable in his letters. "Because of his youth and nervousness," Mme Panaev observes, "he did not know how to conduct himself, and he would only too clearly express his conceit as an author and his high opinion of his own literary talent. Stunned by the unexpected brilliance of his first step in his literary career, showered with the praises of competent literary judges, he could not, as an impressionable person, conceal his pride vis-à-vis other young writers whose first works had started them modestly on the same career. With the appearance of new young writers in the circle, trouble could be caused if they were rubbed the wrong way, and Dostoevsky, as if on purpose, did rub them the wrong way by his irritability and his haughty tone, implying that he was immeasurably superior to them in talent."[11]

All the evidence agrees that Dostoevsky's behavior with the pléiade would have caused difficulties with a group of saints, not to speak of a circle of young and not-so-young writers competing for public attention and each with his own vanity to coddle. The result, only to be expected, was that they turned on Dostoevsky after a certain point and made him the butt of a veritable campaign of persecution. To make matters worse, the leader of the pack, alas, was the very same Turgenev whom Dostoevsky, not very long before, had believed to be his devoted friend. "They began to pick him to pieces," Mme Panaev tells us, "to exasperate his pride by pinpricks in conversation; Turgenev was a past master at this—he purposely drew Dostoevsky into argument and drove him to the farthest limits of irritability. Dostoevsky, pushed to the wall, sometimes defended with passion the most ridiculous views, which he had blurted out in the heat of argument and which Turgenev pounced on and laughed at."[12]

It was clear to an observer like Mme Panaev, who felt genuinely sorry for Dostoevsky, that he was an abnormally high-strung personality whose irritability and susceptibility should be discounted as the symptom of some affliction. This was apparently the view of Belinsky as well, if we are to judge from her account. When Turgenev would gleefully relate some of Dostoevsky's latest enormities to the critic, his response was: " 'Well, you're a fine one! You latch on to a sick man, you egg him on, as if you didn't know that when he gets worked up he doesn't know what he's saying.' "[13] Nor did Mme Panaev herself, for whom Dostoevsky nourished a respectful passion for several months—presumably from a distance—approve of the merciless baiting he had to endure, although she makes amply clear that he was largely to blame for his torments. The situation was only envenomed by Grigorovich, a notorious purveyor of gossip, who carefully reported to Dostoevsky everything said about him in his absence; and he usually arrived at the reunions already boiling with rage.

Matters came to a head one day sometime in the fall of 1846, when Turgenev went too far in his mockery. Mme Panaev describes the scene: "Once, while Dostoevsky was present, Turgenev depicted his meeting in the provinces with a person who imagined himself a genius, and painted the ridiculous side of this individual in a masterly fashion. Dostoevsky, white as a sheet and quivering from head to foot, took flight, not waiting to hear the rest of Turgenev's story. I remarked to them all: why drive Dostoevsky out of his mind like that? But Turgenev was in the very highest spirits and carried away the others, so that nobody paid any attention to Dostoevsky's sudden exit. . . . From that evening, Dostoevsky no longer visited us, and even avoided meeting any member of the circle in the street. . . . He saw only [Grigorovich], who reported that Dostoevsky abused us vehemently . . . , that he had become disenchanted with all of us, that all were envious, heartless, and worthless people."[14] By November 1846, Dostoevsky is writing to Mikhail: "They [the pléiade] are all scoundrels and eaten up with envy."[15]

4
———

All this would have been difficult enough to support even for someone with much better nerves than Dostoevsky. But in his case, and after the triumphant acclaim he had received for *Poor Folk*, the persecution of the pléiade turned his life into sheer torture. His physical and nervous equilibrium, as we know from Riesenkampf, had already shown signs of fragility; and it buckled completely under the new strain. Actually, the first signs of an increasing severity of his ailments appeared even before the resounding success of *Poor Folk*. Grigorovich recalls him collapsing in the street during a walk, sometime in January 1845, when they met a passing funeral procession. This occurred while he was working very intensively on his first novel, and Grigorovich writes: "The unflagging work and totally sedentary life seriously damaged his health; they aggravated his illness, which had sometimes shown up in his youth during his stay at the Academy."[16] This is the only reference made by an eyewitness to Dostoevsky's health as a cadet; and since Grigorovich speaks of the collapse as an "aggravation" of earlier symptoms, we may surmise that these were perhaps attacks of faintness or dizziness—not momentary loss of consciousness as in this case.

Dostoevsky's health became much worse in the spring of 1846, when he suffered what he describes as "a severe shock to the whole nervous system."[17] This shock, according to the diagnosis of the time, had caused an excessive influx of blood to the heart and resulted in an inflammation of that organ; it was checked by the application of leeches and two bloodlettings. Dostoevsky was declared out of danger after this treatment, but advised to follow a severe diet, to avoid strong emotions, and to lead an orderly and regular life: advice much more easily given, in his case, than followed. It was in late spring that Dostoevsky's friend Valerian Maikov suggested that he consult Dr. Stepan Yanovsky, a young medical man just then establishing his practice. Much interested in literature, Yanovsky was quite flattered to number the celebrated author of *Poor Folk* among his patients; and he struck up a friendship with Dostoevsky that lasted for the remainder of their lives. His reminiscences of Dostoevsky in the mid-1840s are an important source of information, and contain some significant details about his health.

Unfortunately, Yanovsky does not tell us what the specific complaint was for which he treated Dostoevsky; he refers only to a "local ailment" which took several months to cure.[18] (Such discretion leads one to suspect that the ailment might have been venereal.) After a few weeks the two young men became fast friends; and Dostoevsky also consulted Yanovsky about the nervous disorders which continued to plague his life. These had grown worse since the days when he believed that someone was snoring beside him at night; now they took the form of veritable "hallucinations," which he was always afraid heralded the onset of what he called a "kondrashka" (apoplexy), that is, one of his fainting fits. Every morning, after taking Dostoevsky's pulse and listening to his heart, Yanovsky would reassure him that his "hallucinations" were the effect of nerves and that his physical condition was perfectly normal; this always succeeded in calming his fears, and he would then settle down to take a cup of tea. Nonetheless, Yanovsky does report one severe attack of such "apoplexy" during the summer of 1847. Writing after Dostoevsky's death, Yanovsky recognizes such attacks as advance signals of "epilepsy"; but whether he thought so at the time is not clear—and very doubtful. If he did have any such suspicion, it was carefully kept concealed from his patient.

So far as Dostoevsky's "hallucinations" are concerned, there is

8. F. M. Dostoevsky in 1847

nothing but the report of their existence to be gleaned from Yanovsky's pages. It is likely, though, that Dostoevsky described them in
The Insulted and Injured, a novel which contains a good many autobiographical details about his life during the mid-1840s. The narrator, an impoverished young author, writes: "I gradually began at dusk
to sink into that condition which is so common with me now at night
in my illness, and which I call *mystic terror*. It is a most oppressive,
agonizing state of terror of something that I cannot define, something ungraspable and outside the natural order of things, but which
may yet take shape this very minute, as though in mockery of all the
conclusions of reason, and come to me and stand before me as an
undeniable fact, hideous, horrible, and relentless. This fear usually
becomes more and more acute, in spite of all the protests of reason,
so much so that although the mind sometimes is of exceptional clarity at such moments, it loses all power of resistance. It is unheeded,
it becomes useless, and this inward division intensifies the agony of
suspense. It seems to me something like the anguish of people who
are afraid of the dead. But in my distress the indefiniteness of the
apprehension makes my suffering even more acute" (3: 208).

Dostoevsky later described the same symptoms in conversation
with Vsevolod Solovyev. "Two years before Siberia," he said, "at the
time of my various literary difficulties and quarrels, I was the victim
of some sort of strange and unbearably torturing nervous illness. I
cannot tell you what these hideous sensations were; but I remember
them vividly; it often seemed to me that I was dying, and the truth
is—real death came and then went away again."[19]

Such onslaughts of "mystic terror," whose effect Dostoevsky compares with the anguish of people afraid of the dead, may perhaps be
seen as an objectification of his sense of guilt about his father. Had
he not used much the same image in his letter to Mikhail just after
the murder, when he spoke about wishing to calm the "restlessness"
of his parents in the grave? Be that as it may, we can assume that
Dostoevsky felt something akin to what he describes, and that such
visitations made him acutely aware of a sharp "inward division" of
his personality between the operations of his rational mind and the
overpowering strength of an irrational apprehension that he was
helpless to master. The importance of such psychic experiences for
the future Dostoevsky is self-evident; clearly, they illuminate the roots
of his grasp of character, and his refusal ever to believe that a self-
confidently purblind rationalism could provide a satisfactory foundation for human existence. But this did not become crucial for Dostoevsky until later; at the moment his "hallucinations" only contributed

to undermine his psychic balance, and to make it impossible for him to control his emotions in the face of opposition or hostility.

5

All sorts of rumors and stories ridiculing Dostoevsky now began to make the rounds in Petersburg literary circles. One anecdote, reported in all the memoirs, is that Dostoevsky had insisted that *Poor Folk* be printed in the *Petersburg Almanac* enclosed in a special border to distinguish it from other contributions. Whether anything of this kind occurred is impossible to establish (there is no border around the novel), but Dostoevsky may well have said something in an argument that gave rise to the charge. This rumor continued to haunt Dostoevsky all his life. Just a year before his death, in 1880, he denied it formally in a letter to A. S. Suvorin, asking him to print a note about it in his magazine, *New Times*.[20]

Another version of this story was that Belinsky, who was gathering material for an almanac of his own to be called *Leviathan*, and who also had asked Dostoevsky for a contribution, found himself confronted with a variation of the same request—Dostoevsky supposedly insisted that his intended contribution be placed either first or last. This whole (probably imaginary) incident gave rise to a satirical poem about Dostoevsky jointly written by Turgenev and Nekrasov at the end of 1846, which pretends to be the answer sent by Belinsky to Dostoevsky's demand. Called "The Knight of the Rueful Countenance," it labels Dostoevsky a "pimple" on the face of Russian literature, jeers at his inflated opinion of his literary prowess, and ridicules him for having fainted dead away on being presented to a beautiful, aristocratic society belle who wanted to meet the author of *Poor Folk*. This humiliating incident actually occurred at a ball given by Count Vielgorsky at the beginning of 1846. K. Chukovsky, who has written the only study of Dostoevsky's relations with the pléiade, remarks: "It is customary to censure Dostoevsky for his caricature of Turgenev in *The Devils*; but it is forgotten that Turgenev, long before the publication of *The Devils*, was the author of a caricature of Dostoevsky deriding—together with Nekrasov—his appearance and his illness."[21]

Even though not very edifying, Dostoevsky's harrowing encounter with the pléiade is worth dwelling on for a number of reasons. The image it gives us of Dostoevsky as a personality does help to illuminate one of the main sources of the characters he created and of the type of world in which they live. If Dostoevsky displays such a remarkable ability to portray feelings and states of suspicion, persecution, and of exasperation reaching a pitch of hysteria, and if he has a tendency to see human relations solely in terms of a struggle for psychic domination, the reason is surely that he was all too familiar with such phenomena in his own psyche. The combination of excessive vainglory and egoism with an equal desire for acceptance, appreciation, and love is one that he often depicted; and these same incompatibles are manifest in his disastrous relations with the pléiade.

Also, these unhappy occurrences undoubtedly led to some critical self-scrutiny, and contributed to a maturation that allowed Dostoevsky to look at himself objectively perhaps for the first time. At any rate, his letters now begin to contain some self-disparaging observations mingled with his customary self-congratulations and accounts of his triumphs. "I have reread my letter," he writes Mikhail in November 1845, "and I find that I am (1) an illiterate and (2) a braggart."[22] This remark still has a jocular tone; but five months afterwards Dostoevsky is in deadly earnest. "I have a terrible defect: an immeasurable egoism and vanity."[23] One of the most poignant letters, half a year later, contains an apology for Dostoevsky's behavior during a holiday at Revel, and reveals his inability—which he would later embody in so many of his characters—to harmonize his true inner sentiments with his outward behavior.

"I remember that you once told me," he writes Mikhail, "that my behavior with you excluded mutual equality. My dear fellow. This was totally unjust. But I have such an awful, repulsive character. . . . I am ready to give my life for you and yours, but sometimes, when my heart is full of love, you can't get a kind word out of me. My nerves don't obey me at such moments. I am ridiculous and disgusting, and I always suffer from the unjust conclusions drawn about me. People say that I am callous and without a heart. . . . I can show that I am a man with a heart and with love only when *external circumstances themselves, accidents*, jolt me forcibly out of my usual nastiness. Otherwise I am disgusting. I attribute this lack of balance to illness."[24] Such self-analysis and self-confession go a long way to explain Dostoevsky's genius for portraying the contradictory fluctuations of love-hate emotions in his characters, and his limitless tolerance for the gap between deeply felt intention and actual behavior in human affairs.

Another reason for dwelling on this spiteful little quarrel of prima donnas is the traces it left behind in Russian literature. The satirical poem of Nekrasov and Turgenev circulated in manuscript and has been preserved for posterity.[25] Dostoevsky himself, of course, became aware of its existence and he had a stormy interview with Nekrasov (duly noted by Mme Panaev) prompted by reports that Nekrasov was reading the poem aloud at various Petersburg gatherings. Panaev satirized Dostoevsky in a malicious little feuilleton included in the fourth issue of *The Contemporary* (April 1847), and in 1855, shortly after Dostoevsky had been released from internment, enlarged on the theme in another sketch called *Literary Idols, Dilettantes, Etc.* Without mentioning any names, Panaev recounts the history of Dostoevsky's discovery by Belinsky and then his "destruction" by the pléiade, not failing to linger at length over the ignominious fainting-scene at Count Vielgorsky's. "Our little idol," he writes, "began to talk his head off, and, after we quickly pulled him down from his pedestal, was completely forgotten. . . . The poor fellow! We destroyed him, we made him ridiculous!"[26] Nekrasov, probably around the same time, returned to the attack with an unfinished story, *What a Great Man I Am!*, which lampoons *both* Dostoevsky and the pléiade, though sparing Belinsky (and of course himself); but this was only found among his papers long after his death and published in 1915.[27]

9. Feodor's older brother, M. M. Dostoevsky, in 1847

Most important of all are the reflections of this conflict in the works of Dostoevsky himself. Both Nekrasov and Turgenev are later particularly singled out by Dostoevsky as the targets of devastating satirical onslaughts. Nekrasov is parodied and ridiculed, directly and indirectly, in *Notes from Underground*; Turgenev is roasted to a turn in the famous portrait of Karmazinov in *The Devils*. There were, to be sure, ample ideological reasons to motivate both these sallies quite aside from personal enmity; but Dostoevsky certainly enjoyed the opportunity to pay back—and with considerable interest!—some of the manhandling he had received himself. Moreover, Dostoevsky's entire attitude to the generation of the 1840s, as he later depicted it in his works, was profoundly affected by his misadventures with the Belinsky pléiade. For he never tired of satirizing the discrepancy between the moral posturings of members of this generation and the petty sordidness of their lives and conduct. And if he felt particularly qualified to undertake the task of unmasking their evasions and hypocrisies, it was because he could always draw on his unhappy memories to confirm his brilliantly devastating exposures.

CHAPTER 13

Belinsky and Dostoevsky: I

Dostoevsky's personal relations with Belinsky were never marred by the petty bickerings that marked his brief membership in the pléiade. Belinsky's age, as well as his authoritative position, excluded the intimate rivalry that soon pitted Dostoevsky against his contemporaries; and Dostoevsky, quite naturally, also felt an immense gratitude toward the man who had catapulted him to fame. Moreover, even when Dostoevsky's relations with the pléiade began to sour, Belinsky never joined in the persecution and openly expressed his disapproval. But, despite all the good will on both sides, Dostoevsky's friendship with Belinsky was also very short-lived: the acquaintance that began so promisingly in the late spring of 1845 ended in a quarrel in the first half of 1847. Dostoevsky's period of close contact with Belinsky thus lasted little more than a year and a half; but this short span of time remained one of the most important and memorable in his whole life.

Belinsky was a powerful and passionate personality, who stood squarely at the center of the Russian culture of his time; and the memoir-literature concerning him is enormous. But the most heartfelt and moving tribute he ever received was that written by Dostoevsky, remembering, almost thirty years later, the exalted state of rapture in which he had emerged after his first interview with the great critic. These reminiscences were evoked by a visit to the sickbed of the dying Nekrasov; and this circumstance, which no doubt swept away the dikes of old rancors and injuries, brought back in a flood the thrilling springtime of days long gone by.

"I left him [Belinsky] in a state of ecstasy. I stopped at the corner of his house, looked at the sky, at the luminous day, at the passersby, and with my whole being I felt that a solemn moment had occurred in my life, a decisive cleavage; something entirely new had begun, but something that I had not anticipated even in my most impassioned dreams. (And I was then a passionate dreamer.) 'And is it really true that I am so great?'—I shamefacedly asked myself in a timid rapture. Oh, do not laugh, never afterward did I think I was great, but then—was it possible to resist? 'Oh, I will be worthy of that

172

praise; and what people, what people! Those are people! I will deserve it, and I will try to be as noble as they are, I will remain "faithful." Oh, how light-headed I am, and if Belinsky only knew how many trashy and shameful thoughts I have! And everyone says that these literary people are proud, vain. True, such men are only to be found in Russia; they are alone, but they alone have the truth, and the truth, the good and the true, always conquer and triumph over vice and evil. We shall win; oh, to be of them, with them!' . . . That was the most wonderful moment in all my life."[1]

This was the joyous mood of the first period of Dostoevsky's intimacy with Belinsky—a mood which, as we have seen, was fully reciprocated on the other side. Dostoevsky spent the summer of 1845 visiting Mikhail and his family in Revel; and the day after arriving back in St. Petersburg he hastens to visit Belinsky. The critic was prodigal with advice, aid, encouragement, and admonition for his new disciple. Dostoevsky reports to Mikhail that Belinsky "explained to me that I unfailingly must, for the salvation of my soul, insist on not less than 200 paper rubles for a folio page."[2] To replenish his funds, Dostoevsky knocked out an insignificant little comic story in one night (*A Novel in Nine Letters*), and he read it the next evening at Turgenev's. There, "it created a sensation . . . and you [Mikhail] will see if it's less good than Gogol's *The Lawsuit*."[3]

10. V. G. Belinsky in 1843

Dostoevsky's period of elation, however, ended with the publication of *Poor Folk* at the beginning of 1846. For its reception was by no means as favorable as he—and perhaps Belinsky as well—had anticipated. The book was attacked vehemently from many sides, the main criticisms being that it was terribly long-winded, very tedious, and its language too obviously an imitation of Gogol's stylistic mannerisms. "*Poor Folk* was published on the 15th [of January]," Feodor told Mikhail two weeks later. ". . . Well, brother! What violent abuse it has met with everywhere!"[4] Dostoevsky consoled himself with the thought that Pushkin and Gogol had also been badly received at first, but had survived to become universally esteemed. He was also cheered by the prospect of an impending critical campaign in his favor led by Belinsky, and which would include lengthy articles by Odoevsky and Sollogub (he now called the latter "my friend"). Attributing the criticisms to a failure to understand his artistic technique ("they don't even suspect that Devushkin is speaking, not I, and that Devushkin is not capable of speaking any other way"), he was reassured by Belinsky's continuing support. "In me they find a new original current (Belinsky and others) consisting in this, that I work by Analysis and not Synthesis, i.e., I go deep and search for the whole by examining the atoms, while Gogol grasps the whole directly and thus is not as profound as I am. When you read, you'll see for yourself."[5]

But the great critical campaign in his favor that Dostoevsky expected never materialized; and the essay that Belinsky published a few weeks later in the *Notes of the Fatherland* must have proved a bitter disappointment. Belinsky, to be sure, was unstinting in his praise of *Poor Folk*, and he greeted its appearance as a major event in Russian literature. Even more, defending Dostoevsky against those who claimed that his reputation had been terribly inflated, he prophesied a dazzling future for the young author. "During the course of his [Dostoevsky's] career many talents will appear and be opposed to his own; but finally they will be forgotten at the very time that he arrives at the apogee of his fame."[6] Nonetheless, for all his warm and flattering words, his article by no means consists entirely of celebration and eulogy. He agrees that the weaknesses in Dostoevsky underlined so forcefully by his critics cannot be overlooked, though he stresses that such defects are the result of youthfulness, literary inexperience, and of an overabundance rather than a lack of creative endowment. All the same, every word of qualification struck a mortal blow at Dostoevsky's boundless vanity and overweening sense of self-importance.

There is some evidence that, even before the publication of this article, Belinsky had begun to nourish reservations about Dostoevsky which he had tried (tactfully but unsuccessfully) to communicate to the young author. During the summer and fall of 1845, Dostoevsky was hard at work on his next important story, *The Double*, and parts of this new production were read at Belinsky's. Grigorovich remembers Belinsky listening with approval, and, from time to time, exclaiming that only Dostoevsky could capture such astonishing psychological subtleties.[7] But P. V. Annenkov, also present at this reading and much closer to Belinsky, was aware of something else in Belinsky's response.

Belinsky, he says, "constantly drew Dostoevsky's attention to the necessity of *getting the knack*, which is what they called in the literary profession acquiring a facility in rendering one's thoughts, ridding oneself of the complexities of exposition. Belinsky apparently could not accustom himself to the author's then still diffuse manner of narration with its incessant returns to what had already been said, its repetitions and rephrasings ad infinitum; and Belinsky put this manner down to the young writer's inexperience, his failures yet to surmount the stumbling blocks of language and form." Dostoevsky, according to Annenkov, "heard the critic's recommendations out in a mood of affable indifference."[8] But while he may have been supremely and self-confidently indifferent to such tentative suggestions, made in the still-friendly and private atmosphere of the pléiade, the same advice had an entirely different edge when confronted in cold print and seemingly echoing the hostile reviews.

The Double had been published in the *Notes of the Fatherland* early in February 1846, and Belinsky's article on Dostoevsky discusses both of these works. His general view of *The Double*, like his view of *Poor Folk*, is highly favorable. "For everyone initiated into the secrets of art, it is clear at a glance that, in *The Double*, there is even more creative talent and depth of thought than in *Poor Folk*."[9] But the negative criticism is equally unequivocal. "It is obvious that the author of *The Double* has not yet acquired the tact of measure and harmony, and, as a result, many criticize even *Poor Folk* not without reason for prolixity, though this criticism is less applicable here than to *The Double*."[10] Such remarks were instantly snapped up by the pléiade and gleefully repeated; their effect may be gauged from a letter to Mikhail in April 1846. Feodor reports on all the excitement and discussion that his work is causing, and then adds: "But this is what sickens and tortures me: Our own circle, Belinsky and all of them, are dissatisfied with me because of Golyadkin [*The Double*].

The first reaction was unquestioning enthusiasm, talk, noise, chatter. The second—criticism: namely, everybody, with one voice, *ours* and all the public, found Golyadkin so boring and dull and so long-winded that it was impossible to read it."[11] Dostoevsky himself now agreed with this judgment. "A great deal of it was written in haste and fatigue. . . . Alongside brilliant pages there is trash and rubbish that turns the stomach; one can't read it."[12]

This was the moment that Dostoevsky suffered the severe nervous illness referred to earlier, and the shock of his disappointment obviously contributed to his malady. "All this," he tells Mikhail, "was hell for me for a time, and I fell sick from chagrin."[13] Dostoevsky managed to survive this blow, however, and his friendship with Belinsky apparently remained unimpaired. Retailing some of the latest literary gossip in the same letter, he informs his brother that Belinsky is leaving the *Notes of the Fatherland* and preparing to take a trip either abroad or to some watering place for his health; to support himself in the near future he plans to publish a gigantic literary almanac. "I am writing two stories: (1) *The Shaved-Off Whiskers*, (2) *A Tale of Abolished Chancelleries*, both of a shattering tragic interest and—also, I answer for it—as concise as can be."[14] It is clear that the criticisms of Dostoevsky's prolixity had hit home and were being taken seriously.

3

During the early fall of 1846, Dostoevsky unwittingly became involved in a rivalry that rocked all of Petersburg literary life and placed an additional strain on his relations with Belinsky. The critic had long been dissatisfied with the terms of his contract with A. A. Kraevsky, the powerful and unscrupulous editor of *Notes of the Fatherland*, who had made a considerable fortune out of the critic's talent and popularity. When two members of the pléiade, N. A. Nekrasov and I. I. Panaev, succeeded in obtaining editorial control of *The Contemporary*—the famous periodical founded by Pushkin, which more recently had fallen on hard times—Belinsky broke with Kraevsky and joined his friends. All of Kraevsky's contributors were now summoned to choose between their old affiliation and their loyalty to Belinsky's literary and moral ideals.

This placed Dostoevsky in an extremely difficult position. In the first place, he had already begun his customary system of taking advances for unwritten work and was heavily in debt to Kraevsky; moreover, his personal feud with the pléiade had steadily been getting worse. Despite his reverence for Belinsky, he was no longer inclined to follow the others out of group solidarity; and he had now become friendly with another coterie of lively intellectuals, one of whose members—the extremely talented young critic Valerian Maikov—had replaced Belinsky at the key post of chief critic of *Notes of the Fatherland*. Dostoevsky thus refused to align himself entirely on the side of *The Contemporary*, and the consequences of his effort to stay above the battle were not long in making themselves felt. "I have to tell you that I have had the unpleasantness of quarreling definitively with *The Contemporary* in the person of Nekrasov," he writes Mikhail in November 1846. "He became annoyed because I continue to give stories to Kraevsky, to whom I am in debt, and because I would not declare publicly that I do not belong to the *Notes of the Fatherland*."[15]

The same letter also contains the first indication of a change in Dostoevsky's unswervingly amicable attitude toward Belinsky. "Nekrasov is getting ready to abuse me. As for Belinsky, he is such a weak person that even in literary matters he keeps continually changing his mind. Only with him have I kept up my former good relations. He is a noble person."[16] From this it would appear that Belinsky had given some indication of beginning to change his mind about Dostoevsky's work. Probably they had had some discussion about Dostoevsky's story *Mr. Prokharchin* (published in the October issue of *Notes of the Fatherland*), and that Belinsky had expressed reservations. This is all the more probable because, the very next month, Belinsky spoke of Dostoevsky again in a survey of Russian literature for 1846; and the terms in which he criticizes him are now much sharper and much less apologetic. Reading between the lines, we can glimpse Belinsky's suspicion that Dostoevsky's work was moving in a direction opposed to the one he would have wished him to follow.

Belinsky, to be sure, does not renounce his protégé, and begins by referring to "the power, depth, and originality of Mr. Dostoevsky's talent"; he also speaks of "the immense power of creative genius" displayed in *The Double*, whose central figure "is one of the most profound and daring conceptions that Russian literature can boast of."[17] But the effect of these soaring compliments is considerably modified by a renewed reference to the tediousness of *The Double*. And Belinsky now adds a much more serious objection, which strikes at the whole conception of the work rather than simply at its execution. *The Double*, he says, also "suffers from another important defect: its fantastic setting. In our days the fantastic can have a place only in madhouses, but not in literature, being the business of doctors, not poets."[18] Such remarks, from the erstwhile ecstatic admirer of Hoffmann, are enough to justify Dostoevsky's charge that Belinsky's literary opinions were perpetually in a state of flux.

As for *Mr. Prokharchin*, the comments of Belinsky show no mercy. He calls it "a disagreeable surprise to all the admirers of Dostoevsky's talent," and finds it "affected, *maniéré* and incomprehensible." Even more, as if accepting the personal accusations of the pléiade against Dostoevsky, he writes that "this strange story" seems to have been "begotten" by "something in the nature of—how shall we say?—ostentation and pretension."[19] Nothing could have been more wounding to Dostoevsky, under the circumstances, than such a thrust from the man whose moral authority still remained for him unimpaired.

4

The final break between the two occurred sometime in the months immediately following the publication of this article. Belinsky had no doubt been disappointed by Dostoevsky's unwillingness to commit himself to *The Contemporary*; and his letters now begin to contain allusions to Dostoevsky which repeat the gossip making the rounds and express dissatisfaction with his work. In a letter to Turgenev early in 1847, Belinsky mirthfully reports that, although Dostoevsky had taken a large advance from Kraevsky for a new novel (*Netotchka Nezvanova*) to be delivered sometime between December 1846 and March 1847, so far no copy had been forthcoming. Rumor had it that one morning Dostoevsky had rung Kraevsky's bell and been admitted to his apartment; but when the editor, hastily dressing, made his appearance in the waiting room, all trace of Dostoevsky had vanished. "Isn't that exactly a scene out of *The Double*?" Belinsky chortles. He also notes that "Dostoevsky's correspondence between two card-sharps,* to my own surprise, simply didn't please me—I could hardly get through it. That's the general impression."[20]

Dostoevsky's stock, quite evidently, was rapidly falling to a new low; and the reports that he may have given Belinsky about his work in progress would hardly have restored him to the critic's esteem. For Dostoevsky abandoned the two stories he had intended to write for Belinsky's proposed almanac, and had now surrendered to a new source of inspiration. From the titles of his two proposed stories, it is clear that they would have remained within the accustomed range of the Natural School; but Dostoevsky had begun to feel that he had worked this vein to death, and he was anxious to make a fresh start.

* This refers to a *Novel in Nine Letters*, published in the first issue of the new *The Contemporary*.

"All that is nothing but a stale repetition of what I have long since said," he writes Mikhail at the end of October 1846. "Now more original, living, and luminous ideas are begging to be put on paper. . . . I am writing another story, and the work goes, as it once did for *Poor Folk*, freshly, easily, and successfully."[21] This new work was *The Landlady*, of which he speaks again enthusiastically three months later.

If, as seems plausible, Dostoevsky confided in Belinsky about the new departure his work was taking, the critic could only have accepted this as confirmation that the hopes he had once placed in the promising young writer had been illusory. For *The Landlady* was quite evidently a return to the style of Russian Hoffmannism that Belinsky now loathed with all the fury of his previous adoration. Dostoevsky no doubt seemed to him to be betraying everything that Belinsky had fought so hard to attain, and the literary ideals they supposedly shared in common. But Dostoevsky had never been as exclusively committed to the poetics of the Natural School as Belinsky probably believed on the basis of his impression of *Poor Folk*. At the very moment Dostoevsky was finishing up this work in 1845, he was also writing Mikhail: "Have you read *Emelya* of Veltman in the last *Library for Reading*?— what a charming thing!"[22] This new work by Dostoevsky's old favorite contains a central character somewhat resembling Prince Myshkin in the absolute purity and simplicity of his soul. Everyone considers him a "fool," and he lives as much in the fantastic world of Russian folklore as in the Moscow of 1812 where the book is set. Veltman continually shuttles back and forth between the real and the imaginary in a Romantic style rejected in the 1840s as completely out-of-date; but Dostoevsky is clearly much less the slave of literary fashion than might have been thought at first sight. One should remember that he chose the epigraph for *Poor Folk* from V. F. Odoevsky's volume, *Russian Nights* (1844), whose stories and dialogues are the literary quintessence of the Romantic Schellingian spirit of the Russian 1830s.

Writing of *The Landlady* early in 1848, Belinsky could not have been more crushing. The author, he says, "wished to try to reconcile Marlinsky and Hoffmann, adding to this mixture a little humor in the latest fashion, and thickly covering all this with the varnish of a Russian folk-style. . . . Throughout the whole of this story there is not a single simple or living word or expression: everything is far-fetched, exaggerated, stilted, spurious and false."[23] Were it not that the story bore the name of Dostoevsky, Belinsky declares, it would not have been worth mentioning at all in his survey of Russian literature in 1847. Whether or not Dostoevsky and Belinsky quarreled over an early draft of *The Landlady* can only remain a matter of speculation; but there can be no doubt that their whole attitude to art had now become diametrically opposed.

5

Even though Dostoevsky, as we know, accepted the new aesthetic of social Realism advocated by Belinsky in the 1840s, he never carried this acceptance to the lengths that Belinsky was prepared to go at the very end of his life. Dostoevsky's view of the nature and function of art had been formed under Romantic influence, and always preserved the Romantic veneration for aesthetic creativity as something sacred and inviolable. During 1846, when he became more and more discouraged because of having to turn out copy for Kraevsky, and dreamed of being able to write in peace and at leisure, he spoke of this desire to Mikhail in words that reveal his fundamental beliefs. What he yearns for, he says, is "at last [to] work for Holy Art, a holy work carried out in purity and simplicity of heart—a heart which has never yet so trembled and been stirred as now by all the new images being created in my soul."[24] It is clear that Dostoevsky has by no means abandoned the Romantic Idealist conception of art as only distinguishable in form, but not in substance, from religion; nor would he ever do so in the future.

At about the same time, Belinsky was firmly rejecting this very conception, which he had once defended with so much ardor, and expressing a preference for a socially didactic art as the only kind he could now endure. In December 1847, he writes to V. P. Botkin: "I no longer require any more poetry and artistry than necessary to keep the story true; that is, to keep it from degenerating into allegory or taking on the character of a dissertation . . . the chief thing is that it should call forth questions, that it should have a moral effect upon society. If it achieves that goal even entirely without poetry and artistry, for me it is *nonetheless* interesting, and I do not read it, I devour it. . . . I know that I take a one-sided position, but I do not wish to change it and I feel sorrow and pity for those who do not share my opinion."[25]

These two quotations about art, read consecutively, clarify one reason why Dostoevsky and Belinsky broke off relations sometime between January and April of 1847. Two years later, Dostoevsky told the commission investigating the Petrashevsky affair that he had quarreled with Belinsky "because of ideas about literature and of the tendency of literature. My view was radically opposed to Belinsky's

180

view. I blamed him for trying to give literature a partial significance unworthy of it, leveling it solely to the description, if one may express it so, *only of journalistic facts* or scandalous occurrences."[26] These words contain Dostoevsky's answer to the position taken by Belinsky in his letter to Botkin—a position Dostoevsky must have been familiar with from Belinsky's own lips, advocated with all the critic's irrepressible vehemence. Dostoevsky probably responded with equal fervor; and since both disputants were known for their lack of restraint in argument, the ensuing rift became inevitable.

Belinsky's final judgment on Dostoevsky was a totally negative one, as we can see both from his published remarks on *The Landlady* and from his comments to P. V. Annenkov early in 1848. "I don't know if I've informed you that Dostoevsky has written a story, *The Landlady* —what terrible rubbish! . . . He's written something after that too, but each work of his is a new decline. . . . I really puffed him up, my friend, in considering Dostoevsky—a genius! . . . I, the leading critic, behaved like an ass to the nth degree."[27] Nor did the usually generous and warm-hearted Belinsky find any more favorable words to say about Dostoevsky as a person. "Of Rousseau, I have only read *The Confessions* and, judging by it . . . I have conceived a powerful dislike of that gentleman. He is so much like Dostoevsky, who is profoundly convinced that all of mankind envies and persecutes him."[28]

Belinsky died several months later, on May 28, 1848, and Dostoevsky's reaction reveals how deeply attached he still was, for all their disagreements, to the combative, volatile, and lovable figure of "furious Vissarion." Visiting Dr. Yanovsky the same day, Dostoevsky made his entrance with the words: "Old fellow, something really terrible has happened—Belinsky is dead!"[29] Dostoevsky remained to spend the night, and, at three in the morning, he suffered an attack of convulsions similar to that of his "kondrashka."

CHAPTER 14

Belinsky and Dostoevsky: II

Dostoevsky's friendship with Belinsky between 1845 and 1847 was the most important relation of its kind in his life. No other person, with the possible exception of Shidlovsky, exercised so powerful an influence on him either then or later, and what he assimilated from Belinsky provides the framework within which his subsequent ideological evolution must be understood.

Even before meeting Belinsky personally, the writings of the critic in the mid-1840s had marked out the path to his own artistic self-discovery. And the memory of the moment when Belinsky had bestowed on him the accolade of fame, whatever the disillusionment following in its wake, served to sustain him in the midst of his worst moments of self-doubt and despair. If for no other reasons, these two would be enough to justify the crucial role that Dostoevsky always assigned to Belinsky in his personal history. But to these public and accessible aspects of their involvement must be added a more private and less visible one—the asserted direct influence of the renowned critic on the formation of the young man's conviction and beliefs. Thirty years later, Dostoevsky published two articles about Belinsky in his *Diary of a Writer*; and their burden is that Belinsky was the ideological mentor responsible for having placed Dostoevsky's feet on the path leading to Siberia. Ever since, these articles have been accepted without question as reliable source material for Dostoevsky's biography.

If we take Dostoevsky's account at face value, it provides an irresistibly hagiographic version of the great drama of his conscience. Before having met Belinsky, he had been a young, pure-hearted, idealistic, naively devout believer in the God and Christ of his childhood faith. It was the passionate and headstrong Belinsky, the revered idol of Russian radical youth, who had succeeded in converting him to Socialism and atheism. The result had been his participation in subversive activity, and then his arrest, conviction, and exile to Siberia. There he rediscovered God and Christ through the Russian people, and came to realize that atheism could lead only to personal and social destruction.

This depiction of events has been eagerly accepted on all sides because it satisfies so many of the differing needs that are fulfilled by Dostoevsky's work. For the believing Christian, who finds spiritual solace in Dostoevsky, it turns the writer's life into a parable illustrating the profound moral of his books. For the Soviet Russian critic committed to a militant atheism, it enables him to locate Dostoevsky as part of that Golden Legend of Russian history first elaborated by Belinsky's followers and, ever since the Revolution, cherished as gospel by a society eager to see its own history in the light of a unified revolutionary tradition. Dostoevsky may have betrayed this tradition in the end, but he nonetheless fits into it very neatly and is not totally unredeemable. Whatever remains valuable in his writings can thus be attributed to the tutelage he received from the great revolutionary forefather. As a result of these opposite but mutually reinforcing interests, there has been very little impetus to examine Dostoevsky's articles of 1873 critically—even though they obviously contradict each other in some respects and, more important, do not quite jibe with what we know of Dostoevsky's life. It is high time, however, that the effort be made to assess the historical veracity of Dostoevsky's testimony and to grapple with some of the problems that it raises.

As a first step, we should keep in mind that these articles were written long after the events they describe and were intended to convey a particular image of Belinsky. By the 1870s, Dostoevsky had come to see Belinsky as the symbolic source of the Russian Nihilism that the novelist had battled with all through the 1860s, and against which he had just launched his most violently anti-radical work, *The Devils*. Belinsky was not simply a person about whom Dostoevsky could discourse objectively or dispassionately; his name had become a slogan and a banner to successive generations of Russian radicals; and it is about this mythical or symbolic Belinsky that Dostoevsky was really writing. In a letter to Nikolay Strakhov, who had objected to the violence of Dostoevsky's language about Belinsky in an earlier missive, Dostoevsky replies in 1871: "I insulted Belinsky more as a phenomenon of Russian life than as a personality."[1] The portrait Dostoevsky sketched of him two years later is dominated by this impersonal perspective; and the result, as we shall see, is that he integrates his own personal history—even when the facts do not quite fit—into the general image he wishes to create of Belinsky's baneful effect on Russian culture as a whole.

2

Let us sketch in first, as succinctly as possible, an account of Belinsky's development from the point at which we dropped him in 1843 up to the end of his life early in 1848. For the Utopian Socialist Belinsky of the early 1840s did not remain unchanged; and by the time he met Dostoevsky in 1845, his point of view had evolved in a manner that took Dostoevsky completely by surprise.

When Belinsky became converted to French Utopian Socialism in 1841-1842, he accepted a doctrine, it will be recalled, strongly informed by Christian moral-religious values. Saint-Simon had entitled the last work he wrote before his death *Nouveau Christianisme*; and all of French Utopian Socialism may be summed up under the same title. "In this way," as V. L. Komarovich has written, "a 'new' and 'true' Christianity was constructed, advocated not only by Saint-Simon but by Cabet, Pierre Leroux, Lamennais [etc.]. Not breaking openly with Christian dogma—not denying, for example, like Voltaire and the Deists of the eighteenth century, divine revelation as the foundation of religion, but not expressing themselves positively on this point—the Utopians directed their main attention to the morality of the Gospel, not refusing, all the same, to recognize its divinity."[2] All the Utopian Socialists of any importance in the 1840s saw Christ (much as Dostoevsky had done in 1838) as a divine figure come to prescribe the laws governing the organization of earthly life in the modern world, and whose teachings, freed from centuries of perversion, were at last to be put into practice.

The "New Christianity" of Utopian Socialism was based on an opposition between the true religion of Jesus Christ—a religion of hope and light, of faith in the powers of man as well as in the beneficence of God—and a false religion of fear and eternal damnation. The second was considered a distortion and corruption of Christ's teaching, an unhappy amalgam of the message of Jesus with doctrines deriving from the fatalism and worldly despair of the "Oriental" cults in whose midst Christianity had come to birth. Victor Considérant makes this contrast very explicit in his *La Destinée sociale*, one of the most widely read of all Socialist treatises in Russia during the 1840s. "Take care!" he warns the supporters of the old religion of fear, "you who condemn God to desire the humiliation and misery of man here on earth, for in a short while man will have conquered God! Your dogma, injurious to God, was able to prevail when man, in his infancy and weakness, trembled before God, believing him to be a barbarous master, a brutal despot whose anger he feared; but he is no longer suitable for man grown in strength and intelligence; man in his strength and intelligence will recognize God his father, will love him with all his love and will know that he has nothing to fear from him, but everything to hope for, to ask for and to expect. . . ."[3]

As we know from *Spiridion*, a devout adherence to the "New Christianity" easily went hand in hand with fierce opposition to the established Church as a source of ignorance and obscurantism and as an ally of political reaction. Hence, in the same letter announcing his conversion to a Socialism in which "Christ will pass His power to the Father," Belinsky scoffs at a friend who still retains "his warm faith in the *muzhik* with the little beard who, sitting belching on a soft cloud surrounded by a multitude of seraphs and cherubims, considers that his might is right and his thunders and lightnings rational demonstrations."[4]

Another feature of this Utopian Socialist "religion" was, as Maxime Leroy puts it, "a divinization of the people,"[5] who were invariably considered morally superior to their upper-class oppressors. Belinsky, accordingly, takes Eugène Sue to task because, in *Les Mystères de Paris*, he portrays the people only "as a hungry and ragged mob condemned by poverty and ignorance to a life of crime," and is not aware that "in the people there are faith and enthusiasm, there is a moral power."[6] Dostoevsky's commitment to this same belief is perfectly evident in *Poor Folk* and may be further illustrated by his enthusiasm for George Sand's *Teverino*—a novel which demonstrates the unspoiled moral sublimity of two outcasts and vagabonds in contrast to the blasé, bloodless, and cynical aristocrats by whom they are surrounded. "Read *Teverino* (George Sand in *Notes of the Fatherland*, Oct.)," Dostoevsky excitedly writes his brother shortly after finishing *Poor Folk*. "Nothing like it has yet existed in our century."[7] Belinsky, who also admired *Teverino*,* correctly sensed a similar conviction to be at the source of Dostoevsky's "humanism" in *Poor Folk*; and the initial accord between the critic and the young novelist was sealed by this community of values. Or so, at least, Dostoevsky thought and believed when he first came into Belinsky's presence.

3

Meanwhile, however, another set of ideas had gradually begun to undermine Belinsky's adherence to the vision and ethos of Utopian Socialism. These ideas were those of the German Left Hegelians, which began to penetrate into Russia almost simultaneously with those of the Utopian Socialists. Left Hegelianism was primarily a critique of religion; and the effect of its influence was to call into question the religious foundation of Utopian Socialist convictions. D. F.

---

* And so, it would seem, did Henry James (1897). ". . . and is there anyone left who remembers *Teverino*?" *Notes on Novelists* (New York, 1914), 161.

Strauss's *Life of Jesus* considered the New Testament to be, not divine revelation, but a mythopoetic expression of the historical aspirations of the Jewish community of the time. It was only a historical accident, Strauss maintained, that these myths had crystallized around the figure of Jesus Christ, who was merely one of the many self-proclaimed prophets of the period. Feuerbach's *The Essence of Christianity* was even more radical in its secularization of the divine, and argued that, instead of God having created Man in His own image, exactly the opposite was true. The human species as a whole had divinized its highest and sublimest attributes by attributing them to supernatural beings, and, in so doing, had alienated its own essence. The task of Mankind was now to reclaim from the transcendent all the qualities that rightfully belonged to humanity, and to realize them on earth by incorporating them into social life.

Such ideas burst like a bombshell among the Russian Westerners, already well-schooled to appreciate them by their previous training in Hegel's thought. A copy of Feuerbach arrived in Russia in January 1842; and Annenkov remembers this book as having been "in everybody's hands" in the mid-1840s. "It can safely be affirmed," he writes, "that Feuerbach's book nowhere produced so powerful an impression as in our 'Western' circle, and nowhere did it so rapidly obliterate the remnants of all preceding outlooks. Herzen, needless to say, was a fervent expositor of its propositions and conclusions; among other things, he connected the upheaval it heralded in the realm of metaphysical ideas with the political upheaval heralded by the Socialists, in which respect Herzen once again coincided with Belinsky."[8]

Belinsky, however, who was kept up-to-date by such friends as V. P. Botkin and Herzen, was not won over as quickly as Annenkov implies. He had, as he confessed himself, a congenital need for religion, and he was still arguing about God with Turgenev—just freshly returned from the philosophical Mecca of Berlin—in the spring of 1843. Reporting on one such interminable colloquy, the novelist recalls Belinsky saying reproachfully to him: "We haven't yet decided the question of the existence of God . . . and you want to eat!"[9] By 1845, though, just a few months before meeting Dostoevsky, Belinsky had come to the conclusion, as he writes Herzen, that "in the words *God* and *religion* I see darkness, gloom, chains and the knout, and now I like these two words as much as the four following them."[10] These phrases mark the moment when atheism and Socialism fused together in Russia into an alliance never afterwards to be completely dissolved (though it weakened somewhat in the 1870s). Not all the Russian Westerners, to be sure, were willing to accept atheism as a new obligatory credo. T. N. Granovsky (who probably later appealed to Dostoevsky for this very reason)* refused to give up his belief in the immortality of the soul and broke with Herzen over the issue—a rift that occurred almost simultaneously with Dostoevsky's first meeting with Belinsky.

4

There is still one other mutation in Belinsky's position that must be taken into account before turning to Dostoevsky's articles. Even though Left Hegelianism was militantly anti-religious, at first it attacked only the historicity and divinity of God and Christ; the moral-religious values that Christ had proclaimed to the world were left untouched. Feuerbach in particular declared Christian moral-religious values to be the true essence of human nature; his aim was not to replace such values by others, but to see them realized in the love of man for man rather than for the God-man. "His only aim," as Karl Löwith has pointed out, "was to remove the 'subject' of religious predicates, God; he had no designs upon the predicates themselves, when interpreted in the proper human sense."[11] Very soon, however, the rejection of the divinity of Christ led to a questioning of the moral-religious ideals that He had proclaimed; and this was greatly aided by the appearance of the last and most sensational of the Left Hegelian treatises, Max Stirner's *The Ego and His Own*. Stirner argued that the acceptance of *any* abstract or general moral value was an impediment to man's freedom, and alienated his personality as much as a belief in supernatural beings. Of no group was he more scornful, no antagonist did he attack more mercilessly, than the Socialists and liberals still clinging to their general ideal of "Humanity." What is fundamental for the individual ego, according to Stirner, is simply the satisfaction of *its own* needs, whatever these may be; his philosophy is that of a totally subjective and totally amoral self-aggrandizement.

Belinsky was familiar with Stirner's book, and mentions it in a letter of February 1847.† From Annenkov, we also know that he was

---

* Granovsky is one of the sources for Stepan Trofimovich Verkhovensky in *The Devils*, Dostoevsky's superbly caricatural but fundamentally sympathetic portrait of the archetypal Russian Liberal of the 1840s.

† By what may be no more than an accidental association, the name of Stirner is closely linked with that of Dostoevsky in Belinsky's letter. Immediately following the reference to Stirner, Belinsky continues: "By the way, I almost forgot—there's a very amusing anecdote about Dostoevsky." Belinsky then goes on

quite concerned with it during the summer of the same year. "It would be juvenile," Annenkov reports him as saying, "to be frightened of the word 'egoism' itself. It has been proved that a man feels and thinks and acts invariably according to the law of egotistical urges, and indeed, he cannot have any others." To be sure, Belinsky did not take the word in Stirner's narrowly selfish sense, and believed that individuals could eventually be made to realize that their own "egotistical interests are identical with that of mankind as a whole."[12] What is important, though, is Belinsky's evident willingness to accept Stirner's non-idealistic view of the roots of human behavior, the critic's desire to search for a new, more "practical" and "rational" foundation for his values. We find the same impulse at work in his attraction for the physiological materialism of Emile Littré; and he now refers privately to the starry-eyed Utopian Socialists, with contemptuous obscenity, as "those insects hatched from the manure heaped up from the backside of Rousseau."[13]

Belinsky's new orientation, not a secret for anybody, was clearly displayed in the pages of *The Contemporary*. His important manifesto in the first issue, defining the ideological line of the rejuvenated periodical, bears unmistakable evidence of the change in his ideas. "Psychology which is not based on physiology," he announces, under the influence of Littré, "is as unsubstantial as physiology that knows not the existence of anatomy." Looking forward to the future triumphs of physical science, he foresees the day when "chemical analysis" will "penetrate the mysterious laboratory of nature," and will "by observations of the embryo . . . trace the *physical* process of *moral* evolution."[14] The excellent Soviet historian of the journal, Evgenyev-Maksimov, also remarks that "the recipes proposed by Utopian Socialism had already (1847) lost credit in the eyes of the majority of the contributors to *The Contemporary*. Skeptical and even contemptuous utterances concerning this tendency in Western European social thought are by no means rare. . . . Especially characteristic in this regard is the judgment of Annenkov in his *Paris Letters*."[15]

These influential articles ridiculed such pillars of Utopianism as Pierre Leroux, Cabet and Victor Considérant, and praised Proudhon's

---

to tell the story (mentioned earlier) of Dostoevsky's failure to turn in a manuscript to Kraevsky, then showing up at his door but vanishing immediately. V. G. Belinsky, *Izbrannye Pisma*, 2 vols. (Moscow, 1955), 2: 294.

This has excited a good deal of speculation, but there is no way of establishing whether it has any relevance. It may mean, however, that Belinsky and Dostoevsky had discussed Stirner, and that the name of the one recalled the other to Belinsky's mind.

just-published *Système des contradictions économiques* for having abandoned fantasy and devoted itself to the study of the economic laws governing actually existing society. "Your letters are our delight," Belinsky writes Annenkov early in the spring of 1847,[16] bearing out Annenkov's observation that, in these last two or three years of his life, Belinsky "was concerned with the new, emerging definitions of the rights and obligations of man, with the new *truth* proclaimed by economic doctrines which was liquidating all notions of the old, displaced truth about the moral, the good and the noble on earth, and was putting in their place formulas and theses of a purely rational character."[17]

As a final touch, we should also note Belinsky's abandonment of his previous idealization of "the people." At the beginning of 1848 he defends Voltaire in a letter to Annenkov, even though the great Frenchman had "sometimes called the people 'vile populace.' " Belinsky justifies this insulting phrase "because the people are uncultivated, superstitious, fanatic, bloodthirsty, and love torture and execution." He adds that Bakunin (now an ardent revolutionary) and the Slavophils, by their excessive idealization, have "greatly helped me to throw off a mystical faith in the people."[18] Such is the atmosphere of the last period of Belinsky's thought, which began shortly after Dostoevsky met him in 1845 and was certainly apparent in 1846. There is every reason to believe, contrary to a widespread opinion,[19] that Dostoevsky was quite familiar with its manifestations.

5
——

During the span of Dostoevsky's friendship with Belinsky, the critic was thus moving (or, more exactly, oscillating) between a Feuerbachian "humanism" with moral-religious overtones and the acceptance of a more "rational" viewpoint shading toward mechanistic materialism and moral determinism. Whether Belinsky, before his death, ever rejected his "humanism" completely is difficult to decide; we shall cite evidence in a later chapter that indicates the contrary. But that he was tending in this direction is unmistakable, even though we should always remember that Belinsky had little use for intellectual consistency as such, and would gladly have adopted as his motto, if he had been familiar with it, the Emersonian dictum that "a foolish consistency is the hobgoblin of little minds."

It is striking to see that the quick portrait of Belinsky sketched by Dostoevsky coincides, in its grasp of the essential, with the image that emerges from a study of all the other materials. "Valuing reason, science, and realism above everything," Dostoevsky writes, "at the same time he [Belinsky] understood more deeply than anyone else that reason, science, and realism alone could construct only an ant-hill and not a social 'harmony' within which it would be possible for mankind to live. He knew that, at the foundation of everything, were moral principles"; and he knew that in attacking Christianity, which was based on the moral responsibility of the individual, he was not only undermining the foundations of the society he wished to destroy but also denying human liberty. But Belinsky also believed, in Dostoevsky's view, that Socialism would restore the freedom of the personality and raise it to hitherto-undreamed of heights.[20] Dostoevsky's two articles of 1873 accurately portray this complex ideological configuration of the last period of Belinsky's life. Indeed, in the context we have sketched, it is clear that one of them depicts the Belinsky who had not yet abandoned the ideals of Utopian Socialism and was perhaps still intermittently a "New Christian." The other, which perhaps incorporates recollections of a slightly later time, shows us the atheistic Belinsky in the process of discarding the old moral-religious basis of his thought. In both cases, however, what Dostoevsky tells us about his relations with Belinsky contain some distortions.

It is the Utopian Socialist Belinsky who dominates in the article called "One of Our Contemporaneous Falsehoods"—an extremely important document, which includes the only direct public testimony that Dostoevsky ever gave about his participation in the Petrashevsky affair and the motives inspiring him at that time. His aim, in this article, was to convince his readers of the 1870s that radicals were by no means people stirred to action by low or dishonorable motives; and he invokes his own past as an ex-Petrashevets to prove the point. In doing so, he brushes in an account of the Utopian Socialism of the 1840s that stresses its moral-religious character. "But in those days the matter was seen in the very rosiest and angelically moral light. Really, truthfully, the Socialism then just being born used to be compared, even by some of its ringleaders, with Christianity, and was regarded merely as a corrective to, and improvement of, the latter in accordance with the century and with civilization. All these new ideas pleased us terribly in Petersburg, and seemed in the highest degree holy and moral and, most important, universal, the future law for all mankind without exception. . . . By 1846 I had already been consecrated into all the *truth* of this 'future regeneration of the world' and into all the *holiness* of the future Communistic society by Belinsky."[21]

What is distorted here is simply Dostoevsky's assertion that it was Belinsky who had indoctrinated *him* with such ideas. We know very well that Dostoevsky had become converted to this sort of moral-religious Socialism at least several years before he met Belinsky—at a time, in point of fact, when Belinsky was still hurling anathema at those benighted souls who believed that "reality" could be improved and refused to "reconcile" themselves to its imperfections. One can only speculate as to why Dostoevsky inverted chronology in this way; the most plausible explanation is that, as a novelist, he instinctively reached after dramatic concentration, and he cast his own life here, as he would have done with any other literary material, in its most effective form. Belinsky, after all, *had* played the role assigned to him by Dostoevsky in Russian culture of the 1840s. Why confuse the reader with the insignificant details of his own *true* personal history, which would have only complicated the picture unnecessarily and lessened the force of the image he was trying to convey? Moreover, just as he identified himself with the characters of his novels at the moment of writing, Dostoevsky was no doubt imagining *himself* as one of the numerous army of young men who *had* caught their first glimpse of the "future regeneration of the world" in Belinsky's pages.

In the other article devoted to Belinsky, however—written a month or two earlier—Dostoevsky paints quite a different picture. For Dostoevsky's purpose is now to convince his readers that Socialism and Christianity are fundamentally incompatible. To be sure, Dostoevsky knew very well that Socialism and Christianity *had* been historically compatible, at least for a brief period; and he also knew, as we see from the article just discussed, that his own Socialism had been precisely of this Christian variety. But since he wishes to show that such an amalgam was really inconsistent with the final doctrine of the Master, he appeals to his own experience of the later phase of Belinsky to prove the point; and once again he dresses up his recollections to convey an impression that is not autobiographically accurate in the strict sense. What he does is to imply (without saying so explicitly) that Belinsky had converted him to atheism, and to that rejection of Christian moral-religious values which usually accompanied such a conversion in the late 1840s. The polemical intent here is clear: Socialism in Russia had been atheistic and totally anti-Christian from the very start, and it was impossible to maintain any connection between it and Christian morality. This was a very important issue in the early 1870s, when a new generation of radicals—the Russian Populists—were returning to a more or less secularized Christianity which their predecessors had abandoned twenty years earlier.

There is only one detail in Dostoevsky's recollections for which we have any historical confirmation. "I by no means exaggerate his [Belinsky's] inclination toward me at least in the first months of our acquaintance," Dostoevsky writes. "I found him a passionate Socialist, and he began immediately with me on atheism."[22] A brief note from Belinsky to Dostoevsky, written in mid-June 1845, verifies the truth of these words. "Dostoevsky, my soul (immortal) longs to see you,"[23] Belinsky writes jocularly. The friendly irony of this parenthesis indicates some serried discussion of the issue which, as we know from Annenkov, was just then also about to be debated in Moscow by Herzen and Granovsky. One surmises, too, that Belinsky was having more trouble overpowering the young man than he had perhaps expected.

It is very probable that Belinsky's onslaught came as something of a surprise to Dostoevsky, and that it was his first jolting awareness of the possibility of conflict between his religious faith and his Socialist convictions. Nourished as he had been on the French social Romantics, he would not have had reason to assume previously that the two could not go quite smoothly hand in hand. However that may be, Dostoevsky's polemical intent in 1873—his desire to show that Socialism and Christianity were then irreconcilable—muddles the terms of the argument on which he reports. "As a Socialist, he [Belinsky] was duty bound to destroy the teaching of Christ, to call it a deceptive and ignorant philanthropy (*chelovekolyubie*), condemned by modern science and economic doctrines."[24] To an incautious reader (and there have been, so far as my knowledge goes, no others), this makes it appear as if Dostoevsky were defending "the teaching of Christ" in some conventional sense—as if he were arguing on the side of "the *muzhik* with the little beard" sitting on his cloud. But it should be obvious that the reader of George Sand, and the author of *Poor Folk*, would not have been guilty of any such naiveté.

If Belinsky was attacking Dostoevsky for continuing to believe in "the teaching of Christ," this could only have meant, in the context of the time, the "New Christianity" of Utopian Socialism. Dostoevsky blurs this fact for evident reasons of ideological strategy, but his choice of terminology in Russian actually gives the show away. He could, it would seem, fudge his historical perspective, but he could not really falsify his style. For it is inconceivable that Belinsky would have argued against the religion of "the *muzhik* with the little beard" by calling it *chelovekolyubie*. This word would only have been appropriate for the Utopian Socialism whose tenets Belinsky was beginning to challenge—and was no doubt vituperating against—with all the excitable bellicosity that he usually displayed on such occasions.* His other objections against the "teaching of Christ" are equally tell-tale— for the connection of Utopian Socialism with a supernatural faith was just then indeed in the process of being condemned in the name of modern "science" (Strauss and Feuerbach), and of the new economic doctrines (Proudhon) that were emerging to take its place.

6

The core of Dostoevsky's portrait of Belinsky is here concentrated in an argument concerning the problem of the moral responsibility of the individual and hence the issue of free will. This issue was of such epochal importance for the later Dostoevsky that one might be inclined to think he had not been able to resist the temptation to smuggle it back anachronistically into the 1840s. In point of fact, however, Dostoevsky's friend Valerian Maikov attacked Belinsky on this very subject in the winter of 1846-1847; and his attack was launched from a Utopian Socialist position appealing to the figure of Jesus Christ as the great symbol of man's moral freedom from material determinism.

As Dostoevsky presents it, the dialogue begins with Belinsky's denial that the suffering and oppressed lower classes had any personal moral responsibility for their actions. " 'But, do you know,' he [Belinsky] screamed one evening (sometimes in a state of great excitement he used to scream), 'do you know that it is impossible to charge man with sins, and to burden him with debts and turning the

---

* The word *chelovekolyubie* in the 1840s was frequently used to characterize the dominating moral-religious "humanism" of the Natural School in Russia and of the related "philanthropic" school in France. Belinsky writes of Eugène Sue that, as a Frenchman, "he is not a stranger to sympathy for the fallen and weak. Humanity and *chelovekolyubie* are one of the most striking national characteristics of the French." V. G. Belinsky, *Izbrannye Filosofskie Sochinenia* (Moscow, 1948), 2: 127. Shevyrev criticized the anthology in which *Poor Folk* was first published because its contributors turned art into "an agent of the *chelovekolyubivoi* tendency." See M. Polyakov, *Vissarion Belinsky* (Moscow, 1960), 419.

The word thus had meant, in general, the application of Christian moral-social ideals to worldly existence. It had no specific theological content; and this is how Dostoevsky continues to use it. Just a year after writing the article under discussion, he jotted down some notes for *A Raw Youth*; and he defines *chelovekolyubie* here as signifying "good deeds without Christ," which he calls a Genevan (i. e., Rousseauistic) idea. This definition, to be sure, gives the word a Feuerbachian nuance of Christian morality combined with doctrinal atheism; while in the article it retains the alternative "New Christian" sense that made it applicable to Dostoevsky's own position in the 1840s. In both cases, however, the emphasis is on "good deeds," not on some extra-terrestrial, purely religious significance. *Literaturnoe Nasledstvo*, No. 77 (Moscow, 1965), 89. See also the discussion of the word in the monumental *Slovar Sovremennogo Russkogo Literaturnogo Yazyka* (Moscow-Leningrad, 1965), 17: 828. It is defined there as "love of people, of mankind; humanitarianism," and no religious usages are cited.

other cheek, when society is organized so vilely that man cannot help committing crimes, when he is economically pushed into crime, and that it is stupid and cruel to demand from men what, by the very laws of nature, they cannot accomplish even if they wanted to. . . .' "[25] The Belinsky speaking here is obviously no longer the old "humanist" who responded to the emotive appeal of Christian moral-religious values; this is the voice of the admirer of Littré and perhaps also the reader of Max Stirner, who would see the moral will as helpless or nonexistent, and the criminal acts of the oppressed only as a natural and legitimate expression of their "egoistic" needs.

The next subject to which the conversation turns is that of the personality of Jesus Christ; and it is revelatory of the time that no discussion of social problems could avoid sooner or later taking a position about Christianity. " 'I'm really touched to look at him,' said Belinsky, suddenly interrupting his furious exclamations, turning to his friend [present at the conversation] and pointing at me [Dostoevsky]. 'Every time I mention Christ his face changes expression as if he were ready to start weeping.' 'Yes, believe me, you naive person'— he turned again to me abruptly—'believe me that your Christ, if he were born in our day, would be the most ordinary and insignificant person; he would simply vanish in the face of contemporary science and of the contemporary movers of mankind.' "[26]

Two observations may be made about this passage. One is that, if Dostoevsky's face registered such extreme emotion at Belinsky's words about Christ, it was because those words were of a harshness and a coarseness of which we know Belinsky to have been fully capable. "That man [Belinsky]," Dostoevsky writes in 1871 to Strakhov, "reviled Christ to me in the most obscene and abusive way, but was never capable of comparing himself and all the agitators of the whole world with Christ."[27] The second is that Belinsky's comments betray the manifest Left Hegelian influence of Strauss, who had attributed Christ's charismatic powers solely to the fact that he lived in a pre-rational world. The reply to this Left Hegelian thrust is uttered by Belinsky's unnamed friend (could Dostoevsky the novelist have invented this interlocutor to speak for his own *true* position?), and is appropriately Utopian Socialist. " 'Well, not at all,' interposed Belinsky's friend. . . . 'Well, no: if Christ appeared now, He would join the movement and would lead it. . . .' 'All right, all right,' Belinsky agreed with surprising suddenness—'He would, as you say, join the Socialists and follow them.' "[28] Belinsky's uncertainty on this crucial point reveals his own transitional state of mind.

Dostoevsky's further comment on the interchange leaves no doubt about the ideological crosscurrents that were really involved. "Those movers of mankind whom Christ was destined to join were the French: George Sand above all, the now totally forgotten Cabet, Pierre Leroux, and Proudhon, then only just having begun his career. . . . There was also a German before whom he bowed to with deference then—Feuerbach (Belinsky, never having been able to master a single foreign language all his life, pronounced it: Fierbach). Strauss was spoken of with reverence."[29] Christ would thus have, quite accurately, joined the movement of the preponderantly Utopian Socialist and moral-religious French; the Left Hegelian Germans are carefully separated from them by Dostoevsky's judicious phrasing. And the argument on which he reports—the argument not only of Belinsky with Dostoevsky, but also of Belinsky with himself—was really being carried on between the two competing doctrines then disputing for the ideological mastery of the Left throughout the world.*

Dostoevsky concludes his portrayal with the following words, which have caused an immense amount of confusion: "In the last year of his [Belinsky's] life I no longer went to visit him. He had taken a dislike to me, but I was then passionately following all his teaching."[30] As should be clear by now, this simple statement contains a quagmire of complexities and possible interpretations: just what Dostoevsky means by "all his teaching" is terribly vague. Is it the teaching of the moral-religious Utopian Socialism which, deceptively, he says he imbibed from Belinsky, and which was only an "improved" form of Christianity? Is it the teaching of Belinsky's insulting Left Hegelian tirade against Christ, and his denial of free will and moral responsibility because of the overwhelming weight of "the laws of nature"? What Dostoevsky evidently wants the reader to understand is that he *was* converted to Belinsky's atheism and materialism; but there is good reason to doubt this very strongly. For Dostoevsky's closest friends in the next several years refused to surrender the moral-religious inspiration of Utopian Socialism and were very critical of Belinsky. And we know from one of his fellow-Petrashevtsy that, as

---

* When Arnold Ruge, the editorial impresario of the Left Hegelians, arrived in Paris in August 1843 to recruit contributors for the *Deutsch-Französische Jahrbücher*, the atheism of the Left Hegelians proved a major obstacle. "Almost without exception they [the French] were believers and held to Robespierre's anathema of godless philosophy." David McLellan, *The Young Hegelians and Karl Marx* (London, 1969), 37-38.

Writing to Feuerbach from Paris in May 1844, Ruge says disgustedly: "All parties base themselves directly on Christianity." Cited in Werner Sombart, *Der Proletarische Sozialismus*, 2 vols. (Jena, 1924), 1: 119.

Dostoevsky was awaiting execution in 1849, he spoke as a believing Christian who had by no means abandoned his hope of an afterlife in which he would "be with Christ."[31]

Dr. Yanovsky saw Dostoevsky almost daily from the late spring of 1846 up to the time of his arrest three years later; and he assures us that his friend Feodor Mikhailovich was an intensely religious person. Indeed, he states unequivocally that they both fasted together, in a spirit of genuine piety, for the Feast of the Ascension in 1847 and 1849. There has been a natural tendency in Soviet scholarship to discount such testimony as tendentious and apologetic; but it seems to me perfectly acceptable in the light of everything else we know about the Dostoevsky of the mid-1840s. Yanovsky also observes that, when Dostoevsky's conversation touched on social-political matters, he always "gave the analysis of one or another fact and situation, which was then followed by a practical *conclusion*, but always of a kind *that did not contradict the Gospel*."[32] To be sure, Yanovsky argues from this that Dostoevsky could not have taken part in any illegal conspiracy; but here Yanovsky is merely assuming—just as do those who reject his recollections as unreliable—that a reverence for the Gospel is totally opposed to any sort of radicalism. This was certainly true in Russia in the 1860s; but it was not at all true in the 1840s; and it was much less true in the 1870s than Dostoevsky would have wished it to be.

7

Even though Belinsky did not play exactly the role in Dostoevsky's life that the latter desired his readers to imagine, the enormous importance of their encounter should by no means be minimized. This importance, however, is more symbolic than historical, more literary than literal. Dostoevsky's verbal skirmishes with Belinsky were of crucial significance for him as the future novelist of the spiritual crises of the Russian intelligentsia; but they did not lead, so far as one can judge, to any decisive change in his ideas and values. The force of Belinsky's impact, though, no doubt explains why Dostoevsky was so determined to tidy up his biography, and to give to life the artistic symmetry which, according to his final view of Russian culture, it should rightly have had. For if Belinsky had not really introduced Dostoevsky to Socialism, he *had* introduced him to *atheistic* Socialism—and this was the only kind that the Dostoevsky of the 1870s believed to be spiritually honest and intellectually self-consistent.

Moreover, the complex of cultural influences whose first stirrings Dostoevsky met with in Belinsky quickly came to dominate the Russian scene, even though Belinsky's views—still embryonic and in a state of flux—should not simply be identified with those of his followers in the 1860s. Nonetheless, the mechanical "scientific" materialism that Belinsky admired in Littré did succeed in becoming the philosophical dogma of the Russian Left for much of Dostoevsky's life. And moral values were derived from a Utilitarian egoism which, if it stemmed more directly from Bentham than from Max Stirner, fully shared the latter's supreme contempt for all sentimental humanitarianism (Engels once aptly called Stirner the German Bentham).* Dostoevsky thus had good reason to regard his disputes with Belinsky as having foreshadowed the major issues posed by the later development of Russian social-political and cultural life; and his encounter with Belinsky certainly colored his own reaction to such changes. In a certain sense, one can say that he continued to carry on the argument all his life. For his Christianity always retained the strongly altruistic and social-humanitarian cast of the 1840s (Konstantin Leontyev bitingly called it "rosewater Christianity" in the 1880s),[33] and it was always pitted against a "rationalism" that served to justify a totally amoral egoism.

There can be no question either that the religious theme of Dostoevsky's great novels was profoundly affected by the challenge of Belinsky. Not, to be sure, that atheism, or doubts about the beneficence of God, first loomed on his mental and emotional horizon in 1845. It would be naive to imagine that the little boy whose consciousness had been stirred by the Book of Job, or the young man who had participated in Shidlovsky's tormented soul-searchings, should have needed Belinsky to introduce him to such matters; but it was Belinsky who first acquainted Dostoevsky with the new—and much more intellectually sophisticated—arguments of Strauss, Feuerbach, and probably Stirner. And though his religious faith ultimately emerged unshaken—even strengthened—from the encounter, these doctrines did present him with an acute spiritual dilemma. Traces of this inner crisis can certainly be found in the wrestlings of Dostoevsky's own characters with the problems of faith and Christ.

Feuerbach had argued that God—and the Son of God so far as He

* According to the most recent Marx scholarship, Marx's own break with the "humanism" of Feuerbach can be attributed to the influence of Stirner's ferocious onslaught. "It is . . . likely that Marx's constant attacks on anything that appeared to be based on 'morality' or 'love' in true socialism was due to Stirner's ruthless criticism of all such notions." McLellan, 132; also Henri Arvon, *Max Stirner* (Paris, 1954), 167-178.

was divine—were merely fictions representing the alienated essence of mankind's highest values. The task of mankind was thus to reappropriate its own essence by reassuming the powers and prerogatives alienated to the divine. The Left Hegelians, to be sure, did not recommend this as a task for any particular individual to undertake; it was only mankind as a whole that could recoup this great human treasure; but Max Stirner comes very close to urging everyone immediately to embark on their own personal deification. The effect of all this on the young Dostoevsky, who had been so fascinated by the character of Alban in *Der Magnetiseur*, is not difficult to foresee. Nobody has grasped more profoundly, or portrayed more brilliantly, the tragic inner dialectic of this movement of atheist humanism; and if Dostoevsky had no effective answer to Belinsky in 1845, he amply made up for it later by the creation of his negative heroes. For when such characters reject God and Christ, they invariably engage in the impossible and self-destructive attempt to transcend the human condition, and to incarnate the Left Hegelian dream of replacing the God-man by the Man-god.[34]

So far as Dostoevsky himself is concerned, the long-range effect of this crisis was probably to sharpen his sense of the absolute incompatibility between reason and faith. This paved the way for his later commitment to an irrationalism for which he had been prepared both by his religious and philosophical education, and by the psychic experience he called "mystic terror." Like Kierkegaard, with whom he has so often been compared in the last half-century, Dostoevsky also later indicated that a paradoxical "leap of faith" was the only source of religious certainty. And the similarity of solution derives from the identity of the point of departure: Kierkegaard greatly admired Feuerbach for stressing how impossible it was to combine religion with the scientific and rational character of modern life. "Feuerbach," writes Karl Löwith, "perceived this contrast in exactly the same way that Kierkegaard did; but the latter drew the equally logical, but exactly opposite, conclusion: that science, and natural science in particular, is simply irrelevant to the religious situation."[35] Dostoevsky too finally chose to take his stand with the existential irrational of the "leap of faith" against Feuerbach's demand that religion be brought down to earth and submit to the criterion of human reason.

It would require many years, however, before Dostoevsky would begin to draw such conclusions. For the moment, what he did was to seek a more congenial atmosphere than he found in the pléiade or with Belinsky personally. A new group of friends, the little-known Beketov circle, provided what he was looking for.

CHAPTER 15

The Beketov Circle

Dostoevsky's character, as he acknowledged himself, was a perverse and prickly one, and the history of his misadventures with the Belinsky pléiade furnished ample justification for the unenviable reputation he soon acquired. At the same time, he was also making friends like Dr. Yanovsky who testify to his amiability, and who remained disinterestedly devoted to him for the rest of his life. When his literary vanity was not involved, and when he could count on unfailing sympathy, he was quite able to adapt himself to social life and even prove very winning in doing so. He no doubt continued to feel the same need for friendship expressed so touchingly after his first meeting with Turgenev; and this need grew all the stronger as his clashes with the pléiade became more frequent and bitter. It was thus only natural that he should reach out now to acquire a whole new circle of friends, and rely very heavily on them for emotional support as his literary reputation declined and relations with Belinsky became tense.

The first mention of these new acquaintances occurs in mid-September 1846–after, that is, the crisis induced by the failure of *The Double*. "I take my dinner with a group," he writes Mikhail. "Six people who know each other, including Grigorovich and myself, have gotten together at Beketovs. Each pays 15 silver kopeks a day, we have two good, simple dishes, and are quite satisfied."[1] Two months later, Dostoevsky speaks of this new circle with the greatest enthusiasm, and attributes to their influence the happiest effect on his physical and emotional well-being. These were months when, as Dostoevsky confesses to Mikhail, he was "almost in a panic of fear about my health";[2] but the psychological aid provided by his friends seems to have restored him completely.

"Brother," he writes, "I am reborn, not only morally but also physically. Never have I felt in myself so much abundance and clarity, so much equanimity of character, so much physical health. I am indebted for much of this to my good friends Beketov, Zalyubetsky and the others with whom I live; they are sensible and intelligent people, with hearts of gold, of nobility and character. They cured me by their company. Finally, I suggested that we live together. We have found a spacious apartment, and all the expenses of the rent and upkeep do not exceed 1,200 paper rubles a year for each person. Such are the great benefits of association."[3] This is the same letter in which Dostoevsky first expresses his critical attitude toward Belinsky's literary judgment; and the security supplied by his new milieu was of great importance in helping him to weather the perturbations brought on by the critic's rejection.

2
———

What was this new group to which Dostoevsky belonged? Unfortunately, the available information is very scanty—there is nothing but the one or two references already cited from Dostoevsky's letters, and a passage in the memoirs of Grigorovich. The center of the group was Aleksey N. Beketov, who had been one of Dostoevsky's intimates at the Academy of Military Engineers, and it included his two brothers—then still students—Nikolay and Andrey. The first later became Professor of Chemistry at the University of Petersburg; the second, Professor of Botany. It was the older Beketov, however, who was the animating spirit of the group, and Grigorovich speaks of him as "the embodiment of goodness and straightforwardness," around whom people unfailingly clustered because of his outstanding moral qualities. He was the sort of person who "became indignant at every sort of injustice and was responsive to every noble and honorable endeavor"; and it was he who set the dominating tone. Even through the veil of Grigorovich's Aesopian language, one surmises that this tone was strongly social-political. "But whoever spoke, and whatever was spoken about—whether we touched on events in Petersburg, in Russia, or abroad, or whether we considered literary or artistic questions—in everything one could feel a rush of fresh strength, the living nerve of youth, the dawning of luminous thought suddenly born in the enthusiasm of a brain that had caught fire; *everywhere one could hear indignant, noble outbursts against oppression and injustice.*"[4] (Italics added.)

Grigorovich, as a matter of fact, attributes to membership in the Beketov circle his true awakening to social-political concerns. "Up to the time that I became one of its regular members my intellectual capacities had been enveloped in a fog. Conversations with Dostoevsky had never gone beyond the bounds of literature; all the interests of life were focused on that alone. . . . I had never thought about anything at all seriously; social questions had not interested me in the slightest. . . . Much that had never entered my mind now began to concern me: a living word, sobering up the mind from frivolity, I first heard only here, in the Beketov circle."[5] It is scarcely credible that Grigorovich should have heard nothing about social questions in the Belinsky pléiade; but perhaps the discussions at Beketov's were more concrete and down-to-earth, more rooted in Russian social reality, than the theorizing at Belinsky's. Such a supposition seems to fit with the important effect of the Beketov group on Grigorovich's literary career. For it was under their influence that, on returning to his family estate in the summer of 1846, he began to work on his first major novel, *The Village*—a pioneer portrayal of peasant life which breaks completely with the pastoral-idyllic tradition, and paints a somber picture of the terrible ravages of serfdom on the character of its unhappy victims.

Nothing more is known about the Beketov circle, which came to an end when the two younger brothers left to continue their studies at the University of Kazan at the beginning of 1847. The impression they created there provides our only precise information on the ideological orientation of the group—though such circles were never monolithic in character, and contained the widest divergence of specific convictions within a general convergence of outlook. N. Flerovsky, whose books later exercised an important influence on the Russian Populists of the 1870s, was a student at Kazan in 1847 and provides a glimpse of the Beketovs. "They propagated the teaching of Fourier," he says, "and here [at Kazan] the results were the same as in Petersburg";[6] presumably he means that they attracted others and formed a circle. The Beketovs were evidently Fourierists; and Dostoevsky's reference to "the benefits of association" points to the Utopian Socialist orientation of the group.

3
———

Dostoevsky's affiliation with the Beketov circle has been more or less neglected in depictions of his career, partly because there is so little direct information available, partly because he focused attention so glaringly on Belinsky. It should be easy to see by now why he did so, and why he preferred not to call attention to this new group. For Dostoevsky's connection with them seriously calls into question the portrait he painted of himself as he was supposed to have been in the 1840s. Far from being a political innocent, abruptly baptized into Socialism, atheism, and materialism all at once by the great intellectual agitator Belinsky, Dostoevsky was a committed moral-religious progressive who stoutly maintained his convictions in the face of

Belinsky's attacks and then allied himself with others of the same persuasion. This is the image that emerges when we take a closer look at some of the people whom Dostoevsky met in and through the Beketov circle.

Besides the Beketovs themselves, it was there that he became acquainted with the well-known poet, then still a student, Aleksey Pleshcheev, whose name turns up everywhere in the annals of the progressive intelligentsia during the 1840s. The attractive and well-bred scion of an aristocratic family—gentle, tenderhearted, cloudily rhapsodic—Pleshcheev became a very close friend of Dostoevsky; and this friendship continued throughout the remainder of their lives, even though, for political reasons, it turned more formal than cordial beginning in the mid-1860s. During the 1840s, however, the two young men were inseparable, not only personally but also politically—they were in exactly the same groups up to the time of their arrest in 1849, and, as public evidence of their amity, dedicated stories to each other (in Dostoevsky's case, his charming little masterpiece *White Nights*). It can scarcely be doubted that the ethos of Pleshcheev's work would have been close to Dostoevsky's heart; and Pleshcheev's poetry, in the words of P. N. Sakulin, "imperceptibly fused the religion of Socialism with the teachings of the Gospel about truth and love."[7] The image of the Utopian Socialist Christ is constantly evoked in his pages; even in a poem which became "the hymn of several generations of revolutionaries,"[8] the poet enjoins his comrades, condemned like himself to torture and execution, to pardon "our senseless executioners"[9] with Christian forgiveness. This rebellious but self-sacrificial mood probably comes as close as we can get to Dostoevsky's own moral-social ideal at the time.

It was also through the Beketovs that Dostoevsky struck up an equally close—and, from a practical point of view, much more important—friendship with Valerian Maikov. Two years younger than Dostoevsky, Maikov had a brief but meteoric career in Russian letters beginning in 1845 and ending with his untimely death by a stroke in the summer of 1847. During this short span, however, he made a considerable splash by taking over the post of chief critic on *Notes of the Fatherland* from Belinsky, turning the journal into an organ of the Utopian Socialist Beketov tendency, and setting himself up as rival of the powerful reigning arbiter of taste and ideas.

An extremely precocious and talented young man, Maikov's interests ranged over a wide field including chemistry (he translated a book of Liebig's into Russian) and political economy as well as literature. Not only did he visit the Beketovs' quarters, but he was also

11. V. N. Maikov.
A portrait from the 1840s

among the early members of the circle gathered around Mikhail Butashevich-Petrashevsky, whose Friday evenings also attracted Pleshcheev and were soon to become the chief rallying place for the progressive intelligentsia in Petersburg. With a friend, R. R. Shtrandman, Maikov wrote most of the articles in the first fascicule of the famous *Pocket Dictionary of Foreign Words* in which Petrashevsky also had a hand. This clever publication, filled with "subversive" ideas, hoodwinked the censorship by its pseudo-scholarly format; the second installment, much more virulently radical, was written largely by Petrashevsky himself and published a year later. There is some question, indeed, whether Maikov really wished to devote himself to literary criticism at all, and would not much have preferred a scholarly career in economics or the new study of society (he was interested in Comte). But, having been offered the chance to replace Belinsky on the recommendation of Turgenev, he threw himself into this task with zest and polemical ardor.

Dostoevsky probably met Maikov early in the spring of 1846 (we know that the latter sent Dostoevsky to visit Dr. Yanovsky later that spring), and the friendship flourished in the succeeding months. Traces of Dostoevsky's intimacy with Maikov soon begin to turn up in his letters. "Grigorovich has written a remarkably good little story," he tells Mikhail in September 1846. "Through the efforts of myself and Maikov—who incidentally wants to write a big article about me for Jan. 1st—the story [*The Village*] will be printed in the *Notes of the Fatherland*."[10] Maikov never wrote the long article that Dostoevsky hoped for; but he did praise him fervently, and was the only voice raised to defend him against Belinsky's criticisms. Several months later, Dostoevsky informs Mikhail that the Belinsky pléiade is spreading the rumor "that I am infected with vanity, have a terribly inflated opinion of myself, and have sold out to Kraevsky because Maikov praises me."[11] A note of Dostoevsky's from the beginning of 1847, referring to a theater party including Maikov and Shtrandman, reveals his participation in the social life of the inner Maikov set.

The death of Valerian Maikov a few months later was a terrible blow to Dostoevsky, and deprived him of the one person in the Petersburg literary world thoroughly in tune with the writing he had been producing after *Poor Folk*. But the memory of Valerian Maikov did not fade for Dostoevsky, and was kept alive by the close ties he had now established with the Maikov family. His affection for Valerian was transferred to Apollon, a slightly older brother, who had already obtained some reputation as a poet and was to remain the most loyal of Dostoevsky's few intimates in later years. The head of the Maikov family was a well-known academic sculptor, the mother a gifted and temperamental woman with literary ambitions herself; their home was the center of a literary-artistic salon at which Dostoevsky, despite his notorious explosiveness, was a frequent and welcome guest. On one occasion, after exchanging unpleasant words with other visitors (probably members of the pléiade), he fled the scene without taking leave of his hostess rather than risk an abusive outbreak, and felt called upon to write a letter of apology. At the time of his arrest in 1849, a manuscript copy of Valerian Maikov's essays (which remained unpublished in book form until the end of the century) was found among his papers. He would scarcely have been lent this treasured memento if the family had not considered him a confidant; and just before departing for Siberia, he could still remember to ask, in the midst of his other woes, whether the manuscript had been returned to the inconsolable mother of his dead friend.

Valerian Maikov was more or less forgotten after his death, and his name vanishes from sight for the next twenty or thirty years. It is only fitting that one of the few references to Maikov, during this period of oblivion, should have come from Dostoevsky's pen. "Valerian Maikov undertook his task passionately," Dostoevsky wrote in 1861, "with enlightened convictions, with the first enthusiasm of youth. But he did not succeed in expressing himself. He died in the first year of his activity [as critic of *Notes of the Fatherland*]. This fine personality held much promise, and perhaps his death deprived us of a good deal."[12] This measured tribute to Maikov is not very revealing, but it does at least testify to a desire not to let the work of Valerian Maikov sink completely out of public view. Nobody reading the passage, to be sure, would have any idea of the crucial role that Maikov had played in Dostoevsky's life; but if we wish to understand the social-cultural climate in which Dostoevsky was living in the mid-1840s, a closer look at Maikov's writings is indispensable.

4
___

Nothing, of course, was of greater moment for Dostoevsky at this juncture than Maikov's vigorous defense of his literary talent and achievements against Belinsky's belittling qualifications. This defense, however, was more than simply a matter of personal preference; it represented an effort systematically to advance beyond Belinsky in a direction that Maikov saw as being that of the future. Hostile to the remnants of German Romantic and Idealist thought still lurking in the background of Belinsky's criticism, Maikov proposed to replace them by a purely empirical foundation drawn from psychology. Art, he said, was grounded in what he called "the law of sympathy" (an idea that goes back both to Adam Smith and Hume, and anticipates as well the late nineteenth century doctrine of aesthetic empathy). According to this "law," man knows and understands everything by comparison with himself; it is through the process of "humanization" that he absorbs the world and domesticates it to his feeling (in art) and his understanding (in science and philosophy).[13] Psychology—the study of the inner life of man—thus becomes the key offering access to the secrets of the universe as a whole. This emphasis on psychology sharply separates Maikov from Belinsky, and reflects a widespread interest among Utopian Socialists who had come under the influence of Fourier's obsessively detailed analysis of human passions.[14] Maikov, as we shall see in a moment, makes extensive use of Fourierist terms; and while he was probably not a Fourierist in the strict sense (there is reason to believe that the image of life in the phalanstery did not appeal to him),* he shared Fourier's

___

* Maikov was a very serious student of Socialist economics, and one of his articles, which remained unpublished in his lifetime, has been called by an authority the first "critical survey [presumably in Russian] of the ideas of the various Socialist schools, [in which] an effort is even made to indicate the path to a solution of the antagonism between labor and capital." K. A. Pazhitnov, *Razvitie Socialisticheskikh Idei v Rossii* (Petrograd, 1924), 49.

Maikov's survey reveals a deep moral sympathy for the aims of Socialism, but

205

preoccupation with the human psyche as an all-important realm that had never been adequately explored.

Such ideas coincided perfectly with Dostoevsky's own artistic inclinations; and the young critic seized on Dostoevsky's work as the best illustration of his critical tenets. Indeed, he viewed both himself and Dostoevsky as the legitimate spokesmen, each in their own domain, for a new generation that was asserting itself against Belinsky's domination. As Maikov saw it, the artistic task of this new generation was to extend Gogol's conquests by pursuing the path he had blazed into the uncharted realms of psychology. The older generation, Maikov wrote, had been frightened and put off by the "analysis" and "negation" of *Dead Souls*; but the younger "was fortunate enough not to have the time, the occasion, nor the means for irresolution; if the author of *The Double* had been born eight years earlier, could he have been such a psychologist?"[15] This question defines the thrust of Maikov's ideas, and the direction in which he wished to go—as well as the central place that he accorded Dostoevsky.

It is highly probable that Maikov's friendship with the famous and slightly older Dostoevsky, already in possession of a considerable (if contested) reputation, had something to do with the formulation of such a critical program. It is certainly not a hazard that Maikov's essays contain the most perceptive specific comments about Dostoevsky made by any of his contemporaries. "Both Gogol and Dostoevsky depict existing society," he writes. "But Gogol is preeminently a social poet, while Dostoevsky is preeminently a psychological one. For the first, the individual is important as the representative of a certain society or a certain group; for the second, society itself is interesting because of its influence on the personality of the individual. . . . Gogol's collected works may emphatically be called the artistic statistics of Russia. Dostoevsky also gives us a strikingly artistic depiction of Russian society, but with him this provides only the background of the picture, and is conveyed, in most instances, with such minute strokes that it is completely swallowed up by the importance of the psychological interest. Even in *Poor Folk*, the interest aroused by the analysis of the people that he brings on the scene is incomparably

---

he is suspicious of Utopian schemes as incompatible with individual freedom. This is probably why he was never entirely won over to Fourierism. "At Petrashevsky's," writes N. A. Danilevsky, "I met Valerian Maikov, who was immersed in the study of political economy. I had many conversations and disputes with him about the teachings of Fourier, thinking I would finally convince him of their truth and that we could together undertake to clear up their obscure aspects." *Delo Petrashevtsev*, 2: 320. Maikov's possible influence on Dostoevsky from this point of view will be discussed in Chapter 17.

stronger than the impression created on the reader by the vivid depiction of the life surrounding them."[16]

This provides an acute insight into the dominating feature of Dostoevsky's talent, which reverses the relation between the individual and society typical of Gogol. After *Poor Folk*, when this reversal becomes more and more pronounced, society appears largely as it is refracted through the consciousness of Dostoevsky's characters. Belinsky disapproved of such internalization; but Maikov welcomes it, with percipient words of praise, as the natural flowering of Dostoevsky's gifts. "In *The Double*, Dostoevsky's manner, and his love for psychological analysis, is expressed with full completeness and originality. In this work he penetrates so deeply into the human soul, he looks so fearlessly and passionately into the secret machinations of human feeling, thought, and action, that the impression created by *The Double* may be compared only with that of an inquisitive person penetrating into the chemical composition of matter." Such a "chemical view of society," he continues, goes so deep that it seems to be "suffused with some sort of mystical light"; but there is nothing "mystical" here at all, and the depiction of reality is as "positive" as can be.[17] These remarks counter Belinsky's charge that *The Double* is too "fantastic" to appeal to contemporary tastes, and that characters like Golyadkin belong only in "madhouses."

Indeed, Maikov then goes on to give a penetrating reading of *The Double* which stresses its social relevance; and we may assume that he comes very close to the manner in which Dostoevsky himself saw the work. *"The Double* develops before us the anatomy of a soul perishing from the consciousness of the disparity of particular interests in a well-ordered society. Recall that poor, sick, egoistic Golyadkin, eternally afraid for himself, eternally tortured by the effort not to give way on any occasion and to any person and, at the same time, continually being crushed even by the personality of his rascally [servant] Petrushka, continually agreeing to cut off his claim to be a personality if only he can *retain his rights* . . . recall all this, and ask yourself: do you not also have in you something Golyadkin-like, something which nobody is eager to acknowledge, but which is fully explained by the surprising harmony reigning in human society?"[18] If the "surprising harmony" reigning in Russian society is based on the Golyadkin-like component in all Russians, this would turn Golyadkin's pathological self-subordination into a terrifying comment on the repressive effects of the existing Russian social order.

Even *Mr. Prokharchin*, about which Belinsky had been so unqualifiedly negative, is not summarily dismissed by Maikov. He agrees that the story suffers from obscurity; but he attributes this to Dostoevsky's having been unduly impressed by Belinsky's complaints against his prolixity. Too much, he says, can be sacrificed "in the interest of that vaunted concision" which no one has ever been able to define satisfactorily. Maikov correctly recognizes the point of the story to lie in Prokharchin's "insecurity," and remarks that, if this character had been treated on the scale of Golyadkin in *The Double*, no perplexity would have existed. He advises Dostoevsky, in the future, to place "more faith in the strength of his talent" than in other considerations—such as, it may be presumed, the advice of critics.[19]

Nor should one overlook Maikov's defense of the freedom of art—a subject very close to Dostoevsky's heart because of his disputes with Belinsky on that subject. Maikov flatly rejects any prescriptive function for criticism, and maintains that "contemporary aesthetics once and for all has renounced the title of a guide to artistic talent." Criticism is—or ought to be—a science, and this ambition "is expressed by nothing else than the total reign of aesthetic liberty."[20] Finally, in a formulation that Dostoevsky repeated in 1861, Maikov declares that "fidelity to reality constitutes such an essential condition for every work of art that a person gifted with artistic talent never produces anything contrary to this condition."* Hence it is not only illegitimate but superfluous to impose restrictions and demands on artistic creation in the name of "reality."

5

Maikov's essays thus provided Dostoevsky both with a heartening defense of his own work and, at the same time, with the expression of a literary-critical position that he could fully accept. But Maikov's writings were also significant for Dostoevsky in a much wider and less specifically literary sense. For the quarrel with Belinsky that Maikov initiated raised far larger issues than merely those of the substance and the form of literary judgment; it went, much more deeply, to the heart of the ideological split between those who still clung to the moral-religious inspiration of Utopian Socialism and those who, like Belinsky, were searching for a more "positive" foundation for their social-political convictions. To be sure, the extent and the se-

---

* In an article aimed at the Utilitarian aesthetics of N. A. Dobrolyubov, Dostoevsky writes: "The most important thing is that art is always true to reality in the highest degree—its deviations are transient and pass away quickly; it is not only always true to reality but it cannot possibly be untrue to contemporary reality." *DW*, 134.

riousness of this cleavage should not be exaggerated. Both sides continued to share the same opposition to existing social evils, and the disagreement did not exclude friendly personal relations nor literary collaboration (at the time of his death Maikov, on Belinsky's invitation, had begun to write for *The Contemporary*). But, all the same, ideological nuances did exist that help to clarify where Dostoevsky stood at that time.

Maikov, as we have remarked, more or less turned the *Notes of the Fatherland* into an organ of the Beketov circle, whose taste and opinions are reflected in its pages after he assumed the editorship. Just as Maikov praised Dostoevsky, so too is he enthusiastic over the poetry of Pleshcheev, whose first volume he hastened to review. What pleases him in Pleshcheev's efforts is that they are in step with the times ("verses to maidens and to the moon are gone for good"), and that the young poet has undertaken to deal with contemporary themes. Russian poetry, in Maikov's opinion, has so far had no voice to express these vital problems; but now, as a successor to Lermontov, Pleshcheev has arrived to become "incontestably our first poet." For "he strongly sympathizes with all the questions of his epoch, suffers from all the illnesses of the century, painfully agonizes over the insufficiencies of society, and burns with an unselfish eagerness to hasten its perfection and bring about the triumph on earth of truth, love, and brotherhood."[21]

There can be no mistaking the Utopian Socialist accents of such declarations; and Maikov's position comes out even more explicitly in the major article which announced his literary program and launched the attack against Belinsky. This article dealt ostensibly with the poetry of A. V. Koltsov, collected and published by Belinsky with a lengthy introductory preface. Not that there was any difference of opinion over the merits of Koltsov. Both critics accord him the highest praise; but Maikov objects to Belinsky's characterization of the writer only as the poet of Russian peasant life and hence as "a type of the Russian nature."[22] In Maikov's judgment, Belinsky sees Koltsov's work and personality too much as a simple product and reflection of his environment; this is not, he argues, an adequate view to take of any individual, much less a creative individual like Koltsov. The issue, as we see, turns on the freedom of the personality to transcend its environment, and hence, by implication, on the question of free will and moral responsibility—the same question that Dostoevsky recalled arguing about with Belinsky at just that moment. Indeed, it is quite likely that Dostoevsky's recollections are strongly influenced (perhaps unwittingly) by memories of this long-forgotten polemic, in which Maikov too was reacting against Belinsky's leaning toward moral determinism.

There is no necessity here to go into the details of Maikov's argument, which, as he acknowledges, draws heavily on the ideas of the French Romantic historian and passionate libertarian Jules Michelet; one quotation will be enough to illustrate the inner social-cultural significance of the debate. For to clinch his point that man cannot simply be seen as a creature of his conditioning, Maikov appeals to the example of Jesus Christ: "The greatest revolution in the life of mankind was produced by God Himself in the image of a man," he writes. "In the aspect of his human substance, Christ reveals himself as the most perfect image of what we call a great personality. His true doctrine stands in such radical opposition to the ideas of the ancient world, and contains such an immeasurable independence from phenomena fateful for millions of beings called free and reasonable—in a word, they are elevated to such a degree above the laws of historical phenomena, that mankind even to this day, in the course of eighteen centuries, has not yet grown up even to half of that independence of thought without which it is impossible to comprehend and to realize them. Such independence, in an incomparably lesser degree, is shown in the ideas of all those truly great people who are responsible for moral revolutions of lesser scope."[23]

To consider Christ the greatest moral revolutionary of all times—a sublime paradigm for all the lesser ones who follow in his wake—was of course to flaunt the banner of moral-religious Socialism in the face of those rallying to another standard. Maikov's words are also of great interest because of their intimations of Dostoevsky's own later Christology. The idea of Christ as revolutionary was quite standard in the 1840s;* but to view Christ as the divine harbinger of man's freedom from the shackles of historical determinism was much less conventional. There can be little doubt that Dostoevsky's own idea of Christ was profoundly affected by Maikov's Utopian Socialist icon, and that Christ for him would always remain, not only the traditional Savior from the bonds of sin and death, but also the sacred pledge of the possibility of moral freedom.

Moreover, Maikov's article also reveals how insistently the issue of free will and moral responsibility had already begun to gnaw at those

---

* "In 1848, at the headquarters of all the worker's organizations and in the homes of a great number of Socialists, one saw an engraving showing Jesus as a carpenter and with the inscription: Jesus of Nazareth, the first representative of the people." Benoît Malon, *Exposé des écoles socialistes de France* (1872), 230; cited in Maxime Leroy, *Histoire des idées sociales en France* (Paris, 1959), 3: 77.

who, like Dostoevsky, refused to surrender the moral-religious basis of their progressivism. For it was by no means a simple matter to continue to believe in the moral power of the personality as the appalling evidence piled up of the human ravages of early capitalism. Even Maikov could not help admitting that it was "stupid and vile" to preach morality to the exploited lower classes because "to be moral and enlightened, that is, civilized, both an individual and a people must first of all live in comfort." But this did not lead him to deny the *possibility* of free will and moral responsibility, even though he agreed that "only heroism can unite moral worth with poverty."[24] Such "heroism," nonetheless, exists; there will always be a small handful, a saving remnant, of such heroes; the human personality will never allow itself to be completely subjugated by material conditions. It is instructive to see here, already adumbrated in Maikov's essays, the same inner debate that will later be so passionately argued in Dostoevsky's pages.* Twenty years later, when Dostoevsky began to break with radicalism entirely, the tendencies evident in the later Belinsky had hardened into dogma, and it was impossible any longer to be a radical and to continue to affirm the existence of free will. In the 1870s, when there was a return to the moral-religious Feuerbachian "humanism" of the 1840s among the Russian Left, Dostoevsky's hostility became considerably mollified.

Still another side of Maikov's thought helps to throw some additional light on Dostoevsky. Man, Maikov writes, using Fourier's terminology, "is endowed with virtues, that is, needs and capabilities that make up his vitality . . . [and] the source of everything vicious can be located in nothing other than the clash between his suffering and acting powers and external circumstances, which create a disharmony between them [man's powers] by the destruction of the proportion of satisfaction for each established by nature."[25] Human nature is thus essentially good, and evil is a result of the arrangements of society that do not allow mankind properly to satisfy its needs and capabilities. In the next chapter we shall see Dostoevsky too, no doubt under the influence of the same current of ideas, also asserting the ego's

---

* There is still another aspect of Maikov's thought that may have influenced Dostoevsky—the sharp distinction he draws between the majority and the minority of a nationality, between ordinary and extraordinary people, which sounds like a passage from Raskolnikov's famous article in *Crime and Punishment*. "Every nationality," Maikov writes, "has two faces; one of them is diametrically opposed to the other; one belongs to the majority, the other—to the minority. The majority of a people always reveal a mechanical submission to the laws of climate, situation, race, and destiny; the minority go to the other extreme in its negation of such influences." Maikov speaks of this division as a "law" (presumably of nature) which has not yet sufficiently been taken into account by ethnographers. *Opyty*, 69.

211

natural and quite justified need for self-expression and self-fulfillment, and noting the unhappy consequences that result when such
needs are frustrated. But in his literary creations he will also place
a burden of responsibility—an increasing burden—on the individual
to overcome the harmful psychic effects of such frustration, and particularly to resist the temptation to take revenge on others for his
own mortifications.

Maikov, however, uses this Fourierist view of human nature to
undermine the assumption that "nationality" is a positive value.
National traits of character, Maikov argues, are the product of
the drives built into the human psyche as they objectify themselves
in one direction or another under the influence of material conditions
(climate, geography, race, history). But the universal human ideal, for
an individual as well as for an ethnic group, is "the harmonious development of all human needs and their corresponding capacities."[26]
Judged by this ideal, all national attributes—even those ordinarily
considered to be virtues—are really defects or vices: they are one-sided
and unbalanced, and distort human nature in its full plenitude. Such
a forthright rejection of nationality was by no means uncommon as
a by-product of Utopian Socialist influence (one can find it expressed
bluntly in the second fascicule of Petrashevsky's *Pocket Dictionary*).[27]
It is unlikely, however, that Dostoevsky agreed with Maikov on this
issue because, in some articles written only a year later, he took an
anti-Slavophil but by no means anti-national position.

6

Belinsky lived for polemics and was at his best when aroused to a
fighting fury; he was not the man to flinch before Maikov's onslaught
in the winter of 1846. And he replied with his famous *A View of
Russian Literature in 1846*, which appeared in the first issue of the
reorganized *The Contemporary*. Here Belinsky takes up the cudgels—
to cite the authoritative Soviet historian of the periodical, Evgenyev-
Maksimov—"not only [against] the young critic of *Notes of the Fatherland*, Valerian Maikov, but against Utopian Socialism in general. At
the end of 1846, Belinsky had not long to go before calling them [the
Utopian Socialists] 'social and virtuous asses.' "[28]

For Dostoevsky, this was the fateful article that certified the total
shipwreck of his literary reputation and his public repudiation by the
critic who had raised him to fame. It was here that Belinsky declared
"the fantastic setting" of *The Double* unsuitable for contemporary
taste and spoke of the "ostentation and pretension" of *Mr. Prokhar-*

chin; and one suspects that Dostoevsky's well-known friendship with Maikov may have had something to do with the new severity of Belinsky's judgment. For it was not Dostoevsky alone who received the back of Belinsky's hand in this unceremonious fashion; anyone else known to have been allied with Maikov, or whose work Maikov had praised, is also treated very harshly.

Poor, inoffensive Aleksey Pleshcheev was caught in the cross fire and contemptuously dismissed as vainly pretending to a nonexistent literary talent (Belinsky even refuses him the dignity of being referred to by name). Pleshcheev, to be sure, was far from being a major poet; but his humanitarian themes would have elicited a word of sympathy under other circumstances. Another unwitting victim of Belinsky's ire was Julia Zhadovskaya, a plaintive lyricist, whose efforts Maikov had greeted with some highly qualified praise. Belinsky brutally makes merry over the heartbroken poetess, wounded by life, who searches for some consolation in the starry heavens. Did she not know, he mocks, that according to modern optics "what charms [her] sight does not exist in reality, but is the product of [her own] vision in which is focused the spherical convexity that [she] sees?" Belinsky is here at his most crudely and scientifically positive; and the same naive scientism is evident in his reply to what he calls "the humanistic cosmopolitans" or "the fantastic cosmopolitans" (Maikov and his friends) with their universal ideal of "humanity" and their repudiation of nationality.

Belinsky's specific answer to Maikov is a curious and contradictory mixture of Littré and Hegel, whose fine points need not concern us and which never really grapples with Maikov's argument against determinism. What is important, however, is his vehement affirmation and defense of nationality against Maikov's deprecation. For Belinsky's polemic with Maikov, as we learn from P. V. Annenkov, marks a decisive moment in the internal evolution of Russian culture in the late 1840s. Up to this time, the debate between the Westerners and the Slavophils had split the Russian intelligentsia into opposing camps; and it was Belinsky who had led the assault against the Slavophil idealization of Russian national virtues as embodied in the backward and illiterate peasantry. Indeed, Annenkov even charges that his articles had encouraged "a tone of haughty, half-patrician and half-pedantic contempt" for peasant life among the intelligentsia.[29] But now, in replying to Maikov, Belinsky declares that "on this subject [nationality] I am rather inclined to side with the Slavophils rather than to remain on the side of the humanistic cosmopolitans."[30] And Belinsky's sensational about-face acted as a catalyst to spur on the process of ideological fusion between the two camps actually begun a few years earlier, and soon to produce the various varieties of Russian Populism (including Dostoevsky's own ideology of *Pochven-nichestvo*)* which dominated Russian culture until the last decade of the nineteenth century.

Indeed, much of what Belinsky says about nationality in this article turns up in the later journalism of Dostoevsky almost word for word. Like Belinsky, and in opposition to the Slavophils, Dostoevsky would always refuse to whitewash or glamorize the Russian past, and to dream of the restoration of some sort of Arcadian, pre-Petrine world; but like Belinsky again he wholeheartedly shared the Slavophil criticism of "Russian Europeanism." Belinsky noted that this automatic and demeaning aping of European civilization, which had been going on far too long, had created "a sort of duality in Russian life, consequently a lack of moral unity"—and what could be more Dostoevskian than such a perception? Would Dostoevsky not later see himself precisely as the chronicler of this "lack of moral unity" in Russian life? Moreover, for Dostoevsky too the remedy would be, not to reject Europe and return to the past (an impossible task in any case), but to realize "that Russia had fully outlived the epoch of reformation, that the reforms had done their business . . . and that the time had come for Russia to develop independently from out of herself."[31] Belinsky here is talking about the reforms of Peter the Great; Dostoevsky would repeat exactly the same argument about those instituted by Alexander II in the early 1860s.

Russian nationality is thus no longer to be neglected, disparaged, or discarded; on the contrary, as the Slavophils argued, it was to become the principle on which the Russia of the future was to be founded. But this made the task of defining such a principle of Russian nationality all the more pressing and important. The Slavophils believed that Russia differed from Europe because its own history had been marked by peaceful Christian concord rather than by the egoistic struggles for power so typical of Western rivalries between classes and nations. But Belinsky disdainfully sweeps aside the idea that Russian history offers any support for the view that Russian nationality can be identified with the principle of love and humility. Even though agreeing with the Slavophils that Russia was destined to give the world "our word, our thought," he wonders whether perhaps the time is yet ripe to try and define this Russian "word" with any clarity. Some clue to what it may be, though, can possibly be found in the "versa-

* *Pochva* in Russian means soil or ground, and also has the sense of foundation or support.

tility" of the Russian character, its seeming amorphousness and un-precedented ability to assimilate and absorb alien cultures. This ca-pacity may seem like a weakness at first sight; but to a mind schooled in Schelling and Hegel, and nurtured on the Messianic speculations of Romantic nationalism, it is child's play to extract the positive from the negative. For the extreme malleability of the Russian folk-psyche may also be "ascribed to natural giftedness," and be the source of future strength. It may mean that "the Russian nationality is foreor-dained to express the richest and most many-sided essence in its nationality, and that it is this which explains its amazing ability to adopt and assimilate all alien elements."[32]

Such ideas would have been familiar to Dostoevsky from the violent nationalism of Belinsky's essays during his Hegelian phase, as well as from numerous other sources. There had been, ever since the end of the eighteenth century, a line of Russian satirical writ-ing directed against excessive Europeanization; and the vision of Russia as charged with a world-historical mission to synthesize the conflicting national cultures of Europe had been much in the air since the 1820s.* But such ideas were given a new vitality and actuality when Belinsky used them to rebut Maikov's "cosmopolitanism" in the 1840s. For in freeing the idea of "nationality" from the negative and limiting connotations given it by Maikov, he adroitly turned it toward a universalism that rescued patriotic emotion and national pride from the Slavophils and reconciled them with progressive Westernism. This is the same vision of Russia as the future creator of a pan-human world-culture that we shall find evoked so often and so eloquently by Dostoevsky; and it will be supported by exactly the same arguments— the ease with which Russians learn foreign languages, their ability to identify with alien cultures, the role of Russian literature as precursor of the new world-synthesis. To these, of course, Dostoevsky will add the Russian Christ as the divine warrant of moral freedom and the triumph of human liberty over the laws of nature. In such a perspec-tive, his post-Siberian "Slavophil" ideology may thus be seen as an amalgam of ideas whose roots go back both to Belinsky and to Valerian Maikov.†

* Alexandre Koyré, surveying the debates about Russian nationality in the 1820s, sums up their conclusions as follows: "Russia has its mission; and this mission consists, not only in equalling the Western peoples by acquiring their civilization, but on the contrary in developing its *own* civilization, a civilization higher and more perfect, which will be, at the same time, the culmination of the entire historical evolution of the West. Thanks to its youth, which constitutes its strength, Russia will be able, in expressing itself and realizing its ideal, to realize that of humanity as a whole." *La Philosophie et le problème national en Russie au debut du XIX siècle* (Paris, 1929), 209.

† One can also find in Maikov, for all his "humanistic cosmopolitanism," the

It is important to sketch such lines of continuity if we are to restore the true historical picture that Dostoevsky himself did so much to blur. For the moment, though, let us note only the general tenor of Belinsky's article. "Europe today is engrossed with great new problems . . . but . . . it would be quite futile to treat these problems as our own. . . . We ourselves, in ourselves, and around ourselves— that is where we should seek both the problems and their solutions."[33] These words translate the mood of Belinsky's disillusionment with Utopian Socialism; but they also reflect a general trend among the progressive intelligentsia. Even those who still clung to some remnants of Utopian Socialist hopes now began to reinterpret and to readapt them, partly under the stimulus of Slavophil thought, in terms of Russian social problems. This movement will be described at greater length when we depict Dostoevsky's participation in the Petrashevsky circle. Before doing so, however, we must first analyze a group of feuilletons that he wrote in the spring of 1847. These offer an extremely valuable access to some of the feelings and ideas agitating him, and also serve as a partial self-commentary on his literary creations.

Slavophil contrast that became so important for Dostoevsky between the purity of Christian doctrine in the Russian Church and the distortion of the Christian message by Roman Catholicism.

"Everyone knows," Maikov writes, "that Russia . . . preserved them [the dogmas of the Christian faith] in such purity and immutability that only the Russian Church fully has the right to its historical name of Orthodox." On the other hand, "at the same time as Byzantium was concerned with searching for and guiding its flock to the kingdom of heaven, Rome was dreaming of spiritual power over earthly kingdoms." *Opyty*, 398-399.

CHAPTER 16

The Petersburg Feuilletons

During the first flush of the success of *Poor Folk*, the future shone for Dostoevsky in the most resplendent colors. It was not only that he saw himself as a famous and fêted writer, all of whose boyhood dreams of glory were at last to be realized; critical success and public acclaim would also mean the end of the financial worries that had plagued him ever since his resignation from the Army. A few months after his discovery by Belinsky, he reports to Mikhail that "Kraevsky, hearing that I had no money, entreated me most humbly to borrow 500 rubles from him."[1] At the beginning of 1846, after citing some of Belinsky's still-laudatory opinions, Dostoevsky adds jubilantly: "Brother, my future is as brilliant as it can possibly be!"[2]

Very soon, however, the letters begin to sound another and much more depressing note. There was, in the first place, the appalling crash of his literary reputation, with its shattering effect on his fragile nervous equilibrium. And then there are complaints about his economic subservience to the editor, A. A. Kraevsky, whose obliging willingness to advance funds to impecunious authors turned out to be a trap baited with honey. Kraevsky, notorious for his ability to exploit literary talent, made a fortune out of Belinsky during the years that the critic worked for the *Notes of the Fatherland*; and he used the same methods on the needy Dostoevsky.

Soon finding himself totally dependent on the editor for his sustenance, Dostoevsky was forced to turn out copy against his will to pay his debts. In a letter of October 1846, he tells Mikhail of his desire to go to Italy so as to write a novel there at leisure and in freedom —to write "for myself, and so make it possible to raise my price. And the system of eternal debt, which Kraevsky tries to extend to everybody, is the system of my slavery and literary vassalage."[3] Laments of this kind can be found repeated endlessly in Dostoevsky's letters beginning in 1846 and continuing up to his arrest in 1849. Despite all his efforts, however, he could never succeed in breaking loose from his servitude to Kraevsky and attaining the security he craved to create in peace. "It's awful to work like a day laborer. You ruin every-

217

thing, your talent and youth and hope, you loathe your work, and you finally become a sloppy scribbler and not a writer."[4]

Dostoevsky's chronic indebtedness not only forced him to write more rapidly than he would have liked, and to hurry the completion of work that should have matured; it also impelled him to keep a sharp eye on the literary marketplace, and to snap up any assignments that could bring a little extra cash. In the winter of 1847, we find him doing editorial work for an encyclopedia and complaining about the difficulty of correcting in galley proof an article about the Jesuits. Dostoevsky evidently had a special interest in the history and character of this Roman Catholic order, whose worldwide influence was later to become one of his persistent obsessions. Earlier, in the spring of the same year, he had picked up a more important assignment from the *St. Petersburg Gazette*. The writer who regularly supplied the feuilletons for this newspaper died unexpectedly; and the editor hastily filled the gap by appealing to some of the young St. Petersburg literati to furnish him with copy. Aleksey Pleshcheev wrote one for the issue of April 13, and it was perhaps through him that Dostoevsky learned of this journalistic opportunity. The next four feuilletons, signed F. D., were written by Dostoevsky himself.

These feuilletons completely vanished from sight after their ephemeral appearance, and were only unearthed and republished in the 1920s.* Why Dostoevsky did not later himself reprint these four extremely interesting specimens of his early journalism is difficult to say; we shall offer a possible reason farther on. It could not have been, however, that the mature novelist was ashamed of having once turned his hand to a demeaning journalistic task. All the up-and-coming young talents of the Natural School—Grigorovich, Panaev, Turgenev, Goncharov, Sollogub, Pleshcheev—also wrote feuilletons, and Dostoevsky was simply joining a general literary trend. It will be recalled that he had already written one such article for the ill-fated *Jester*, and had compared his own sprightliness and humor with Balzac's Lucien de Rubempré, who became the toast of Paris overnight after dashing off a brilliant piece that became the prototype of the new genre. Balzac's *Illusions perdues*, published in 1843, had glorified the feuilleton as a form created to capture all the glitter, excitement,

---

* Three of the feuilletons were reprinted in 1922; another in 1927. A feuilleton of Pleshcheev's was mistakenly included as one of Dostoevsky's in the 1922 volume, but the error was corrected in the later publication (XIII: 594; 608).

Unfortunately, this mistake continues to be perpetuated in English. David Magarshak prints the Pleshcheev feuilleton in his volume, *Dostoevsky's Occasional Writings* (New York, 1963), 3-9, and assumes it to be written by Dostoevsky. I have used Mr. Magarshak's translation of the three other feuilletons as a basis for my own quotations, with corrections where appropriate.

and variety of Parisian social-cultural life. Eagerly on the alert for the latest literary novelties, the younger Russian writers immediately adopted it as a vehicle for their own self-expression.

The invention of the feuilleton in France had been stimulated by a new, popular mass-circulation press which served as a medium of publicity and could influence the success or failure of books, plays, operas, and public spectacles of all kinds. Originally, the feuilleton had been simply a column of information about all such cultural novelties; but it quickly developed into the form of the modern book or theater review. Lucien de Rubempré's famous column was a scintillating account of a new play in which a young actress, his future mistress, was making her first important appearance. The feuilleton, however, in branching out to describe urban types and social life, also gave birth to the physiological sketch. Once the taste for such sketches had caught on, it occurred to Frédéric Soulié to unite them week by week with a loose narrative line; and this was the origin of the feuilleton-novel.

It is difficult to distinguish the feuilleton from the physiological sketch in any clear-cut fashion. One can say that the former is less marked by the ambition to portray the life of a particular social environment, and allows more freedom for the writer to roam wherever his fancy pleases and to display his personality. A lesser French practitioner, Nestor Roqueplan, spoke of "ce droit de bavardage" that, in his view, gave the feuilleton its special charm.[5] The writer of feuilletons ordinarily used this privilege to indulge in lyrical effusions and pseudo-personal "confessions"; and these created an atmosphere of intimacy between writer and reader that became a stylistic convention. Indeed, as we learn from Belinsky, the persona of the feuilletonist was always understood to be highly conventional and stylized. The writer of a feuilleton, he says, is "a chatterer, apparently good-natured and sincere, but in truth often malicious and evil-tongued, someone who knows everything, sees everything, keeps quiet about a good deal but definitely manages to express everything, stings with epigrams and insinuations, and amuses with a lively and clever word as well as a childish joke."[6]

These words fit the personality assumed by the young Dostoevsky to the life. At first sight, his feuilletons may seem little more than unpretentious familiar essays, leaping from topic to topic solely according to the whimsical moods of the narrator. Depictions of Petersburg life and landscape, sketches of various social types, reflections and reminiscences, the stereotyped purveyance of the latest cultural tidings —all the standard ingredients are there, thrown together haphazardly to distract the casual reader. But the moment one reads a little less casually, it is evident that the feuilletons mean much more than they appear to say. With all their reticences and sly evasions, they do "definitely manage to express everything" (or at least a good deal) of what was preoccupying Dostoevsky—and many others like him—in the spring of 1847.

2

Nobody reading Dostoevsky's first feuilleton could have any doubt that its author was very much dissatisfied with the existing arrangement of social-political life in his fatherland. It is quite evident that he is smarting under the total lack of freedom in Russia to be informed about, and to discuss, matters of "public interest" for every thinking citizen. This point is made immediately in the sketch of two Petersburgers venturing into the street to welcome the arriving spring, and greeting each other after the long winter hiatus. The first question they invariably ask is—"What's the news?"; and at this point the Petersburg chronicler notes a curious phenomenon. There is, he says, always "a piercing feeling of desolation in the sound of their voices, whatever the intonation with which they may have begun their conversation." No explanation is offered for such a strangely despondent mood, which hardly suits the time of year; but Dostoevsky's reader, accustomed to the Aesopian language of Russian journalism, would understand very well that the question was asked hopelessly because no answer of any interest could possibly be forthcoming: there was just no "news" of any kind worth talking about. Nonetheless, the question continues to be asked "as if some sort of propriety requires [Russians] also to participate in something involving society and to have public interests" (XIII: 8-9).

This vivid sketch is a good example of one of the techniques of insinuation that Dostoevsky uses—the device of what may be called the "unexplained enigma," to which the knowing reader supplies the proper solution. To make doubly sure that his readers get the point in this instance, Dostoevsky also uses hyperbolic irony to satirize the usual function of a feuilletonist—which was to supply "news" about public entertainment as a substitute for more substantial and potentially dangerous fare. "But I am a feuilletonist, gentlemen," exclaims the chronicler, "I must tell you about the latest news, the newest, most *thrilling*—it is fitting to use this time-honored epithet, no doubt invented in the hope that the Petersburg reader will tremble with joy at some sort of thrilling news, for example, that *Jenny Lind* has left

for London." Each time that Dostoevsky refers to his conventional obligations as a feuilletonist to provide *such* "news," his tone is invariably one of withering scorn (XIII: 12).

Not only does Dostoevsky protest, in his first feuilleton, against the
lack of a free press in Russia; he also alludes in the same fashion to
the lack of free speech, the complete impossibility of any public discussion of vital social-political issues. "It is well-known," writes the
chronicler, "that all Petersburg is nothing other than a collection of
small circles, each of which has its statutes, its decorum, its laws, its
logic, and its oracle." He wonders, with a knowing naiveté, why such
"circles" are "so much a product of the [Russian] national character,
which is still somewhat shy of public life and looks homeward." The
answer provided is necessarily evasive, but could hardly have been
misunderstood—life in a "circle" is "more natural, skill is not required,
it is more peaceful. In a 'circle' you receive a bold answer to the question—*What's the news?*" In other words, one speaks more freely in a
circle, one relaxes in relative security without having to worry about
spies and informers (XIII: 9).

Life in "circles" is thus a Russian device to carry on some sort of
social-political life in the absence of civil freedoms enjoyed elsewhere;
but it is, at best, only a feeble substitute for the real thing. One type
of "circle"—the chronicler calls it "patriarchal"—exists, in any case,
solely to provide a place where its members can talk cynically and
amusedly, and conversation there never gets past "gossip or a yawn."
There are, however, other "circles"—evidently those of the progressive
intelligentsia—in which "a group of educated and well-intentioned
people . . . with inexplicable enthusiasm interpret various important
matters" and come to general agreement "about several generally
useful questions." But then, after the first upsurge of excitement, "the
whole 'circle' falls into a kind of iгitation, into a kind of unpleasant
enfeeblement," and gradually sinks into a state of cynicism much like
that of the "patriarchal" assemblage. There is no way for Russians to
participate actively in the social-political affairs of their country; and
this, as the chronicler intimates here for the first time, helps to explain
a good deal about the Russian character (*ibid.*).

It explains, for one thing, the kind of person who flourishes in
"circles," and who is the bane of existence there for others. "You
know this gentleman very well, gentlemen," the chronicler observes
to his readers. "His name is legion. This is the gentleman with *a good
heart*, and possessing nothing but *a good heart*." Actually, though he
spends his time assuring all and sundry of his sterling moral qualities, this gentleman is a consummate egotist and perfectly oblivious

of the rest of humanity. The comment of the chronicler about such a type already reveals Dostoevsky's sharp eye for—and intense dislike of—the "liberal" affectation of moral compassion that he would later pillory so brilliantly. Such a man, writes the chronicler, does not even suspect that "his hidden treasure, his good heart, can be ground and polished into a precious, sparkling, and genuine diamond" only when he begins to identify his interests "with those of society," only when he "shows sympathy for society as a whole" (XIII: 10-11).

Dostoevsky's portrait of the gentleman with "a good heart" is the first of a series of such derisive character sketches that take up most of the remainder of this feuilleton. Each deals with a personality who, behind a façade of virtue, conceals some defect of character or some form of vice. At this point Dostoevsky drops the technique of irony he has been using up to now—the technique of the *faux naif* so beloved of eighteenth century satirists, the *naif* whose incomprehension of what he sees enables the reader to see much more clearly—and shifts to that of simulated identification with what is being satirized. The Natural School had devoted itself to delineating much of Russian life precisely in terms of the contrast between a glittering surface of impeccable virtue and an underside of vicious corruption. What Dostoevsky now does is to *identify himself*, as chronicler, with the *opponents* of the Natural School, who were furiously protesting against its scandalous attempt to expose the injustices of Russian life. And while pretending to speak in the name and from the point of view of such critics, he cleverly makes his own contribution to the genre of social muckraking they were attacking by relying on innuendo and hyperbole to convey his real meaning.

3

"Good Lord!" the chronicler exclaims. "Where are the old villains of the old melodrama and novels, gentlemen? How pleasant it was when they were about in the world! It was pleasant because instantly, right at hand, was the most kindhearted of all men, who of course defended innocence and punished wickedness. That villain, that *tiranno ingrato*, was born a villain, ready-made in accordance with some secret and utterly incomprehensible predestination of fate. Everything in him was the personification of evil." In those happy days, there was no gap between appearance and reality; good and evil were clearly delimited, and no confusion between them was possible. But now, alas, "you are somehow suddenly faced with the fact that the most virtuous man, a man, besides, who is quite incapable of committing a crime, suddenly appears to be a perfect villain without even being aware of it himself." Even more, such a man lives and dies "honored and exalted" by all who knew him; quite often he is sincerely and tenderly mourned even "by his own victims" (XIII: 11).

As an example of this type of man, who is unforgivably now being slandered, the chronicler instances "my good friend Julian Mastako-vich, a former well-wisher and even to some extent a benefactor of mine." Julian Mastakovich is a character in two of Dostoevsky's short stories; and he is here given a nonfictional existence, we may assume, because of the "confessional" convention of the form. Poor Julian Mastakovich, a high bureaucratic official, is a man with a problem. He is about to marry, at the ripe age of fifty, a charming and perfectly unspoiled girl of seventeen; but he is troubled by the difficulty he may have in continuing to visit the apartment of a handsome widow, whom for the last two years he has been benevolently helping to conduct a lawsuit. The chronicler sympathizes with his dilemma, though he does not conceal his envy. How nice to have found such a charming young bride to console one's declining years! (XIII: 11).

Another example of the same type of eminently respectable person, who for some inexplicable reason has begun to be portrayed in the most unfavorable light, is culled by the chronicler from the pages of a recent story in the Notes of the Fatherland.[7] One episode, which Dostoevsky singles out for the attention of his readers, recounts the accidental breaking of a mirror at a children's party in the absence of the master of the house, a low-grade Moscow civil servant of unimpeachable respectability. "Ivan Kirilovich is a good man," the chronicler assures us; but he is also a petty family tyrant and a drunkard to boot, who tortures his ailing and long-suffering wife by his uncontrollable temper. The broken mirror predictably leads to a storm, and "a month later [the wife] dies of consumption . . . a kind of Dickensian charm fills the description of the last moments of the gentle, obscure life of that woman" (XIII: 15).

Biographers have of course seen in Ivan Kirilovich a reminiscence of Dostoevsky's father, especially since the chronicler remarks that the story "brought back many things to my mind! . . . I personally knew a man like Ivan Kirilovich. There are lots of them everywhere" (ibid.). Whether this assertion means any more than the similar reference to Julian Mastakovich is difficult to say; such claims of personal acquaintance in a feuilleton cannot be taken too literally. But even if we assume that Dostoevsky was struck by this story because he was reminded of his father, it is more important to note that he sees Ivan Kirilovich, not so much as an individual, but as a type. His father, that is, had now become fused in his sensibility with a whole class of similar individuals, whose domestic cruelties were being exposed by the Natural School as a widespread social abuse. Dostoevsky's resentment against his father for having maltreated his mother—if we believe such resentment to have existed—was no longer a purely personal trauma festering in the depths of his subconscious; it has now become part of all the moral-social evils that were being attacked by the literary school to which he belonged.

In closing this first feuilleton, Dostoevsky appends some remarks on the past literary season which epitomize the procedure he has used throughout—oblique social criticism, combined with a disparagement of the traditional function of a Petersburg chronicler. "Gogol's book created a great deal of noise at the beginning of the winter," he remarks casually. "It's especially noteworthy that almost all newspapers and journals agreed about it, even those whose ideas continually contradict each other" (XIII: 15). The book referred to is Gogol's ill-starred *Selected Passages from My Correspondence with Friends*, which had been unanimously condemned for its glorification of all the existing institutions of Russia (including serfdom) as God-given and sacred.* Dostoevsky thus indicates, by this concluding reference, the underlying moral-social evil of Russian life infecting all the rest; and he then shifts into a mockery of his obligation to be informative about the social season—a mockery whose words take on a special edge just after the reference to serfdom. "Sorry, I forgot the most important things . . . Ernst is giving still another concert; this occasion will be a benefit for the Home Aid Society for the Poor and the German Beneficial Society" (XIII: 15).

4

To a large extent, Dostoevsky's second feuilleton merely picks up and elaborates certain themes already begun in the first. It opens with a lengthy—far too lengthy—variation on the topic of the lack of "news" in Russian life and its deleterious effects on social behavior. One result is that a person who has "some kind of news in store, not yet known to anybody, and above all possessing the talent of narrating

---

* As Sir Isaiah Berlin has pointed out, Gogol's book could not have appeared at a worse moment. For it had just then become generally recognized that "agricultural slavery was an economic as well as a social evil. Count Kiselev [Nicholas's adviser on the issue of serfdom] held this view strongly . . . and even the landowners and reactionary bureaucrats who did their best to put difficulties in the path of positive reform had not, for some years, thought it profitable to question the evil of the system itself." "Russia and 1848," *Slavonic and East European Review* 67 (1948), 351.

it agreeably," is someone of great importance in Petersburg. The most unlikely people—people who, under ordinary circumstances, would never get past the lackey at the door—are allowed to penetrate into closely guarded inner sanctums so long as they have "news." And the chronicler portrays the doglike servility of such personages, as well as the condescending tolerance of those on whom they dance attendance; each flatters the vanity of the other quite self-consciously, and both are perfectly content. "Duplicity, concealment, masks—agreed, it's a nasty affair; but if at the present moment everybody appeared in public as they really are, my God! it would be even worse" (XIII: 15-17).

This contrast between appearance and reality is then illustrated by the chronicler in a very daring manner. For Dostoevsky now returns to the theme he had already alluded to in mentioning Gogol's book— the theme of serfdom; and this of course was a very ticklish matter. To refer to such a subject directly was naturally impossible, and the chronicler takes a very circuitous route to reach his destination. Once again the technique adopted is that of ironical identification—this time an identification, not with the opponents of the Natural School, but with the kind of people who feel no need at all to gather in "circles," and who seem perfectly satisfied with things as they are. "I am sometimes even ready to burst into song from sheer joy," the chronicler declares, "when entering some social gathering and seeing such well-bred and respectable people sitting and discussing something decorously without at the same time losing a jot of their dignity" (XIII: 19).

For all his ecstasy, however, the chronicler admits that it is often very difficult for him to grasp what is being discussed by such eminently seemly upper-class people. "Goodness only knows what they talk about! Something, no doubt, quite inexplicably charming, for they are all such charming and respectable men of the world, but it is difficult to grasp all the same. . . . Occasionally you get the impression that they were talking about some highly serious subjects, something calling for thought; but afterward when you ask yourself what they were talking about, you simply cannot find an answer: was it about gloves, the state of agriculture, or about whether 'a woman's love is lasting'? So that, I confess, sometimes I am overcome by a feeling of melancholy" (*ibid.*). To help his reader understand the reason for such a feeling, apparently so inappropriate in such delightful company, the chronicler has recourse to an extended comparison —every word of which, we may be sure, was carefully chosen.

Imagine, he says, that you hear the captivating music of a gay fancy-dress ball sounding from some stately residence filled with light and laughter and the bustle of society. You listen "elated, excited, a desire for something has stirred in you, an aspiration. You seem to have heard life; and yet all you carry away with you is only a pale, colorless motif, an idea, a shadow, almost nothing. And you pass by as though distrusting something; you are hearing something else, you hear—sounding through the pale motif of our everyday life—another note, piercingly alive and sad, like Berlioz's ball at the Capulets.* Anguish and misgiving gnaw and tear at your heart *like the anguish that lies in the endless refrain of the despondent Russian song that rings out in such a native, familiar tone"* (italics added). Then follows this quotation from a poem:

> "Listen, . . . Other sounds are heard . . .
> Sounds of despondent, desperate revelry.
> Is it a highwayman singing there,
> Or a maiden weeping in the sad hour of parting?
> No, it is haymakers homeward bound . . ."
>
> (XIII: 19-20)

This passage is a superb illustration of Belinsky's point that a feuilletonist could "definitely manage to express everything" in the midst of what seems like inconsequential chatter. For Dostoevsky here is pointing his finger at the greatest moral-social blight on Russian society, and scornfully condemning those who nonetheless continue, with an untroubled conscience, to lead their dignified, civilized, self-satisfied lives. The juxtaposition of the fancy-dress ball with the peasant "revelers" speaks for itself; so does the "anguish and misgiving" that gnaw at the heart of the chronicler, and the "melancholy" that overcomes him while attending the festive gatherings of polite society. For the "reality" of Russian life is to be found, not in the social rituals of the ruling strata, but in the suffering and heartbreak of the enslaved peasantry.

Both of the topics so far broached in this second feuilleton are, it is clear, developments of themes which have already appeared in the one preceding. But there is also a third theme anticipating what is to come later—the theme of Petersburg as a symbol of Russian enlightenment and Russian assimilation of European progress. Descriptions of Petersburg, as we have mentioned, were part of the feuilletonist's stock-in-trade; and Dostoevsky scatters them through his articles with a fairly liberal hand. Such urban landscapes are invariably in the gray and depressing tonality of the Natural School, which concen-

---

* Berlioz conducted a number of concerts in St. Petersburg during the late winter of 1847, and included parts of his new Romeo and Juliet symphony in the program.

trated on the inclemencies of the Petersburg climate and the shabby squalor in whose midst its poorer inhabitants dwelled. The architectural glories of the Palmyra of the North (as earlier poets liked to call the city) are reduced to an image of "huge, damp walls . . . marbles, bas-reliefs, statues, columns which . . . shivered and chattered with the damp cold." What the chronicler picks out for notice is a tired and hungry cab horse, a funeral procession gloomily making its way through the streets with "strained, mournful faces" peeping from the carriages, passersby "looking pale green and stern, terribly angry with something." Even the Petersburg spring is compared to a sickly young girl, ailing and tubercular, whose cheeks suddenly flame into life and beauty for one moment only to fade the very next day (XIII: 13, 26).

At first glance, it might seem as if Dostoevsky would have nothing good to say for the city, which appears only as an inhuman and oppressive environment ruled by the crushing might of the Bronze Horseman and his descendants in the seats of power. But, like other Westerners of the 1840s, Dostoevsky's attitude toward Petersburg was ambiguous: the city was not only the nerve center of tyranny and despotism, it was also, compared to Moscow, the symbol of Russia's desire to absorb Western progress and enlightenment; and it is in this latter guise that it shows up at the end of the second feuilleton. For here the chronicler compares Petersburg to the young, rather naughty son of an old-fashioned country gentleman who is himself quite content to vegetate in his comfortable, patriarchal existence. He wants his son, however, to "become a young European," even though he has heard about "enlightenment" only through rumor. But when the son throws himself into the process with noticeable enthusiasm, the old gentleman exhibits alarm at the foreign exterior and spendthrift ways of his offspring, "grumbles, becomes angry, [and] condemns both enlightenment and the West" (XIII: 17-18). Petersburg thus appears in a new guise and a much more favorable light; and Dostoevsky develops this theme at length in the next article.

5

Dostoevsky's third feuilleton stands somewhat apart from the others, and is much less intimately confidential and unbuttoned in manner. Abandoning the motley of the amuser and satirist, the chronicler dons the more dignified garb of the cultural commentator and makes his own modest contribution to the Westerner-Slavophil controversy then raging in Russian culture. Dostoevsky's little article can scarcely compete with the much weightier ones written by Belinsky and Herzen on the same subject at much the same time; but it is of great interest as the only semi-conceptual formulation of his ideas at this period. Some of these ideas are so much at variance with his later convictions that, if he ever went back to read this feuilleton, he must have regarded it with a shudder of distaste as a glaring example of the aberrations of his youth. Perhaps this is why he never resurrected his four pieces, and allowed them to remain buried in the files of the *St. Petersburg Gazette.*

The chronicler begins his reflections with a picture of the empty city vacated for the summer, and filled now only with workmen cleaning and rebuilding the winter-worn metropolis. "A fine, thick layer of white dust hangs in the torrid air," and the pedestrian, *"flâneur* or spectator,"* is advised not to venture into the Nevsky Prospect "if he does not have the serious desire to resemble the Pierrot of the Roman carnival who is doused with flour." How, then, is a person who remains in the city to occupy his time? Well, he can, for example, look around at the architecture, "an important occupation, and even, truly, an educational one" (XIII: 21).

This thought recalls to the mind of the chronicler that, some time ago, he "had happened to read a French book entirely given over to contemporary conditions in Russia." What book is being referred to has never been satisfactorily established (my own candidate is the famous work of the Marquis de Custine, *La Russie en 1839*); but Dostoevsky culls from its pages some uncomplimentary remarks about Petersburg architecture. The chronicler recalls this acerbic French view as being that "there [was] nothing there particularly striking, *nothing national,* and the whole city [was] just a ridiculous caricature of several European capitals." On the other hand, the cultivated French tourist "is lavish in his praise of Moscow because of the Kremlin, utters a few florid, rhetorical phrases about it, and is gratified by how much nationality he finds in Moscow" (XIII: 21-22).*

* The one or two efforts so far made to identify this work are not convincing. V. Kirpotin speaks vaguely of "the notes of A. Dumas's voyage in Russia"; but Dumas made his journey in 1858. The editor of one of the volumes in a recent French translation of Dostoevsky (Gustave Aucouturier) believes the book to be Xavier Marmier's *Lettres sur la Russie, la Finlande et la Pologne* (1843). But Marmier's innocuous travel notes are hardly "entirely given over to contemporary conditions in Russia"; nor would Dostoevsky have referred to them as "a book by a celebrated tourist read all over Europe with avidity." Such words apply much more aptly to Custine. Moreover, I have been unable to find very much in Marmier that would justify Dostoevsky's attack.

On the other hand, Custine *is* directly concerned with the social-political situation ("contemporary conditions"); and his remarks on Petersburg architecture

Waxing merry over this search by the foreign visitor for visible signs of the Russian soul, the chronicler ridicules his dislike of droshkys "because they diverge from the old, patriarchal wagonette, thus testifying to the manner in which everything indigenous and national in Russia disappears." But the chronicler's target turns out to be, not so much the visiting tourist himself, as those in Russia who adopt a similar point of view. For, he notes, such ideas "coincide with some—we shall not say Russian—but idle ideas of our own, conceived in the study." This is of course an allusion to the Slavophils, who are also delineated as those who search for Russian nationality in "a dead letter, an outworn idea, a heap of stones [the Kremlin] presumably recalling ancient Rus, and, finally, in a blind unconditional reversion to a slumbering native antiquity."

For the chronicler, this identification of Russian nationality with the Kremlin may have been true in the past; but it hardly exists any longer in the present. "It [the Kremlin] is an antiquarian rarity that you look at with special curiosity and with great reverence; but why it should be the height of nationality—that is beyond my understanding! There are some national monuments which outlive their time and cease to be national";—presumably the Kremlin belongs in this category. Even going so far as to deny that the Kremlin serves as a focal point for the religious-national feelings of the Russian people, he points out that they flock to other monasteries as well, and to foreign places of devotion such as Mt. Athos and Jerusalem. And do the Russian people, he asks, really know much more about their history than the names of Dimitry Donskoy, Ivan the Terrible, and Boris Godunov? (XIII: 22). Such arguments reveal to what extreme Dostoevsky was prepared to go in order to counter the Slavophil position.

Like a good Westerner, of course, he takes the opposite tack and celebrates the new capital over the old. It is no doubt true, the chron-

---

are well calculated to stir Dostoevsky's ire. "Je vous ai décrit," he says, "une ville sans caractère, plutôt pompeuse qu'imposante, plus vaste que belle, remplie d'édifices sans style, sans goût, sans signification historique." Marmier says nothing about the Kremlin as the site of Russian nationality, but Custine does go into a flight of rhetoric: "Espèce d'Acropolis du Nord, de Panthéon barbare, ce sanctuaire national pourrait s'appeler l'Alcazar des Slaves." V. Kirpotin, *F. M. Dostoevsky: Tvorcheskii Put*, 1821-1859 (Moscow, 1960), 176; Dostoevsky, *Récits, chroniques et polémiques*, ed. Gustave Aucouturier (Paris, 1969); 1682; Marquis de Custine, *La Russie en 1839* (Paris, 1843), 2: 90; 3: 162.

Shortly after writing this note, I came across a just-published article which also identifies the book referred to in Dostoevsky's feuilleton as the Marquis de Custine's *La Russie en 1839*. No argument is given to establish the point, however, except a general reference to the popularity of the book in Russia, and the fact that it was read by Belinsky and known in the Petrashevsky circle. See E. I. Kyko, "Belinsky i Dostoevsky o Knige Custina 'Rossia v 1839,' " in *Dostoevsky: Materiali i Issledovania*, ed. G. M. Fridlender (Leningrad, 1974), 1: 196-200.

icler concedes, that Petersburg architecture is a chaos and a medley
of styles, and that "much may furnish nourishment for caricature;
but for all that, everything is life and movement." Petersburg is full
of dust and plaster because it is still in the process of being built;
"its future is still an idea; but this idea belongs to Peter the Great,"
and it is taking on flesh and blood and growing every day. Indeed,
the medley of architectural styles in the city "all together recall the
history of the European life of Petersburg and of all Russia." Petersburg is the living symbol of Peter's "great idea," and it supports and
activates everything vital in the country—"industry, trade, science,
literature, civilization, the principle and the organization of social
life." Nor does this assimilation of Western culture, contrary to the
fears of its opponents, involve any surrender to a foreign principle or
way of life. "No, we do not see the disappearance of nationality in
the contemporary effort, but rather the triumph of nationality, which,
in my opinion, will not succumb so easily to European influence as
many believe" (XIII: 23).

For all his pro-Westernism, we see that Dostoevsky is by no means
willing to follow Maikov in rejecting nationality as a value. On the
contrary, Dostoevsky's visceral nationalism is quite evident in the
feuilleton, and sets up a perceptible tension between his ideas and his
feelings. For while his main aim is to belabor the Slavophils, he does
not miss the occasion to take a xenophobic sideswipe against foreigners who fail to understand Russia because "we stubbornly have refused up to now to be measured by the European standard." French-
men in particular refuse to recognize "anything not-French, either
in art, literature or science, not even in the history of a people, and,
most important, [they are] capable of flying into a rage because there
exists some sort of other people with their own history, their idea,
their national character and their development" (XIII: 21-22). This
emphasis on Russian historical "uniqueness" is very close to Slavophilism, even though thrown out in the midst of an anti-Slavophil
polemic. Herzen, with his usual aphoristic brilliance, wrote of the
Slavophils in *My Past and Thoughts* that "like Janus, or the two-
headed eagle, they and we [the Westerners] looked in different direc-
tions while one heart throbbed in us";[8] and this was already beginning
to be true in the late 1840s.

Still, in 1847 Dostoevsky differs sharply from the later view he
expressed of the relation between the people and the educated class.
As we have just seen, Dostoevsky desired nothing more fervently than
the liberation of the serfs and was deeply troubled by the suffering of
the people. But, for all his nationalism, he had not yet accepted the

Slavophil view of the Russian people as endowed with any extraordinary moral qualities and virtues. "What are the people?" asks the chronicler. "The people are ignorant and uneducated," and they look for leadership "to society, to the educated class" (XIII: 23). This is exactly the reverse of what Dostoevsky would say after Siberia, when he advised the educated class to look for guidance to the people. It is thus the intelligentsia who must lead the people along the path hewn out, with a giant hand, by Peter the Great, to the fulfillment of "his great idea."

Finishing off the third feuilleton with a general celebration of the intellectual and cultural activity of Petersburg in the past winter season, Dostoevsky continues the motif of the "great idea" embodied in the city and its key role as the crucible of Russian culture. As a footnote to this survey of the cultural scene, the chronicler praises the illustrations in a new edition of *Dead Souls* (also singled out for favorable comment by Valerian Maikov), and remarks that "in truth, it would be difficult to find a more auspicious time than the present for the appearance of a caricaturist-*artist* (XIII: 26). The italicizing of this last word is quite significant. For to be an artist, in Dostoevsky's terminology, means precisely to transcend caricature in the direction of the "humanization" that Maikov had declared to be the source of aesthetic appeal. There can be little doubt that Dostoevsky was defining himself and his own artistic ambitions in lauding the illustrator who managed to hold a balance between these two conflicting tendencies.

6

If Dostoevsky's first three feuilletons are of great interest because of the information they supply about his ideas and attitudes in general, the fourth is of particular significance because it provides a partial self-commentary on his literary work. Here Dostoevsky returns to the important theme he had approached gingerly in his first feuilleton—the theme of how the oppressive conditions of Russian life influence the Russian character—and develops it in a very illuminating fashion. For it is these conditions, the chronicler now suggests, that create the type of characters we find portrayed in Dostoevsky's fiction of the same period.

Written in early June, this fourth feuilleton evokes the yearly exodus from the city of all those who, like the chronicler and his friends, are able to enjoy the pastoral delights of the countryside. But the chronicler immediately suggests that true relaxation and *dolce far niente* are not for the likes of himself and his readers (now presumed to be members of the intelligentsia). For, he says, Russians of this kind always carry with them the blighting pall of "analysis and comparison, a skeptical outlook, a secret thought, and always the obligation of some eternal, never-ending everyday task" (XIII: 27)—that ubiquitous and inescapable "task" which haunted educated Russians trying to take a rural holiday in 1847.

This manifest incapacity of Russians—more exactly, a certain kind of Russian—to benefit emotionally from their sojourn in the bosom of nature, leads the chronicler to diagnose their situation a little more at length. Why should Russians have developed this "most unpleasant characteristic" of continual self-analysis and eternal dissatisfaction with life? The answer, he suggests, is that they "are tormented by a desire for external, spontaneous activity which they cannot satisfy." Indeed, this passion "for some sort of activity reaches a point of feverish and uncontrollable impatience; we all long for some serious occupation, many of us are full of evident desire to do good"; but all this pent-up emotion leads nowhere. "The trouble is that if anything has to be done we only become aware of it, as it were, from the outside. . . . Russians do things badly and sloppily because we do not really care how they are done." Why should they care, in other words, when their lives are completely in the hands of an all-powerful government which does not even allow them the right publicly to discuss its fiats? (XIII: 27-28).

As a result, Russian life does not cultivate any sense of inner discipline in the individual, or encourage a feeling of personal responsibility. And Dostoevsky then describes, in an extremely important passage, the psychological consequences of this unhappy situation. "When a man is dissatisfied, when he is unable to express himself and reveal what is best in him (not out of vanity, but because of the most natural necessity to become aware of, to embody and to fulfill his Ego in real life), he at once falls into some quite incredible situation; one, if I may say so, takes to the bottle in a big way; another becomes a gambler and cardsharp; another a quarrelsome bully; another, finally, goes off his head because of *ambition*,* at the same time completely despising ambition and even suffering because he has had to suffer over such nonsense as ambition." All this leads Dostoevsky to "an almost unfair, offensive *but seemingly very probable* conclusion," namely, that Russians "have little sense of personal

* The Russian word "ambitsia" does not have the same neutral meaning as its English synonym. In Russian, the word has the pejorative sense of self-love, pride, and arrogance.

dignity" and very little of what he calls "necessary egoism" (XIII: 29).

Such a revaluation of egoism, as we have noted earlier, was very much in the foreground of Russian awareness in 1847; the combined influence of Fourier and Max Stirner had been working to transform this idea from the negative to the positive. It was in the summer of this year that Belinsky felt called upon to mull over the lessons of Stirner; and Herzen—whom Dostoevsky was reading with envy and admiration*—had published his own conclusions a few months before Dostoevsky's feuilleton. "To eradicate egoism from a man's breast," Herzen wrote, "means to eradicate his vital principle, his leaven, the salt of his personality . . . I dare say that *a rational acknowledgment of self-will is the highest moral acknowledgment of human dignity and that all can aspire to it.*"⁹ Dostoevsky's remarks on "necessary egoism" spring from a similar conviction; and this favorable attitude toward personal self-assertion as a manifestation of "human dignity" furnishes an important clue (though by no means an exclusive one) to the interpretation of Dostoevsky's early work.

In the list of psychic malformations given above, we can easily recognize most of the character-types of Dostoevsky's fiction in the 1840s. Drunkards (old Pokrovsky, Devushkin in despair, Emelyan Ilyich in both *Poor Folk* and *An Honest Thief*); those who go mad out of "ambition" while despising the very idea (Golyadkin in *The Double*); those whose lack of "necessary egoism" leads to a pathological fear and neurotic insecurity (Mr. Prokharchin in the story by that name, Vasya Shumkov in *A Weak Heart*). The remarks in the feuilleton thus help to clarify the implicit social-psychological presuppositions of Dostoevsky's creations. Even though, as we shall see, these presuppositions were not understood by most of Dostoevsky's contemporaries—and perhaps he did not do enough to make their presence felt artistically—it is reasonable to assume that he conceived his characters as instances of the prevailing difficulty for Russians "to become aware of, to embody, and to fulfill [their] Ego in real life." But, it should be stressed, this does not mean that he absolves

---

* As late as 1873, Dostoevsky advised a young woman writer, aspiring to educate herself, to obtain old issues of *Notes of the Fatherland* from the public library and read what Herzen had published in the mid- and late-1840s. He refers specifically to Herzen's *Letters on the Study of Nature* (1845-1846), which he calls "the best philosophy" not only to have appeared in Russia, but also in Europe.

Herzen's *Letters* are a lively résumé of Hegel's *History of Philosophy*, written from a Left Hegelian point of view but still idealist in character. Eighteenth century materialism is rejected by Herzen, as it was by Hegel, because it is solely a philosophy of "negation," *DVS*, 2: 138; see also Dimitri Chizevsky [Tschiževskij], "Hegel in Russland," in *Hegel bei den Slaven*, ed. Dimitri Tschiževskij (Darmstadt, 1961), 271-274.

such characters from all individual responsibility for whatever lack of "personal dignity" they may exhibit.

7

Dostoevsky's fourth feuilleton thus gives us an illuminating glimpse into the ideological matrix of those works that remain within the stylistic orbit of the Natural School. In addition, however, it also furnishes insight into a new vein of his production that begins in 1847—a vein which no longer focuses on a *chinovnik* of limited mental capacities but rather on a character-type of the intelligentsia: "the dreamer." The appearance of this type, like so much else in Dostoevsky, has usually been traced exclusively to the peculiarities of his psyche and seen in narrowly biographical terms; but it is impossible to accept this view as adequate. For one thing, impractical idealists in the grip of Romantic vagaries are by no means unknown in earlier Russian literature—Pushkin's Lensky (in *Eugene Onegin*) and Gogol's unhappy artist Piskarev (in *Nevsky Prospect*) both exemplify a similar cultural-spiritual dilemma. And, even more important, Dostoevsky's "dreamer" emerges exactly at the moment when a general campaign was being carried on against the dangers of *mechtatelnost* (dreaming, reverie) as a congenital malady of the Russian intelligentsia.

Everywhere one turns in Russian culture of the mid-1840s, one finds evidence of this campaign. High-flown Romantic ideals and attitudes are denounced as leading to a debilitating withdrawal from the world and the cultivation of a purely passive and self-satisfied attitude of exalted contemplation. Herzen published a series of slashing articles ridiculing the absurdity of Romantic affectations in the midst of "this bustling age, occupied with material improvement, social questions, science."[10] Belinsky inveighed against those who, modeling themselves on Schiller's ideal of "the beautiful soul," believed they could transcend the conflicts of ordinary life. Such people, he says, "know 'the sublime and the beautiful' only in books, and then not always; in life and reality they know neither the one nor the other."[11] The literary sensation of the early spring of 1847 had been Goncharov's *An Ordinary Story*, which contains a devastating portrait of a typical young provincial Romantic brought down to earth by contact with life in Petersburg, and by the admonitions of the chief "positive" character—a busy, disabused, cool, and hard-headed bureaucrat in charge of running a very efficient factory for the government.

Dostoevsky is merely echoing this widespread devaluation of Romantic *mechtatelnost* when, in a letter to Mikhail at the beginning of 1847, he remarks that while a rich and intense inner life is a spiritual good, those who live such a life too fervently are also in danger. For, he explains, "there is a terrible dissonance, a terrible disequilibrium, that comes to us from society. The *external* should be balanced with *the internal*. Otherwise, in the absence of external events, the internal acquires a much too threatening supremacy. Nerves and fantasy assume a very great place in one's existence."[12] This has often been taken as a self-confession; and there is no reason to deny that the young Dostoevsky who suffered from "hallucinations" may well have felt threatened by his own propensity to give way to "nerves and fantasy." It can scarcely be a hazard, though, that he expresses this fear only in 1847; nor should we overlook that the blame for the failure to find any appropriate external outlet is attributed to "society." Dostoevsky's own experience of psychic imbalance was certainly poured into his imaginative realization of "the dreamer"; but the significance that he assigns to the type in his feuilleton is inspired by the dominant social-cultural situation.

Dostoevsky's letter, indeed, jibes perfectly with the analysis of the dreamer that we find in his feuilleton. What is a dreamer? He is, we might say, the cultivated variety of the type of character produced by the frustrations of Russian life. Like the others, the dreamer too is "eager for activity, eager for spontaneous life, eager for reality"; but since this need cannot be satisfied, and because his character is "weak, womanly, soft," he is the kind of person who takes refuge in dreams and fantasies rather than in the more vulgar outlets of the less educated or the more virile. The cultured dreamer develops to an excessive degree the typical Russian practice of living completely in the world of "our illusions, our invented chimeras, our reveries, and all those extra remedies with which people nowadays try in any way to fill up all the dull emptiness of their everyday colorless life." It is in such natures that "little by little develops what is called reverie (*mechtatelnost*), and a man finally becomes something not a man at all but some kind of strange neuter being—*a dreamer*" (XIII: 29-30). The marvelous portrait given of this type is too long to quote entire; but it is one of the gems of Russian prose. To paraphrase lamely, the dreamer is absent-minded and detached, temperamentally very unstable, solitary and self-absorbed, incapable of sustained effort even in his favorite occupation of reading. Everything serves to nourish his capacity for living in an artificial universe of his own creation—a world of imagination and illusion far surpassing the real in attractiveness. "Sometimes entire nights pass imperceptibly in indescribable pleasures; often in a few hours he [the dreamer] experiences the heavenly joys of love or of a whole life, gigantic, unheard of, wonderful as a dream, grandiosely beautiful" (XIII: 30).

The cultivation of such delights brings with it an increasing incapacity to tolerate reality ("the moments of sobering up are dreadful"), and the dreamer becomes totally alienated from his real existence, with all its anxieties and demands. "Little by little our prankster begins to shun crowds, to shun general interests, and gradually, imperceptibly, his talent for real life begins to dull. Finally, in his delusion, he completely loses that moral sense which enables a man to appreciate all the beauty of the actual. . . ." And the chronicler ends by labeling such a life a tragedy, a sin, a caricature; but—"are we not all more or less dreamers?" (XIII: 31). Whether or not he considers himself to be (or to have been) a "dreamer," Dostoevsky makes clear that the time has come for the intelligentsia to stop nourishing itself on such dreams and to turn to the enormous tasks confronting them in Russian life. Just two years later, he was to try to put such convictions into practice.

8
––––––

Dostoevsky's feuilletons have received very little attention in the immense critical literature about their author; and of course they cannot compete in interest with his more important creations of the 1840s. Nonetheless, it should be obvious by now that they yield more of interest than may be thought at first sight. They are, if nothing else, the only first-hand documents that give us some specific notion of Dostoevsky's ideological position at this crucial moment; and they also provide an invaluable context for interpreting his early work. Moreover—a point not touched on so far—they initiate one current of Dostoevsky's literary activity that will take on increasing importance in the future.

Dostoevsky is usually not thought of as a journalist at all, perhaps because so many of the ideas he expresses are so distasteful to admirers of his art. But he *was* a journalist all the same—and an immensely successful and influential one during the 1870s, when his *Diary of a Writer*, published in monthly installments, was the most widely read broadsheet ever to have appeared in Russia. Even earlier, during the 1860s, he was an indefatigable contributor of polemical articles to the two magazines he edited jointly with his brother (*Time* and *Epoch*). This is not the place to discuss his work as a publicist any further; but it is relevant to note that all his writing in this format bears the stamp of the feuilleton style.

Dostoevsky evidently found that the easy, casual manner of the feuilletonist fitted him like a glove; and one never finds him later, even when presumably expounding ideas, writing anything that can be considered ordinary expository prose. His stance is always personal and intimate; his points are made not by logical persuasion but through sketching character-types, dramatizing attitudes, narrating experiences and observations. To be sure, the whimsical tone of the feuilletonist of the 1840s, though never abandoned completely, is replaced by that of the serious and sometimes choleric social observer; but his use of irony and persiflage remains the same, and so does the identification with the reader who becomes an implicit partner in a dialogue. From this point of view, Dostoevsky's five-finger exercises in the 1840s mark the début of an essential aspect of his career.

V. L. Komarovich is the only critic to have speculated on the possible artistic influence of the feuilleton style; and while his observations are still of considerable interest, he misses the one instance where it seems to have been decisive.[13] Among the most striking features of *Notes from Underground* is its artistic singularity and unprecedentedness; it seems to come, formally speaking, from nowhere; but in fact it probably comes from the feuilleton. There is good reason to believe that this work began as a critical article on two recent novels—Pisemsky's *The Troubled Seas* and Chernyshevsky's *What Is To Be Done?*; and if so, Dostoevsky must have started to write it in his usual feuilleton manner. But then, we may assume, the richness of the subject took over, and the quondam article developed into the unique little masterpiece that we know. Such an origin would account for all of the original formal features of the novella, which are so baffling otherwise—the first-person narrator who takes us into his confidence to the point of embarrassment; the direct address to the reader who is treated as an interlocutor; the apparent fortuitousness and haphazardness of the narrative sequence; the blend of irony and pathos.

These are matters, however, that must be left for more ample discussion to a later volume. Here we need only point out the skill with which the Petersburg chronicler, throughout his seemingly casual *causerie*, conveys all the smoldering frustration undoubtedly felt by the progressive intelligentsia of the mid-1840s at their social-political helplessness. Nowhere else in the writing of the time is this note struck so clearly and distinctly; nowhere is the tempting siren song of *mechtatelnost* rejected with more inner awareness of its delights and dangers. And the feelings these articles convey were undoubtedly shared, to a greater or lesser degree, by all the people he encountered at the meetings of the Petrashevsky circle—a group he began to frequent just at the very time they were being written.

CHAPTER 17

The Petrashevsky Circle

The spring of 1847 was an extremely difficult period in Dostoevsky's personal life. The breakup of the Beketov circle at the beginning of the year deprived him of the crucial emotional support he had received from having shared common quarters with a congenial group of friends. Just a few months earlier, he had quarreled decisively with the Belinsky pléiade; his estrangement from Belinsky was increasing with every passing day; and the final split between them occurred sometime between the beginning of the year and early spring. What he himself called "the dissolution of my fame in the journals" was proceeding apace; and he informs Mikhail, in the same letter, that his funds are so low that "if there had not been some kind people, I would have gone under."[1] Only Valerian Maikov was left to afford him some comfort; but Maikov lacked Belinsky's authority, and his praise could not offset the older critic's condemnation.

Dostoevsky moved to new quarters in the early spring of 1847, and began to live a lonely, bachelor existence. There were, of course, people he saw frequently like Yanovsky, and he could rub elbows with literary-artistic Petersburg society of all levels at the Maikovs; but he clearly felt the need for a closer and more intimate group of friends. It must have been about this time that he took to organizing dinners on a cooperative basis for the people he knew best—Pleshcheev, the two Maikov brothers, Yanovsky, the minor writer Yakov Butkov (Dostoevsky's competitor as a portrayer of Petersburg slum life); somewhat later, the schoolteacher and critic Alexander Milyukov, whose memoirs of Dostoevsky are quite valuable. These dinners were held in the Hôtel de France, reputed for its cuisine and located on the avenue where Dostoevsky now lived; and he took a great deal of pleasure, according to Yanovsky, in arranging such convivial occasions. He was well aware, as we know, of the importance of maintaining a psychic balance between the external and the internal, and fearful of "nerves and fantasy" obtaining the upper hand in his own life. No doubt it was partly to counteract his new isolation that he now began to frequent the gatherings of the Petrashevsky circle.*

The opportunity to do so, as a matter of fact, had been offered to him a good while before. Dostoevsky first met Petrashevsky at a coffee shop in the spring of 1846, where he had gone with Pleshcheev to take some refreshment and read the newspapers. He noticed Pleshcheev stopping to chat with an unknown person, whose face he could not see and to whom he was not introduced. When Dostoevsky left a moment later, the unknown followed him into the street and unexpectedly shot out: "May I ask what will be the idea of your next story?" By this time Pleshcheev had hastened up, and he introduced the stranger as Petrashevsky. A few further words were exchanged (Dostoevsky does not say whether he answered the question), and the three men separated.[2] This was Dostoevsky's first encounter with

12. M. V. Butashevich-Petrashevsky in 1840

* I should like to acknowledge my debt, in the following three chapters, to the unpublished Princeton dissertation of Francis Michael Bartholomew, *The Petrashevsky Circle* (1969). Although I disagree with some of Mr. Bartholomew's interpretations, I found his careful collations of testimony an invaluable aid in getting a clear picture of the aims and activities of the group and its various satellites.

Another work I have consulted with great profit, and which I shall not otherwise have occasion to cite, is the short but substantial book of V. R. Leikina, *Petrashevtsy* (Moscow, 1924).

the figure whose eccentricities had already made his name a byword in Petersburg; and his abrupt manner of accosting Dostoevsky was only a mild sample of the behavior that had gained him his reputation.

A month or two later Dostoevsky left Petersburg for the summer, and, on returning, continued to meet with Belinsky, moved in with the Beketovs, and did not use his introduction to Petrashevsky to pursue the acquaintance any further. Both Pleshcheev and Valerian Maikov had known Petrashevsky ever since 1845, and he could easily have done so. But relations between Valerian Maikov and Petrashevsky had become very strained for some unknown reason (perhaps disagreements over the editorial policy of the *Pocket Dictionary of Foreign Words*), and the picture that Dostoevsky probably received of the gatherings was far from enticing. It was not until a year later that he began to drop in at the meetings of the Petrashevsky circle.

2

In 1847, Mikhail Butashevich-Petrashevsky was a young man of twenty-six, just about a half-year older than Dostoevsky. Educated in the Alexander Lyceum at Tsarkoe Selo—the most exclusive school in Russia for children of the nobility, which was housed in a wing of the Imperial Summer Palace—he had acquired a reputation even there for refractoriness and opposition to authority. Barely managing to graduate, he obtained a post in the Ministry of Foreign Affairs as a translator, and continued his studies by acquiring a diploma in law at the University of St. Petersburg. Petrashevsky, however, also attended the courses in political economy given by Professor V. S. Poroshin, who lectured on the various new Socialist systems with a good deal of sympathy. This initiation into Socialist ideas influenced Petrashevsky very strongly, just as it had done with many others—Valerian Maikov among them—who had sat in Poroshin's classroom. Fourierism in particular made a great impression on Petrashevsky, as he candidly confessed to the investigating commission. "When I read his [Fourier's] writings for the first time, it was as if I had been reborn," he writes. "I did homage to the greatness of his genius."[3] From that time on he became a convinced Fourierist, and devoted himself to propagating his new faith.

Sometime in the early 1840s, Petrashevsky began to invite his immediate friends to drop in for conversation; and this was the nucleus of what became his "circle." An indefatigable reader and book collector, he acquired a sizable library of "forbidden" books in various languages dealing with the most important historical, economic, and social-political issues of the day. Despite the censorship, it was comparatively easy to obtain almost anything from abroad in a foreign language; and since one of Petrashevsky's functions was to help foreigners in their difficulties with the Petersburg police, he often enriched his collection by acquiring books from those he met in this fashion. Indeed, one of the greatest attractions at Petrashevsky's was his possession of an extensive library, which he was only too eager to make accessible to others. After a time, the library was maintained and enlarged with the aid of subscriptions paid by his regular visitors.

By 1845 the circle had extended much beyond the bounds of Petrashevsky's old schoolfellows at the Lyceum or the University, and he had become a well-known figure in Petersburg social life. In a verse drama called *Two Egoisms* published in that year, and written by the noted poet and critic Apollon Grigoryev—later to be very close to Dostoevsky in the 1860s—he is good-naturedly satirized as a character named Petushevsky, who, in a discussion with a Moscow Slavophil at a masked ball, recommends that his opponent read Fourier's *Nouveau Monde* if he wishes some enlightenment on the problem of the family.

This is enough to show the reputation that Petrashevsky had already acquired. He was by no means, however, a fanatical follower who took every word of the Master as a sacred text from which it was forbidden to diverge. On the contrary, Petrashevsky quietly dropped all of Fourier's fantastic cosmology and natural history; nor did he indulge in any of the wish-fulfilling fantasies of a future world in which every possible variety of sexual appetite would be fully gratified. Moreover, having read and assimilated Strauss and Feuerbach, he did not share the religiosity either of Fourier, or of his successor as the head of the movement Victor Considérant. "Naturalism" is defined approvingly in the *Pocket Dictionary* as a modern philosophy which, considering "divinity nothing other than the general and higher function of human thought," has led to "anthropotheism"—the recognition that all positive religions based on revelation or tradition are really man's deification of himself or of the laws of nature.[4] In a letter, Petrashevsky refers sarcastically to Christ as "the well-known demagogue, whose career finished rather unsuccessfully."[5] And like a good Left Hegelian, he believed that religion was not only an error but positively harmful: having robbed man of his highest attributes by making them supernatural, it condemned humankind to inactivity and stagnation and stood in the path of progress.

What impressed Petrashevsky most of all in Fourierism was "everything relating to the organization of the phalanstery," which, he declared staunchly, "I fully accept as just and capable of being put into practice."[6] He was firmly persuaded that the establishment of a phalanstery, and the application of Fourier's theory of human nature to the organization of its work, would transform human labor from a burden and a curse to a joyous, self-fulfilling activity. Indeed, according to one generally accepted source, he was so convinced of the feasibility of Fourier's Utopia that in 1847 he tried to realize it on his own small estate. Enlisting the support of his peasants, who obligingly agreed to all his proposals (or so he believed), he proceeded to build a fully equipped phalanstery for them. The great day arrived; the forty-odd peasant families left their miserable *izbas* for their new residence; but the next morning the ideal dwelling, with all its comforts and amenities, had been burned to the ground.

Far from disillusioning Petrashevsky, this only convinced him all the more that a preparatory period of intellectual enlightenment was absolutely essential if any social progress was to be successfully realized. Age-old ignorances and prejudices would first have to be uprooted and destroyed; and so he devoted himself even more fervently to the task of spreading enlightenment everywhere he could. Petrashevsky had a still-untarnished eighteenth century faith in the power of ideas to bring about social change, and was quite certain that, if he encouraged enough people to think critically about whatever affected their lives, this would eventually lead to action. It was to this task that he dedicated himself with untiring zeal, not only at his open-house "Fridays," but also at various clubs and organizations that he joined (including a dancing class for tradesmen and shopkeepers) specifically to meet as many people as possible and spread the ferment of dissatisfaction.

Despite his wide range of acquaintances, which he made such strenuous efforts to extend, Petrashevsky as a man had no close friends. Always courteous and well-mannered with members of his circle, there was yet something angular and grating about his personality which perhaps sprang from the firmness of his convictions, and his self-appointed role as an intellectual *agent provocateur*. D. D. Akhsharumov, who later became a doctor and a pioneer in Russian social hygiene, says that "he spoke in a low and mild voice. His conversation was always serious, often in a scoffing tone: his look expressed, above all, thoughtfulness, contempt, and a biting derision."[7] Petrashevsky was respected for his wide erudition, his staunchness of character, and the inexhaustible energy he displayed in carrying out his mission as an apostle of social discontent; but he rarely inspired any feelings of cordiality or affection. Dostoevsky, under questioning, denied any real intimacy with him but felt obliged to add: "To be sure, I always respected [him] as an honorable and noble human being."[8] This attitude was more or less typical.

Most of the visitors who came to Petrashevsky's, moreover, could not help harboring somewhat mixed feelings about him because of his reputation as a strange and capricious eccentric. "Many people, everybody who knows or has heard about him," Dostoevsky writes, "talk about his eccentricities and singularities."[9] Some of the stories about him derived simply from the striking individuality of his personal appearance: he wore a short beard (government employees were supposed to be clean-shaven), and he walked around town in a large sombrero and cape rather than in more conventional European attire. There were also endless anecdotes about his hassles with various bureaucratic officials, whom he constantly provoked by insisting that they obey to the letter the prescriptions of the Russian legal code. He was once supposed to have gone to church dressed as a woman; on another occasion, having been ordered to cut his hair, he arrived at the office with luxuriant locks that turned out to be a wig! How many reports of this kind are apocryphal is impossible to say. But they all obviously derive from his mockery of the innumerable petty regulations governing every aspect of ordinary life in Russia, and his stiff-necked and courageous refusal to submit to them tamely. The result was, nonetheless, that he acquired the reputation of being a jester and a laughingstock rather than a person of sense and responsibility; and it was difficult even for most of the members of his circle to accept him without inner reservations.

3

This was the unusual and already notorious personality whom Dostoevsky began to visit in the spring of 1847. It should not be imagined, however, that he would have considered such a step of any great importance; he went to Petrashevsky's as he would have gone to any other social gathering. There was nothing secret or conspiratorial about Petrashevsky's "Fridays" any more than there had been about the reunions of the Belinsky pléiade or the Beketov circle. After all, people came together there only to talk a little more freely about the same matters that were being broached month after month in the literary journals. It was generally believed that, so long as such conversation was carried on behind closed doors, there was nothing to fear from the government. The reputation of the Petrashevsky evenings as an interesting and stimulating place to visit, if one could manage to wangle an invitation through a friend, was very widespread. A lively young Petersburger, in a letter dating from the beginning of 1848, lists among the attractions of the city "the sermons of Nilson, the propaganda of Petrashevsky, and the public lectures and feuilletons of Pleshcheev"[10]—all seemed to him to exist on the same level of tolerated public diversion and expression of opinion.

The atmosphere of these Petrashevsky gatherings has been described by many of the participants. In the early years, when attendance was sparse, the circle was more of a study group than anything else; books and articles were read in common, and occasionally a member would expound some topic in which he had a particular interest. Later, when the gatherings became larger, the membership of the circle fluctuated from week to week and conversation was usually carried on in small groups. If some impassioned argument attracted general attention, a referee was appointed to supervise the controversy and ensure the rights of both parties. In the late spring of 1848, it was suggested that the meetings be organized a little more formally, with a speaker assigned in advance for each meeting and a presiding chairman to supervise the interventions of the audience. The meetings thus turned into a sort of debating club or parliamentary assembly, and a small bell, with a handle suspiciously carved in the figure of a statue of liberty, was used to regulate the ebb and flow of talk and to call the various speakers to order.

D. D. Akhsharumov writes that the gatherings were "an interesting kaleidoscope of the most diversified opinions about contemporary events, the decisions of the government, about the creations of contemporary literature in various fields of knowledge; happenings in the city were brought up, everything was talked about at the top of one's voice, without the slightest restraint. Sometimes one of the specialists would give a report in the form of a lecture. . . . Because of the content of the conversations touching primarily on social-political questions, these Petrashevsky evenings interested us enormously; they were the only ones of their kind in Petersburg. The gatherings usually continued far into the night, until two or three in the morning, and ended with a modest supper."[11] One of the earliest and most faithful members of the circle, Alexander Balasoglo, wrote that the guests were usually between seven to ten in number; this would sometimes rise to fifteen, and, on Petrashevsky's name day or birthday, about twenty to thirty people would gather. "About what was the talk, disputes, judgments? Absolutely about everything," though "the balance was tilted, without any doubt, in favor of social theories."[12]

Dostoevsky did not frequent the Petrashevsky meetings very assiduously during the first year and a half; and his attitude toward the group seems to have been quite ambiguous. Yanovsky says that he spoke of the gatherings rather contemptuously, attributing their popularity both to the free refreshments and to a desire "to play at liberalism, because, you see, which of us mortals does not enjoy playing that game."[13] What Dostoevsky wrote about the group for the investigating commission is in the same tone, and agrees with the picture given by others. "In the society gathered around Petrashevsky there was not the slightest unity, neither in thought nor in the tendency of ideas. It seemed as if this was a dispute which had begun at one time for the purpose of never having to end. . . . Without dispute at Petrashevsky's it would have been very dull, because only dispute and contradictions could unite people of such diverse character."[14] Such testimony, of course, must be approached with some skepticism; but there is good reason to believe that it expresses much of Dostoevsky's genuine feelings. For the Petrashevsky milieu could hardly have replaced either the pléiade or the Beketov circle in his affections.

Both of these had been small and tightly knit groups bound together by ties of personal friendship and common aims and interests. At Petrashevsky's, there was only a more or less haphazard conglomeration of people whose membership constantly fluctuated, and who had little or no underlying bond of unity except curiosity and the desire freely to speak their mind. Moreover, there were other and more particular reasons why this circle would not have attracted Dostoevsky irresistibly week after week. Even though externally Dostoevsky and Petrashevsky remained on the best of terms—and Petrashevsky, from time to time, paid a call on the young writer who was the most famous catch he had succeeded in hauling in—the two did not get on very well together. Dostoevsky writes in his deposition that both of them "took care not to carry on a conversation with each other for very long because we would have begun to fight after ten words, and this annoyed both of us."[15] This assertion may perhaps again be suspect as an effort by Dostoevsky to dissociate himself from a dangerous acquaintance; but there are once more good reasons for taking him at his word.

In the first place, Dostoevsky would certainly have disliked Petrashevsky's rampant Left Hegelian atheism as much as he had disliked that of Belinsky; as a matter of fact, we can imagine him disliking it a good deal more. Belinsky's tempestuous explosions were at least indicative of a genuine emotional concern for the dilemmas of religious faith; and the warmth and good-heartedness of his character, as well as his genius as a critic, no doubt made up for a good deal. Petrashevsky was of an entirely different temperament, and always spoke of religion with coldly hostile sarcasm or scornfully mocking irreverence. After Dostoevsky's death, Nikolay Speshnev—about whom we shall soon be hearing a good deal—told Mme Dostoevsky that "Petrashevsky had produced a repulsive impression on [Dostoevsky] because he was an atheist and mocked at faith."[16]

Also, Petrashevsky had very little respect for literature except as a means of propaganda; and he once attacked fables and fairy tales as harmful for the education of children. This produced a heated argument with all the literati of the circle, eliciting in particular an impassioned eulogy of the Russian fabulist Krylov from Dostoevsky. Petrashevsky is also recorded as having said that he had quarreled with the Dostoevsky brothers (Mikhail had come to live in Petersburg in the fall of 1847) because he had "upbraided them for their manner of writing, which could not lead in any way to the development of ideas in the public."[17] This statement, though made quite late in the history of the circle, reflects an attitude that Dostoevsky had surely become aware of much earlier, and which echoes the view at least partially responsible for his break with Belinsky—the view that art should limit itself to serving the cause of social advancement. Petrashevsky's opinions would not have had the slightest importance for Dostoevsky; but they would nonetheless have detracted from the appeal of his Friday night reunions.

Finally, there is one other background factor that must be mentioned in gauging Dostoevsky's attitude toward the Petrashevsky circle at this time. Like all of the intelligentsia, he was of course oppressed by the general lack of freedom in Russian social life; but the most glaring and insufferable injustice—the issue that stirred his deepest emotional responses—was that of the enslavement of the peasantry. On May 18, 1847, however, Nicholas I strongly insisted, in a speech to a delegation of nobles, that peasants could not be considered "as private property, and even more as goods,"[18] and he asked for the aid of the nobility in helping him to convert the status of the peasants from serfs to that of tenants. News of this pronouncement, spreading like wildfire through the capital, aroused the highest hopes; even Belinsky became convinced that Nicholas was at last determined to cut out the deadly cancer threatening the life of Russian society. There was, as a result, very little sense of political urgency in the talk at Petrashevsky's before the fall of 1848. Articles were read and views exchanged on every conceivable subject; the advantages of one or another Socialist system were pondered and weighed; the rigors of the censorship were condemned; the malfeasance of various highly placed bureaucratic officials exposed. But the final effect must have been that sense of exasperated impotence which Dostoevsky had already diagnosed in his feuilletons, and which, we may assume, he could tolerate only in small and intermittent doses.

4

This atmosphere of stagnation was swept away by the outbreak of the revolutions of 1848 in Europe, which caused panic in Russian ruling circles and a wild excitement among the intelligentsia. The Tsar himself, when the news arrived, was supposed to have erupted in the midst of a ball clutching the telegraphic dispatch, and ordered his dancing officers to saddle their horses. Herzen has left a picture of frenzied Petersburgers snatching the newspapers from each other's hands at cafés until, finally, someone clambered on a table and read to all the others at the top of his voice. Alexander Milyukov well conveys the rebellious mood that swept over the intelligentsia as the astonishing news kept pouring in from abroad.

"I met F. M. Dostoevsky in the winter of 1848. That was a difficult period for the educated youth. From the first day of the February revolution, the most incredible events succeeded one another in Europe. The unheard-of reforms of Pius IX provoked uprisings in Milan, Venice, Naples; the surge of liberal ideas in Germany provoked revolutions in Berlin and Vienna. It seemed as if some general rebirth was on the way for the entire European world. The rotten foundations of the old reaction were falling, and a new life was beginning for all of Europe. But, at the same time, the most oppressive stagnation reigned in Russia; thought and the press were confined more and more, and no activity appeared anywhere since social life had been crushed. . . . Practically with every mail delivery from abroad, we heard about new rights granted to the people, whether willingly or not, while in Russian society we heard only rumors of more limitations and constraints. Whoever remembers that period knows how all this worked on the minds of the youthful intelligentsia."[19]

The first effect of this mutinous restlessness, which began to be manifest in the spring of 1848, was to swell the ranks of the Petrashevtsy with an influx of new members. Never before had the gatherings been so well attended and so lively; and it was beginning in the fall of 1848 that Dostoevsky began to show up at Petrashevsky's "Fridays" with some regularity. In the back of everyone's mind, of course, was the question of whether the Russian régime itself could indefinitely escape the fate that had overtaken the absolute monarchs of Europe. "A terrifying spectacle is occurring in the West," Dostoevsky wrote in his deposition, "an unprecedented drama is being played out. The age-old order of things is shaking and breaking up. The very foundations of society threaten at every moment to fall in and to carry along an entire nation in its collapse."[20] Such an apocalyptic vision of impending social chaos inevitably led to much deeper and more fundamental questionings of the old order in Russia, and the talk at Petrashevsky's began to focus much more directly on Russian social-political problems. All the more so because, as Herzen noted, "all the rumors about the intention of the Tsar to declare the liberation of the peasants, which had become very widespread . . . instantly ceased."[21] It was at this time that the Petrashevsky gatherings were organized on a more formal basis, and the practice was initiated of choosing a "president" each Friday to take charge of the animated arguments.

With the crisis atmosphere in the country brought on by the revolutions, it was inevitable, sooner or later, that the meetings at Petrashevsky's would arouse suspicion. His escapades, as a matter of fact, had already called him to the notice of the secret police, and he had been placed under discreet observation in 1844. But since no action was taken, we may assume that he was dismissed as an inoffensive crank. At the beginning of 1848, however, he incautiously circulated a petition among the St. Petersburg nobility calling for a revision of the law governing the sale of estates. The ostensible purpose of this proposal was to raise the value of such property by making it available to non-noble buyers; but such a buyer would be required to change the status of peasants, after purchase, from serf to tenant. Petrashevsky thought this a very clever maneuver to enlist the greed of the landowners on the side of peasant emancipation. Its only result, however, was to alert the authorities once again to his irritating, gadfly existence.

Deciding to investigate him a little more carefully, both the secret police and the Ministry of Internal Affairs placed him under secret surveillance. To avoid confusion the job was finally assigned to the Ministry, whose agents reported, after ten months, that meetings were taking place in his home every Friday lasting until three or four in the morning. "They [the guests] did not play cards, but instead read, spoke, and disputed; but what exactly they spoke about it was impossible to determine because of the caution and secrecy with which Petrashevsky surrounded himself."[22] Accordingly, a secret agent named Antonelli—an ex-student, and the son of a well-known painter of Italian descent—turned up as a fellow employee of Petrashevsky at the Ministry in January 1849. Antonelli furnished his superiors with regular reports of his conversations with the suspect; and though Petrashevsky was suspicious of his efforts to ingratiate himself, and wondered about his liberal supply of funds, Antonelli was present at the last seven meetings of the circle between March 11 and April 22.

5

The information regarding Dostoevsky's participation in the debates of the Petrashevsky circle is quite scanty. As he told the investigating commission, "I am far from being a loudmouth, and everybody who knows me will say the same. I do not like to speak noisily and lengthily even with friends, of whom I have a very few, and still more in society, where I have the reputation of being an uncommunicative, reserved, unsociable person."[23] There are, indeed, few traces of Dostoevsky as an active presence in the ample material about the circle that has become available since the 1920s. Only in the very last weeks of its existence does his name figure at all among those who took a leading part in discussion.

Denying to the investigating commission that he had ever held forth at Petrashevsky's about social or political matters, Dostoevsky does admit that he took the floor on other subjects. "I spoke at his place only three times, or better, twice. Once *about literature*, on the occasion of a dispute with Petrashevsky about Krylov, and the other time *about personality and egoism*."[24] The argument about literature arose because of Petrashevsky's already mentioned attack on fables. Dostoevsky explains his own position as having been "that art has no necessity to have a tendency, that art is an end in itself, that an author should concern himself only over artistic quality and the idea will come by itself; for this is a necessary condition of artistic quality. In a word, it is well known that this is a tendency *diametrically opposed to the journalistic and inflammatory*."[25] These words are very similar to those already quoted* in which Dostoevsky explains his break with Belinsky as having been caused by disagreements over the role of literature in society.

* See pp. 180-181.

The elucidation he offers of his talk on "personality and egoism" strongly recalls the passage in his feuilleton on "necessary egoism"—with, however, a significant modification. "I wished to show," he says, "that there is more *ambition* among us than genuine human dignity, that we tend to fall into belittling ourselves, into a pulverization of personality out of trivial self-love, egoism, and the aimlessness of our occupations."[26] The stress in this sentence, for obvious reasons, is much more on personal character than on the obstacles placed by Russian society in the path of individual self-fulfillment; but the latter idea is vaguely suggested ("the aimlessness of our occupations"). It is likely that Dostoevsky had been much more explicit on this point even than he had been in the feuilleton, and was allowing for the possibility that others would report his speech in such terms; if so, the reference to "occupations" would allow him to rebut any charge of deliberate concealment.

Some members of the circle thought that Dostoevsky's evident reluctance to participate more vigorously in their debates sprang simply from ignorance. This can be inferred from Balasoglo's slurring remark that, despite his years of association with the circle, Dostoevsky had not taken advantage of Petrashevsky's library to "educate" himself and had not read one single "proper" book—i.e., by Fourier, Proudhon, or Helvetius![27] Count Semenov, however, knew Dostoevsky quite intimately, and the lonely young writer frequently visited him in the apartment Semenov shared with N. A. Danilevsky (later the famous theoretician of Pan-Slavism, and reputed to be, in the 1840s, the most thorough expert on the intricacies of Fourierism among the Petrashevtsy). Semenov, who may be accepted as qualified to judge, ridicules the notion that Dostoevsky was "uneducated." On the contrary, he remembers him as one of the best-informed and most erudite of the people he knew; not only was Dostoevsky familiar with Russian, French, and German literature, but, according to Semenov, he had read very extensively in the history of the French Revolution (Thiers, Mignet, Louis Blanc), as well as in Socialist theory (Saint-Simon, Fourier).[28]

Even if such testimony were not available, Balasoglo's charge would be belied by the list of works that Dostoevsky actually withdrew from Petrashevsky's ample collection. He may not have used its resources as extensively as some others; but the range of material he consulted spans the whole gamut of problems that were being discussed at the meetings. For a firsthand contact with Left Hegelian thought, Dostoevsky took out D. F. Strauss's *Life of Jesus*. Louis Blanc's three-volume *Histoire des dix ans* covered recent French history between 1830 and 1840, and brought him up-to-date on the social-political conditions that had led to the creation of Utopian Socialism. He also withdrew several works of Proudhon (the titles are not recorded), and a book by an obscure author named Paget with the bland title *Introduction à l'étude de la science sociale*–which turns out to be one of the best popularizations of Fourierism then available. In Étienne Cabet's *Le Vrai Christianisme suivant J. Christ*, Dostoevsky came across the argument, which he violently rejected, that total Communist egalitarianism was the only true Christianity (he remarks in his deposition that "nothing in the world stupider than *Cabetism*"[29] has ever been invented). Gustave de Beaumont's *Marie ou l'esclavage* (a work also diligently perused by Karl Marx, who quotes from it extensively in *The Jewish Question*) exposed the horrors of Negro slavery in the United States and gave a very unflattering picture of the supposed land of liberty.

6

If Dostoevsky did not throw himself more wholeheartedly into the fray at Petrashevsky's, it was not, then, because of ignorance. It is much more likely that he was simply uninterested in the interminable debates over the merits or demerits of one or another Socialist system. For many in the circle, Socialist ideas were still a titillating novelty; and those already familiar with them were fanatics eager to proselytize others. Dostoevsky, however, had nothing to learn about Socialism from such zealots as Petrashevsky or Danilevsky; nor had he become a disciple himself dedicated to spreading the gospel. He was wholeheartedly in accord with the moral impulse inspiring the various Socialist systems, but he was not persuaded that any of their panaceas could be put into practice. "Socialism offers a thousand methods of social organization," he comments, "and since all these books are written intelligently, fervently, and often with genuine love for mankind, I read them with curiosity. But precisely because I do not adhere to any of the social systems, I studied Socialism in general, all of its systems, and this is why (though my knowledge is far from complete) I see the faults in every social system. I am convinced that the application of any of them would bring with it inescapable ruin, and I am not talking about us but even in France."[30]

Commentators have hesitated to accept such a declaration, made under duress, as defining Dostoevsky's relation to Socialism with any exactitude; but it expresses an attitude that he shared with many of his contemporaries and friends. Valerian Maikov too had been sympathetic to Socialist ideals, but quite skeptical about the feasibility of any of the specific programs advanced by the various schools; and the same position inspired an important series of articles published in *The Contemporary* in 1847 by Vladimir Milyutin, a brilliant young economist who was an intimate of Valerian Maikov and also turned up at Petrashevsky's. As the first public discussion of Socialist economics in the Russian press, these articles aroused a great deal of interest—not only because of their dangerous subject matter, but also because, as Evgenyev-Maksimov remarks, they were "absolutely free of the disapproving aftertaste which one feels at that time in the judgments of Belinsky and Annenkov [about Utopian Socialism]: Milyutin sympathizes with these new schools. . . ."[31] A member of a very prominent family (his uncle, Count Kiselev, headed a commission appointed by Nicholas to study the abolition of serfdom), Milyutin was also, as we shall see further on, much more intimately connected with Dostoevsky than anyone had until recently suspected.

Milyutin saw Socialist theories as inspired by an admirably humanitarian aim; but like Maikov he found it impossible to accept any of their concrete proposals. Concerned, like Maikov again—and also like Dostoevsky—with the freedom of the individual, Milyutin criticized the "new schools" for limiting this freedom much too drastically. "In those forms of social organization worked out by the new schools," he writes, "the personality of the individual either vanishes entirely, or is contained within the most confining limits. Instead of finding the means of reconciling the two equally necessary principles of individualism and sociality (*obshchinnost*), contemporary schools, for the most part, sacrifice the first in the interests of the second, and subordinate the activity of the individual to certain rules that cannot be complied with except through self-restraint or self-sacrifice."[32]

Using the language of Auguste Comte, Milyutin describes all Socialist theories as not yet having reached the stage of "positivity," the stage of being a true science capable of giving a satisfactory account of the laws governing empirical phenomena. The Utopias of the Socialists are constructed to satisfy the dreams of mankind about an ideal social order; but they are still in what Milyutin calls their mythological-metaphysical phase: they are the harbingers of a future science of society which one day will be capable of solving social problems, but they are not yet that science itself. As P. N. Sakulin has pointed out, exactly the same idea and terminology is used more concisely in Dostoevsky's deposition. "Socialism is a science in ferment," he explains to his judges, "a chaos, alchemy rather than chemistry, astrology rather than astronomy. It seems to me, however, that out of the present chaos something consistent, logical, and beneficial will be worked out for the common good."[33] The unusual perspicacity of this evaluation, which seems to foresee the rise of Marx's so-called scientific Socialism, reflects the influence of the most sagacious student of political economy in the Russia of the 1840s.*

The memoirs of Alexander Milyukov help to support the view that Dostoevsky's attitude toward Socialism was genuinely what he stated it to be under investigation. Milyukov was not a member of the Petrashevsky circle, but belonged to one of the several satellite groups that had formed around the parent body. His testimony, however, is all the more valuable because Dostoevsky—one of the organizers of this smaller group—probably spoke there with less inhibition. "Talk about the New Lanark of Robert Owen, the Icaria of Cabet, and particularly about the phalanstery of Fourier and Proudhon's theory of a progressive tax sometimes took up a major part of the evening," he writes. "We all studied the Socialists, but all were far from believing in the possibility of the practical realization of their plans. Among these latter was F. M. Dostoevsky. He read the Socialist writers, but regarded them critically. Agreeing that at the foundation of their doctrines there was a noble aim, he nonetheless considered them only as estimable visionaries."[34]

Far from having been captured by these Utopian fantasies, Dostoevsky was thinking along much more concrete and down-to-earth lines. He especially insisted, Milyukov writes, "that all these theories had no importance for us, that we should seek for the sources of a development of Russian society not in the doctrines of Western Socialists, but in the life and age-old historical organization of our people, where in the *obshchina* [communal ownership of land], *artel* [worker's wage-sharing cooperative], and in the principles of mutual village responsibility [for the payment of taxes] there have long since existed much more solid and normal foundations than in all the dreams of Saint-Simon and his school. He said that life in an Icarian commune or phalanstery seemed to him more terrible and repugnant than any prison."[35] The remark about prisons seems almost too prophetic of Dostoevsky's future to be true; but it is by no means implausible that he might have used some such image. Maikov and Milyutin had both criticized Socialism for its constraints on individual freedom; Dostoevsky speaks of "the relentless necessity" of Fourierism in his deposition; and Apollon Maikov, when called in for questioning, expatiated

---

* This was not only the evaluation of his contemporaries, but continues up to the present day. Milyutin's most important articles were republished in the Soviet Union in 1946 with an extremely laudatory introduction. Vladimir Milyutin, *Izbrannye Proizvedenia* (Moscow, 1946).

on the lack of privacy in the phalanstery and compared life there to living in an army barracks.[36]

Even more important, however, is that we see another idea emerging in Milyukov's account. This idea is that, since "true" or "natural" Socialism is *already* contained in the social institutions of the Russian peasantry, these furnish a basis for the construction of a new social order superior to the artificial Utopias of the Western Socialists. Because this idea is the heart of Russian Populism, and was to prove of such tremendous importance for Dostoevsky in the future, Milyukov has been accused of smuggling the opinions of the post-Siberian and more "Slavophil" Dostoevsky back into the 1840s.[37] A closer study of the available evidence, though, tends to confirm Milyukov's words. Franco Venturi, in his massive history of Russian Populism, has noted the existence of an embryonic "Populist" wing among the Petrashevtsy.[38] It is within this group—who were following Belinsky's recent injunction to work out the solution to Russian social problems in Russian terms—that Dostoevsky must be placed.

A crucial catalyst in this development of Populist ideas was the book of the German agronomist Baron Haxthausen, *Studies on the Interior of Russia* (1847), which depicted the Russian peasant commune as remarkably similar "to the utopia which modern political sects, namely, the Saint-Simonians and the communists, have imagined to represent the perfect society."[39] Petrashevsky was familiar with this work, and, under the influence of Haxthausen, began to think of the phalanstery as an improved and amplified *obshchina*. Other Petrashevtsy stressed another point made by Haxthausen—that the *obshchina* protected Russia against the acute pauperism and the growth of a landless proletariat which had led to Utopian Socialism as a remedy. One of the people most impressed with this thought was a young civil servant, V. A. Golovinsky, whom Dostoevsky considered to be among his closest friends.[40] "The Slavic principle contains a foundation—the *obshchina*—which will save Russia from the terrible consequences of Socialism," writes Golovinsky. "Since there exist two kinds of property in Russia—*personal and communal*—village, that is, peasant land does not belong to any particular individual but to the whole village community—the *obshchina*, which distributes it among the community."[41] Another friend of Dostoevsky, the young Army lieutenant Nikolay Grigoryev, expressed similar views about the *artel* and the *obshchina*, which he called "Socialism without stupidity."[42]

Ideas very close to these proto-Populist formulations can be found in Dostoevsky's deposition. "Fourierism, and along with it every Western system, is so unsuited for our soil, so strange to our conditions, so not in the character of our nation—and, on the other hand, so much an outgrowth of the West, so much a product of the Western order of things, where the proletarian question has to be solved by any means whatever . . . [that] for us now, among whom there is no proletariat, it would be killingly ridiculous."[43] Since Dostoevsky had recently insisted on the impossibility of understanding Russian history and national character in European terms, the appeal of such "Slavophil" ideas, freed from the onus of their suspect origin by Haxthausen's approval, would clearly have been very powerful.

7

Dostoevsky's thoughts, as we see, were thus immovably riveted on Russia and Russian problems. These subjects were rarely discussed at Petrashevsky's in terms he thought sensible; and so he took the floor only when he felt personally attacked as a writer, or to expound some idea close to his heart and important for his literary work. But if Dostoevsky was known for his tepidity and indifference whenever the talk revolved around the fine points of Socialist doctrine, he was equally notorious for his impassioned intensity whenever it focused on the problem of serfdom. For there is one overwhelming impression that emerges from all the accounts of Dostoevsky given in the memoirs: he was, literally, someone who found it impossible to control himself whenever he spoke about the mistreatment of the enslaved peasantry.

I. M. Debu—a Fourierist belonging to Petrashevsky's inner circle—recalls Dostoevsky in this fashion: "As if it were now, I see Feodor Mikhailovich before me at one of the evenings at Petrashevsky's. I see and hear him telling us how a sergeant of the Finnish regiment was made to run the gauntlet because he had taken revenge on the squad commander for the barbarous treatment of his comrades; *or about how the landowners behave with their serfs*."[44] (Italics added.) Count Semenov, present on the same occasion, hits very close to the mark in diagnosing the emotive source of Dostoevsky's radicalism in the 1840s. "Here I can only say," he writes, "that Dostoevsky was never, and could never be, a *revolutionary*; but, as a man of feeling, he could be carried away by a wave of indignation and even hatred at the sight of violence being perpetrated on the insulted and injured. This happened, for example, when he saw or heard about the sergeant of the Finnish regiment having had to run the gauntlet. Only in such moments of outrage was he capable of rushing into the street with a red flag."[45]

Clearly, Dostoevsky spoke with uncontrollable fervor at such moments, whether at Petrashevsky's or elsewhere. "I cannot now give his speeches exactly," writes Milyukov, "but I remember very well that he always spoke energetically against all measures that would hamstring the people in any way, and he was particularly outraged at the mistreatment from which both the lowest class and the youth in school suffered."[46] What swept over him was no doubt a combination of all the old emotions connected with his traumatic experience of the beating of the peasant coachman on the road to Petersburg; his memory of the routine sadism at the Academy of Engineers; and the nightmare images and suffocating sense of complicity arising from guilt over his father's death. All these horrors, working together, evidently inspired Dostoevsky to sudden outbursts of blazing eloquence; and some members of the circle even felt him to have the makings of a born agitator and rabble-rouser. (His later triumphs as a public reader of his own works, and as a soul-stirring orator, prove them to have been right.) In any case, nobody could have the slightest doubt that Dostoevsky was filled with a burning urgency to remedy the intolerable social injustice in whose midst every Russian was forced to live.

It was perhaps Dostoevsky's volcanic eruptiveness, whenever he came to speak about serfdom, that may have first brought him to the attention of the enigmatic and fascinating figure of Nikolay Speshnev. For within the amorphous agglomeration of the Petrashevsky circle, the iron-willed Speshnev was one of the few ruthlessly determined to turn words into deeds; and he was continually on the watch for people he might recruit for this purpose. He formed a little circle—partly among the Petrashevtsy, partly through his own contacts—which was the only true secret society to emerge from the Petrashevsky "Fridays." Very little is known for certain about this underground organization, but one fact is incontestable: Dostoevsky was among its members. Not Belinsky or Petrashevsky but Speshnev was Dostoevsky's mentor in revolutionary radicalism; it was Speshnev who shaped Dostoevsky's conception of what underground conspiracy really meant in practice. The relations between the two, so far as they can be unraveled, thus deserve to be treated in some detail.

CHAPTER 18

Dostoevsky and Speshnev

Nikolay Speshnev—who unquestionably furnished Dostoevsky, twenty years later, with some of the inspiration for the character of Nikolay Stavrogin in *The Devils*—stood out among the rather drab personages clustering around Petrashevsky as a bird of a quite different and much more brilliant plumage. He was, in the first place, a very wealthy landowner (Petrashevsky was also a landowner, but of a small and impoverished estate). Like Petrashevsky, he had attended the Alexander Lyceum and the two had known each other as students; but with an arrogant off-handedness typical of his character, Speshnev had not bothered to graduate. He was the only member of the circle who did not have to earn a living either in the Army or the bureaucracy, or, like Dostoevsky, eke out a precarious existence as a free-lance writer. And he was the only one who had traveled to Europe, and had enjoyed the cultural advantages of the disorganized but extremely cosmopolitan life of the Russian gentry.

Speshnev, moreover, was not only different from the others because of his wealth and social status; he was also an extraordinary person in his own right. Bakunin—a product of the same milieu, and who knew a fellow aristocrat when he saw one—was much impressed with Speshnev when they met in Siberia in 1860. "Speshnev," he wrote to Herzen, "is a remarkable man in many ways: intelligent, cultivated, handsome, aristocratic in bearing, not at all standoffish though quietly cold, inspiring confidence—like every one possessing a quiet strength—a gentleman from head to foot."[1] The wife of Nikolay Ogarev, who met him just before his arrest in 1849, describes him as being tall, with finely chiseled features and dark brown hair flowing in waves down to his shoulders; his large blue-gray eyes were, she thought, shadowed by a look of gentle melancholy.[2] Count Semenov, who is anything but sentimental, also comments on Speshnev's masculine good looks: "He could well have served as a model for sketches of the head and type of the Savior."[3]

Speshnev had lived in Europe between 1842 and 1847, and, when he returned to Petersburg in December of that year, was surrounded with the aureole both of a romantic and a revolutionary legend.

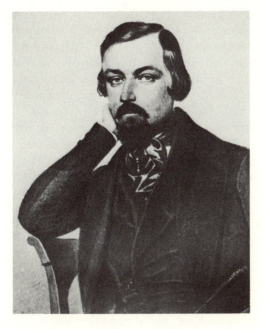

13. N. A. Speshnev

Rumor had it that he had run away with a Polish beauty, the wife of a neighboring landowner, who had died a few years later in Vienna—perhaps having poisoned herself because of jealousy—leaving him with two illegitimate children. Women, as Bakunin notes somewhat enviously, found Speshnev irresistible. "Women are not opposed to a bit of charlatanry," he sagely informs Herzen, "and Speshnev creates quite an effect: he is particularly good at wrapping himself in the mantle of a deeply pensive and quiet impenetrability."[4] If we are to believe Bakunin, Speshnev cut a wide swath during 1846 in the Russian-Polish society of Dresden. Whether old or young, whether mother or daughter, all the women were mad about him. Even more dazzling than this Byronic reputation as a Don Juan was the report that he had taken part in the *Sonderbund* war, which had broken out in 1843 between the liberal and Catholic cantons in Switzerland over the expulsion of the Jesuits; Speshnev was said to have fought as a volunteer with the army of the liberal cantons.

Whether true or not, this rumor is enough to indicate the complexion of Speshnev's politics. He began, under the influence of his reading of the French Romantic historians, as a political liberal; but if he was still such a liberal in 1843, he quickly evolved leftward toward a much more radical position. Steeping himself in the literature both of orthodox political economy and its Socialist critics, he very soon passed through Utopian Socialism to egalitarian Communism. He also had a very considerable philosophical culture, and was widely read in Left Hegelian thought up to and including Max Stirner. His contact with Polish emigré circles both in Germany and France had acquainted him with the methods of underground conspiracy, and, becoming fascinated with the history of secret societies, he read everything he could find on the subject. He was familiar with Buonarotti's *La Conspiration de Babeuf* (which served as a handbook on conspiratorial tactics for all the French secret societies up to 1848), as well as with the compendious tome of the Abbé Barruel, *Mémoires pour servir à l'histoire du Jacobinisme, de l'impiété et de l'anarchie*, which described in detail the supposed success of the Masons and Jacobins in secretly engineering the French Revolution. Everywhere he went, Speshnev moved in left-wing or (as in the case of the Poles) oppositional political circles. In Paris, through a Polish friend named Edmond Chojecki (who was later close to both Herzen and Proudhon), he became acquainted with the group around the *Revue Indépendante* and was invited to furnish articles about Russia.

Unlike Belinsky, however, Speshnev seems never to have been strongly influenced by the sentimental humanitarianism and the religious-philosophical Messianism of the Sand-Leroux school. He was much more attracted by the doctrines rampant among the extreme French secret societies that preached the necessity of violence, and whose Communism was combined with a philosophy of materialism, atheism, and Utilitarian self-interest rather than with an updated version of Christianity. One of the most articulate spokesmen for this position, who received an approving nod from Karl Marx in *The Holy Family*, was Theodore Dézamy.[5] A fiery young French ex-schoolteacher and journalist who had once been Cabet's secretary, he broke with his erstwhile patron in the mid-1840s and ferociously attacked his Christian Communism as vacillating and cowardly. Dézamy was as committed as Cabet to a totally egalitarian and leveling Communism of the crudest kind; but he believed that it could be realized only by the seizure of power and the ruthless application of terror to crush all the enemies of the new ideal order. One of Dézamy's books, *Le Jésuitisme vaincu par les socialistes*, was found in the search of Speshnev's quarters; and the young Russian was very familiar with the obscure details of the fratricidal struggle being waged just before 1848 by these two minuscule Communist sects.

There is also very good reason to believe that Speshnev, during his sojourn in Paris, was influenced by the fathers of Marxism themselves (not yet Marxists, to be sure). In the fall of 1844, Engels wrote a letter to the *New Moral World*, an Owenite-Communist journal, proudly claiming that "we are having much success among the Russians living in Paris. There are three or four Russian nobles and landowners here who are declared radical Communists and atheists." V. I. Semevsky, writing before the Russian Revolution, and a historian of scrupulous objectivity with an unrivaled knowledge of Russian radicalism, thinks "we can scarcely doubt that one of these Russians was Speshnev."[6]

2

The dossier about Speshnev compiled in 1849 for the investigating commission has unfortunately been lost, and what we know about him comes largely at second hand through the testimony of others and the summary of his case made for Nicholas I. Recently, however, the drafts of two letters written by him sometime in 1847 have been published—one originally in French, the other in German, and both containing a liberal sprinkling of Polish words and phrases. Both are presumed to have been addressed to Chojecki; and they furnish striking confirmation of the qualities in Speshnev that so impressed his contemporaries. Even now one cannot help admiring his easy erudition in philosophical and social-economic matters, and the lucid, ironic, coldly incisive quality of his mind. This quality is revealed most fully in his discussion of political tactics—a discussion arising from a purely philosophical disagreement over whether the final results of a certain action could be unified if it originated from divergent sources lacking such unity. Or, more practically, should one co-operate with others in a social-political movement in the absence of complete ideological agreement?

From Speshnev's reply, we surmise that Chojecki was arguing against any surrender of principle; but Speshnev is in favor of more flexible tactics. "I also am fully persuaded," Speshnev writes, "that if, today, the early Christians living in communes and the Jesuits of Paraguay were suddenly to rise from their graves, and were invited by Dézamy's present-day atheist-Communists to live together in a community, such a community would produce only friction, dispute, and conflict."[7] Indeed, he remarks, one does not even have to be as far apart ideologically as the early Christians and modern atheist-Communists for this to be true. Even people as close together as "the

Deist and moralist Cabet and the atheist and materialist Dézamy cannot live in the same world: they will fight to the death until the moralistic Deist has seated his 'amoral opponent' in jail."[8]

Nonetheless, Speshnev makes a careful distinction between such long-range irreconcilabilities—which presumably can be eliminated only by force—and a temporary union of differing factions to achieve a limited goal on which they all concur. Just imagine, he tells Chojecki, that there are believing Christians and dyed-in-the-wool atheists who both agree that private property is evil, and that earthly goods should be distributed according to need. Even if they differ about ultimate aims, "why should [they] not agree on the establishment of a communal organization of society as long as both value this? . . . You think that all the Byzantine metaphysics in my head can only cause trouble? Fine, but what stops you from condemning it after we accomplish what we have both been striving for?" And Speshnev assures Chojecki that, unless one adopts such a course, "your party will rightly consider you to be a very unpractical fellow."[9] This ironic advocacy of political Machiavellianism helps to light up some of the shadowy background of Speshnev's machinations in the Petrashevsky circle.

What Speshnev says about philosophy in these letters further illuminates his personality and jibes perfectly with his tactical opportunism. A good deal of space is devoted to refuting the views of a Polish Left Hegelian named Kamieński, whose book Speshnev compares with Proudhon's *Système des contradictions économiques*; but the most important remarks are those that show how strongly he had come under the influence of Max Stirner. Rejecting all attempts to establish any sort of metaphysical system, Speshnev writes: "Anthropotheism [the position of Feuerbach] is also a religion, only a different one. It divinizes a new and different object, but there is nothing new about the fact of divinization. . . . Is the difference between a God-man and a Man-god really so great?" Both, he says, are abstractions, which do not concern the actually existing individual of flesh-and-blood. "Am I, writing to you now, really identical with humanity or 'the human'? . . . If not, then 'humanity' and 'the human' are also alien, foreign beings, not identical with me, and, though rather similar, still alien authorities." Accordingly, Speshnev concludes that "such categories as beauty and ugliness, good and bad, noble and base, always were and always will remain a matter of taste."[10]

There is no way of establishing for certain whether Speshnev ever uttered such thoughts to Dostoevsky. He did, however, lecture on religion from a "philosophical" point of view during one of the evenings at Petrashevsky's when Dostoevsky was probably present. But even if we assume that Dostoevsky totally invented the ideological motivation of Stavrogin, this merely verifies the astonishing capacity of his imagination, at what may seem to be its wildest flights, to intersect with some of the historical reality of Russian culture. For Stavrogin's "Confession" contains the following passage, which offers the rationale for his behavior: "I have neither the feeling nor the knowledge of good and evil, and not only have I lost the sense of good and evil, but good and evil really do not exist (and this pleased me) and are but a prejudice; I can be free of all prejudices, but at the very moment I achieve that freedom I shall perish" (12: 113).

Speshnev's appearance at the Petrashevsky "Fridays" early in 1848 naturally stirred a good deal of interest and excitement, if only because the widely traveled new visitor could provide first-hand information about Socialist circles in Europe. But his strong and striking personality also produced its effect, greatly aided by his posture of reticence and the air of mystery that he assumed—the air of a man perfectly poised and self-secure, who knew much more than he was willing to disclose to the uninitiated. He rarely entered into the current of the conversations at Petrashevsky's, spent most of his time in the host's study consulting his library, and would only condescend now and then to drop a laconic word. From the summary of what Speshnev said about himself, we see that he deliberately cultivated such a stance to increase his authority and prestige. "He stood among the others implicated as completely independent, needing no one while others needed him; he spoke little, spent most of his time at home reading, and must have seemed a secretive person; he was sometimes very sharp in speech, to prevent others from hiding from him, and succeeded in recognizing all hidden thoughts so as to know with whom he was dealing."[11] The manner in which Speshnev was treated by the others, including Petrashevsky, suggests that he was suspected of being the emissary of some European revolutionary organization.

Whenever Speshnev *did* speak, he injected a new note of steely decisiveness into the somewhat desultory atmosphere of the meetings; no one had ever expressed himself there with such brutality and frankness. In the talk on religion already mentioned, he remarked that, in Russia, it was possible to propagandize ideas only by word of mouth. "And therefore, gentlemen, since only the spoken word remains to us, I intend to use it without any shame or conscience, with no sense of dishonor, in order to propagandize for Socialism, atheism, terrorism, everything, everything that is good in the world. And I advise you to do the same."[12] Speshnev was of a totally different moral temper than Petrashevsky, and the two men were, ideologically, poles apart. Both were revolutionaries in the sense that both wanted fundamental social changes in Russia. But Petrashevsky pinned his hopes to a gradual, long-range evolution, decried precipitous political action, and rejected egalitarian Communism as economic barbarism. Speshnev openly called himself a Communist, believed in the nationalization of all means of production in the hands of a strong central power, and felt that the initial and most important step should be the seizure of such power by the revolutionaries at the first favorable opportunity.

3

During the winter of 1848-1849, a number of incidents occurred in the Petrashevsky circle that betrayed an increasing radicalism among some of the participants—or at least an increasing need for some sort of positive action. This restlessness took the form of various tentative proposals to turn the "Fridays" into a genuine political organization. Speshnev was either directly involved in all these incidents, or was suspected by others to be working in the background. And there can be no doubt that he seized whatever possibilities he could sense to move beyond the cautiousness and hesitancy invariably displayed by Petrashevsky.

The most curious episode of this kind involved the flamboyant figure of Rafael Chernosvitov, a Siberian gold-prospector who floated into the Petrashevsky orbit one day in November 1848, prompted more by curiosity than anything else. An ex-Army officer, about ten years older than most of the other Petrashevtsy, he had knocked about a good deal, been decorated for bravery, and was the proud possessor of a wooden leg replacing one lost in battle. A garrulous and expansive personality, he evidently enjoyed bedazzling his young and gullible audience with portentous hints about his enormous influence over the wild and unruly population of his Siberian district and his contacts with the Governor-General. Dostoevsky, who enjoyed the pithiness of Chernosvitov's language, compared his racy Russian to that of Gogol; but he also remarked to Speshnev that the colorful newcomer was probably a police spy. Speshnev thought he was the agent of a revolutionary organization in Siberia sent to feel out the ground in the heartland of the Empire; so perhaps did Petrashevsky.

At the same time, Chernosvitov suspected *them* of being the leaders of a movement preparing an uprising in European Russia.

It is indicative of Speshnev's status that Petrashevsky invited him to participate in a series of private conversations with Chernosvitov. Each of the three tried to feel out the other as the talk turned on the possibility of a revolution. Chernosvitov assured his interlocutors that, beyond the Urals, the free Siberian peasants all possessed arms and were ready to massacre any invading Army. Speshnev pointed out that, if the bulk of the Russian Army could be decoyed into Siberia, and if this could be coordinated with uprisings in the two major cities, the fate of Tsarism would be sealed. Declaring his readiness to participate in such an undertaking, Chernosvitov tried to elicit admissions from the other two that they were indeed organizing for such a revolt. Speshnev was willing to play along in the hope of extracting more information from Chernosvitov; but Petrashevsky flatly refused to participate in outright deception. The talks broke down as a result of this refusal.

The next incident involved an ex-naval officer, Konstantin Timkovsky, who held a post in the Ministry of Internal Affairs. During the winter of 1848 Timkovsky spoke two or three times at Petrashevsky's, and left a lasting impression. He seems to have been a hotheaded Socialist neophyte who struck everyone by his rashness and naiveté. "Some regarded him with mocking curiosity," Dostoevsky writes; "others skeptically, not believing in his sincerity. Several took him for a genuine, true-to-life daguerreotype of Don Quixote and, perhaps, they were not mistaken."[13] It is impossible to know exactly what he said because no copy of any speech has been preserved; but he apparently changed course in the interval between his various interventions. At first he spoke of the need to organize, and to carry on a united effort of propaganda so as to influence people in high places in favor of Fourierism; but then, it is generally agreed, he fell under the influence of Speshnev. What he said later, according to one account, definitely bears the Speshnevian stamp. "Timkovsky declared . . . that the efforts of all true fighters for progress should be directed toward hastening a rebellion," which, in any case, he believed was certain to occur, and which he implied *could* occur in the next several weeks. Proclaiming his readiness to sacrifice his own life for the sacred cause, he insisted that "the first condition for success lay in the unity of all fighters and in the cessation of all disputes over systems, and also in the establishment of a firm principle for propaganda."[14]

Timkovsky's tirade was very badly received, leading some to suspect him of being a police spy and causing others to blanch with fear at such dangerously subversive talk. Only his brother—a naval officer—and (naturally) Speshnev expressed approval. Petrashevsky, as host, preserved his decorum, but later sent a long and disapproving letter to Timkovsky, who by this time had left Petersburg to take up a post in Revel. The letter is an eloquent statement of Petrashevsky's own convictions, written with considerable dignity and rebuking Timkovsky for his vanity and brashness in displaying his revolutionary fervor à la Karl Moor. Fourierism, he explains, "does not desire to squander the results of a thousand years of mankind's bitter toil for one moment of upheaval, sublime if you will but unhealthy and feverish."[15]

Nonetheless, Timkovsky's speech served as a catalyst to bring into the open half-formulated thoughts (or, perhaps, fully formulated but as yet still too-frightening thoughts) that were fermenting among the group. The next person to take them up was a young Army lieutenant named Nikolay Mombelli, who spoke privately to Petrashevsky about the formation of a secret mutual-assistance society. The aim of this organization, so far as one can judge, would have been to infiltrate the bureaucracy; its members would secretly aid each other in every possible way, attempting to use their influence to bring about reforms and to counter the oppression of the authorities. This led to another series of private conversations, which took place about the same time as those with Chernosvitov, again with Speshnev and Petrashevsky as the main participants.

Mombelli, as we now know, was a member of Speshnev's secret organization, and his suggestion may have been part of a more elaborate plan. Speshnev, in any case, immediately seized the opportunity to outline his own idea of what a secret society should be. He explained that "there are three illegal methods of action—Jesuitical [i.e., infiltration], propaganda, and revolt; that neither of these is certain, and thus there is a better chance if all three roads are taken, and for this a central committee [is] necessary whose function would be to form auxiliary ones: a committee of brotherhood to set up a school of Fourierist, Communist, and Liberal propaganda, and, finally, a committee to form, behind all this, a secret society for revolt."[16] Mombelli suggested that all members of the proposed organization begin by writing their biography (perhaps for purposes of pressure and blackmail?), and that traitors were to be executed. But Petrashevsky engaged in delaying tactics, constantly warned about the necessity for being prudent and practical, and said that, even though he did not approve of violent revolution, he still believed he would live in a phalanstery during his lifetime. Speshnev finally lost patience, refused to attend any more such futile meetings, and broke off relations with Petrashevsky temporarily sometime in December 1848.

4

It is against the background of these various attempts by Speshnev to form a secret society, all frustrated and thwarted by Petrashevsky, that we must place what we know of Dostoevsky at this time. For it was shortly after these abortive efforts that, one evening in January 1849, he visited the flat of Apollon Maikov and stayed to spend the night. He told Maikov that he had been delegated to make him a proposal—the proposal to join in a new secret group that had been formed. "Petrashevsky," Dostoevsky said, "well, he's a fool, a play-actor and a chatterbox; nothing sensible would ever come out of him." More practical people had, as a result, thought up "a plan of action" without telling Petrashevsky anything about it. The idea was "to set up a secret printing press and print, etc."; seven others had joined, and Maikov was invited to be the eighth; no others were to be approached. "I remember Dostoevsky," Maikov writes, "like the dying Socrates before his friends, sitting in his nightshirt with an unbuttoned collar and lavishing all his eloquence on the sanctity of this action, on our obligation to save the fatherland, etc.—so that I finally began to laugh and crack jokes."[17] Maikov warned Dostoevsky that the whole adventure was very dangerous, and that he was heading for certain ruin; but he promised not to breathe a word of the proposal to anyone and remained true to his pledge during Dostoevsky's lifetime.

This attempt to enlist Maikov was first revealed in a letter written after Dostoevsky's death (but never sent) and published only in 1922; it contains the names of Speshnev and Pavel Filippov as two other members of this secret group (Filippov was an ex-student at the University of St. Petersburg whom Dostoevsky listed, along with Golovinsky, as among his closest friends). Maikov told the same story verbally to a friend, a minor poet, who transcribed it in a diary that came to light in 1956. Here we learn the names of all the other members: Nikolay Mordvinov, Mombelli, Nikolay Grigoryev, Vladimir Milyutin; and the purpose of the organization is bluntly stated to be that of "producing a revolution in Russia."[18] In his letter, Maikov also mentions having learned later that the parts for a handpress had been gathered together and assembled shortly before the arrest of all the Petrashevtsy. The activities of this underground group, so far as they are known, will be detailed in the next chapter. What is important here is simply to establish that Dostoevsky *was* a member of such an organization beginning at least in January, and that he had accepted the responsibility of actively recruiting on its behalf.*

Nothing further has been unearthed for certain about this Speshnev fraction, although its existence was not a secret from the more penetrating observers who came to Petrashevsky's. D. D. Akhsharumov remarks, in his memoirs, that Speshnev had formed "his own circle, with, so far as I know, its own tendency, as it were competing with Petrashevsky."[19] What this tendency was may be gathered from Speshnev's testimony about his social-political ideas. "When he [Speshnev] heard in 1848 that this question [the liberation of the serfs] had been put aside, it seemed to him that to postpone this question meant voluntarily to prepare in Russia the sole possible aim of a peasant insurrection."[20] Many years later, Dostoevsky gave some additional information to his close friend and official biographer, Orest Miller. "For Feodor Mikhailovich himself," Miller writes, "the memory evidently remained that a conspiracy *in intent* had existed—that is, existed for the future. It sprang, evidently, from the general discontent, which was the most important link between the members of 'the society for propaganda,' as it was accurately named in the Leipzig book.† The aim was to spread discontent with the existing order everywhere, beginning with the schools: to establish connections with everybody who was already discontented—with the religious dissidents (*raskolniki*) and the peasant serfs."[21]

Some further light on the organization is also cast by a document found among Speshnev's papers—the draft of an oath of allegiance to a secret group called the "Russian Society." The person signing this oath pledged himself to obey the orders of the central committee whenever this executive body decided that the time for a revolution

---

* There is some dispute over the date of Dostoevsky's nocturnal visit. Leonid Grossman, in his authoritative chronology of Dostoevsky's life, places it sometime in March-April 1849. No reason is offered for this change, though I suspect it was motivated by a desire to make the formation of the Speshnev group coincide more closely with the period when the handpress (so far as we know) was assembled.

However, even though Maikov himself makes a numerical error in dating Dostoevsky's visit as January 1848 (it could only have been a year later), this hardly seems sufficient to disregard entirely the only first-hand evidence we have. See Leonid Grossman, *Zhizn i Trudy Dostoevskogo* (Moscow-Leningrad, 1935), 54; Belchikov, *Protsesse*, 265.

† The reference is to a book published in Leipzig in 1875, which contained some documents pertaining to the Petrashevsky affair. It was entitled: *The Society for Propaganda in 1849 (Obshchestvo Propagandy v 1849)*.

had arrived. He promised to take part in the battle at the appointed time and place; to come equipped with firearms, or cold steel, or both; and to fight "without sparing himself" for the success of the cause.[22] Speshnev asserted that this document stemmed from his past study of secret societies, and had never been meant to be used. Luckily for him, no copies of it were turned up in the various searches by the secret police. The authorities, though, were properly skeptical of Speshnev's explanation and pressed him for more details.

It was only Speshnev, among all those under arrest, who was threatened with the use of more severe methods of extracting information. Permission was requested of Nicholas I to put him in shackles if this became necessary; but though the request was granted, it was never, so far as the record shows, put into practice. Under the threat, however, Speshnev disclosed the existence of the smaller groups that had grown out of the Petrashevsky "Fridays," and also the secret conversations with Chernosvitov and Mombelli: none of this had been known before. These new leads succeeded in throwing the commission off the scent of the "Russian Society"; but the oath gives us a lurid glimpse into the kind of society that Speshnev would have formed, and allows us to imagine some of the atmosphere of its deliberations. Dostoevsky was speaking very seriously when, thirty years later, he remarked in the *Diary of a Writer* that while he could never have become a "Nechaev"—the *leader* of a clandestine revolutionary group that murdered one of its members in 1869—"as for becoming a Nechaevets, I can't certify, perhaps, possibly . . . in the days of my youth."[23]

5

Dr. Yanovsky became aware of a notable change in the character of his friend Feodor Dostoevsky between the end of 1848 and the time of his arrest three months later. "He became somewhat melancholy," he writes, "more irritable, more touchy, ready to quarrel over the merest trifle, and very often complained of giddiness." Yanovsky reassured his patient that there was no organic cause for these symptoms, and predicted that his gloomy state of mind would probably soon pass away. To which Dostoevsky replied: "No, it will not, and it will torture me for a long time. For I have taken money from Speshnev (he named a sum of about five hundred rubles) and now I am *with him* and *his*. I'll never be able to pay back such a sum, yes, and he wouldn't take the money back; that's the kind of man he is." And Dostoevsky repeated several times, so that the sentence engraved itself in Yanovsky's memory: "Do you understand, from now on I have a Mephistopheles of my own!"[24] Dostoevsky, we may assume, was not a man to use his literary comparisons lightly. If he identified Speshnev with Mephistopheles, it must have surely meant that he felt he had been tempted, by a force stronger than he could resist, to embark on a dangerous and grandiose enterprise in which he might not otherwise have chosen to engage.

Just what Dostoevsky was feeling and thinking in these last few months of his freedom is difficult to determine with any certainty: the evidence is all inferential and quite contradictory. It is clear from Maikov's account, and from everything else we know, that Dostoevsky—passionately committed to the aim of liberating the serfs—had agreed to cooperate with Speshnev in his secret society. On at least one occasion, according to an eyewitness, when the question arose of what action to take if it proved impossible to free the serfs except through an uprising, "Dostoevsky, with his usual impressionability, exclaimed: 'And so let there be an uprising!' "[25] On the other hand, Milyukov recalls another debate over the perennial question of whether the people would be freed "from above" or "from below." Dostoevsky, according to this source, was among those who said that "our people would not follow in the traces of European revolutionaries, and, not believing in a new Pugachev revolt, will patiently await the resolution of their fate by the supreme power."[26] The best way to reconcile such conflicting accounts is to assume that Dostoevsky was genuinely beset by inner doubts over the course he had chosen—or which may have seemed to have chosen *him*—and that his various utterances faithfully portray the oscillation caused by his uncertainties.

This is all the more likely because, throughout these months, the risks and dangers of the enterprise must have begun to assail him once the first flare-up of the moment of decision had passed. The warnings of disaster given by Maikov in their nighttime conversation possibly began to sink in. Even long before this conversation, there is evidence that Dostoevsky had been continually anxious over the perils of his Petrashevsky involvement. It was he who first voiced the suspicion that Chernosvitov was probably a police spy; and he became increasingly uneasy about the unknowns who crowded into Petrashevsky's flat week after week. Haunted by the possibility of betrayal and arrest even for assisting at these relatively innocent Petrashevsky gatherings, whose toleration by the authorities for so long seemed to guarantee a certain security, how much more would he have been agitated, how much more a prey to extreme fluctuations of emotion, because of his relations with the Speshnev group!

There is still another piece of evidence provided by Yanovsky that must be taken into account. Both Dostoevsky and his brother Mikhail were visitors to Petrashevsky and to one of the smaller gatherings; both had always been more or less in agreement on all important questions. But Yanovsky noted that, after Dostoevsky began to see Speshnev frequently, this fraternal harmony was shattered. One day, Yanovsky overheard a quarrel in which Mikhail, now a dedicated Fourierist, told his brother firmly that he hewed to the line of this non-political credo. Dostoevsky urged him to read a book by Louis Blanc, and assured him that, if he did so, he would change his mind.[27] Since Louis Blanc was the great Socialist advocate of the use of state power to implement social change, one can deduce that the controversy had arisen over Dostoevsky's conversion to political activism under the influence of Speshnev. Writing years later of his brother in *Diary of a Writer*, and praising him for not having given anyone away during his incarceration (Mikhail was arrested, but released after two months), Dostoevsky stated that "although he took no part in anything, *he did know many things*."[28] The italics can be taken to imply that he had been made privy to the existence and the plans of the Speshnev group; and if so, Dostoevsky would have been constantly assailed, not only by his own misgivings, but by Mikhail's arguments and presages of disaster as well.

In the light of all this, we can better appreciate the full implications of what seems, at first sight, Dostoevsky's totally misleading statement to Yanovsky. To be sure, the loan itself was not the source of Dostoevsky's jumpiness and irritability. After all, Dostoevsky had been in debt often before (he was, as a matter of fact, rarely *out* of debt), and the indebtedness itself would not have agitated him so strongly. What disturbed him was the extra tie of *personal* obligation to Speshnev that the debt fastened on him, and which reduced the margin of inner freedom he would have liked to preserve. In this sense, Dostoevsky's explanation was by no means false—he indicated both the person and the event at the root of the trouble; but he could not of course reveal his conspiratorial commitment to the innocent doctor, whom he had refused even to take to Petrashevsky's. Moreover, the remark about Speshnev declining to take back the debt, even if Dostoevsky could afford to return it, hints at a suspicion—which may by this time have been based on some experience—that Speshnev was not a man easily to relinquish a hold he had once acquired over

271

another person. No wonder Dostoevsky was plunged in gloom and melancholy: he felt inextricably trapped in a labyrinth from which there was no escape except through catastrophe; and he later told his second wife that, if not for the providential accident of his arrest, he would certainly have gone mad.[29]

CHAPTER 19

The Palm-Durov Circle

During the last period of the existence of the Petrashevsky circle, the sudden popularity of the gatherings and the increase in their size led to the formation of several satellite groups organized to take account of differing interests. Such groups did not compete with the Petrashevsky circle, and their members, by and large, continued to attend the "Fridays"; but these were no longer the exclusive center of debate and discussion. Even though it is usual to associate Dostoevsky only with the parent body, in fact he practically ceased to frequent Petrashevsky's during his last two months of freedom. And if we are to understand the intrigues of the underground organization of which he is known to have been a member, we must follow him, as best we can, through the maze of testimony compiled about these minor groupings.

The Petrashevsky circle split into two main factions. One, the Kashkin circle, was composed of pure Fourierists who felt that too little time was spent in discussing and explaining the doctrines of the Master. It was they who arranged the famous banquet in honor of Fourier's birthday on April 7, 1849, and invited Petrashevsky to be one of the speakers. Dostoevsky, not a Fourierist, was neither asked to join this circle nor invited to the banquet. He belonged to another group—the Palm-Durov circle—composed of people whose interest in Fourier was minimal, and who, indeed, felt that there was already far *too much* discussion of his ideas at the regular Petrashevsky sessions.

What eventually became the Palm-Durov circle seems to have arisen from gatherings held during the fall and winter of 1848 at the home of Pleshcheev. These were casual and impromptu, and included all of the literati who came to Petrashevsky's, as well as most of the people known to have belonged to Speshnev's secret society (Speshnev himself, Dostoevsky, Mombelli, Grigoryev, Filippov, Vladimir Milyutin). On one such occasion, Herzen's essay *Petersburg and Moscow* was read by Milyukov, and Pleshcheev also read aloud—whether at the same meeting or another is not clear—a speech by Felix Pyat, the well-known radical French playwright and journalist

273

elected to the Constituent Assembly after the revolution of 1848. When the Dostoevsky brothers, as well as Danilevsky and Butkov, complained bitterly about the rigors of the censorship, Speshnev offered to arrange to have any works they wished to give him published abroad (probably through Chojecki, who intended to establish a Russian Free Press in the West). Mikhail Dostoevsky, however, flatly refused the proposition, and the others were confused and hesitant. This is by no means the only time we shall see Mikhail taking a firm public stand against outright illegality, while his brother remained in the background and, by his silence, at least implied consent and approval.

Sometime beginning in March 1848, or perhaps a bit earlier, many of the people who had met at Pleshcheev's decided to hold regular meetings, usually on Saturday, in the spacious apartment jointly shared by Alexander Palm and Sergey Durov. The first was a lieutenant in the Life Guards, who also, to increase his meager income, contributed to literary journals; the second, a few years older than most of the Petrashevtsy (he was born in 1816), was a graduate of the University of St. Petersburg and a free-lance writer and translator. There are conflicting accounts of why this group became dissatisfied with Petrashevsky and decided to unite independently. One version—which may be called "official," and was offered by all but one of the participants—maintained that it grouped people who were put off by Petrashevsky's narrow range of interests and fanatical fixation on social-political issues. Palm wrote in his deposition that the people who formed this group (including the two Dostoevskys) "discussing the evenings at Petrashevsky . . . and finding that they were sometimes tedious and monotonous because of the speeches, had the idea of organizing evenings devoted exclusively to music and literature. When Mombelli asked whether Petrashevsky would be invited, Durov said: 'Petrashevsky, like a bull, sticks to philosophy and politics; he has no understanding of fine art and will only spoil our evenings.' "[1] Dostoevsky himself told the authorities ingenuously that the Palm-Durov circle arose out of a plan to publish a literary almanac, which required all the literati to meet together very often for discussion.[2]

This account cannot of course be taken at face value; but neither is it entirely false. The Palm-Durov circle did group the people who had argued with Petrashevsky over literature, and who refused to consider art only a means for transmitting "useful" social ideas. It is also true that a literary almanac was being planned (such a publication, if successful, could be very profitable) and a good deal of time at the meetings *was* devoted to reading literary works. Music was also regularly performed because the group included a pianist, two violoncellists, and a singer; part of the subscription paid by each guest (three silver rubles a month) was even used to rent a piano. A number of people in the Palm-Durov circle were undoubtedly attracted by these innovations, which provided a welcome relief from the more Spartan social-political atmosphere at Petrashevsky's.

There is, however, another version of the origin of the circle that comes from Speshnev. He told the investigators that Dostoevsky and Pleshcheev once paid him a visit "and said that they wished to meet with their acquaintances in some place other than Petrashevsky's, where it was boring, and one spoke only about learned subjects and one hardly knew the people, so that it was dangerous to utter a word; that they would invite only those among their acquaintances who they were sure were not spies, and that he, Speshnev, could do the same. This society he [Speshnev] could only label as one formed because of fear of the police."[3] These words put a different complexion on the entire organization, which could hardly have been conceived only as an assembly of aesthetes desiring to escape from the burden of politics. The group—or at least some of its members—knew very well that it would be preoccupied with matters other than purely literary or artistic.

2

Much of what went on in the Palm-Durov circle is still obscure, and will probably continue to remain so unless new material is uncovered. Some facts, however, are indisputable. The most important is that this circle included *all* the members of Speshnev's secret society (there is some doubt about Milyutin, but he was absent from Petersburg in the early spring of 1849). Another is that the secret society and the Palm-Durov circle are not identical. The Speshnev group, as will appear, tried to mobilize the circle for the purposes of reproducing and distributing revolutionary propaganda (the plan outlined by Dostoevsky during his midnight visit to Maikov); but they never succeeded in doing so. Finally, there is no doubt that Dostoevsky, as a member of the secret society, was immersed in conspiratorial activity all through this period.

The first meeting of the Palm-Durov circle, at the beginning of March, had a very pronounced literary-musical character. Both hosts took the occasion to read some of their own works—Palm a story entitled *Tragicomedy, or Brother and Sister*, and Durov "a dramatic story" called *A Petersburg Don Juan* (which sounds like a physiological sketch). He also read his own introduction to a new edition of the works of his uncle, the early nineteenth century satirical dramatist Khmelnitsky. Most revealing, however, was Durov's reading of his translation of Auguste Barbier's *Chiaia*, a long narrative poem with a distinct social-political edge. It is in the form of a dialogue between the painter Salvator Rosa and a fisherman plying his trade in the bay of Chiaia, near Naples, who discuss the unhappy state of their country groaning under despotic rule. The painter has lost hope and bitterly bewails the passivity of the people; but the sturdy fisherman, a man of action, is convinced that one day

> En mon golfe divin je ferai bonne pêche,
> Aux rives de Chiaia, sur ce sable argenté,
> Dans mes larges filets viendra la Liberté.[4]*

Even if the meetings had really been meant to be as free of politics as was claimed, it is clear that the literary tastes of the participants allowed for no such exclusion. And, in fact, talk about the liberation of the serfs and the tyranny of the censorship flowed as freely there as at Petrashevsky's. Moreover, one incident at this very first meeting is highly significant. Mombelli, a member of the Speshnev society, told the circle that its reunions would unquestionably be considered those of a social-political "club," whatever the participants may have intended. Hence, he suggested, they might as well form a mutual-assistance society—presumably the same kind of organization that he had discussed a few months previous during the secret negotiations with Petrashevsky. This early attempt to introduce an overtly political note, however, was not well received. Mombelli ran into severe resistance from those attracted to the group because of its literary-musical character and, though he did not insist, but for several weeks afterwards he was not present at the Palm-Durov reunions.

Exact chronology is difficult to establish for the events at these meetings, but there is additional information regarding some literary discussions in which Dostoevsky took an active part. Once, we learn from Milyukov, Dostoevsky's old favorite Derzhavin—the court poet of Catherine the Great—was sharply criticized. "Someone declared that he saw in [him] much more a bombastic rhetorician and servile panegyrist than the great poet he was proclaimed to be by his contemporaries and by scholastic pedants. At this, F. M. Dostoevsky leaped up as if stung and exclaimed: 'What? Can you deny that

---

* "I shall have good fishing in my heavenly gulf / By the banks of Chiaia, on the silvery sand / Liberty will come into my spacious nets."

Derzhavin has his flights of poetic inspiration? Look here, is this not great poetry?'—and he recited from memory the poem *Rulers and Judges* with such passion, with such enthusiasm, that everybody was carried away by his declamation, and without further commentary the stature of the singer of Felitsa [Catherine] rose in general esteem." *Rulers and Judges*, it should be noted, is a version of the 81st Psalm (the 82d in the Bible of Western Christians), admonishing earthly rulers to deal justly and charitably with the humblest of their subjects. "On another occasion," writes Milyukov, "he read several poems by Pushkin and Victor Hugo that were similar in theme and imagery, and proved, in a masterly fashion, to what extent our poet was artistically superior." Dostoevsky also read aloud the uncensored version of Pushkin's *The Village*, with its evocation of the dawn of a radiant new day for Russia when serfdom would be abolished "by the hand of the Tsar."[5]

The next important event in the history of the circle occurred approximately three or four weeks later, sometime toward the end of March. Pavel Filippov, another Speshnevite, suggested that it was time for the members of the group, now that they had come to know each other so well, to think of sharing their social-political ideas with others. He proposed that "they undertake, as a united effort, the composition of articles in a spirit of liberalism [which meant "revolutionary" in those days] concerning questions that touch on the contemporary condition of Russia, in a juridical and administrative sense." It was necessary, Filippov explained, to strip bare "all the injustice of the laws . . . [and] all the corruption and deficiencies in the organization of our administration."[6] Once such articles had been written, they could be reproduced on a home lithograph and distributed. Another member of the circle, F. N. Lvov, was a staff captain in the Army who taught chemistry at a school for cadets. He declared himself willing and able to set up an apparatus of this kind, and promised to make an estimate of the costs.

This proposal, enthusiastically supported by Grigoryev, Mombelli, and Speshnev, seems to have been accepted. Topics were taken by each of the members of the circle according to their predilections, and Dostoevsky assumed the obligation to write an exposition of Socialism. The initial excitement caused by Filippov's proposal, however, soon gave way to sober second thoughts. Opposition to his plan came to the fore in the days following the reunion, and was voiced most vigorously by Mikhail Dostoevsky. If we are to believe his brother, some dissatisfaction was exhibited, if not openly declared, at the moment the idea was first suggested. "I am not sure, perhaps I am mistaken," he told the commission, "but it seemed to me that half of those present did not speak out against Filippov's idea only because they were afraid the others would suspect them of cowardice, and they wished to reject the proposal not directly but in some sort of indirect fashion."[7]

Dostoevsky's testimony on this point is extremely interesting, not only because remarks like the one just cited anticipate certain scenes in *The Devils*, but also because a careful reading of what he says reveals his own complicity. For it is remarkable that Dostoevsky never states anywhere, as he could easily have done, that *he personally disapproved of Filippov's idea*. Instead, he reports on the disapproval of others—particularly his brother—and then associates himself with this disapproval *so that the entire Palm-Durov circle should not break up entirely*. "The next day [after the meeting] my brother told me that he would no longer go to Durov's if Filippov did not withdraw his proposal; he told Filippov the same thing, I remember, when he met him about two days later. I noticed, by my own observations, that many would act in the same way as my brother. I positively know, at least, that Durov wished to end his evenings as quickly as possible. Finally, when we met the next time, I asked for the floor and talked them all out of it, assuming in my talk a tone of light mockery and sparing as much as possible everyone's susceptibilities."[8]

Dostoevsky's intervention on this issue of the lithograph has often been cited as proof that he was among those who opposed Filippov, and hence could not be considered in favor of revolutionary action.[9] There is, however, another equally plausible explanation that should not be overlooked. From his own words, and from the testimony of others, it is clear that his brother took the lead in openly rejecting the plan for a lithograph. And if we assume that this proposal sprang from the attempt of the Speshnev society to manipulate the Palm-Durov circle, whose literary-musical character it was using as a screen for its activities, then Dostoevsky's testimony and behavior take on quite a different meaning. When the Speshnev group became aware that the Palm-Durov circle might dissolve entirely, Dostoevsky was assigned (or took on himself) the job of smoothing matters over so that the group could continue to be used as a cover. The commission, it is relevant to note, distinguished very sharply between the two brothers and was not impressed by Dostoevsky's speech against the lithograph. Mikhail was freed two months after the investigation began, and was even indemnified for his loss of income.*

---

* Much attention has been paid recently to the possibility that Mikhail Dostoevsky may have "betrayed" the Petrashevtsy because he was released after several

Feodor was sentenced for, among other reasons, "the attempt, along with others, to write works against the government and circulate them by means of a home lithograph."[10]

Despite Dostoevsky's effort to calm the agitation, the Filippov proposal marked a turning point in the history of the Palm-Durov circle. Both hosts became increasingly uneasy about continuing the gatherings; and when Durov asked impatiently if they could not be held elsewhere, Mombelli suggested they might assemble at Speshnev's in the future. Mombelli's behavior, as we shall see more clearly in a moment, was not distinguished by conspiratorial prudence; and though the idea was a reasonable one—Speshnev was a wealthy bachelor living alone in spacious quarters, who could easily have received the circle—it probably sprang from an unreflecting impulse to keep the group together at all costs. For the Palm-Durov circle to have met at Speshnev's, however, would have negated its usefulness to his secret society. Refusing to entertain the proposition, he offered only to arrange a dinner the following week to demonstrate his good will. Two or three further meetings were held in the Palm-Durov apartment, but both men were anxious to terminate them. Just before the roundup of the Petrashevtsy on April 22, 1849, Palm wrote to all members canceling the next date and Durov made sure not to be home that evening.

3

From Dostoevsky's account of the Filippov proposal, one has the impression that it was very rapidly rejected. In fact, however, an interval of several weeks went by during which it continued to be discussed. Also, while the mention of the lithograph first arose in connection with the idea of writing articles on "the contemporary condition of Russia in a juridical and administrative sense," nobody seems to have taken this assignment very seriously. Dostoevsky did not pro-

---

months and indemnified by the government with two hundred rubles. Such a suspicion was first voiced by A. S. Dolinin, and then repeated by Leonid Grossman and others.

A recent article, however, which includes the official documents concerning his case—never before published—clears him of all such accusations. Nothing in the record indicates that Mikhail Dostoevsky gave information damaging to any of the other prisoners. It is also noted that General Dubelt, the head of the secret police, followed the invariable practice of paying informers only thirty rubles—the reward of Judas—and that the reputation of Mikhail Dostoevsky did not suffer at all during his lifetime, even though he made no secret of having received compensation for the time he spent under arrest. Indeed, other radicals were indignant at the miserliness of the sum awarded, given the needs of his family. For the documents and other relevant references, see "Sledstvennoe Delo M. M. Dostoevskogo–petrashevtsa," in *Dostoevsky: Materiali i Issledovania*, ed. G. M. Fridlender, I: 254-265.

duce his exposition of Socialism, nor were any of the other promised articles forthcoming. However, several manuscripts did appear in the next few weeks that seemed eminently suitable for propaganda purposes, and the question of the lithograph was debated in connection with the possibility of their reproduction and distribution.

Not surprisingly, the first manuscript of this kind to surface was written by Grigoryev, a lieutenant in the Horse Grenadiers and a member of the Speshnev society. Called *A Soldier's Conversation*, it was first read at Speshnev's dinner for the Palm-Durov circle. This little work is a physiological sketch consisting of a brief descriptive introduction and then a monologue. The speaker, a peasant-veteran of the Russian Army reduced to beggary, has taken refuge from the freezing cold of a Petersburg winter in a guardhouse. Invited by the younger soldiers to recount his life, in return for warmth and food, he does so in simple, peasant language. His fate had been decided when, having attacked a landowner who had abused his sister, he was shipped off to the Army as punishment. A soldier in 1812, he had participated in the invasion of Europe and gotten a taste there of another kind of life. He speaks wonderingly of what he had seen in France, where the people had thrown out a king and "now they do not want Tsars and run things for themselves, just like we do in the villages."[11] The sketch is full of this sort of pseudo-naive social protest, couched in terms that peasants would understand and calculated to appeal to their mentality and values. It is, to use the modern term, an early example of agit-prop literature.

Grigoryev's literary effort caused a good deal of discussion at Speshnev's. Mikhail Dostoevsky advised him to destroy it, but others urged him to make it even more sharp and forceful. The version we have is probably a reworking of the original, whose conclusion, Grigoryev said, "had been more moderate."[12] Without naming those who encouraged him to strengthen it, he mentions having lent a copy to Mordvinov, who passed it on to Speshnev before it was returned. The only copy of the work unearthed by the investigating commission was found among Speshnev's papers; and Grigoryev said that Speshnev had asked his permission to read *A Soldier's Conversation* "practically in the public street." Feodor Dostoevsky did not join his brother in warning Grigoryev (he explicitly denied ever having spoken to the latter about his manuscript), and he pretended not to have known who the author was and what was being read at Speshnev's because no announcement had been made in advance.

There is every reason to believe that Grigoryev's work was only one example of the kind of material being produced by the Speshnev group for propaganda purposes, and which they were also encouraging others to produce. A manuscript by Filippov—which never saw the light, but was found among his papers—is exactly of the same character: a new, revolutionary version of the Ten Commandments, written in a combination of Church Slavonic and modern Russian. Each commandment is interpreted in a manner to persuade the reader (or listener) that a revolt against oppression and social injustice is in conformity with the will of God. The authorities were particularly disturbed by Filippov's comments on the sixth commandment, which "said that if peasants kill their master, they are obeying the will of God; that whoever goes to war is sinful, and the Tsar in particular sins when he leads his people to commit murder."[13] Such material could only have been intended for circulation among the peasantry, and particularly, perhaps, the *raskolniki*. Dostoevsky, who included in his deposition a long and laudatory analysis of Filippov's character, was surely aware of its existence and may well have taken a hand in its composition.

From the evidence gathered about Speshnev's dinner, it appears that he had not originally intended to have Grigoryev read *A Soldier's Conversation* on that occasion; instead, he had expected Alexander Milyukov to present his translation and adaptation of some chapters from Lamennais's famous *Paroles d'un croyant*. But Milyukov never showed up, and Grigoryev was called on to fill the gap. These facts indicate that Speshnev had been in contact with Milyukov (not, so far as we know, a member of his secret society) about his plan to translate this work, and had encouraged him to do so. Milyukov read his version a week or so later at a Palm-Durov meeting; and it is easy to see how well it fits into the pattern of propaganda material favored by the Speshnevites. Lamennais's work, written in a French that attempts to imitate the majesty of the biblical Hebrew, is a powerful and moving "New Christian" attack on social injustice and inequality. Milyukov used a stately Church Slavonic for his rendering, and gave it a homespun Russian title—*The New Revelations of the Metropolitan Antonio*. Dostoevsky, who had certainly also encouraged Milyukov's efforts (he may have informed Speshnev about the project), told the translator that Lamennais sounded much better in the severe Church Slavonic than the original. In its new guise, the work which Harold Laski once called "a lyrical version of the *Communist Manifesto*"[14] was no doubt felt to be very well suited to stir up the latent dissatisfactions of the Russian peasant by its appeal to the egalitarian roots of primitive Christianity.

There is still another work that the members of the Palm-Durov circle spoke about reproducing and distributing. Belinsky's famous *Letter to Gogol* had been written in the summer of 1847 as an answer to Gogol's *Selected Passages* (more accurately, as an answer to a letter of Gogol's about Belinsky's unfavorable reaction to the book), and was then circulating in manuscript. Pleshcheev, who had gone to Moscow in mid-March for family reasons, obtained a copy there and sent it to Dostoevsky through Durov. He also told a group of students at the University of Moscow, from whom he probably obtained the text, that "it is necessary to stir up self-consciousness in the people, and that the best means to do this would be to translate foreign works into Russian, adapting them to the speech-style of the simple people and distributing them in manuscript. And who knows, maybe some way will be found to print them. A society in Petersburg had been formed for this purpose, and . . . if we [the students] wished to cooperate with it we could begin with Lamennais's *Paroles d'un croyant*."[15] From a letter of Pleshcheev's to Dostoevsky, we know that Milyukov had promised to send a copy of his translation to Moscow. Pleshcheev asks Dostoevsky to tell Milyukov to hurry, and that "the sooner the better. . . . There are people here who sympathize with our ideas about the possibility of action."[16] Both Belinsky's *Letter* and Milyukov's translation were read at the same meeting of the Palm-Durov circle in early April.

However, even though Lvov estimated that the costs of a home lithograph were well within the means of the circle, the idea of setting one up was finally rejected. It may have been in the course of these discussions—perhaps in his speech against the lithograph—that Dostoevsky made the enigmatic remarks recorded in the testimony of Golovinsky. Dostoevsky is quoted as having said, at one of the meetings in early April, "that one should not act illegally against two points; one should not condemn society, and [should] work on it not by gall and mockery but by revealing one's own shortcomings." A draft version of these words reads: "Dostoevsky condemned an (illegal) kind of action (against two points) and said that all the blame was heaped on the government and not society; that before condemning, one should be better oneself."[17]

Commentators have leaped on this testimony as evidence that Dostoevsky was beginning to flinch under pressure, and was already advocating his famous doctrine of "self-purification through suffering" as a means of changing society for the better. But the meaning and context of these fragmentary statements is very obscure; and Golovinsky—singled out by the commission as one of the most hostile and un-cooperative of all the prisoners—may well have been only trying to exculpate a friend. If uttered, however, the words are of great interest because they coincide with an inner evolution observable—as we shall see in later chapters—both in *The Landlady* and, more emphatically, in *Netotchka Nezvanova*. Both these works show Dostoevsky shifting some of the onus for unhappiness and human misery to the moral failures or weaknesses of individuals themselves, and thus removing it from society; to this extent one may see here the first intimations of the doctrine of self-purification. There is no evidence, however, that *at this time* Dostoevsky was undergoing any social-political change of heart, or that his commitment to the aims of the Speshnev group was in any way faltering. No hint of repentance or remorse shows up in his deposition, although many other defendants *did* blame themselves and beat their breasts in humiliating contrition.

It was after the plan for a lithograph was defeated that, we may infer, the Speshnevites decided to act alone. Filippov, with funds provided by Speshnev, began to order the parts for a handpress in various establishments in Petersburg. It is not clear whether these parts were taken to Speshnev's quarters and, after his arrest, smuggled out to Mordvinov (not called in for questioning until several months later), or whether they were at Mordvinov's in the first place. The authorities learned about the handpress from both Filippov and Speshnev, each of whom tried to shield the other by taking the blame for the idea; both insisted that only they had been involved in the plan. Dostoevsky, when questioned about the handpress, adroitly evaded the issue. "The question speaks of a *home printing press*. I never heard anything from anybody at Durov's about *printing*; yes, or anywhere else. . . . Filippov suggested a *lithograph*."[18] Not finding any trace of the handpress, and unable to establish that others were involved in attempting to set it up, the commission made no further effort to pursue this line of inquiry. The existence of the Speshnev secret society was never discovered; and Dostoevsky later told his biographer Orest Miller that "many circumstances [of the case] completely slipped from view; *an entire conspiracy vanished*."[19]

4

The police spy Antonelli furnished his superiors with a detailed, informative, and quite objective account of the last seven meetings of the Petrashevsky circle. Most of this material is not relevant for our purposes; but Dostoevsky was present at two of these meetings (April 1 and April 15), and what occurred on one other evening throws some light on the people with whom he was most closely associated. In general, the activities of Dostoevsky and his friends (whether or not known to be members of the Speshnev society) were dedicated to radicalizing the sluggish Petrashevsky meetings and stirring their members to address themselves to the immediate revolutionary issue: the liberation of the serfs.

At the meeting of March 25, only Mikhail Dostoevsky was present (Antonelli lists a "Dostoevsky," but the commission accepted Feodor's denial that he was in attendance). Antonelli, who arrived a bit late, reports on a dispute between Durov and Filippov already in progress. The issue at stake involved the technique of propaganda. Should one attack the laws and the Tsar directly, or try to arouse enmity only against the lower officials with whom the people were in actual contact? Durov was in favor of attacking the source of evil directly because the lower officials were themselves oppressed and should not be made to bear the brunt of the blame. Filippov, on the other hand, vigorously maintained that the people were already so terrorized of higher authority that any propaganda directed against "the source of the evil" would be useless. People "will run away from you waving their arms and stopping up their ears." This argument sounds very much like an overflow of one that had been carried on in the Palm-Durov circle; and such an inference is supported by Filippov's clinching words: "Our system of propaganda is the best, and to depart from it means to depart from the possibility of putting our ideas into practice."[20] Filippov's allusion to "our system" seems to refer to those who were intending to circulate *A Soldier's Conversation* and his own commentary on the Ten Commandments; and it hinted at the existence of an organized propaganda group. Antonelli, who was far from being a fool, realized the importance of Filippov's declaration and underlined it in his report.

Petrashevsky was well aware of the activist current at work in his circle, and had perhaps gotten wind of the plan for propaganda being discussed among the Palm-Durov group. This may explain why, at the meeting of April 1, he launched a full-scale attack against the hotheads dreaming of the possibility of a putsch. Petrashevsky began by outlining three problems as being of paramount social-political importance. These were, he said, the abolition of censorship, the reform of the judicial system, and the liberation of the serfs. How should they be rated in urgency? Which one should receive the priority of the efforts of those working for progress? Petrashevsky's answer, which he developed with great ingenuity, was that the reform of the judicial system should be ranked as the first and most pressing goal.

So far as the censorship was concerned, Petrashevsky expressed sympathy for those who had to struggle with its tentacles; but he refused to regard it only negatively. In his view, it did some good by eliminating stupidities and absurdities and compelling writers to watch over what they said very carefully. Many books, he remarked with a touch of malice, "even though deserving a place in the history of literature because of their talent," serve, all the same, as "obstacles in the development of mankind and to the achievement of the goal so dear to all of [us]."[21] So much for the literati among his audience, Dostoevsky included! The liberation of the serfs, to be sure, was a question of great seriousness; but it involved the lives of only twelve million people. On the other hand, a reform of the courts so as to ensure public hearings and trial by jury would have a happy effect on the destinies of sixty million people. Every Russian had had to suffer from the corruption and inequities of the present legal system. Its reform would correspond to the wishes of the vast majority of the people, and stood the best chance of being implemented.

The fiery twenty-year-old Golovinsky, whom Dostoevsky had brought along that evening for a first visit to Petrashevsky's, bounded to his feet after this and launched into a passionate refutation. Even Antonelli was impressed: "Golovinsky spoke with heat, with conviction, with genuine eloquence, and it was evident that his words came straight from the heart." He said that "it was sinful and a shame against humanity to look on indifferently at the sufferings of twelve million unhappy souls. That everybody's idea should be to try to liberate these oppressed sufferers. That the liberation of the serfs presented no particular difficulties because they themselves at this moment recognized all the burden and all the injustices of their situation and were striving to free themselves in every way."[22]

Golovinsky's arguments reveal how concretely Dostoevsky and his friends had been mulling over the social-political situation. It was impossible for the government to liberate the serfs, Golovinsky maintained, because if it did so with land, it would have to pay compensation to the gentry. But for this the necessary funds were lacking. If it liberated the peasants without land, or refused to compensate the gentry for their loss of revenue, it would be behaving in a revolutionary fashion (meaning it would stir up opposition in one or another class), and would thus be acting against its own political stability. The obvious conclusion was that the liberation of the serfs could only come "from below."

Not discomfited in the slightest by this tirade, Petrashevsky took the floor after dinner to question whether the peasants were as unhappy with their lot as Golovinsky believed. A good half of them, who paid rent to their landlords rather than furnishing services, probably preferred this arrangement for economic reasons. The taxes they would be forced to pay if liberated would certainly exceed their quitrent. Further, the liberation of the serfs would probably lead to a class conflict that might result in a military or a clerical despotism. "To bring about the improvement of the judicial system," Petrashevsky concluded, "was much less dangerous and more realizable."[23] Golovinsky, perhaps replying to Petrashevsky's remark about class war, observed that a change of régime could not occur all at once and that a dictatorship would probably be necessary during the period of transition. Outraged at talk of dictatorship, and a declared admirer of the republican institutions of the United States, Petrashevsky retorted that he would be the first to raise his hand against any dictator.

This heated interchange brought into the open the conflict between the activists around Speshnev and the Fourierists or moderates for whom Petrashevsky spoke. It also uncovers some of the agitated atmosphere and extreme political conclusions being drawn in Dostoevsky's immediate circle. Political democracy was a very secondary consideration in their ideology, and they contemplated the idea of a revolutionary dictatorship—no doubt exercised by a body similar to Speshnev's secret central committee—without repugnance. Where Dostoevsky stood is perfectly clear: Antonelli records that he intervened to support Golovinsky.

5

Two weeks later, the same argument was resumed in another form during the famous session at which Dostoevsky read Belinsky's *Letter to Gogol*, which he had already read twice at the Palm-Durov apartment. Dostoevsky explained that he brought the letter to Petrashevsky's because, just after he had picked it up from Durov, Petrashevsky had walked in and inquired about the bundle of manuscript in his hand. Dostoevsky told him what it was, and spontaneously offered to bring it along when next he came for a visit. This may have been true; but if so, Dostoevsky could not have found a more propitious moment to introduce the weight of Belinsky's *Letter* in the controversy already raging over tactics. Belinsky's epistle is the most powerful indictment against serfdom ever penned in Russian, and Dostoevsky and his friends used it very effectively to reinforce their argument that serfdom was too morally intolerable to be endured a moment longer.

Dostoevsky read two of Gogol's letters as well as Belinsky's text, and the effect of his rendition, as described by Antonelli, was sensational. "This letter [of Belinsky] produced a general uproar of approval. Yastrzhemsky shouted, at all the passages that struck him: 'That's it! That's it!' Chirikov, though he did not say a word, smiled all the time and muttered something to himself. Balosoglo went into hysterics, and in a word, the whole group was electrified."[24] The copy read by Dostoevsky belonged to Filippov, but the latter explained that it had been made from the one furnished by Dostoevsky, who then took both copies back and asked him "to keep [the matter] a secret."[25] Dostoevsky also passed the text to Mombelli, who, with incredible rashness, gave it to his regimental scribe and asked him to make several more copies. This evidence that Dostoevsky was actively circulating and propagandizing Belinsky's *Letter* weighed very heavily against him.

Gogol's *Selected Passages* is a very curious book, which still continues to baffle and irritate admirers of his work. Here the erstwhile pitiless satirist of Russian life displays his conversion to a religious pietism which, if it continues to remain aware of social injustice, nonetheless sees the only remedy in the inner striving of each Christian soul for moral self-improvement and self-perfection. The work was an abrupt slap in the face for all those who believed (as did many Slavophils, not to mention the progressive Westerners) that serfdom was incompatible with genuine Christianity. Belinsky was outraged by the book, not only because of its possible social repercussions, but also as a personal insult—a betrayal of everything he had fought for under the banner of Gogol's name. He could not, of course, attack the book too violently in public print; but when he received a private letter from Gogol expressing surprise at his unfavorable reaction, his anger burst forth in a raging flood of invective. Herzen called this white-hot torrent of words Belinsky's last "testament," and even Lenin, in the late nineteenth century, still continued to admire the fiery ardor of its indignation.[26]

Despite its reputation as a revolutionary manifesto, however, Belinsky's *Letter to Gogol* is far from being ideologically extreme, and its indignant rhetoric should not be allowed to conceal that its concrete demands are relatively moderate. Moreover, for reasons that remain unclear, Belinsky responds to Gogol in the accents of a Utopian Socialist "New Christian," even though he had presumably by this time abandoned the "sentimental" values of this credo for a more "rational" ideology. Whether this was only a tactic to reply to Gogol's own "Orthodox Christian" position, or whether it reflects the genuine inner uncertainty in Belinsky that Dostoevsky depicted, is difficult to decide.* Whatever the reason, Belinsky's view of Christ as moral revolutionary is completely in harmony with the moral-religious Socialist ideas that Dostoevsky shared with the Beketov circle and which he had never abandoned.

"That you [Gogol] base your teaching on the Orthodox Church," Belinsky writes, "I can understand: it has always served as the prop of the knout and the servant of despotism; but why have you mixed Christ up in this? What in common have you found between Him and any church, least of all the Orthodox Church? He was the first to bring the people the teaching of freedom, equality, and brotherhood and set the seal of truth to that teaching by Martyrdom."[27] Belinsky flatly contradicts Gogol's assertion that "the Russian people are the most religious in the world," and calls them, on the contrary, "profoundly atheistic"; but he means only that their religion is one of superstition and ritual rather than of true inward faith. "Superstition" (the purely external and mechanical performance of religious ritual) is barbarous and backward, but Belinsky makes clear that genuine "religiousness" can well go hand-in-hand with progress and enlightenment;[28] and no doubt Dostoevsky felt his own faith to be of such an "enlightened" variety. It is noticeable that one finds no Left Hegelian attack on religion *as such* in Belinsky's *Letter*, no rejection of it as a noxious hindrance to mankind's progress on the path toward self-realization and self-deification.

---

* A similar note is struck in Belinsky's last important essay, *A View of Russian Literature in 1847.* "The Redeemer of mankind," he writes, "came into the world for all men. . . . His loving and merciful glance was not offended by the sight of festering sores on a body barely covered by filthy rags. He, the Son of God, loved people with a human love and commiserated with their poverty and squalor, their shame, wickedness, vices and sins," etc.

The Soviet editor of the English translation of Belinsky I am using does not quite know what to make of this text. He excuses it by saying that Belinsky included it for the censorship. But Belinsky was not the man to betray his deepest convictions only to fool the censor. One should remember that, when he wrote these words, he knew that he was dying of tuberculosis. Belinsky, *Selected Philosophical Works* (Moscow, 1948), 420-421, 524.

Nor is Belinsky's *Letter* revolutionary in any Socialist sense at all; there is nothing in it calling for a fundamental transformation of society on new principles. It is a fervent democratic protest against despotism and serfdom, which does not go beyond political liberalism in its demands. What Russia needs, Belinsky tells Gogol, "is not sermons (she has had enough of them!), or prayers (she has repeated them too often!), but the awakening in the people of a sense of their human dignity lost for so many centuries amid the dirt and the refuse; she needs rights and laws conforming not with the preaching of the Church but with common sense and justice. Instead of which she presents the dire spectacle of a country where men traffic in men, without even having the excuse so insidiously exploited by the American plantation owners who claim that the Negro is not a man." Hence, for Belinsky, "the most vital national problems in Russia today are the abolition of serfdom and corporal punishment, and the strictest possible observance of at least those laws that already exist."[29] This is the "minimal program" that Belinsky actually advocated in the very last year of his life. Dostoevsky, it will be recalled, misleadingly said that he had "accepted" all of Belinsky's ideas in the late 1840s, depicting Belinsky in the context of that statement as a Left Hegelian atheist, incipient materialist, and moral determinist. But if we assume that he was really thinking about Belinsky's *Letter to Gogol*, his assertion becomes perfectly acceptable: he unquestionably accepted *these* ideas and *this* program with all his heart and soul.

Even though placed at a disadvantage by the wave of excitement caused by Dostoevsky's reading, Petrashevsky valiantly took the floor and tried to counter its heady effects. He returned to the question debated two weeks earlier, and argued once more that a change in the judicial system should take preeminence over all other issues. Antonelli found his reasoning this time "metaphysical," but said it boiled down to this: "One should not undertake any uprising without being certain at the start of complete success, which was not possible at the present time. While a reform of the judicial system could be achieved in the most legal fashion, by demanding from the government those things it could not refuse, being aware that they were just."[30] Golovinsky, taking a conciliatory line, pointed out that the liberation of the serfs might perhaps be obtained through the courts, particularly in the western provinces; and he asked permission to pursue this topic at the next two meetings. "In general," writes Antonelli with a flourish, "the meeting of the 15th, as the foreign newspapers express it, was *très orageuse*."[31]

April 22, the date of the last meeting at Petrashevsky's, was a day of pouring rain, and at about six o'clock Dostoevsky stopped in at Dr. Yanovsky's to dry off and drink a glass of tea. Yanovsky assumed that Dostoevsky was going to Petrashevsky's, and nothing was said that gave him any other impression. Dostoevsky even borrowed money for a cab because of the considerable distance between where Yanovsky lived and Petrashevsky's home. Either Yanovsky's memory played him false in this instance, or Dostoevsky was deliberately concealing his destination. For he spent the evening at Grigoryev's, perhaps talking over plans with him and others for the operation of the handpress.

At four in the morning he returned home and went to bed; but shortly thereafter was awakened by a faint metallic sound in the room. Opening his eyes sleepily, he saw standing before him the local police official of his quarter, sporting a pair of luxurious sideburns, and a lieutenant-colonel dressed in the light blue uniform of the secret police whose dangling sword was clinking against his boots. Told very politely by the officer to rise and dress, he did so while his room was searched and his papers sealed. A much-rubbed fifteen copek piece on his table attracted attention; and when Dostoevsky jestingly inquired whether it was counterfeit, it was solemnly added to the evidence. A sergeant was ordered to inspect the shelf above the stove and climbed on a table; but he fell down heavily as the cornice of the shelf gave way, and the search was given up. Finally, Dostoevsky was conducted to a waiting carriage, accompanied by the local police official, the lieutenant-colonel, his frightened landlady, and her servant Ivan, who was also frightened but "looked around with an air of stupid solemnity appropriate to the occasion."[32] When Dostoevsky left the room and entered the carriage, he stepped out of the relatively normal life he had been living up to that time—with the exception of his brief apprenticeship as an underground conspirator—and into an extraordinary new world.

This new world would strain Dostoevsky's emotional and spiritual capacities to the utmost, and immeasurably widen the range of his moral and psychological experience. What he had only read about previously in the most extravagant creations of the Romantics, whether metaphysical or social, would now become for him the very flesh and blood of his existence. He would know the creeping and chilling despair of total solitude in prison; he would feel the desperate anguish of the hunted; he would live through the terrifying agony of the condemned clinging desperately to the last precious moments of life; he would sink to the lowest depths of society, rub elbows with outcasts and criminals, and listen to the talk of sadists and murderers for whom the very notion of morality was a farce; and he would have instants of sublime inner harmony, moments of fusion with the divine principle ruling the universe, in the ecstatic "aura" preceding an epileptic attack. When he returns to society again and begins to rediscover himself as a writer, the horizon of his creations will now be defined by this new world and its overwhelming revelations. And this will enable him to create works of incomparably more profound imaginative scope than had been possible in the 1840s, when his only approach to such a world had been through its Romantic stereotypes.

PART IV

The Road to Self-Discovery

CHAPTER 20

The Double

To attain a proper perspective on Dostoevsky's minor fiction in the 1840s after *Poor Folk* is by no means an easy task. It is impossible, of course, to agree with the almost totally negative evaluation of his contemporaries, especially since we can discern, with the benefit of hindsight, so many hints of the later (and much greater) Dostoevsky already visible in these early creations. On the other hand, in rejecting what seems to us the distressing myopia of his own time, we should not fall into an equally flagrant and perhaps less excusable error. We should not blur the line between potentiality and actuality, and read this earlier work as if it *already* contained all the complexity and profundity of the major masterpieces. Some of the more recent criticism, especially outside of Russia, has fallen into this trap; and these slight early works—*The Double* is a good case in point—have sometimes been loaded with a burden of significance they are much too fragile to bear.

It should be stated at once that Dostoevsky's production between 1846 and 1848 can boast of no work that matches *Poor Folk* as a successful and fully rounded creation. Indeed, at the time of his imprisonment he was generally considered a writer who had failed lamentably to live up to his earlier promise. This prevalent opinion was of course unjust and untrue; but it is not as outrageous as it may seem at first sight. Between 1846 and 1848 Turgenev published a good many of the stories included in *A Sportsman's Sketches*; Herzen produced *Who Is To Blame?* and a series of brilliant short stories; Goncharov made his impressive début with *An Ordinary Story*, and followed it with a chapter from his novel in progress, "Oblomov's Dream"—and we have not yet mentioned either Grigorovich's two novels of peasant life, *Anton Goremyka* and *The Village*, or A. V. Druzhinin's *Polinka Sachs*, which raised the banner of female emancipation. Compared to the array of such works, Dostoevsky's publications seemed very small potatoes indeed; and the longer book that he counted on to reestablish his credit with the reading public, *Netotchka Nezvanova*, was never completed because of his arrest.

Part of Dostoevsky's problem was unquestionably his straitened circumstances, which required him to turn out work too quickly. Part was also his artistic restlessness and ambition, which impelled him to abandon the vein of sentimental Naturalism and, after the triumph of *Poor Folk*, to shift disconcertingly to what seemed an unhealthy fascination with mental disorder and to lyrical explorations of the theme of *mechtatelnost*. It is clear to us now that Dostoevsky was experimenting with styles and character-types that he was later to fuse together superbly. But it was difficult at the time not to feel that, compared with the other young writers on the rise, he had simply lost his way.

2

Dostoevsky's next important work, which followed hard on the heels of *Poor Folk*, was *The Double*. In May 1845, while putting the finishing touches to his first novel, he tells Mikhail that he already has "many new ideas"[1] for other works; and the initial conception of *The Double* was probably among them. From other references in letters, we know that he discussed the novel (as he called this long story) during the summer of 1845, and got down to work on it seriously in the fall. In a letter of October 1845, parodying the speech-style of the main character, he informs Mikhail that "*Yakov Petrovich Golyadkin* . . . [is] a rascal, a terrible rascal! He will not agree, under any circumstances, to finish his career before the middle of November. He has just cleared things up with Your Excellency, and, if it comes to that (and why not?), is ready to hand in his resignation."[2] But, as was to become usual with Dostoevsky, work dragged on longer than expected, and he was still revising at the end of January 1846 just a few days before the magazine version was published.

The origins of the novel, both in Dostoevsky's personal life and in literary tradition, are not difficult to discern. It is interesting to note that, in a letter referring to Netotchka Nezvanova, he remarks that this projected novel "will also be a confession like *Golyadkin*, but in another tone and style."[3] This observation is made in a context of some personal self-criticism which reminds one of Golyadkin because of Dostoevsky's protest against the view taken of him by others. "I am ridiculous and disgusting, and I always suffer from the unjust conclusions drawn about me."[4] Like his character again, Dostoevsky was subject to "hallucinations" which may very well have included delusions similar to Golyadkin's; and he was shy to a degree border-

14. A caricature (1848) showing F. M. Dostoevsky in conversation with his editor, A. A. Kravsky

Dostoevsky: "Allow me to ask whether you have read my story?"

Kraevsky: "I've read it; it's so-so, not bad, there are gaps here and there, a superficial view of the subject . . ."
(With deeply pondered seriousness) "You know, your story isn't really a story but a psychological study."

Dostoevsky: "Very true, sir . . . You perhaps have deigned to forget that this is the opinion of Mr. M[aikov], which I explained in the letter I sent you along with the story?"

ing on the abnormal. From Belinsky's already-quoted remark to Annenkov that, like Rousseau, Dostoevsky was also "firmly convinced
that all of mankind envies and persecutes him," we know that he
exhibited more than a trace of Mr. Golyadkin's paranoia.

Such aspects of self-portraiture in *The Double*, however, furnish
only one element of its composition; others were provided both by
Dostoevsky's own earlier work and by external literary influences.
There is, in the first place, an obvious continuity between the character of Devushkin and that of Golyadkin. During one of the crucial
moments of *Poor Folk*—at the point where Devushkin, in complete
despair, is summoned for his interview with the General—his feelings are described as follows: "My heart began shuddering within
me, and I don't know myself why I was so frightened; I only know
that I was panic-stricken as I had never been before in all my life.
I sat rooted to my chair—as though there was nothing the matter, as
though it were not I" (1: 92). Here is exactly the reaction of terror
that leads to the splitting of Golyadkin's personality and the appearance of the double: the internal process is simply given dramatic
reality.

Poor Folk thus constitutes the most obvious literary source for *The
Double*; but there are several others that should be mentioned. Dostoevsky's employment of the device of the *Doppelgänger* links his new
novel with E.T.A. Hoffmann; and the possible relations between *The
Double* and various Hoffmannian prototypes have been thoroughly
investigated.[5] The direct influence of Hoffmann, however, is much
less important than his assimilation by the Russian Hoffmannists as
it came to Dostoevsky particularly in the writings of Gogol. V. V.
Vinogradov has defined the subject of *The Double*, formally speaking,
as consisting of "a naturalistic transformation of the Romantic 'doubles' of Russian Hoffmannism,"[6] presumably on the analogy of the
naturalistic transformation of the sentimental epistolary novel in
Poor Folk. But *The Double* is much less original in this respect. Gogol
himself—not to mention others—had already begun this process of
"naturalistic transformation," and Dostoevsky simply carries it one
step further.

Golyadkin's courtship of the appetizing Klara Olsufyevna recalls
the similar infatuation of Gogol's Poprischin, in the *Diary of a Madman*, with the daughter of *his* office-chief. The young lady pays no
more attention to him than to the furniture in her father's bureau,
and the baffled Romeo ends up in a madhouse firmly believing himself to be the King of Spain. In another of Gogol's stories, *The Nose*,
this irreplaceable organ becomes detached from its proper location

on the face of collegiate assessor Kovalyov (who prefers the military title of major) and darts about town in the uniform of a much more exalted rank under the bewildered eyes of its former possessor. Both stories use the same technique of the fantastic grotesque combined with themes of social ambition that we find in Dostoevsky, who clearly is working in the same tradition.

These two stories, however, are by no means the only Gogolian sources for *The Double*. There is external evidence that Dostoevsky himself (as well as others) thought of his new work primarily in relation to *Dead Souls*. "Golyadkin is ten times better than *Poor Folk*," he writes Mikhail jubilantly on the day his new work was published. "They [Belinsky and the pléiade] say that after *Dead Souls* nothing like it has been seen in Russia. . . . You will like it even better than *Dead Souls*, that I know."[7] Dostoevsky evokes this linkage quite self-consciously in his original subtitle, *The Adventures of Mr. Golyadkin*, which recalls Gogol's *The Adventures of Chichikov*. Just as Gogol had written a mock-heroic account of Chichikov's "adventures" in trying to rise in the world, so Dostoevsky was doing the same for Mr. Golyadkin. The relation between *The Double* and *Dead Souls* has been more or less neglected because, in revising the story nineteen years later, Dostoevsky eliminated most of the traces pointing from one to the other. But the best way to understand *The Double* is to see it as Dostoevsky's effort to rework *Dead Souls* in his own artistic terms, just as he had already done with *The Overcoat*.

The effect he obtains, nonetheless, is quite different in the two cases, even though both are part of the same artistic endeavor to penetrate into the psychology of Gogol's characters and depict them from within. Golyadkin may be described as a composite of the timidity and pusillanimity of Poprischin imbued with the "ambition" of Chichikov; but the closeness of vision, the descent into his inner life, hardly creates any feeling of sympathy. The mock-heroic tonality taken over from *Dead Souls*, which Gogol used for purposes of broad social satire, is now applied to a world shrunk to the level of slightly off-color vaudeville farce; the picaresque adventure involves the search, not even for a large fortune, but for a slightly higher office post and acceptance into the charmed circle of a corrupt bureaucratic hierarchy. Dostoevsky thus once again takes his departure from a Gogolian model and intensifies its effect; but this time his aim is not to bring out more unequivocally the "humanitarian" component of the original. Rather, it is to reinforce Gogol's acute perception of the grotesque effects on character of moral stagnation and social immobility. The result is a new synthesis of Gogolian elements, transformed and recast not by sentimentalism but by a deepening of Hoffmannian fantasy into a genuine exploration of encroaching madness. In this way, Dostoevsky accentuates the humanly tragic aspect of Gogol's still relatively debonair portrayal of social-psychic frustrations.

3

In *The Double*, we are once more in the same *chinovnik* atmosphere, and confront the same world of the St. Petersburg bureaucracy, as in *The Overcoat* or *Poor Folk*. But Golyadkin is by no means an Akaky Akakievich or a Devushkin, living at the very edge of poverty and destitution. On the contrary, he is not impoverished at all, lives in his own flat with his own servant (rather than in a "corner" somewhere behind a screen), and has piled up a tidy sum in savings which he keeps at hand to gloat over for reassurance. Golyadkin's position in the bureaucratic hierarchy is by no means exalted, but he is nonetheless the assistant to the chief clerk of his office. As the story opens, he has just hired a carriage, outfitted his servant Petrushka with a livery, and is nervously making preparations to crash the birthday party of Klara Olsufyevna to which he has carefully *not* been invited.

In other words, Mr. Golyadkin has climbed high enough on the social ladder, at least in his own estimation, to aspire to climb a bit higher; he is suffering not from grinding poverty but from "ambition." Dostoevsky thus breaks the connection maintained in *Poor Folk* between Devushkin's poverty and his struggle for self-respect, and now emphasizes this latter motif. His focus, becoming internal and psychological, concentrates on the effort of Golyadkin to assert himself; but this inevitably brings him into opposition with the existing rigidities of the social order. And Dostoevsky's theme now becomes the crippling inner effects of this system on the individual—the fact that, to quote his feuilleton, Golyadkin "goes mad out of *ambition*, while at the same time fully despising ambition and even suffering from the fact that he happens to suffer from such nonsense as ambition."

The first several chapters of *The Double* give a brilliant picture of Golyadkin's split personality before it has disintegrated entirely into two independent entities. On the one hand, there is Golyadkin's evident desire to pretend to a higher social station and a more flattering image of himself—hence the carriage, the livery, the simulated shopping spree for elegant furniture as if he were a new bridegroom, even the marvelous detail of changing his banknotes into smaller denominations to have a fatter pocketbook. His pretension to the favors of Klara Olsufyevna is only an expression of this urge for upward mobility and ego-gratification, not its cause. Indeed, the novel originally contained a passage that explicitly motivates Golyadkin as indulging in ego-enhancing daydreams. Mr. Golyadkin, Dostoevsky wrote, "very much loved occasionally to make certain romantic assumptions touching his person; he liked to promote himself now and then into the hero of the most ingenious novel, to imagine himself entangled in various intrigues and difficulties, and, at last, to emerge with honor from all the unpleasantnesses, triumphing over all obstacles, vanquishing difficulties and magnanimously forgiving his enemies" (1: 335). Mr. Golyadkin as first conceived thus had a streak of Don Quixote in him, or, if one prefers, Walter Mitty.

This motivation was part of the original mock-heroic framework of the novel, which was eliminated in the revised version we are familiar with. Each chapter, for example, was introduced by a series of parodistic descriptive sentences outlining, in a format that began with *Don Quixote*, the action to come. "Of the awakening of the titular councilor Golyadkin," we read in the first chapter. "Of how he outfitted himself, and set forth on the path that lay before him. Of how he justified himself in his own eyes, and then correctly concluded that it was best of all to act boldly and openly, though not without nobility. Of where, finally, Mr. Golyadkin arrived to pay a call" (1: 334). This parody of the heroic convention is supplemented, in the unaltered last chapter, by another parody of the romantic intrigue of the sentimental adventure novel, with its eloping lovers escaping the vigilance of recalcitrant parents and Golyadkin cast in the role of reluctant seducer.

With one part of his character, then, Mr. Golyadkin likes to imagine himself as an all-conquering hero; but with another he knows that he is quite incapable of sustaining such a role, and is, in fact, as timid as a mouse. He shrinks from the sight of two young colleagues in the street as he is rolling along impressively in his carriage, and is positively petrified when overtaken by the smart droshky of his office superior, Andrey Filippovich. His reaction to this event releases the psychic mechanism—the same one we have already seen in Devushkin—that will soon lead to the appearance of the double. " 'Bow or not? Call back or not? Recognize him or not,' our hero wondered in indescribable anguish. 'Or pretend that I am not myself, but somebody else strikingly like me, and look as though nothing were the matter. Simply not I, not I—and that's all' " (1: 113). Golyadkin is pathetically unable to live up to the part he is trying to play, and can only escape from it by this evasion of responsibility; but the moment Andrey Filippovich disappears, the all-conquering hero comes to the surface again. "Then, suddenly recalling how taken aback he had been, our hero flushed as hot as fire, frowned, and cast a terrible defiant glance at the front corner of the carriage, a glance calculated to reduce all his foes to ashes" (*ibid.*).

It is clear from the very start that Mr. Golyadkin, for all his assumed heroism, is not setting out on the road to adventure with a light heart. And his visit to his German doctor, Krestyan Ivanovich Rutenspitz, reveals some of the reasons for his discomfiture. A young competitor, the nephew of Andrey Filippovich, has received the office promotion to which Mr. Golyadkin aspired, and is now the leading (and far more suitable) aspirant for the hand of the beauteous Klara. Mr. Golyadkin, unable to control his displeasure at these frustrating events, had created a scandal only a day or so before by overtly displaying his hostility to his rival and the latter's powerful uncle. Moreover, Golyadkin is also aware that word has gotten round of some disreputable behavior in his own past involving the German landlady of a lodging house where he had once lived. At the beginning of the novel, he is desperately trying to suppress his awareness of both these disturbing events, and has already transferred them, with paranoiac logic, into the idea that he is being hounded and persecuted, and that only *he* is acting openly, straightforwardly and honestly. The scene with the doctor thus serves to fill in the background of the action, to indicate that Mr. Golyadkin's behavior is distinctly abnormal, and to reveal the pathos of his plight when he suddenly breaks down and starts to weep.

Mr. Golyadkin's crisis is precipitated by his efforts to gain admittance to Klara's birthday party. The wonders of this occasion are described by the narrator in a splendid outburst of Gogolian mockery underlining the ludicrous mediocrity of the sphere to which Mr. Golyadkin aspires. "Oh, if I were a poet! Such as Homer and Pushkin, I mean, of course; with any lesser talent one would not venture—I should certainly have painted all that glorious day for you, O my readers, with a free brush and brilliant colors," etc. (1: 128). This passage is worth dwelling on for a moment because, aside from its interest as an example of Dostoevsky's rhetorical skill, it is also of some thematic importance. For the narrator makes clear, amidst all his flowery, self-negating phrases, that the group being celebrated is really a hotbed of bribetaking and corruption. The worthy Olsufy

Ivanovich, Klara's father and Golyadkin's patron, "is a hale old man and a privy councilor, who had lost the use of his legs in his long years of service and been rewarded by destiny for his devotion with investments, a house, some small estates, and a beautiful daughter," etc. (1: 129). Mr. Golyadkin's rival Vladimir Semyonovich, who has been promoted because of nepotism, inspires the remark that "everything in that young man . . . from his blooming cheeks to his assessorial rank, seemed almost to proclaim aloud the lofty pinnacle a man can attain through morality and good principles" (1: 130). Compared to such hardened reprobates, Golyadkin himself is the soul of innocence and virtue.

It is after Mr. Golyadkin has been ignominiously evicted from this worthy gathering that his double finally materializes. The arrival is preceded by another rhetorical set-piece, a parody of the style of the historical novel. "It was striking midnight from all the clock towers in Petersburg when Mr. Golyadkin, beside himself, ran out on the Fontanka Quay," etc. (1: 138). And the double comes on the scene when, as we are told explicitly, "Mr. Golyadkin was killed—killed entirely, in the full sense of the word" (*ibid.*). When he first looms out of the darkness of the stormy night, the double of Mr. Golyadkin unquestionably seems a purely psychic phenomenon. But there are certain scenes (such as those in the office) where the presence of an actually existing double is affirmed by other characters; and Dostoevsky deliberately keeps the reader in a state of uncertainty about how much of what occurs is the result of Golyadkin's hallucinations and growing loss of objective awareness. Whether the double is psychic or material, however, his function is never left in doubt: he is used to confront Mr. Golyadkin with everything the latter cannot endure to contemplate about himself and his own situation. This situation has been caused by his social temerity, the suspicions about his tawdry peccadillo in the past, and his fear of the consequences of having offended his superiors. Golyadkin's relation with his double mimics one or another of these three facets of his position vis-à-vis himself and his world, and sometimes several of them blended together in a superbly subtle admixture.

4

The first five chapters of *The Double* describe the "adventures" of Mr. Golyadkin trying to assert himself in the real world. The remainder, which begin a new sequence, depict his unsuccessful struggle to keep from being replaced by his double everywhere and finally sinking into madness. At first, the double is deferential, ingratiating, obsequious, and begs Mr. Golyadkin for protection. Such comportment is probably meant to recapitulate the start of Mr. Golyadkin's own career, when he must have behaved in the same fashion; the sad tale told by the double of early poverty and humiliation may be taken as a flashback to Golyadkin's own life. The subordinate status of the double expresses the position of relative self-confidence that Mr. Golyadkin has just managed to attain and which has nourished his "ambition." But then, after the double worms his way into Mr. Golyadkin's confidence and learns all his secrets, the double "betrays" him (as Mr. Golyadkin is "betraying" his superiors by his insubordination) and begins to act out Mr. Golyadkin's mingled hopes and fears.

The double obtains all the success in the office that Mr. Golyadkin would like to have had, constantly humiliates him by allusions to his amorous dalliance with the German landlady ("'he's our Russian Faublas, gentlemen; allow me to introduce the youthful Faublas,' piped Mr. Golyadkin junior, with his characteristic insolence"), is on the best of terms with Klara Olsufyevna, and baffles and frustrates the real Mr. Golyadkin in every possible way (1: 195). Some of the episodes are purely slapstick—such as the consumption of ten pies by the double on the sly, which requires Golyadkin, who has eaten only one, to pay for eleven and to suffer the embarrassment of a reprimand. But, for the most part, the double's behavior both mirrors the suppressed wishes of Mr. Golyadkin's subconscious and objectifies the guilt feelings which accompany them.

During the first part, Mr. Golyadkin's "ambition" dominates his feelings of inferiority and guilt and manages to keep them in check. The movement of the action shows him, however unsuccessfully, still trying to impose himself on the world despite its rebuffs. Once the double appears, however, the process is reversed, and we find Golyadkin striving by every means possible to prove himself a docile and obedient subordinate, who accepts the dictates of the authorities ruling over his life as, literally, the word of God. It is in this latter part of the work that Dostoevsky's social-psychological thrusts become the sharpest. Golyadkin struggles against becoming confused with his double, who behaves in a fashion that the real Golyadkin would dearly like to emulate but which he has been taught to believe is morally inadmissible. The double is of course "a rascal," but the *real* Golyadkin is "honest, virtuous, mild, free from malice, always to be relied on in the service, and worthy of promotion . . . but what if . . . what if they get us mixed up" (1: 172)! The possibility of substitution leads Mr. Golyadkin to accuse his double of being "Grishka Otrepeev"—the famous false pretender to the throne of the true Tsars in the seventeenth century—and introduces the theme of impostorship, so important for Dostoevsky later and (with its evocation of *Boris Godunov*) so incongruous in this context.

The more threatened Mr. Golyadkin feels because of the machinations of his double, the more he is ready to surrender, give way, step aside, throw himself on the mercy of the authorities and look to them for aid and protection. He is ready to admit that he may even truly be "a nasty, filthy rag"—though, to be sure, "a rag possessed of ambition . . . a rag possessed of feelings and sentiments" (1: 168-169). The inchoate phrases that tumble off his tongue are filled with the mottoes of the official morality of unquestioning and absolute obedience encouraged by the paternal autocracy. " 'I as much as to say look upon my benevolent superior as a father and blindly trust my fate to him,' " he tells Andrey Filippovich, in his desperate efforts to "unmask the impostor and scoundrel" who is taking his place. "At this point Mr. Golyadkin's voice trembled and two tears ran down his eyelashes" (1: 196). As the double, "with an unseemly little smile," tells Golyadkin in the important dream-sequence of Chapter 10: "What's the use of strength of character! How could you and I, Yakov Petrovich, have strength of character? . . ." (1: 185.)

This depressing process of Mr. Golyadkin's capitulation is lightened somewhat, in the final chapters, by his belief that he has received a letter from his beloved Klara setting a rendezvous for an elopement. Since Poprishchin was able to read the delightfully chatty correspondence of the two dogs Madgie and Fido in the *Diary of a Madman*, there is no need to speculate, as so many commentators have done, about the ontological status of the epistle that represents Mr. Golyadkin's heart's desire. Or does it really? Some of the most genuinely amusing moments in the novel occur as Mr. Golyadkin, taking shelter from the pouring rain under a pile of logs, sits waiting in the courtyard of Klara's house for her to keep their supposed assignation—and, at the same time, inwardly protests against such an unforgivable breach of the proprieties.

" 'Good behavior, madame'—these are his ruminations—'means staying at home, honoring your father and not thinking about suitors prematurely. Suitors will come in good time, madame, that's so. . . . But, to begin with, allow me to tell you, as a friend, that things are not done like that, and in the second place I would have given you and your parents, too, a good thrashing for letting you read French books; for French books teach you no good,' " etc. (1: 221). The original version of *The Double* concludes shortly thereafter as Mr. Golyadkin is driven off in a carriage by his doctor, Krestyan Ivanovich, who suddenly becomes a demonic figure and—but we are left hanging in the air! The work is abruptly cut short at this point on a note of Gogolian flippancy and irresolution: "But here, gentlemen, ends the history of the adventures of Mr. Golyadkin" (1: 431).

5

The haunting brilliance of Dostoevsky's portrayal of a consciousness pursued by obsessions of guilt and ultimately foundering in madness has been recognized from the very first moment that *The Double* was published. What occurs in the novella is clear enough in its general outline; but there has been continual controversy over just how to interpret its significance. Does Mr. Golyadkin's double represent, as one Soviet critic has put it, "the meanest and most degrading qualities of [Golyadkin's] soul"?[8] Or does the double, as another has argued, represent only a hallucinatory image of the external social forces that threaten Golyadkin's existence as an individual?[9] It seems to me impossible to choose between such alternatives because, if Golyadkin's existence *is* threatened socially, it is precisely because he has dared to assert himself in a manner that *does* reveal something about his soul (or his subconscious).

Such disagreements arise, however, because it is genuinely difficult to pinpoint Dostoevsky's moral focus in *The Double*. It is, for example, clearly impossible to identify with Golyadkin sympathetically to the same degree as with the kindhearted and self-sacrificing Devushkin. If nothing else, the nature of his "ambition" as revealed through his double is hardly one of which Dostoevsky wishes us to approve unconditionally—as he makes amply clear by the unflagging mockery of his narrative tone. At the same time, the radical critic of the 1860s, N. A. Dobrolyubov, is undoubtedly right in characterizing Golyadkin as one of the early Dostoevsky's "downtrodden people," struggling desperately to assert their dignity and individuality in a social hierarchy that refuses to acknowledge their right to the luxury of such sentiments.[10] But how can we reconcile Dostoevsky's irony with his compassion?

One way of dealing with this problem has already been indicated in passing. For all his taunts at Golyadkin, Dostoevsky is even more sarcastic about the exalted eminences of the bureaucratic realm that glimmer before Golyadkin as his unattainable ideal. *They* are clearly corrupt to the core, and lack even that minimum of moral self-awareness responsible for Golyadkin's plight.[11] Golyadkin at least *believes* in the pious official morality to which everybody else gives lip service; and his struggle with the double is an effort to defend that morality from being betrayed. In fighting off the double, Golyadkin is really fighting off his own impulses to subvert the values presumably shared by his official superiors. This is probably what Valerian Maikov meant when he said that Golyadkin perishes "from the consciousness of the disparity of particular interests in a well-ordered society," i.e., his realization of the impossibility of asserting himself as an individual without violating the morality that has been bred into his bones and which keeps him in submission.

Such an answer, however, is only partially satisfactory, and still leaves in the dark the question of why Dostoevsky should have treated Golyadkin satirically at all. Here, it seems to me, we must have recourse to a document that has been neglected in this connection—Dostoevsky's remarks on "necessary egoism" in his feuilleton. Russian life, he said there, offered no outlet for the ego to assert itself normally, and the Russian character as a result tended not to exhibit a sufficient sense of its own "personal dignity."* Such an analysis contains exactly the same mixture of sympathy and critical reserve that he incorporates in *The Double*: there is commiseration for Golyadkin's desire to rise, but also a certain disdain for his inability to sustain the combat and for the paltriness of his aims. Dostoevsky's genuine indignation at the crippling conditions of Russian life, in other words, did not turn him into a moral determinist willing to absolve the victims of all responsibility for their conduct. Indeed, his very portrayal of a figure like Devushkin implied that debasing social conditions were far from being able entirely to shape character. As a result, Dostoevsky's work of this period often contains a puzzling ambiguity of tone because a character is shown *simultaneously* both as socially oppressed and yet as reprehensible and morally unsavory because he has surrendered too abjectly to the pressure of his environment.

The same ambiguity of attitude is also reflected in the narrative technique of the story, which has attracted a good deal of attention in Soviet criticism. Both Bakhtin and Vinogradov have rightly noted that, while the narrator begins as an outside observer, he becomes more and more identified with Golyadkin's consciousness as the story progresses.[12] More recently, it has been stressed with equal justice that this identification is never total: the narrator keeps his distance by parodying Golyadkin, even when he uses the character's own

* See pp. 232-233.

speech-style and seems to limit himself to Golyadkin's horizon.[13] This mixture of identification and raillery creates the peculiar blend of tragicomedy in *The Double* that most readers find so difficult to accept (if we are to judge from the inclination of critics to read the work exclusively in one or the other perspective), and yet which exactly translates Dostoevsky's own point of view.

6

As we know, Dostoevsky's high hopes for the success of *The Double* were quickly dashed. The work met with a withering fire of criticism for two main reasons. One was simply because—to quote the Russian Symbolist Andrey Bely, both a connoisseur of Gogol and an admirer of Dostoevsky—"*The Double* recalls a patchwork quilt stitched together from the subjects, gestures, and verbal procedures of Gogol."[14] In this respect *The Double* suffered from being too imitative; but in another it was too original to be fully appreciated. For the complexities of Dostoevsky's narrative technique did pose a special problem for the readers of his time.

The Double is narrated by an outside observer who gradually identifies himself with Golyadkin's consciousness and carries on the narrative in the speech-style of the character. Its verbal texture thus contains a large admixture of stock phrases, clichés, mottoes, polite social formulas, and meaningless exclamations, which are obsessively (and excessively) repeated as a means of portraying the agitations and insecurities of Mr. Golyadkin's bewildered psyche. This is a remarkable anticipation, unprecedented in its time, of Joyce's experiments with cliché in the Gerty McDowell chapter of *Ulysses*, and of what Sartre so much admired in John Dos Passos—the portrayal of a consciousness totally saturated with the formulas and slogans of its society. The effect in *The Double*, however, was a tediousness and monotony that Dostoevsky's readers were not yet prepared to put up with either for the sake of social-psychological verisimilitude or artistic experimentation.

And even though Dostoevsky's narrative technique *per se* no longer creates any barrier for the modern reader, the complexity of Dostoevsky's attitude still creates problems of comprehension. In isolating Golyadkin's imbroglio from any overt social pressure, and by treating both Golyadkin *and* the world he lives in with devastating irony, Dostoevsky tends to give the impression that Golyadkin is simply a pathological personality who has only himself to blame for his troubles. Even Belinsky, who might have been expected to grasp the social implications of Golyadkin's psychology as Dostoevsky had explained them in his feuilleton, remarked that his life would not really have been unbearable except "for the unhealthy susceptibility and suspiciousness of his character," which was "the black demon" of his life.[15] In other words, Dostoevsky was simply portraying a case of paranoia and mental breakdown with no larger significance than that of a case history.

This judgment set the pattern for a view of Dostoevsky's early work (and for much of his later work as well) that dominated a good deal of Russian criticism until the end of the nineteenth century. In 1849 P. V. Annenkov, echoing Belinsky, accused Dostoevsky of being the leader of a new literary school (which included his brother Mikhail Dostoevsky and Butkov) specializing in the portrayal of "madness for the sake of madness."[16] Annenkov severely criticized this unhealthy taste (as he saw it) for rather sensational and grotesque tragicomedy, in which he could discern no more serious or elevated artistic aim. Such an accusation was of course unfair to Dostoevsky, whose "abnormal" and "pathological" characters can all be seen, on closer examination, to make a social-cultural point. But Dostoevsky perhaps relied too much on the reader to grasp the ideological implications of his psychology, and to understand that the "abnormalities" of his characters derived from the pressure of the Russian social situation on personality. The result was an artistic lack of balance that led to a good deal of misunderstanding, and has caused unceasing critical disagreement.

7

The overwhelmingly hostile reaction to *The Double* spurred Dostoevsky to think of revising it almost from the moment of its publication. This did not prove possible before his arrest, however, and he could only return to the project in the 1860s. His notebooks contain a series of jottings, not so much for a revision as for an entire recasting of *The Double*, with the same characters and sentimental intrigue but with new ideological motifs deriving from this later period. Golyadkin would become a radical, attend a meeting of the Petrashevsky circle, "dream of being a Napoleon, a Pericles, the leader of the Russian revolt," learn about science and atheism—and his double would denounce the radicals to the authorities.[17] These notes show how the double-technique had begun to expand in Dostoevsky's imagination, and to incorporate the major ideological motifs that would characterize his post-Siberian creations. But he never got around to rewriting *The Double* as he had intended, perhaps because the same artistic impulse was already being channeled into new productions. It was only while finishing *Crime and Punishment* in 1866 that he revised *The Double*, and gave it the form it has retained ever since.

For the most part, Dostoevsky's revisions consist in little more than cutting out many of the verbal repetitions that were the butt of so much criticism.[18] More important, however, is that he also eliminated the entire mock-heroic framework. He struck out all the chapter headings, and for the original subtitle—*The Adventures of Mr. Golyadkin*—substituted *A Petersburg Poem*. This concealed the stylistic relation to *Dead Souls*, and was perhaps meant to dissociate *The Double* from the elements of radical social critique and the memories of Belinsky still connected with Gogol's novel. The new subtitle did not betray the work (Golyadkin *was* a Petersburg type), and was vague and noncommittal enough not to be compromising; it had the further advantage of correctly assigning *The Double* its place in the Russian literary tradition initiated by *The Bronze Horseman*.

In addition, Dostoevsky shortened the work by a full chapter and simplified the intrigue, excising almost entirely the motif of the double as "Grishka Otrepeev" (this was given much more space in the original), and truncating Golyadkin's xenophobic fear of being poisoned in a plot woven by his German ex-landlady in cahoots with the equally German Krestyan Ivanovich. Some passages connected with this poison-motif are much more obscure in the final version. By contrast, the central social-psychological emphasis was strengthened by a change in the ending, which now provides chilling confirmation of Golyadkin's madness and ultimate destination, along with a last thrust of his sense of guilt: "You get free quarters, wood, with light and service, which you deserve not" (1: 229).

Despite his dissatisfaction with *The Double*, Dostoevsky always continued to maintain his belief in its great significance. Writing to Mikhail in 1859 about his plans to improve it, and to publish it with a new preface, he says: "They [his critics] will see at last what *The Double* really is! Why should I abandon a first-rate idea, a really magnificent type in terms of its social importance, which I was the first to discover and of which I was the herald?"[19] Twenty years later, in the *Diary of a Writer*, he confessed that "my story was not successful"; but he continued to claim that "its idea was clear enough, and I have never contributed anything to literature more serious than this idea. But I was completely unsuccessful with the form of the story."[20] Just what Dostoevsky means by "form" here is unclear; but one suspects that he was referring to the "fantastic" aspect of *The Double*, the uncertain oscillation between the psychic and the supernatural. The double as an emanation of Golyadkin's delirium is perfectly explicable; the double as an actually existing mirror-image of Golyadkin, with the identical name, is troubling and mysterious. Dostoevsky never leaves any doubt in the future about this alternative: his doubles will either be clear-cut hallucinations, or they are what may be called "quasi-doubles"–characters who exist in their own right, but reflect some internal aspect of another character in a strengthened form.

It is not difficult to understand, though, why Dostoevsky thought the "idea" embodied in *The Double* to have been of such importance. Golyadkin's double represents the suppressed aspects of his personality that he is unwilling to face; and this internal split between self-image and truth–between what a person wishes to believe about himself, and what he really is–is Dostoevsky's first grasp of a character-type that became his hallmark as a writer. Golyadkin is the ancestor of all of Dostoevsky's great split personalities, who are always confronted with their quasi-doubles or doubles (whether in the form of other "real" characters, or as hallucinations) in the memorable scenes of the great novels. The similarity of personality-structure between Golyadkin and his successors–such as the underground man, Raskolnikov, Stavrogin, and Ivan Karamazov–has led some critics to interpret *The Double* as if all the philosophical and religious themes of the mature Dostoevsky were *already* present in its pages;[21] but this is an untenable anachronism. The Dostoevsky of the 1840s is not that of the 1860s and 1870s, and his frame of reference in *The Double* is still purely social-psychological.

The mature Dostoevsky later felt that the discovery of this "underground" type, whose first version is Golyadkin, constituted his greatest contribution to Russian literature. For such a type represented, in his view, the true state of the Russian cultural psyche of his time, hopelessly split between competing and irreconcilable ideas and values. In this early phase of Dostoevsky's work, Golyadkin's intolerable guilt feelings at his own modest aspirations disclose the stifling and maiming of personality under a despotic tyranny. Later, the same character-type will be employed to exhibit the disintegrating effect of the atheistic radical ideology imported from the West on what Dostoevsky believed to be the innately moral-religious Russian national character, with its instinctive need to believe in Christ and God. Dostoevsky's notes for the rewriting of *The Double* thus reveal the process both of continuity and metamorphosis between his earlier and later creations. The character-type discovered in the 1840s, and used to further the progressive social ideals of the Natural School, becomes in the later Dostoevsky a weapon against radical ideology. One may perhaps conclude from this that its ultimate source lay in Dostoevsky's own psychology; but such a conclusion provides only the beginning, not the end, of a comprehension of Dostoevsky's achievement.

CHAPTER 21

Petersburg Grotesques

Several other short stories that Dostoevsky produced at this time are written from the same perspective as *The Double* and raise much the same critical issues. In each, Dostoevsky continued to explore the pathological effects on personality of the Petersburg world of giant chancelleries and terrified *chinovniks*, but without portraying this environment as in any way *specifically* responsible for the abnormalities he depicts. The result was a continuation of the confusion that had been caused by *The Double*, and an increasing dissatisfaction with Dostoevsky's works by all the critics and, presumably, by most of the reading public as well.

Hard on the heels of *The Double* followed *Mr. Prokharchin*, which was hardly calculated to recoup any of Dostoevsky's waning fortunes. This story probably arose from one of the projects that Dostoevsky mentioned he was working on in April 1846 for the anthology that Belinsky planned to issue. It was to be called *A Tale of Abolished Chancelleries*; and since the prospect of losing his position frightens the wits out of poor Mr. Prokharchin, it is likely that his story represents a development of this idea. Written during the summer of 1846, *Mr. Prokharchin* appeared in the October issue of *Notes of the Fatherland*. Before publication, however, it was badly mangled by the censorship. Dostoevsky complains, in a letter to Mikhail, that "all the life [in it] has vanished. What remains is only a skeleton of what I read you. I renounce my story."[1]

2

Mr. Prokharchin (the name evokes, ironically, someone who spends an excessive amount of money on food) is a rather distressing mélange of macabre farce with the much more harrowing themes of insecurity and guilt. The story once again concerns a poor, downtrodden clerk on the lowest level who is, at first, presented somewhat like Akaky Akakievich as a totally insensitive and subhuman grotesque. All his life he has either attended punctiliously to his insignificant duties in his bureau, or lain on his filthy mattress in the sordid

313

boardinghouse where he vegetates "without talking or having any sort of relations with anyone" (1: 246). His existence becomes transformed, however, when an unexpected external shock—similar to Akaky's need to acquire a new overcoat—suddenly intrudes on his life. A new group of younger lodgers invade his formerly peaceful abode, and Mr. Prokharchin's inevitable involvement with them precipitates his catastrophe.

These new lodgers, several of whom are endowed with comic Gogolian names, are described in a tongue-in-cheek narrative tone whose strained jocularity clashes unpleasantly with the sinister quality of the events that take place. "We must observe here that all of Ustinya Feodorovna's new lodgers without exception got on together like brothers; some of them were in the same office; each one of them by turns lost all his money to the others at faro, preference, and *bixe*; they all liked in a merry hour to enjoy what they called the fizzing moments of life in a crowd together; they were fond, too, at times of discussing lofty subjects, and though in the end things rarely passed off without a dispute, yet as all prejudices were banished from the whole party the general harmony was not in the least disturbed thereby" (1: 241).

Mr. Prokharchin, though, *does* disturb the general harmony by his silence and his surliness. His fellow lodger Mark Ivanovich, "an intelligent and well-read man," diagnosed the source of his unpleasant demeanor, to the general satisfaction of all, as being caused by "nothing else but lack of imagination" (*ibid.*). No one seems to have noticed the importance of this motif of "imagination" in *Mr. Prokharchin*; but it is, in my view, the key to this somewhat baffling story. For Dostoevsky's point is to show that the inhuman grotesque Mr. Prokharchin is really more "imaginative" than all his stupidly complacent detractors put together.

With the exception of one exploration of his subconscious, Mr. Prokharchin is presented only indirectly through his violent and abusive reactions to the prodding and suggestions of his companions. The casual remark that he might be "hiding" something in the box under his bed leads to an explosion, and then to a continual litany about being "a poor man" who has to support a "sister-in-law." But this is only the beginning. For the jolly *bons vivants* begin to torment him purposely with all sorts of stories and rumors about new requirements for retaining his job that he could not possibly satisfy. Mr. Prokharchin, as a result, is simply driven out of his mind. He ends up "looking more like the shadow of a rational being than that rational being itself," and finally—after a rebuke from his office-superior, frightened by his strange behavior—entirely disappears from sight (1: 243, 245).

What occurs to Mr. Prokharchin during this escapade is not recounted, but may be pieced together from hints and allusions. The lodgers hear that he has been seen among the crowd at a fire, and in the company of a well-known "drunken cadger"—a discharged clerk turned beggar and toady, who is quite shameless in his servility. Mr. Prokharchin is brought back to the lodginghouse totally unconscious, but mysteriously not either drunk or the victim of a beating. And while he lies on his bed in a delirious trance, a whole series of disconnected images—some stemming from his past life, and others connected with the fire—run through his brain crazily to reveal the secret of his life.

These images are of a fellow clerk, barely able to feed his large family, who looks at Prokharchin reproachfully as the latter hides his salary, and for whose plight, somehow, he feels responsible; of an old woman "in wretched bark shoes and rags" driven into the street by the fire, shouting that "her own children had turned her out and that she had lost two coppers in consequence"; of a peasant who incites the crowd watching the fire against Mr. Prokharchin, and whom he recognizes as a cabman he had cheated "in the most inhuman way" five years ago. With its visible threat of possible destruction and destitution, the fire had evidently given the final push to Mr. Prokharchin's already pathological sense of insecurity, and has stirred up his subconscious fears of an imminent vengeance by fate for all his misdeeds. He regains consciousness only to feel that his own head is on "fire." Leaping up from the bed clutching "his precious mattress," he has to be dragged back by main force (1: 250-251).

The remainder of the story recounts the irritated attempts of his fellow lodgers to "reason" with Mr. Prokharchin, who, they now realize, has lost his wits completely because of their "playful" conspiracy. Nothing will convince him that his life is secure, and he turns every idea offered to reassure him into an additional confirmation of his fears. Even the "drunken cadger," who is unexpectedly able to subdue Mr. Prokharchin by telling him sternly to "behave yourself . . . or I'll give you away," has no success with persuasion. When he yells at Prokharchin that the latter is a "free-thinker" for imagining he will simply be discharged from his post without cause, Prokharchin uses this to feed his persecution complex: " 'Well, that's just it. . . . I am meek. I am meek today, I am meek tomorrow, and then all of a sudden they kick me out and call me a free-thinker.' " The upshot is a complete breakdown of Mr. Prokharchin again, who subsides into hysterical tears and then unconsciousness, "so that they almost thought of sending for a doctor" (1: 256, 258).

The story concludes in an atmosphere of grisly farce as the "drunken cadger" and another lodger invade Mr. Prokharchin's corner during the night, begin to slit his mattress, and are stopped as he gives a bloodcurdling shriek and rolls under the bed. He dies during the ensuing confusion, whose significance becomes clear only when money begins to drop from a rent in the mattress made by the culprits. Even after his death, however, Mr. Prokharchin's head plunges through a broken slat in the bed, "leaving in view only his two bony, thin, blue legs, which stuck upwards like two branches of a charred tree." It is as if he were continuing to protect his precious treasure (described in an epic enumeration recalling a similar catalogue in *Eugénie Grandet*) from beyond the grave; and two lodgers crack their heads together, in a low-comedy routine, when they crawl under the bed to investigate the situation. The "clever" Mark Ivanovich, asked to explain why Prokharchin had not deposited his money in a bank, replies with his predictable penetration: " 'He was too simple, my good soul, he hadn't enough imagination.' " But the narrator sees him otherwise: "There was a look of deep reflection in his face, while his lips were drawn together with a significant air, of which [Mr. Prokharchin] during his lifetime had not been suspected of being capable." And the lodgers gathered round the bedside seem to hear the rasping ejaculations of his voice again as if he were threatening to come back to life (1: 260, 262).

3

Mr. Prokharchin is a difficult story to interpret for a number of reasons. In the first place, Dostoevsky was determined to be laconic because of the charges of long-windedness leveled against *The Double*; and, as Valerian Maikov suggested, he probably did not leave himself enough room to develop his theme. Also, if the censors caused as much damage as Dostoevsky claimed, this would have added considerably to the obscurities that make the work so much of a puzzle. Finally, so far as one can judge, Dostoevsky seems to have been aiming at an almost impossible goal in *Mr. Prokharchin*. Its nature may be suggested by a remark of Maikov's, made in a review of Butkov's *Petersburg Heights*, that Butkov was incapable of coping with "the gigantic task of *humanizing*, or in other words, *giving an artistic depiction of*, a scoundrel."[2] Pleshcheev, around the same time, also raised the question in a feuilleton of how to portray people "in whom every germ of goodness has been crushed by the terrible weight of the circumstances to which they have been sacrificed since childhood"; and his answer is that such people could be "humanized" only if the author delved into their inner lives.[3] In *Mr. Prokharchin*, it seems to me, Dostoevsky was wrestling precisely with this very dilemma, which represented a natural extension of the artistic and "philanthropic" objectives of the Natural School.

For Prokharchin's fellow lodgers, he is scarcely human at all and lacks "imagination"; but in point of fact, possessing far too much "imagination" for his own good, he has been haunted by the terror of insecurity all his life. Moreover, though his miserliness is a sordid and despicable trait, its existence does not mean that he has become completely dehumanized. We see that he is capable of feelings of pity and remorse (even though they have no effect on his conduct), and what brings on his final delirium is as much a guilty conscience as a fear of losing his treasure. This thematic point, however, does not really emerge because of the repulsive squalidness of Prokharchin himself, the gruesomeness of the details, and the difficulty once again, as in *The Double*, of locating any moral center in the work. Dostoevsky's irony undercuts the perspective of the lodgers about Prokharchin, but the latter is also treated—except in the one account of his delirium—only as an object of grimly sinister ridicule; and this self-negating clash of perspectives nullifies the single effort made to "humanize" Prokharchin from within. If we assume (consistently with everything we know about Dostoevsky at this time) that such "humanization" was intended, then the story must be pronounced a failure. Indeed, the impression created is rather that the author shares a good deal of the incomprehension and callousness that he presumably wishes to hold up to ridicule. This impression is further strengthened by the insertion, here and there, of a self-consciously "literary" stylistic flourish. Such passages are probably what prompted Belinsky to call the work "affected and *maniéré*," and they work to distance the reader even more firmly from any possible identification with Prokharchin as a suffering human being.

Whatever its deficiencies, however, *Mr. Prokharchin* is interesting for several reasons. Most importantly, it is Dostoevsky's first attempt to portray the psychology of avarice—a motif he will later develop on a grand scale in such works as *The Gambler*, *The Idiot* (the character of Ganya), and particularly in *A Raw Youth*, where the young hero is determined "to become a Rothschild." Avarice as a literary motif has a long history, and numerous prototypes for Dostoevsky's handling

317

of it have been suggested: Molière's Harpagon, Gogol's Plyushkin in *Dead Souls*, Pushkin's *The Covetous Knight*, Balzac's Papa Grandet. It can be assumed that Dostoevsky was familiar with all these predecessors; but Pushkin's poetic fragment is probably most closely related to his own treatment. Like Pushkin, Dostoevsky focuses on the *inner emotional need* satisfied by avarice, the need, in the case of Mr. Prokharchin, to secure and to defend a life inwardly threatened at every moment. No such need, to be sure, troubled Pushkin's covetous knight, who thoroughly enjoyed the feeling of limitless power over others given him by his wealth—the gloating *knowledge* that the world was at his command. Both Dostoevsky and Pushkin nonetheless emphasize the psychological importance of wealth as ego-support, even if in one case the support is needed because of genuine weakness and social vulnerability, while in the other it stems from an overriding sense of power.

To be sure, there is one hint of this Pushkinian linkage between avarice and the will-to-power in *Mr. Prokharchin*. When the lodgers realize that Mr. Prokharchin has become totally obsessed with himself, the "clever" Mark Ivanovich shouts: " 'Why, are you the only person in the world? Was the world made for you, do you suppose? Are you a Napoleon? What are you? Who are you? Are you a Napoleon, eh?' " (1: 257). This incongruous comparison surely is not meant to be taken seriously, but only to illustrate the exasperation that all have begun to feel at Mr. Prokharchin's stubborness. All the same, this has not prevented some critics from trying to read Mr. Prokharchin's avarice as if it were stimulated by a desire for power (at least over his own life).[4] Such an interpretation, however, once again views the early work too much in the light of Dostoevsky's later use of this motif, when the "covetous knight" equation of avarice with a will-to-power is perfectly clear and explicit. Nothing in the text of *Mr. Prokharchin* really justifies attributing anything that could properly be called a will-to-power to the pitiably deranged *chinovnik*. But it is striking to see how early—even if only ironically—Dostoevsky identifies the idea of a total and exclusively self-centered egoism with the symbolic name of Napoleon.

4

Another story that may be grouped in this category of Petersburg grotesques, is *A Weak Heart*. The chief character is a bureaucratic scribe (but this time a young man, rather than the middle-aged or elderly Devushkin, Golyadkin, and Prokharchin); once again he ends

in madness; and no more than in the case of Golyadkin or Prokharchin is the existing social order manifestly responsible for his mental
collapse. On the contrary, Dostoevsky even stresses the kindness and
generosity of his immediate superior, Julian Mastakovich, who is the
same high bureaucrat mentioned in the Petersburg feuilletons. But
this is only meant to accentuate the extent to which the character's
self-esteem has been crippled and crushed by the general conditions
of his life. *A Weak Heart* happily avoids some of the blemishes that
marred both *The Double* and *Mr. Prokharchin*. In this case, the character's inner struggle is not portrayed as a morally dubious self-assertion; nor is he so odious that *any* sympathy with him is impossible.
Moreover, Dostoevsky does provide a symbolic clue that connects his
character's abnormality to a wider social-cultural cause; but this is
still too vaguely allusive to offset the prevailing view that he loved to
dwell on psychopathology for its own sake.

Dostoevsky here takes one side of his earlier characters (the component of fear and submissiveness) and makes this, in an exaggerated form, the exclusive personality-trait of his new figure, Vasya Shumkov. Vasya is a small, delicate, slightly deformed clerk, who at the
beginning of the story informs his bearlike, rowdy but tenderhearted
roommate Arkady Ivanovich that he has just become engaged. The
relation between these two—the impulsive strength of the one, the
troubled wistfulness and melancholy sensitivity of the other—seems
like a faint pencil-sketch for the friendship between Razumikhin
and Raskolnikov in *Crime and Punishment*. Vasya's courtship has led
him to neglect some extra copying entrusted to him by his office superior and benefactor, Julian Mastakovich, who in the past had even
rescued him from military service.* Since his patron had been so
unusually kind to Vasya, he is overcome with a sense of guilt at the
idea of letting him down. In reality, the task confided to Vasya is
totally unimportant, and there is no objective reason whatever for
the overweening guilt-feelings that finally drive him mad.

The mood of the first part of the story, devoted largely to a visit of
the two roommates to Vasya's fiancée, is much like that of *Poor Folk*,
with its sentimental stress on the simple joys of humble, unpretentious

---

* This detail of the story has led some scholars to conclude that the character
of Vasya is based on that of Dostoevsky's friend and fellow writer, Yakov P.
Butkov. It was known that Butkov had been saved from being drafted only by the
intervention of A. A. Kraevsky, who purchased a substitute for him. Butkov was
also very poor, very humble, and lived in a constant state of fright and anxiety.
However, while Dostoevsky may have used this fact of Butkov's life for his own
purposes, the close resemblance of Vasya Shumkov to other Dostoevsky characters
argues against taking Butkov as the "source" of Vasya's creation. See the editorial
comments in 2: 475-476.

people who nourish such a commonplace (and yet so touching) image of earthly bliss. The narrator, even while underlining their naiveté, does so without a trace of superciliousness; his tone is one of humorous tenderness, not the grating sarcasm of *Mr. Prokharchin*. A hint is dropped of Vasya's concern over his special assignment, but Arkady sweeps away all worry in his exuberant joy at the great news of Vasya's betrothal. It is only in the second half of the story that the note becomes more menacing, and the focus shifts to Vasya's increasingly manic behavior and final breakdown. Vasya becomes possessed by the idea that, if his copying is not completed on schedule, his exemption from military service will be withdrawn. Such fear, the narrator makes clear, is groundless in this instance; but it nonetheless concretizes the very real menace hanging over those whose inferior social status subjected them to conscription.

Unlike *The Double*, where the narrator remained very close to the consciousness of Mr. Golyadkin, Dostoevsky does not give us any inside view of Vasya at all. He is seen primarily through the affectionate and increasingly perturbed eyes of his comrade Arkady Ivanovich, who serves as the center of consciousness; and Arkady's analysis of Vasya's character is crucial for understanding Dostoevsky's theme. In one exchange with Vasya, Arkady tells him: " 'Because you are happy, you want everyone, absolutely everyone, to become happy at once. It hurts you and troubles you to be happy alone. And so you want at once to do your utmost to be worthy of that happiness, and maybe do some great deed to satisfy your conscience' " (2: 38). What has undermined Vasya is not really any sense of being unable to meet his external obligation; it is rather that, for the first time in his life, he has become "happy." This has overcome him to such an extent that he has begun to feel "guilty"; and the burden of this guilt has been transferred to the neglected copying for Julian Mastakovich. Vasya, in other words, has been so beaten down by life that the attainment even of the simplest and most natural human satisfaction is enough to inspire him with a sense of guilt.

This is also the interpretation of the story in a review attributed to Mikhail Dostoevsky. "Weak and tender hearts," he writes, ". . . subordinate themselves to a crushing fate so completely . . . that they regard their occasional joys as the manifestation of something supernatural, as an illicit deviation from the ordinary course of events. . . . This is why even these very joys are poisoned for them . . . [because] conditions have been able to such an extent to humiliate them in their own view." The outstanding trait in all these heroes of the early Dostoevsky, the reviewer concluded, is "the sentiment of the awareness

of their inequality" (2: 477).* It might also be mentioned that Mikhail Dostoevsky himself gained a small reputation with stories related
in conception to those of his brother, though written in a humorous
rather than a tragicomic vein. For in his works too, insignificant incidents and events are blown up out of all proportion and become menacing simply because of the constant insecurity and fear of the "little
man" exposed to the caprices of an authority against whom no recourse is possible or even thinkable.[5]

A *Weak Heart* ends with the demented Vasya, saluting like a soldier,
being led away to an asylum under the grieving and bewildered eyes
of Julian Mastakovich and the rest of his office comrades. One clerk
in particular is terribly excited and "particularly distressed." He is,
we are told, "pale as a sheet, trembling all over and smiling queerly,"
and he insists to everyone, plucking at their elbows, "that he knew
how it had happened, that it was not so simple, but a very important
matter, that it couldn't be left without further inquiry," etc. In the
1848 version of the story, Dostoevsky adds: "In his circle, he [the
clerk] had the reputation of a desperate free-thinker"; but these words
were eliminated when he revised the text in 1865 and they no longer
appear in the editions generally read (2: 47, 416). It is clear that
Dostoevsky was trying to clue in the reader to seek for a more general
significance to Vasya's fate—a significance that might be considered
"free-thinking." The behavior of the agitated clerk is thus a preparation
for the epilogue, which concerns Arkady rather than Vasya and symbolically crowns the story.

Arkady goes to visit the family of Vasya's fiancée, and a tearful
little scene takes place as they all bemoan the madness that has
struck poor Vasya down. Then, on the way home, Arkady experiences
the famous "vision on the Neva"; this is the context in which Dostoevsky first uses the passage.† And if we accept the view that this
"vision" of Petersburg is organically linked with *The Bronze Horse-*

---

* Vasya's psychology seems to fit perfectly with Freud's description of those
people who are "wrecked by success." "As a rule," Freud writes, "people fall ill as
a result of frustration, of the non-fulfillment of some vital necessity or desire.
But with these people, the opposite is the case; they fall ill, or even go entirely
to pieces, because an overwhelmingly powerful wish of theirs has been fulfilled."
In one group of such cases, Freud explains, this paradoxical reaction occurs because "we find a sense of guilt or inferiority, which can be translated: 'I'm not
worthy of such happiness, I don't deserve it.'" Freud sees this feeling as a "ma-
terialization of our conscience, of the severe super-ego within us, itself a residue
of the punitive agency of our childhood."
These words apply very well to Vasya, except that his psychology is meant to
be understood in social rather than personal-familial terms. Sigmund Freud, "A
Disturbance of Memory on the Acropolis," in *Character and Culture*, ed. Philip
Rieff, 35.
† The text is quoted on p. 134.

man and the madness of Pushkin's Evgeny, then it is not difficult to
see what Dostoevsky was trying to convey. For it does not seem to
have been noticed that *A Weak Heart*—though of course in a gro-
tesquely miniature and sentimental-naturalistic key—exactly parallels
the main theme of Pushkin's poem. In both works, the joys of the
individual ("family happiness") are pitted against an obligation to
the state (Vasya's copying); both Pushkin's Evgeny and Vasya choose
the individual over the state (Vasya's neglect of his work because of
his betrothal); both go mad because the power embodied in Petersburg inevitably crushes the idyllic dream of a tranquilly mediocre
private existence. Dostoevsky's Petersburg, to be sure, is not that of
Pushkin, and instead of the splendors of imperial majesty our attention is drawn to the social stratifications of the city ("the refuges of
the poor, or the gilded palaces for the comfort of the powerful of this
world"). But the psychic consequences are the same in both cases, and
now not even any willful gesture of defiance (as in the case of Evgeny)
is required to stir up the terror of the Bronze Horseman's wrath.

From this point of view, we can understand the momentous effect
of the "vision" on Arkady: "He started, and his heart seemed at that
instant flooded with a hot rush of blood kindled by a powerful, overwhelming sensation he had never known before. He seemed only now
to understand all the trouble, and to know why his poor Vasya had
gone out of his mind, unable to bear his happiness." What is responsible is simply the order incarnated by Petersburg itself, the absolutism
that had destroyed Evgeny and had now succeeded in stamping out
the slightest spark of self-respect in those of even lower status. It is
little wonder that the effect of this "vision" on Arkady is disastrous,
and eradicates all of his previously cheerful and buoyant attitude toward life. "He became gloomy and depressed and lost all his gaiety"—
this is the sad and hopeless note on which the story ends (2: 48).

5

The two stories just discussed are Dostoevsky's most ambitious efforts
in the vein of the Natural School after *The Double*; all the rest are
little more than physiological sketches or comic anecdotes, and, most
often, combinations of the two.

In the fall of 1846, while still at work on *The Double*, Dostoevsky
dashed off an insignificant little story in one night called *A Novel in
Nine Letters*. It was intended for inclusion in the biweekly almanac
The Jester, to be edited by Nekrasov, Grigorovich, and Dostoevsky
himself; and its expected inclusion in the pages of a humorous

(which meant satirical) journal helps to explain its character. Written, like *Poor Folk*, in the form of an exchange of letters, the story is a comic anecdote belonging to the ample Russian tradition of plays and tales about gambling and cardsharping (for example, Gogol's *The Gamblers*). Like the play, Dostoevsky's story also employs the hoary comic *topos* of "the cheater cheated."

The anecdote concerns two swindlers in Petersburg who set out to fleece a wealthy young man from the provinces. One, an acquaintance of the young man's family, introduces him to the home of the other, who proceeds to clean him out thoroughly at cards every night. An arrangement had been made to divide the spoils, but the Petersburg cardsharp, a debonair man-about-town, avoids meeting his erstwhile accomplice and an exchange of letters takes place. These are amusing enough, as they contrast the increasingly absurd and farfetched excuses of the one for never being available with the growing suspicion and indignation of the other. At the dénouement, the cardsharp learns that he has been made a cuckold by his willing victim; the family friend also learns that his new wife, expecting a child, had previously been the young man's mistress. The letter of the wife to her ex-lover, full of genuine feeling, introduces an unexpectedly serious note; but the story is otherwise of little value except as an indication of Dostoevsky's range. This, as a matter of fact, is exactly how it was taken by Belinsky. "Belinsky said that he is now completely sure of me," Dostoevsky writes to Mikhail about this story, "because I can handle completely diverse material."[6]

Of much greater interest is *Polzunkov* (the name evokes someone crawling or creeping), which unites a farcical anecdote of bureaucratic skullduggery with a brief but penetrating character analysis of a down-at-heels ex-clerk who lives by playing the buffoon for his fellows. Beginning as a physiological sketch (a provisional title, *The Buffoon*, indicates its origin), it retains, in the tone of the frame-narrator, some of the impersonal, quasi-scientific stance appropriate to this genre. Polzunkov, classified as belonging to the order of "voluntary buffoons," arouses no sympathy in the narrator because "voluntary buffoons are not even to be pitied." What is interesting about him, however, is that he does not—or cannot—accept his degrading status. "He seemed afraid of jeers, in spite of the fact that he was almost getting his living by being a buffoon for all the world, and exposed himself to every buffet in a moral sense and even in a physical one, judging from the company he was in." The trouble with Polzunkov was that, while he was "what is called a 'rag' in the fullest sense of the word," no more than Mr. Golyadkin could he inwardly accept such a status, "and [he] actually had pretensions to respectability and personal dignity" (2: 5-6).

Polzunkov could thus never emotionally come to terms with his social position. Even though he lived by cadging, each appeal for a loan was a new martyrdom, and the narrator explicitly labels him "a comic martyr." "Everything was there—shame and an assumption of insolence, and vexation at the sudden flushing of his face, and anger and fear of failure, and entreaty to be forgiven for having dared to pester, and a sense of his own dignity, and a still greater sense of his own abjectness—all this passed over his face like lightning." The subtlety of this analysis already foreshadows the tormented dialectic of pride and humiliation in *Notes from Underground* (to mention only one example); and the resolution of this dialectic is also sketched with the same economy. "If he had been convinced in his heart (and in spite of his experience it did happen to him at moments to believe this) that his audience were the most good-natured people in the world, who were simply laughing at something amusing, and not at the sacrifice of his personal dignity, he would most readily have taken off his coat, put it on wrong side outwards, and have walked about the street in that attire for the diversion of others and his own gratification" (*ibid.*). In other words, the feeling of being accepted as an equal (later, the feeling of being genuinely loved as a spiritual equal) is the only solution for the torments of humiliation.

Polzunkov, as we have said, is a combination of a "physiology" with a comic anecdote, the latter delivered in the form of what Russians call a *skaz*, that is, a first-person oral narrative highly colored by the speech-style and personality of the narrator. Polzunkov, at this point, takes over from the frame-narrator and tells the sad tale of his downfall to the vast amusement of his audience. Resentful because he has unsuccessfully courted the daughter of his office superior in some provincial town, who is waiting for a more prosperous aspirant to her hand, Polzunkov threatens to inform about her father's peculations and takes a bribe to remain silent. But then, when accepted lovingly (or so he thinks) as an intended son-in-law, he lets down his guard for a moment and is himself hoodwinked in return. Just for one instant he believes in the genuineness and sincerity of the sentiments expressed by her family—and he promptly finds himself out on the street without a job, having been previously gulled as well into returning the money paid to keep him silent! It is true that, as a result, he escapes becoming the father of his erstwhile fiancée's child by a passing cavalry officer. But this is scarcely any consolation and indeed a further humiliation; the young lady did not even consider him good enough to serve as a substitute.

This "cheater cheated" *topos* scarcely gives any distinction to *Polzunkov*, though it does throw a vivid light on the bureaucratic *mores* of his time. What raises the story above the commonplace, however, is the depiction of the destructive effect of this experience on Polzunkov himself, who now becomes excruciatingly aware of being a social inferior. But where Devushkin and Golyadkin struggle helplessly in various ways, he has, when we first meet him, apparently given up the fight and accepted his own degradation. He thus belongs to another line of characters, which begins with old Pokrovsky in *Poor Folk* and includes "the drunken cadger" in *Mr. Prokharchin*. This type has apparently surrendered all public claim to self-respect, but nonetheless constantly reveals in behavior a sense of self-abasement. Polzunkov is the first of such "suffering buffoons" (as they have been called) with any degree of spiritual complexity; and the brief analysis quoted earlier already shows Dostoevsky's mastery of their psychological intricacies. (2: 473).

Polzunkov's *skaz*-rendition of the comic anecdote, with everything it reveals about the world in which he lives, is superbly expressive. The great "confessions" and self-revelations of the later novels are already in embryo in this unpretentious little tale. But there is also a more complicated relation between Polzunkov and his audience that has so far gone unnoticed. Polzunkov is, to be sure, humiliating himself in the story; but he is also confronting his listeners with an image of themselves. For, he tells them unmistakably, they all share in the world of bribery and corruption that he describes: "She is our Mother, gentlemen, our Mother Russia; we are her babes, and so we suck her!" (2: 8). What has undone him is the one moment of genuinely honest sentiment in his whole life; presumably those to whom he is talking would never have been so incautious. And so, in laughing at Polzunkov's failure to survive in the bureaucratic jungle, they are, unawares, laughing at the exposure of their own turpitudes. This is a first sketch for the much more complex (but nonetheless similar) relation between the underground man and *his* interlocutor in Part I of *Notes from Underground*. For the latter too is ready to despise the underground man, without realizing that he is really looking at a more honest image of himself than he is willing to contemplate.*

* This point will be discussed at much greater length when I come to analyze *Notes from Underground* in a succeeding volume. Since it may surprise some readers, however, I can only refer them to my interpretation of this work contained in "Nihilism and *Notes from Underground*," *Sewanee Review* 1 (1961): 1-33.

Several other sketches written during 1847-1848 are in the same form of the *skaz*, preceded by some sort of brief introduction. There is evidence that Dostoevsky, perhaps inspired by the success of Turgenev's stories (later collected in *A Sportsman's Sketches*) planned to write a whole series of works of this type. Traces of this plan can still be found in *An Honest Thief*, which bears the subtitle, *From the Diary of an Unknown*. This "unknown," the frame-narrator of the series, is a youngish, cultivated, and reserved bureaucrat leading a "hermit's existence" (2: 83), who rents a corner of his kitchen to a retired soldier on a pension. It is this retired soldier, Astafy Ivanovich, who is the *skaz*-narrator, and the cycle as a whole was to be called, after him, *The Tales of a Man of Experience*. Two stories of this cycle— *The Pensioner* and *An Honest Thief*—were published in the *Notes of the Fatherland*; the fragment of another, *Domovoy*, was found among Dostoevsky's papers. Another cycle, this time with "the unknown" as sole narrator, includes *A Christmas Tree and a Wedding* and *Another Man's Wife Or The Husband Under the Bed*. Dostoevsky's later alterations and revisions of these early stories eliminated the outline of this overall plan.

The first sketch of the *skaz*-cycle, *The Pensioner*, is very little known. Dostoevsky discarded most of the story in 1860 and combined what was left with *An Honest Thief*, cutting out a physiological sketch of the pensioner as a social type and a *skaz*-narrative in which Astafy Ivanovich recounts some of his adventures in the campaigns of 1813 and 1814. This "physiology" is of considerable interest, however, because of the glimpse it affords into some of Dostoevsky's notions about "the people" at this time.[7]

"The pensioner is much more civilized than the peasant," says the frame-narrator, "and a hundred times higher morally than the manor servant." Presumably, the pensioner is more "civilized" because he has been trained and disciplined by Army life. "He doesn't run away from work; he works, because work is part of his life; you'll never scare him with work. Skill, know-how, and sharp wits are present in him to a greater degree than in the peasant." He "doesn't like to holler bloody murder, like a muzhik in trouble, but does everything necessary himself, without whimpering and in an orderly fashion." Such remarks indicate how far Dostoevsky was in the 1840s from any sentimentalizing or idealizing of the Russian peasant. After this sketch, Astafy takes over with military reminiscences that reveal his courage, fortitude, and basic humanity, as well as the instinctive linkage made by the Russian people between religion and politics: "And it was presented to Bonaparte that he should have himself baptized in the Russian faith and swear allegiance to it. But the Frenchman wouldn't agree; he would not sacrifice his faith . . . ," etc. (2: 422, 426).

Dostoevsky later took the framing section of this story, which depicts Astafy's arrival as a lodger of "the unknown," and fused it with the second of the tales by the voluble pensioner, *An Honest Thief*. This tale centers on a hopelessly destitute and incurable drunkard Emelyan Ilyich (perhaps the same ex-clerk for whom Makar Devushkin had felt sorry in *Poor Folk*), who attaches himself to Astafy and lives off his charity. Hapless Emelyan has sunk to the very lowest depths. " 'Such a pitiful, God-forsaken creature,' Astafy says, 'I never did set eyes on. And not a word said either; he does not ask, but just sits there and looks into your eyes like a dog. To think what drinking will bring a man down to!' " (2: 85). Driven to desperation by his craving for alcohol, Emelyan steals a pair of breeches from Astafy to go on a spree. Returning, he stubbornly denies the theft; but he feels the distrust and disapproval of Astafy and this drives him away again. He finally comes back to die of fever and remorse, confessing the theft with his last words and asking Astafy to sell his ragged overcoat as compensation rather than using it for his burial.

An Honest Thief is in the purest style of sentimental Naturalism, with the innate "good" qualities of Emelyan shining through all the degradation and hopelessness of his life. To make the point perfectly clear, Dostoevsky has Astafy explain this to "the unknown" of higher social rank, who might have been inclined to regard a creature such as Emelyan with contempt and disgust:

> "And as a depraved man can't have a strong will, and his judgment isn't always sound, so then he does this shameful thing, and on the spot his impure thought becomes a deed. And if it's done, and if, for all his depraved life, he still hasn't killed off everything human in him, if he still has some kind of heart left, then it will begin to ache and to bleed, remorse will gnaw at him like a snake, and the man will not die because of a shameful act but because of grief, because what was best in him—what he had clung to more than anything, and what lets him call himself a man—has been destroyed for nothing, just as Emelyan destroyed the one thing left him, his honesty, for a bottle of stupid, rotgut vodka. It's only an example, sir, out of the life of our simple, working people, but still it happens in all ranks, only

327

in a different way. So don't you despise my little story. Yes, and pardon poor, unlucky Emelyan too; he wanted to drink, sir, only it looks like he wanted it too much. And you, sir, don't despise a man who has fallen; that's what Christ, who loved all of us more than himself, told us not to do. My Emelyan, if he had stayed alive, wouldn't have been a man but some sort of trash to spit on. But here he died from grief and a bad conscience and it's like he showed the world that, whatever he might be, he was a human being all the same; that a man can die from vice as from a deadly poison, and that vice, it must be, is a human thing, something you pick up, it's not born with you—here today, it can be gone for good tomorrow; otherwise, if we were destined to stay depraved all through the ages because of original sin, Christ would never have come to us." (2: 426)[8]

Dostoevsky eliminated this important speech when he republished the story in 1860, perhaps because it had been specifically criticized by P. V. Annenkov for being out of character. This is all the more reason, however, to believe that we hear the voice of Dostoevsky himself speaking; and it is an extraordinarily interesting voice for anyone concerned with studying his evolution. For Astafy's words, it seems to me, light up the path leading from the early to the later Dostoevsky. They show, in the first place, how deeply concerned he was with the theme of moral freedom even in this "radical" phase of his literary career (we shall see this even more clearly in the next chapter), and help to buttress some of the conclusions already drawn in discussing the Beketov circle and Valerian Maikov.

More importantly, they show how natural it was for Dostoevsky to transpose the "philanthropic" inspiration of his moral-religious Socialist idealism in the 1840s—with its belief in the existence of conscience, and in the moral freedom of the human personality—into terms that seemed to him quite congruous with the traditional Christian faith of the Russian people. Dostoevsky probably felt no opposition in principle between the two at this time, perhaps considering the first a "purified" form of the second. It was, at any rate, crucially important for him that he could later shift from one to the other—as we see him doing here momentarily—without any sense that he was really betraying the bedrock moral-religious convictions and values to which he had always adhered. Emelyan's deathbed repentance is the prototype of many such memorable scenes in which moral truth and the power of conscience finally prevail. And Dostoevsky, all through his life, will continue to reaffirm that only the inexpugnable existence of moral conscience makes man a truly human being.

7

The second cycle of stories has a less colorful narrator in Astafy's landlord, "the unknown," who also speaks in the first person; but since he remains unobtrusive, the stories are not in the *skaz*-form. What characterizes this narrator is simply a sharp eye for the social incongruities of a world that he observes with caustic detachment; and the most important story in which he figures is *A Christmas Tree and a Wedding*.

Present at a New Year's party in the home of a highly placed acquaintance, the narrator notices that all human relations at the festivity are governed either by bureaucratic rank or by fortune. A gentleman from the provinces, come to ask help from the host on some important matter, sits alone without being introduced to anyone at all. On the other hand, the powerful Julian Mastakovich (again!) is the center of the most flattering attention. Even the gifts for the children are carefully graded according to the rank of the parents; the son of the governess of the family "got nothing but a book of stories about the marvels of nature and tears of devotion, etc., without pictures or even woodcuts." The children are less affected and more democratic; but even so the son of the governess has already learned the way of the world—"he longed to play with the other children, but did not dare." However, he is finally able to join a little girl engaged in dressing a doll (2: 96-97).

This little girl, as it happens, is the daughter of a wealthy contractor, who trumpets to all the world that he intends to settle an extravagant dowry on his child. Julian Mastakovich makes some rapid calculations, and then suddenly takes a piercing look at the little heiress. "Either his calculations had affected his imagination or something else, for he rubbed his hands and could hardly stand still." He frightens the child when he kisses her unexpectedly, and tries unsuccessfully to shoo away the inconvenient little boy—who stubbornly remains, however, because of the obvious alarm of his playmate. Julian Mastakovich is vexed by this embarrassing scrutiny; and when his host charitably asks him later to afford his protection to the governess's son, he irritably refuses. The future prospects of the boy have thus been irrevocably damaged by his concern for his playmate. The evening ends with Julian Mastakovich graciously accepting an invitation to come to visit the little girl's parents. Five years later the narrator accidentally stumbles on a wedding, which turns out to be that of Julian Mastakovich and his sixteen-year-old bethrothed; now a "marvelous beauty," she looks "pale-faced and sorrowful" as she is led to the altar (2: 97, 100).

This story is linked with two others—*Another Man's Wife* (*A Street Scene*), and *A Jealous Husband* (*An Extraordinary Occurrence*) which may be considered its continuation. Both deal with the theme of cuckoldry and are also narrated by "the unknown," who suggests that the wedding of Julian Mastakovich may well lead to the torments of jealousy being experienced by Ivan Andreevich, another middle-aged gentleman of rank and dignity with a considerably younger wife. These two stories about Ivan Andreevich were later shortened and made into a single work, *Another Man's Wife Or The Husband Under the Bed*. One episode depicts the husband's vigil before an apartment house in which he suspects his frivolous spouse to be keeping a rendezvous. Another episode finds the bewildered Ivan Andreevich mistakenly dashing into a strange apartment, believing himself to be in pursuit of his erring wife, only to end up under a bed in the company of a young man similarly intent on hiding from *another* elderly husband of a beauteous young wife.

Both these stories are perfectly routine comic anecdotes turning on the always effective theme of sexual misconduct. Dostoevsky does not make any effort to transform this material and raise its level; but one cannot help being impressed with his skill in carrying off this narrative version of French bedroom farce. "Who in Russian literature," as Victor Terras remarks, "has done a better imitation of Paul de Kock than Dostoevsky?"[9] Indeed, the very triviality and conventionality of these stories allows us to catch one of the outstanding features of his art in—as it were—a pure state. Their humor arises from the unwillingness of people involved in a compromising situation to speak plainly and openly. Each suspects and tries to read the thoughts of the other *through* the words, in terms of the common imbroglio which they both understand. Such works are successful if the author is able to write crisp dialogue presupposing a common understanding referred to only by hints and allusions; the interchanges acquire in this way a special inner tension noticeably lacking when characters simply express what they mean unambiguously.

Dostoevsky succeeds brilliantly in sustaining this sort of rapid-fire dialogic exchange, which derives from the implication of all his characters in a situation involving sexual scandal. But while, on this occasion, he uses this skill only for farcical comedy, the same gift is employed for much more serious purposes in other works. Bakhtin has perceptively remarked that Dostoevsky's dialogues are never between two people totally alien or closed off from each other. "Dostoevsky always introduces two characters in such a way that each of them is intimately connected with the interior voice of the other. . . . The profound essential bond, or, to express it otherwise, the partial coincidence of one character's word with the interior secret word of the other is an indispensable element in all of Dostoevsky's most important dialogues."[10] It is not surprising to note such a feature in Golyadkin's dialogue with his double, where the psychic identity between the two is postulated by the situation. But the ability to achieve the same sort of dialogic interpenetration with *any* set of characters, solely on the basis of their mutual involvement in a common situation, explains the unusual sense of excitement that Dostoevsky manages to create from page to page, and the almost hypnotic fascination, quite aside from plotting, that he never fails to exercise on his readers.

CHAPTER 22

Reality and the "Dreamer"

Simultaneously with the works discussed in the last two chapters, Dostoevsky also composed others quite different in style and theme: *The Landlady* and *White Nights*. Dostoevsky is once supposed to have said that all the Russian literature of his time emerged from Gogol's *The Overcoat*; and even though the alleged utterance is probably apocryphal, *se non è vero*, as the Italians say, *è ben trovato*.[1] Russian literature of the 1840s *was* dominated by the rise of the Natural School, and the most important writers of the time, including Dostoevsky, did emerge originally from the capacious folds of Gogol's overcoat. But the stories we are about to consider belong to a different Gogolian tradition. To vary the trope slightly, we might say that the inspiration for them came to Dostoevsky as he accompanied Gogol for a stroll along the Nevsky Prospect.

Russian fiction of the 1830s, strongly influenced by Hoffmann and German Romanticism, is filled with the dissonance between the ideal and the real, the spiritual and the material. N. A. Polevoy, who contributed importantly to this mode, explained his artistic aim as being "to show that the mad dreams of the poets do not fit in with the world of material existence."[2] In those days, this lack of adjustment was felt to be a crushing indictment of the narrowness and limitations of the quotidian. And since it was only artists (and philosophers) who, according to the metaphysics of Romantic Idealism, were in inspired contact with the realm of transcendental truth, artists invariably turned up as the heroes of such creations. The classic expression of this theme in Russian literature is Gogol's *Nevsky Prospect*.

Gogol's story follows the contrasting experiences of two characters who meet by chance while ambling along the Nevsky at dusk. One is the idealistic young artist Piskarev, who becomes enraptured by the seraphic beauty of a girl flitting by just as the lamps are being lit. To his horror, he discovers that this incarnation of divine harmony is a prostitute; and the shock of encountering such a degradation of beauty shatters his entire spiritual world. He dreams of setting her in a more appropriate and honorable environment, and takes opium to make his visions of their future bliss more gorgeous and richly embroidered. Finally, deciding to rescue her from a debasing fate, he plucks up the courage to offer marriage. But she only laughs in his face at the idea of abandoning her luxurious life of sin; and he commits suicide in despair at this defilement of his dreams. At the same time, the ineffable Lieutenant Pirogov, one of the supreme embodiments of Gogolian *poshlost*—that elusive word which may be unsatisfactorily rendered as "self-complacent mediocrity," and on which Vladimir Nabokov has written some sparkling pages[3]—is busily pursuing a tempting little blonde on the same thoroughfare. The enterprising lieutenant ends up being ignominiously beaten by her husband and his close friend—named, not by accident, Schiller and Hoffmann—but nonetheless bounces back with india-rubber resilience and undisturbed aplomb.

Gogol's story stands at the borderline between the purely Romantic delineation of this clash between the ideal and the real and its later development in the 1840s. For while Piskarev is still a positive figure compared to Pirogov, Gogol does not weight the values of the story heavily in his favor; there is something pathetic and pitiful, rather than sublimely tragic, about his ignorance of the ways of the world.

15. View of the Nevsky Prospect

Only a short step separates this portrayal of the artist-"dreamer" from Dostoevsky's own portrait of the type in his Petersburg feuilletons. And in the interval between the two had come Belinsky's attack on Romanticism in the mid-1840s, which led to a complete reversal of the original Romantic relation between the ideal and the real. Now the dreamer (no longer a true artist, but an abortive or inauthentic one) becomes a symbol of the failure to grapple with and master the demands and challenges of life. This is the context in which, along with Goncharov, Herzen, the early Turgenev and many others, Dostoevsky offers his own version of the "dreamer" character-type and his conflicts.

2

It was after the publication of *Mr. Prokharchin* that Dostoevsky began to work on *The Landlady*. At the end of October 1846, he writes to Mikhail that he has abandoned his plans to do another story in his old manner and that his work has now taken a new turn. Part of the reason was no doubt the failure of all his work after *Poor Folk*, but part too was a weariness with the narrow stylistic range of the Natural School: Dostoevsky felt his shift to a new style and subject matter as an inner release. "I am writing my *Landlady*," he tells Mikhail three months later. "It's already turning out to be better than *Poor Folk*. It's of the same kind. My pen is guided by a source of inspiration rising directly from the soul. Not like *Prokharchin*, over which I agonized all summer."[4] Just what Dostoevsky means by saying that *The Landlady* and *Poor Folk* are "of the same kind" is difficult to explain; two works more different in character can scarcely be imagined. Perhaps the assertion is meant to be taken with the sentence following, which stresses a spontaneity of inspiration and ease of composition that may have resembled what Dostoevsky felt during the writing of *Poor Folk*.

While the new turn taken by Dostoevsky's work in *The Landlady* is in the tradition of *Nevsky Prospect*, the style and plot-motifs have been more directly traced to an earlier work of Gogol's, *A Terrible Vengeance*. This story is part of *Evenings on a Farm near Dikanka*, where Gogol was still drawing his inspiration from Ukrainian folklore and imitating the epic-ballad style of Cossack folk-tales. *A Terrible Vengeance* has a heroine of the same name as that of *The Landlady* (Katerina); she too is loved incestuously by her father—a sorcerer and magician—who murders her mother; he exercises a mysterious and irresistible power over her that drives her to madness; and the story is composed in the highly stylized language of folk-poetry. Comparisons have also been drawn between *The Landlady* and various works of Hoffmann, as well as a whole host of minor stories exploiting the popular conventions of Russian Hoffmannism.

Whether Dostoevsky was directly inspired by such predecessors or not, there can be no doubt that *The Landlady* attempts to revitalize this tradition in the late 1840s—by no means an easy task. Gogol's use of the Romantic supernatural, as well as of a heightened epic-ballad style of narration, sprang naturally from the superstitions and beliefs of the vanished world he was depicting. Dostoevsky tries the much more difficult feat of utilizing the same Romantic conventions and melodramatic events for a story set in modern Petersburg and focusing on the contemporary character-type of the "dreamer." He was, as will soon become clear, drawing on these conventions quite self-consciously for a specific symbolic purpose; but it cannot be said that he successfully brought them back to life. *The Landlady* does not really work because Dostoevsky failed to endow his out-of-date Romantic framework with the same new significance that he had managed to give to sentimentalism in *Poor Folk*, and to the equally Romantic *Doppelgänger*-motif in *The Double*.

3

The "dreamer"-character of the story, Vasily Mikhailovich Ordynov, is supplied with all the essential traits of this type. The last survivor of an aristocratic family fallen on evil days, he has inherited a small sum of money allowing him to live a lonely and secluded life devoted to study. Ordynov's passion is for "science" (which in this Russian context has the broad meaning of "philosophy"), and he is at work on a "system"; but as yet "he had only the first ecstasy, the first fever, the first delirium of the artist" (1: 266). It has been suggested that Ordynov's "system" is really Utopian Socialist in character; and it is true that the same word "science" (*nauka*) was currently used to refer to Utopian Socialist theories. But such a hypothesis does not jibe with the imagery used to describe Ordynov's "system," nor with the fact that he is called an "artist." This seems to make him much more an old-fashioned Romantic Idealist "dreamer," for whom art and philosophy provide equal and eventually converging paths to discovery of the highest truths. Moreover, the image given of his character also speaks against the view that he was really elaborating a Utopian Socialist "system."

If this interpretation were correct, one can hardly imagine Dostoevsky stressing so strongly Ordynov's isolation and sense of estrangement from other people and from the throbbing life of the Petersburg in which he lives. At the beginning of the story, Ordynov's need for new living quarters compels him to wander through the streets and to discover a whole new and previously unknown world. And this sudden immersion in everyday existence makes him realize to what extent he has always been cut off from the human community. "A thought suddenly occurred to him that all his life he had been solitary and no one had loved him—and, indeed, he had succeeded in loving no one either." He recalls that even in childhood, "sympathy for people had always been difficult and oppressive for him, and had been unnoticed by others, *for though it existed in him there was no moral equality perceptible in it*" (1: 267; italics added). This is hardly the description of a Utopian Socialist, presumably sensitive to the sufferings of mankind and yearning to lighten their burdens; it is much more suitable for a Romantic Idealist "genius," nourishing in proud solitude the flattering belief that he has been singled out for great creative achievement. In any case, here we have the first hint of the connection between egoism and the "dreamer"-intellectual that will later flower so luxuriantly in Dostoevsky's work.

Like the unhappy Piskarev, a chance encounter has the most fateful consequences for Ordynov. He falls under the spell of the beauty of a young woman whom he first sees praying fervently in a church, and in whose face he discerns "traces of childlike fear and mysterious horror." Accompanying her is a considerably older man dressed in the Old Russian fashion of the merchant class, and of an imposing and forbidding mien. "His thin, long, grizzled beard fell down to his chest, and fiery, feverishly glowing eyes flashed a haughty, prolonged stare from under his frowning, overhanging brows" (1: 267-268). Moved by an irresistible impulse, Ordynov forces his way into their cramped flat and asks to rent a room; much against his will, the old man (Murin) bows to Katerina's desire and accedes to the request. From this point on, the story becomes a string of incidents, one more incredible and sensational than the last.

Ordynov falls ill and lies in a constant state of delirium; when not out of his mind with fever, he is swooning with sensual ecstasy at Katerina's caresses. She alternates between passionate embraces with Ordynov and enraptured attention to Murin as he reads from the heretical books of the *raskolniki*, or tells wild tales of bandit exploits on the Volga. Murin tries to shoot Ordynov and falls into an epileptic fit. Ordynov, spurred on by Katerina, is on the point of killing the unconscious Murin after a drinking bout, but fails when "he fancied that the old man's whole face began laughing and that a diabolical, soul-freezing chuckle resounded at last through the room" (1: 310). His failure to carry out this deed and free Katerina from Murin's spell marks the "dreamer's" defeat by the malignant power that also holds his beauteous landlady in thrall.

Much of what occurs is so extravagant that Ordynov himself wonders repeatedly if he is not living through some sort of hallucination. This has led one critic to suggest that the events supposedly occurring in Murin's apartment are purely imaginary, and only a dramatization of Ordynov's delirious fantasy which he takes as objectively real.[5] With good reason, this view has not been generally accepted; but that it should have been offered at all well conveys the mystery that surrounds everything in *The Landlady*. It is never clear whether Katerina is really mad and suffering from hallucinations herself, or whether the frenzied tale that she narrates so poetically is true. Nor is it possible to decide whether Murin is really only an old merchant whose possessions have been destroyed by fire (this is the prosaic view taken by the police official, Yaroslav Ilyich), or a Volga robber chieftain with mysterious occult powers.

Dostoevsky definitely overdoes the use of Gothic and Romantic accessories in *The Landlady*, and one can well understand Belinsky's violent antipathy to the story. Murin's eyes, he jibes, "hold so much electricity, galvanism, and magnetism that he might have commanded a good price from a physiologist to supply the latter . . . with their lightning-charged crackling glances for scientific observation and experiments."[6] Such a response is perfectly justifiable in terms of the taste of the time; but it is of course not the final word that needs to be said about *The Landlady*. If it is difficult to argue that the work is an artistic success, the passage of time has nonetheless revealed it to be among the richest of Dostoevsky's early works in important anticipations of the future. And even if we remain within the boundaries of the 1840s, a closer study of the story shows it to be much more than the overheated Romantic phantasmagoria that Belinsky and all the others took it for. In fact, Dostoevsky was struggling here to give the basic theme of his *chinovnik* stories—the theme of the crushing of human personality in the Russian world of despotism and unconditional subordination—a much wider symbolic resonance in terms of Russian history and folklore.

4

To illustrate this point, it is necessary to examine more closely the relation between Murin and Katerina as we glimpse it darkly through Katerina's allusive words to Ordynov. Even though she may be demented and her words untrustworthy, this does not diminish their thematic importance; the secret of her enslavement by Murin lies in what Katerina *believes* to be true, not in what may actually be the case. What Katerina believes is that Murin was (and still perhaps is) a robber chieftain of Volga bandits who was once the lover of her mother, and that she is his illegitimate daughter. Nonetheless, she accepted his advances and ran off with him after her father died (presumably murdered by Murin) in a fire that destroys all his possessions and while her mother was expiring in her death agony. What won Katerina was Murin's superb self-assurance that she could not fail to obey his wishes, and his pledge to release her if she so desired it—"but stir only your sable eyebrows, turn your black eye, stir only your little finger and I will give you back your love with golden freedom" (1: 298).

Katerina, however, discovers that once she has placed herself in Murin's power there is no longer any means of escape. The source of this power at first was clearly sexual; but, by the time Ordynov meets her, Murin is a sickly old man, and his power has taken another and much more subtle form. He has made her realize that she has committed "the unpardonable sin" (incest), and frightens her with the specter of eternal damnation. "He tortures me," she tells Ordynov, "he reads to me from his books" (the manuscript volumes of the Old Believers), and she is continually tormented by the thought that "my prayers will not reach the saints, and they will not save me from cruel grief." The "mysterious horror" that Ordynov had first noticed in Katerina's face in church derives from this source. Worst of all, Katerina has reached the point where she has begun to enjoy and to savor her own sorrow and sense of irremediable sinfulness. Her true "grief," she tells Ordynov, is not that "I have sold myself to the evil one and abandoned my soul to the destroyer"; it is, rather, that "my shame and disgrace are dear to me, shameless as I am," and that "it is dear to my greedy heart to remember my sorrow as though it were joy and happiness; that is my grief, that there is no strength in it and no anger for my wrongs! . . ." (1: 293, 299).

Katerina's psyche has thus become crippled and distorted by her belief in Murin's occult powers. And these are not, it should be noted, presented as purely magical and pagan but are intertwined with the Christian symbols of Russian Orthodoxy. Also, it is striking that only *this* aspect of Katerina's story receives external confirmation (the "educated" and pretentious Yaroslav Ilyich also believes in Murin's capacities as a seer and a prophet). What ties Katerina to Murin are the fears and horrors he has managed to instill into her, and which have now become transformed into a strange kind of "enjoyment" released through fervent prayer. Murin himself is perfectly (and even cynically) aware of what he has done to Katerina, and generalizes it, for the benefit of Ordynov, into a universal law. "Let me tell you, sir," he explains to the thunderstruck Ordynov, "a weak man cannot stand alone. Give him everything, he will come of himself and return it all. . . . Give a weak man his freedom—he will bind it himself and give it back to you. To a foolish heart freedom is no use!" (1: 317).

It is thus the theme of "freedom" that emerges at the center of *The Landlady*, and which links the story very firmly, on this level, with Dostoevsky's other works of the same period. Just as he has dramatized the fashion in which Devushkin and Golyadkin have been psychically crippled by the prevailing conditions of Russian life and society, so now he explores the same subject in a totally different style and manner. And to drive the point home even more decisively, he provides Ordynov, at the conclusion of the story, with the following reflections:

> He fancied that some mystery, some secret, bound her to the old man, and that Katerina, though innocent of crime as a pure dove, had got into his power . . . he had constant visions of *an immense, overpowering despotism* over a poor, defenseless creature, and his heart raged and trembled in impotent indignation. He fancied that before the frightened eyes of her suddenly awakened soul *the idea of its degradation* had been craftily presented, that the poor *weak* heart had been craftily tortured, that the truth had been twisted and contorted to her, that she had, with a purpose, been kept blind when necessary, that the inexperienced inclinations of her troubled passionate heart had been subtly flattered, and by degrees the free soul had been clipped of its wings till it was incapable at last of insurrection or of a free movement toward real life . . . (1: 319; italics added, except for word "weak").

Seen in this light, the folklore aspect of the story and its evocation of the Old Russian past also takes on a new significance. For it is the dark superstitions of this past—its religion of fear and eternal damnation—that has succeeded in inculcating Katerina (really innocent, in Ordynov's view) with a terrible sense of guilt, and has furnished the arms by which Murin has subdued and broken her spirit. Dostoevsky, we know, was working on *The Landlady* at the very same time he was writing his Petersburg feuilletons. And is not the symbolism of the story a reflection of his criticism of Slavophilism, with its "blind, unconditional conversion to a slumbering native antiquity"?*

Indeed, one little-noticed passage seems to contain a satirical allusion to this enthusiasm of "educated" society for the folk-traits of the people presumably surviving from a morally purer time. Murin has just been craftily playing the simple, subservient man of the people for the benefit of Yaroslav Ilyich, and explaining how happy he would have been, under other conditions, to have welcomed Ordynov into his home as a sacred "guest":

> Murin bowed down from the waist. Tears came into Yaroslav Ilyich's delighted eyes. He looked with enthusiasm at Ordynov.
> "What a generous trait, isn't it! What sacred hospitality is to be found in the Russian people."
> Ordynov looked wildly at Yaroslav Ilyich. He was almost terrified and scrutinized him from head to foot.

Such details have prompted Rudolf Neuhäuser to suggest recently that *The Landlady* should be interpreted as a consistent allegory, in which every episode may be correlated with the Russian social-cultural scene in 1846-1847. Even though his attempt to provide such a reading is not persuasive, he does furnish a penetrating statement of the main symbolic theme: "The Russian soul enslaved by centuries-old national and religious traditions has become intoxicated by a narcissistic complex of self-lacerations and enjoyment of humiliation and lacks the power to renounce the oppressive traditions."[7] This view of the story also helps to explain the shattering effect of the whole experience on Ordynov, which foreshadows the similar collapse of Arkady Ivanovich in *A Weak Heart*. (The title of this latter work in Russian, *Slaboe Serdtse*, is a phrase originally used in Ordynov's just-quoted reflections on Katerina.)

After his defeat by Murin, Ordynov finds that he cannot return to his old life and loses faith in himself as "destined to be an artist in science." For "genuine faith is the pledge of the future"; but now the future seems closed. He had also, we learn, previously jotted down notes for "a work relating to the history of the Church, and his warmest, most fervent convictions were expressed in it" (this is *not* the same work, though the two are often confused, as his "system"). But now he abandons this project too, and "something akin to mysticism, to fatalism and a belief in the mysterious began to make its way into his mind." Presumably, such convictions were quite the

* See p. 229.

opposite of those that his history of the Church would have developed. And the relation of this spiritual breakdown to the symbolic theme of the story is clinched by an ironical sentence: "The German's servant [Ordynov is now living in the apartment of a German artisan], a devout old Russian woman, used to describe with relish how her meek lodger prayed and how he would lie for hours together as though unconscious on the church pavement" (1: 318). What Dostoevsky seems to be suggesting here is the opposition between a religion of light and hope and faith in man, and one—more traditional—of mysticism and fatalism: the same contrast we have seen made both by Considérant and Belinsky.* From this point of view, it seems to me very likely that Dostoevsky meant *The Landlady* not only as a symbolic critique of Slavophilism but also of Orthodoxy, so far as he, like Belinsky, then saw the latter as a religion of fear or terror.

The Landlady is thus of considerable interest as Dostoevsky's laudable (even if artistically unsuccessful) attempt to transpose into another key and tonality the major theme of his works written according to the poetics of the Natural School. It is of even greater interest when we become aware that this story marks a decisive moment of transition in Dostoevsky's artistic maturation. The character of Katerina is the first in which Dostoevsky focuses on the psychology of masochism, and begins to explore the subtle and unhealthy "enjoyment" that can be derived from self-laceration and self-punishment. Glimpses of such a psychology can of course be found earlier—for example, in *The Double*. At one point, after a report in direct speech of some of Mr. Golyadkin's self-reproaches, the narrator continues: "So Mr. Golyadkin taunted himself as he jolted along in the vehicle. To taunt himself and so to irritate his wounds was, at this time, a great satisfaction to Mr. Golyadkin, almost a voluptuous enjoyment" (1: 170). But this remark is made only in passing, and Mr. Golyadkin's "enjoyment" is not used for any thematic purpose. It is only in *The Landlady* that Dostoevsky begins to grasp the implications of this psychology and to exploit it seriously. His artistic focus thus shifts from the inner conflict within the individual caused by socially conditioned attitudes to the struggle of the individual with his own character. Katerina is still a victim of Murin and all the dark forces that he represents; but she is also a victim of her inability to conquer the "enjoyment" that she derives from her enslavement and degradation. A new dimension is thus added to Dostoevsky's portrayal of personality, which now moves in the direc-

* See pp. 148-185.

tion of transferring to the individual some of the moral responsibility for his own plight.

Of crucial importance in the Dostoevsky canon as the first hint of this evolution from a social-psychological to a moral-psychological grasp of character, *The Landlady* also contains more limited anticipations of things to come. Dostoevsky never again tried to write so extensively in an epic-ballad style; but a similar haunting note of folk-poetry occasionally appears, most notably in the lyrical accents of the crippled Marya Lebyadkina in *The Devils*. And there is, indeed, a certain similarity in situation between Katerina and Marya that explains the stylistic echo. Katerina hopes that Ordynov has come to rescue her, just as Marya waits for Stavrogin and imagines him to be her "deliverer"; but in neither case is the Russian folk-maiden delivered from the enchantment of evil by her "false" swain from the intelligentsia. In addition, it has frequently been pointed out that Murin's contemptuous opinion about mankind's inability to endure "freedom" anticipates one of the most famous passages of the Legend of the Grand Inquisitor. The physical description of Murin—his grizzled, emaciated features, and the "galvanism" of his eyes at which Belinsky poked fun—clearly prefigure the awesome majesty of the Inquisitor; so does Murin's symbolic role as the representative of a religion of tyranny and oppression based on fear and leading to the enslavement of the human personality.

5

Even though *The Landlady* is the first of Dostoevsky's works in which the figure of the "dreamer" makes his appearance, the story itself does not center thematically on this type at all. As the title indicates, the focus is on Katerina and her relation both to Murin and Ordynov; the psychology of the latter is sketched in briefly but not really developed. One expects him somehow to come into contact or conflict with the "real"; but instead, Ordynov's first, faltering emergence from isolation leads into a realm far more strange and fantastic than anything he had ever imagined. To be sure, the world that Ordynov encounters—and which, alas, is evoked in such hackneyed prose—is intended to represent the psychic "reality" of the Russian past impinging on the present. But Dostoevsky was not yet master of the artistic means that could have made this "reality" seem anything more than what Belinsky called it—an attempt "to reconcile Marlinsky and Hoffmann," in which everything was "far-fetched, exaggerated, stilted, spurious, and false." Dostoevsky's next effort in the same direction, however, happily corrects these two defects of *The Landlady*. Romantic folklore is dropped entirely; and the psychology of the "dreamer" is now placed squarely at the center of the artistic perspective.

The result is that charming little story, *White Nights*, one of the two minor masterpieces (the other is *The Double*) that Dostoevsky wrote after *Poor Folk*. Charm is not a literary attribute that one ordinarily associates with Dostoevsky; but he was versatile enough to be able to capture this elusive quality on the one or two occasions when he tried for it. *White Nights* stands out from the tragicomic and satirical universe of his early creations by the beautiful lightness and delicacy of its tone, its atmosphere of springtime adolescent emotionality, the grace and wit of its good-natured parodies. Several allusions to Rossini's *The Barber of Seville* are interwoven into the main episode, and *White Nights* is filled with some of the exuberance and gaiety of this effervescent little operatic romp.

Doubly subtitled—it is called *A Sentimental Novel*, which comes from *The Diary of a Dreamer*—*White Nights* is written in the first person by the "dreamer" himself. What strikes the reader, especially after coming to this story after *The Landlady*, is the total difference in mood and temperament between this new "dreamer" and Ordynov. There is nothing of Ordynov's portentous, pseudo-Faustian preoccupation with "science" about him, though he is clearly a sensitive and extremely cultivated young man. Nor—since he has a very ordinary job in a very ordinary government office—is he cut off from the rest of the world. Both are similar, however, in their sense of isolation and loneliness; but the "dreamer" of *White Nights* looks with friendly curiosity and benevolent interest on the rest of humanity, and even strikes up acquaintance with the houses that he passes everyday. "I have my favorite among them, some are dear friends; one of them intends to be treated by an architect this summer. I shall go every day on purpose to see that the operation is not a failure" (1: 103).

Just as in *The Landlady*, the "dreamer" of *White Nights* makes his contact with "reality" by meeting a young girl—not, however, a pain-racked beauty like Katerina, but a pert little miss of seventeen named Nastenka, who knows that the time has come for her to find a husband. A year before, she had become betrothed to a young man who had gone to Moscow to establish himself, promising to return in the same season and to keep a rendezvous, in the eerie incandescence of the Petersburg springtime "white nights," on the very bridge where she is first seen by the "dreamer" leaning pensively over the side. The time is up, the fiancé has not yet manifested himself, and Nastenka is troubled. She and the "dreamer" meet for several enchanted nights at the same spot; he falls head over heels in love with her (as she expects, since she expressly forbids him from doing so); and there is one moment when she is ready, with a healthy feminine instinct of self-preservation, to transfer her affections. "I love him; but I shall get over it," she says firmly; "I must get over it, I cannot fail to get over it; I am getting over it, I feel that" (1: 136). For one dazzling moment, encouraged by Nastenka, the "dreamer" obtains a glimpse of "real" happiness; but she flies to the arms of her intended when he does appear at last, and the "dreamer" is left to mull over this last of his "dreams" and what it has meant to him.

The action is nothing but a bare schema of the most banal and insignificant sentimental intrigue; but it is enough to allow Dostoevsky to make his two characters talk about themselves. And once they begin, the story takes wing. Nastenka is delightful in her spontaneity, her capacity to enter into the "dreamer's" dilemma, her warmth and vivacity—and her staunch loyalty to her first love. The wistfully humorous lyrical extrapolations of the "dreamer" are, in part, taken over word for word from the portrait of this type in the fourth Petersburg feuilleton; and Dostoevsky conjures up once again, with even more detail, all the enchantments and fascinations of the extraordinary world in which he lives.

"Poor things! thinks our dreamer" [about ordinary people]. "And it is no wonder that he thinks it. Look at these magic phantasms, which so enchantingly, so carelessly and freely group before him in such a magic, animated picture, in which the most prominent figure in the foreground is of course himself, our dreamer, in his precious person." The most famous passage in this lengthy tirade is one that Dostoevsky added in 1860, when he revised the story and decided to give the "dreamer" a more specific cultural genealogy. "You ask, perhaps, what he is dreaming of? . . . of friendship with Hoffmann, St. Bartholomew's Night, of Diana Vernon, of playing the hero at the taking of Kazan by Ivan Vasilievich, of Clara Mowbray, of Effie Deans, of the council of the prelates and Huss before them, of the rising of the dead in *Robert the Devil* (do you remember the music, it smells of the churchyard!), of Minna and Brenda, of the battle of Berezina, of the reading of a poem at Countess V. D.'s, of Danton, of *Cleopatra ei suoi amanti*, of a little house in Kolomna," etc. (1: 115-116). The passage contains allusions, so far as they can be identified, to Hoffmann, Merimée, Sir Walter Scott, Karamzin, George Sand (perhaps!), Meyerbeer, Zhukovsky, and Pushkin.

Dostoevsky inserted this kaleidoscope of Romantic influences into *White Nights* about the same time (1860-1861) that he wrote his *Petersburg Visions in Verse and Prose*; and the similarity of inspiration is evident.* Its sparkle, though, now tends to conceal what probably stood out more prominently in the original text—the parody of Romantic novels depicting desperate and undying love in high society and exotic climes. Hitherto, the narrator's inflamed imagination has battened on such enticing fare; and while his declamation for the benefit of the open-mouthed Nastenka is too extended to quote in full, one extract is indispensable to give the flavor of Dostoevsky's witty deflation:

> Surely they must have spent years hand in hand together—alone the two of them, casting off all the world and each uniting his or her life with the other's? Surely when the hour of parting came she must have lain sobbing and grieving on his bosom, heedless of the tempest raging under the sullen sky, heedless of the wind which snatches and bears away the tears from her black eyelashes? . . . And, good Heavens!, surely he met her afterwards, far from their native shores, under alien skies, in the hot south in the divinely eternal city, in the dazzling splendor of the ball to the crash of music, in a *palazzo* (it must be in a *palazzo*), drowned in a sea of lights, on the balcony, wreathed in myrtle and roses, where, recognizing him, she hurriedly removes her mask and whispering "I am free," flings herself trembling into his arms, and with a cry of rapture, clinging to one another, in one instant they forget their sorrow and their parting and all their agonies, and the gloomy house and the distant garden in that distant land, and the seat on which with a last passionate kiss she tore herself away from his arms numb with anguish and despair . . . etc. (1: 117).

By the time he meets Nastenka, the bloom of such imaginary romances has long since begun to fade, and the dreamer has become aware of the insubstantiality of their deceptive delights. He has begun to feel that "for him, too, maybe, sometime the mournful hour may strike, when for one day of that pitiful life he would give all his years of fantasy, and would give them not only for joy and happiness, but without caring to make distinctions in that hour of sadness, remorse and unchecked grief" (1: 116). The meetings with Nastenka finally provide him with that one day (or rather, several "white

* See p. 133.

nights") of real life; and he knows that, as a result, his own existence will be changed forever.

The dreamer's love for Nastenka, however, is untainted by selfishness, and he even tries to help her make contact with her elusive fiancé. Moreover, when the latter appears at last, there is not a trace of jealousy or resentment in his response, even though he knows he is condemned once again to vegetate in the gloom of his lonely chamber. And as he sits and reads her note of apology and gratitude—in which, with feminine sophistry, she asks him to keep on loving her "as a brother" just *as before*—he cannot find it in his heart to cast any shadow on her joy. "Oh, never, never! May your sky be clear, may your sweet smile be bright and untroubled, and may you be blessed for that moment of blissful happiness which you gave to another, lonely and grateful heart! My God, a whole moment of happiness! Is that too little for the whole of a man's life?" (1: 141).

White Nights thus terminates on a note of benediction for the one moment of "real" happiness that the dreamer has been vouchsafed. The splendors of the ideal and the imaginary fade into insignificance before the reality of love for a sprightly snip of a girl of glowing flesh-and-blood. This is Dostoevsky's vibrantly poetic contribution to the attack on Romantic *mechtatelnost* so common in Russian literature of the late 1840s; and though his little story cannot compete with the novels of Herzen and Goncharov on the same theme, nowhere in Russian literature is it expressed with more sensitivity and lyrical grace. *White Nights* was the only one of Dostoevsky's minor stories to be greeted favorably by the critics; but it also provided the occasion for a friendly polemic with Aleksey Pleshcheev. As we have noted earlier, the story was dedicated to Pleshcheev, who in response wrote his own *Friendly Advice* dedicated to Dostoevsky.

Pleshcheev's main character, also a "dreamer," sounds very much like Dostoevsky's and even echoes some of his phrases. But he manages to attain the object of his heart's desire, marries a wealthy and very ordinary young lady—and then settles down to lead the most Philistine existence imaginable! For Pleshcheev, the "dreamer's" passion for Nastenka, however real it may be, is itself only a less grandiose, more commonplace form of Romantic self-delusion. The Soviet critic who makes this point, in an informative article, also remarks that the enticements of *mechtatelnost*, even though thematically condemned, are nonetheless painted by Dostoevsky in the most glowing colors.[8] The power of imagination is glorified in the very act of seeming to pass censure upon its effects; and a good deal of the story's appeal certainly derives from this ambiguity. Indeed, Dostoevsky pronounces his negative judgment with such elegiac tenderness that one cannot help suspecting a greater sentimental attachment to the richness of Romantic culture than he would perhaps have been willing to acknowledge.

Dostoevsky was tied to Romanticism by too many emotional fibers of his being to be able to detach himself from it entirely. If he was always ready to satirize and parody the fatuity of Romantic attitudes, or their use as a screen for egoistic impulses ("in the foreground is of course himself, our dreamer, in his precious person"), he would nonetheless always continue to believe in the importance of maintaining the capacity to be stirred by the imaginative and the ideal. During the 1860s, the theme of Dostoevsky's early story would become one of the main issues at stake in the battle between the generations. And no matter how much Dostoevsky would later belabor the pretensions and the moral vacuity of the Romantic generation of the "fathers," he would always prefer the latter to their offspring, who fanatically insisted on reducing "real life" exclusively to the matter-of-fact, prosaic, and even grossly material.

CHAPTER 23

Netotchka Nezvanova

Even during his darkest days of despair over the poor reception of his works, Dostoevsky continued to cling to one hope which, he was convinced, would reverse the process of his downfall. He had begun to block out a new major novel probably as early as October 1846; and he was relying on this to restore his reputation. His plan, as he tells Mikhail, was to go to Italy and there write the first section of this novel "in three or four parts for *The Contemporary*"; the rest could be completed on his return after a stay of about eight months. "The subject (and the prologue) and the idea are all in my head," he reassures his brother.[1] By the end of October, however, he informs Mikhail that he has given up the idea of going abroad and has begun to write *The Landlady*, but is nonetheless continuing to think about the novel, "which even now gives me no rest."[2]

Dostoevsky's quarrel with *The Contemporary* occurred in the next month, and in December we learn that he has agreed to give Kraevsky "the first part of my novel *Netotchka Nezvanova*, about whose publication you [Mikhail] have certainly already read in *Notes of the Fatherland*."[3] At the beginning of the New Year, he repeats to Mikhail that "soon you will be reading my *Netotchka Nezvanova*."[4] But Mikhail did not read the first installment as rapidly as his brother had expected. Dostoevsky was forced to break off work on the book repeatedly in 1847 to satisfy other and more immediate literary obligations, though no doubt doing so with great reluctance. He knew that only a substantial literary success could halt his precipitous decline in public favor, and he was well aware that a new group of literary competitors were looming on the horizon. "A whole host of new writers have begun to appear," he remarks uneasily to Mikhail in April 1846. "Some are my rivals. Herzen (Iskander) and Goncharov stand out the most among them."[5] Eight months later, he confesses to Mikhail: "I can't help feeling that I've begun a campaign against all our literature, journals, and critics, and that with the three parts of my novel in *Notes of the Fatherland* this year I will again affirm my superiority in the teeth of all who wish me bad

348

luck."[6] It was to take another year, however, before the novel finally began to appear at the beginning of 1849.

2

The unfinished state of *Netotchka Nezvanova*, which breaks off when the heroine is barely eighteen years old, makes it difficult to obtain any overall sense of what Dostoevsky was trying to do; but some speculations may plausibly be ventured. It seems clear, in the first place, that the work was designed as a *Bildungsroman*, depicting the life history of Netotchka written in maturity or old age and reflecting the experiences that have formed her character and shaped her life. It is generally thought that Netotchka was to develop into a great singer, like so many heroines of George Sand; and this is very likely. Not only was Dostoevsky an ardent opera lover, who assiduously attended the performances of the Italian Opera in Petersburg as one of his few diversions,* but there is also evidence that George Sand was much on his mind as he wrote about Netotchka. In a letter mingling an analysis of his own character with comments on his novel, Dostoevsky compares himself in passing with Prince Karol, the central male figure of Sand's then-famous *Lucrezia Floriani*.† This work was written in the last stages of Sand's notorious liaison with Chopin; and Prince Karol has been identified as a portrait of the great Polish composer and pianist. An aristocrat of exquisite refinement, sensitivity, and spiritual distinction, Prince Karol's admirable qualities only make him overly demanding, terribly susceptible, and ultimately unbearable even for those he loves, and who, in return, are devoted to him heart and soul. (One wonders what Chopin must have felt when, as we know to have been the case, Sand read her manuscript to him as it was being written.)

Dostoevsky's reference to Prince Karol is significant both because of what it tells us about himself, and also because it documents the inspiration he derived from Sand. Indeed, the direct influence of George Sand is felt in this novel-fragment more strongly than anywhere else in Dostoevsky; and his young heroine, who begins to take singing lessons in the last episode he managed to write, was thus

---

* Dostoevsky was regularly attending the opera while at work on *Netotchka Nezvanova*. "I am loaded down with work and have promised to give Kraevsky the first part of my novel *Netotchka Nezvanova* by February 5th. . . . I am writing this letter in snatches because I write day and night, except that at seven in the evening for relaxation I go to the gallery of the Italian Opera to hear our incomparable singers." *Pisma*, 1: 104; December 17, 1846.

† Dostoevsky remarks on his own character have already been cited on p. 169.

probably intended as a Russian analogue to Lucrezia, or to Sand's even more famous Venetian *cantatrice* Consuelo (in the novel by that name). The book would have been the Romantic autobiography of an artist so beloved of novelists in the 1830s; and in choosing this old-fashioned genre as his model, Dostoevsky was following the same stylistic impulse that had led him to the sentimental-epistolary novel in *Poor Folk*, the *Doppelgänger* technique in *The Double*, and the Romantic folktale in *The Landlady*. In each case, he took a form that had become outmoded and attempted to revitalize it with a new, contemporary significance.

If we are to judge from the three episodes that Dostoevsky completed, this significance would have centered on a very immediate cultural issue. As a result of the concerted attack on Romantic values, doubts about the function and the status of art had begun to be expressed everywhere in Russian literature of the late 1840s. For all his criticism of *mechtatelnost*, however, we have seen that Dostoevsky could not accept the total subordination of art and the imagination to social concerns. And what he wished to do, in my opinion, was to portray a character who unites a dedication to art with an equally firm commitment to the highest moral-social ideals. Netotchka's life begins in the shadow of an artistic obsession that perverts her character and disorients her moral sensibility. But, triumphantly overcoming this initial handicap, her love of art would go hand in hand with a sensitive and fearless moral-social conscience. With this work, then, Dostoevsky was endeavoring to steer a middle way between the discredited Romantic glorification of art on the one hand, and the temptation to discard the values of art entirely in favor of the utilitarian and the practical on the other.

It is from this point of view, perhaps, that we can best understand Dostoevsky's remark to Mikhail that *Netotchka Nezvanova* "will be a confession like *Golyadkin*, but in another tone and style."[7] Ordinarily, this is taken to refer only to the character of the musician Yefimov in the first section, whose desperate struggle to sustain his faith in his own talent is seen as a portrait of Dostoevsky's self-doubts under the blows dealt him by Belinsky. Dostoevsky certainly worked some of his own misgivings during these years into his depiction of Yefimov; but there is no reason to limit the scope of his emotional involvement to this single feature of the book. The question of the supreme moral-spiritual significance of art was one that concerned Dostoevsky very deeply. He had, after all, suffered a good deal of material hardship and psychic anguish because of his insistence on following his own literary path; but he firmly believed that in doing so he was by no means betraying the humane outlook that he fully shared with the Natural School. Dostoevsky's novel may thus be seen as an effort at self-vindication in the form of a new artistic creation.

The book can also be considered a "confession" in another and much more intimately personal sense. The main theme of the first part, at least on the purely moral-psychological level, is the unjust and cruel hatred of a child for its parent—a hatred springing from a false belief that this parent blocks the way to the self-fulfillment of an artist, and to the life of ease and glory that artistic success would bring in its train. The child in this case is a little girl, the parent is her mother, the artist her stepfather; but this conflict can well be seen as a barely disguised transposition of Dostoevsky's own resentment against his father for having insisted that he become a military engineer and for having forbidden any thought of a career as a writer. Netotchka's terrible sense of guilt for having hated her poor, long-suffering and hard-working mother, whom she even cheats out of money to aid her miscreant artist-father, can also be interpreted as a reflection of Dostoevsky's own guilt-feelings connected with his father's murder. The process of Netotchka's moral and emotional maturation is portrayed as the overcoming of such hatred—and of the guilt it has engendered—by an expansion of the ego to identify with the suffering of others. If such suppositions are correct, *Netotchka Nezvanova* would be truly a "confession"—and perhaps to a greater extent than even Dostoevsky himself was fully aware. Seen in this light, the novel takes on a good deal of poignancy as Dostoevsky's effort to do justice to the memory of his father, and to depict himself as accomplishing the moral obligation of overcoming his Oedipal antagonism.

As always, however, Dostoevsky transforms his own psychic dilemmas into artistic structures relevant to the moral-social issues of his time. And even though, as we shall see more clearly later, *Netotchka Nezvanova* marks the point at which Dostoevsky moves decisively beyond the literary confines of the Natural School, the novel still has a good deal of overt social resonance. There is some evidence that an earlier version was even more forthright in posing moral-social problems. I. M. Debu remembered Dostoevsky, at one of the Petrashevsky meetings, "narrating *Netotchka Nezvanova* much more fully than the published text; I recall," he says, "with what lively human feeling he spoke even then of that social 'percentage' whose embodiment he later delineated in Sonechka Marmeladova (not without the influence of Fourier's doctrines, to be sure)."[8] Nothing of this sort occurs in the novel; but it is quite likely that the original plan included some "philanthropic" treatment of the theme of prostitution, and particularly of the rehabilitation of such "fallen women."* This was a very popular subject at the time—it inspired, for example, Nekrasov's famous poem, "When from thine error, dark, degrading," which Dostoevsky derided mercilessly in *Notes from Underground*—and continued to remain so for the next two decades.[9]

It seems clear that an earlier version—whether or not it contained anything about prostitution—was much more explicit on the subject of adultery. In the only surviving fragment of this original text, an important symbolic function is given to a famous engraving of the period, Emil Signol's *Christ and the Adultress*, inspired by the words from St. John: "He that is without sin among you, let him first cast a stone at her" (2: 411-417). There is no reference to this engraving in the published version; but the entire third episode dramatizes this theme in a bowdlerized form. The subtitle of the book—*The History of a Woman*—also suggests that Dostoevsky intended to emphasize similar motifs involving the status of women as the work proceeded. Moreover, what little we know of Netotchka is enough by itself to give her history a "philanthropic" stamp. Born of humble parents and living her earliest years in abject misery, Netotchka's success in becoming a great artist would reveal all the wealth of neglected talent hidden in the socially outcast and despised as well as in her supposedly inferior sex.

In all these ways, Dostoevsky was endeavoring to tap some of the lively interest in "the woman question" then so prominent on the Russian literary scene, and which had already been utilized in such novels as *Polinka Sachs* and in Herzen's story *The Thieving Magpie* (*Soroka-Vorovka*). Herzen anticipates Dostoevsky in also having taken a female artist (a gifted serf-actress) as the heroine of his tale; but his point is simply to show her destruction when she rejects the sexual advances of her owner and patron. Dostoevsky's

---

* There is reason to believe that Dostoevsky himself was personally involved, at least as an observer, in one such attempt. In a letter to him from Moscow (March 14, 1849), Pleshcheev inquires about someone named Naste (Nastasya). "Kiss her for me," he tells his friend. "I would give a good deal to have her beside me right now. Lately I have loved her even more, and I am terribly sad that it's impossible to reeducate her . . . or if it's possible, that it would cost money; I confess to you that this was the chief cause of my melancholy before departure. I am grateful for the pleasure she has given me, and would like to reward her with something. . . ."

A few weeks later (March-April 1849), in a letter written both in Russian and French, Pleshcheev appeals to Dostoevsky: "If you have some money, don't forget her [Nastasya], my dear fellow; as you owe me a bit, give her that trifle. I shall try to send her something also, but nothing is certain in this cruel world. . . . *If you only knew how sad I would be if she went again to where she was before.*" (Italics added.) It seems obvious that Pleshcheev is referring to a brothel. *Delo Petrashevtsev*, 3: 290, 296.

aim, unprecedented in the Russian novel of his time, was to depict a talented and strong-willed woman who refuses to allow herself to be crushed—who becomes, in short, the main *positive* heroine of a major novel. In so doing he hoped once again, as with *Poor Folk*, to reestablish his independent position on the Russian social-cultural scene, and offer an alternative both to Goncharov's unappealing submission to *meshchantstvo* (bourgeois practicality) as well as to Herzen's bleakness and despair.

3

The first part of *Netotchka Nezvanova*, entitled *Childhood*, focuses on Netotchka's earliest years as the stepdaughter of the down-and-out musician Yefimov, whom she believes at that age to be her real father. Yefimov's ancestry as a character has been traced both to E.T.A. Hoffmann and to Balzac (*Gambara*); but it is more enlightening to see him in terms of Dostoevsky's own work. Clearly related to Golyadkin, he wrestles with the same sort of inner conflict in other terms: he too refuses to acknowledge the truth about himself, and, when forced to do so by circumstances, also goes mad. Yefimov's "ambition," however, takes the form of a maniacal *idée fixe*—the belief that he is the greatest violinist, if not in the world, then at least in Russia; and his character is entirely free of Golyadkin's timidity and servility. In Yefimov, Dostoevsky heightens Golyadkin's urge for self-assertion into megalomania, unites this trait with the thematic complex of Romanticism and the "dreamer," and transforms this type, for the first time, into a very unsympathetic character. For Yefimov's artistic obsession leads to an exacerbated egoism whose consequences are literally monstrous in their effect on the lives of others.

The source of Yefimov's delusion, presented rather enigmatically, stems from his relation to an Italian violinist—his first instructor in that instrument—who dies under suspicious circumstances after willing his violin to Yefimov; and this section of the book is invariably considered "Hoffmannesque." Dostoevsky places considerable emphasis on the demonic and extra-social (or asocial) features of Yefimov's mania, and his discontent and extravagant self-glorification have often been attributed to the lowliness of his social condition. But he is not a serf like Herzen's actress, and his employer—a wealthy landowner, with a passion for music—prides himself on treating his musicians with respect for their dignity. Dostoevsky even takes pains to underline that Yefimov's incomprehensible behavior has no simple social cause. For after repaying the kindness of his employer with the blackest ingratitude, Yefimov himself finds it impossible to explain the impulse that has caused him to insult and slander all those who have befriended him. " 'God knows why I insulted you, sir,' " he tells the landowner, waving his hands; " 'it's probably the devil who has misled me. I don't know myself what has pushed me to all this' " (2: 147).

Yefimov's uncontrollable egoism makes him entirely unfit for ordinary social life, and is depicted as fiendishly mysterious in origin—similar to the inexplicable criminal impulses that so often seize some of Hoffmann's characters. And since this Hoffmannesque atmosphere is confined only to Yefimov, it is tempting to interpret it as having some symbolic value. Yefimov, we might say, is possessed by the demon of the old-fashioned Romantic conception of art, which was indeed largely a glorification of the ego of its creator. Such a reading can be supported by the satire of Romantic egoism that Dostoevsky works into this first section, using Nestor Kukolnik's pompous Romantic tragedy, *Jacopo Sannazaro*, as his target. Both Yefimov and his friend Karl Feodorovich—an unsuccessful ballet dancer, a purely comic replica of Yefimov—are wild with enthusiasm over this work, and spend their time, as they sit in Yefimov's miserable attic, declaiming it aloud with delectation. "This play deals with the misfortunes of a great artist, some Gennaro or Jacopo," writes Netotchka, "who on one page cries: 'I am unrecognized!' and on another: 'I am recognized!' or: 'I have no talent!' and then, several lines later: 'I have talent!' It all ended very tearfully" (2: 168). Such a scene parodies the total self-absorption of the Romantic artist, whose consequences are shown in Yefimov to be so morally disastrous.

Possessed of genuine talent and a fine understanding of music, Yefimov is incapable of self-discipline because convinced in advance that he is a genius of the first order. Dostoevsky contrasts him with his close friend, the Russo-German violinist B., who, lacking Yefimov's natural gifts, makes up for them by hard work and unstinting devotion to his art. " 'He's a dreamer,' " explains B. to Prince X., later to play an important part in Netotchka's life. " '. . . He thirsts for glory. If such a feeling becomes an artist's sole and only motive, then that artist is no longer an artist because he has lost the main artistic instinct, that is, love of art solely because it is art and not something else, not glory' " (2: 175). The opposition between Yefimov and B. parallels the one in Goncharov's *An Ordinary Story* between the Romantic illusions of the young Aduev and the sober common sense of his hard-working uncle; but instead of satirizing the illusions of art in contrast to "real life," Dostoevsky juxtaposes the egoism of the

Romantic artist against a disinterested devotion to art as a value of the highest spiritual importance. It can scarcely be a hazard that, except for Yefimov, the characters genuinely devoted to music—Yefimov's original employer, the violinist B., Prince X., his stepdaughter Alexandra Mikhailovna—are all depicted as kind and unselfish in their relations with others.

Yefimov's character is Dostoevsky's first fully developed portrait of a masocho-sadistic personality. Unable to face the contrast between his megalomania and the humiliations of his actual status in society, he takes refuge in paranoia. He believed, writes Netotchka, that he was "persecuted by fate, injured, misunderstood because of various intrigues and therefore unknown. This last idea even flattered him because there are characters like that who dearly love to consider themselves insulted and oppressed, and to complain about this loudly or console themselves under their breath while doing reverence to their own unacknowledged grandeur" (2: 157). Yefimov thus derives a masochistic satisfaction from his own degradation; and this masochism becomes transformed into sadism with a suitable victim. Unable to accept responsibility for the abyss between his self-image and reality, Yefimov fastens the guilt onto his poor slavey of a wife who actually keeps him alive. She becomes the scapegoat for all his misfortunes—a living "pretext" for his idleness and dissipation. The "blindness, the unshakable idea of my stepfather, his folly, made him inhuman and insensible . . . [and] he swore never to take up his violin again until his wife's death, as he told her with brutal frankness" (2: 155).

Netotchka's first memories go back to her ninth year, and they are all dominated by the strange figure of her stepfather. Her earliest notions of art are colored by her stepfather's cruelty and moral irresponsibility in refusing to lift even a finger to support the family. To his wife's reproaches, Yefimov always replied haughtily that he was an "artist," and Netotchka comments that "the idea became instantly established in my imagination that an artist was a special kind of person not like other people" (2: 62). Infected by her father's fantasies of artistic triumphs, and of a life of ease and luxury to arrive after her mother's death, Netotchka begins to wish her already in the grave so that the glorious day should finally be at hand. Netotchka's emotions become identified with those of Yefimov to such an extent that she even steals money badly needed for food from her mother to supply him with alcohol. "How could I have developed such cruelty toward such an eternally suffering being as my mother?" Netotchka asks wonderingly. "It's only now that I understand her tormented life,

and I cannot remember that martyr without a pang in my heart"
(2: 163).

The *dénouement* of this part of Netotchka's life occurs when the
world-famous European violinist S. arrives to give a concert in Petersburg. Yefimov begins to be tortured by the possibility that he will not
be able to dismiss him—as he has done, in the past, with so many
others—as infinitely inferior to his own talents. S.'s playing confirms
his fears; and Yefimov returns home from the recital shaken and distraught, to find his wife dead and all possibility of self-evasion
stripped away at last. The eerie efforts of the demented "artist" to
scrape out a tune on his violin, after having buried his dead wife
under a mountain of clothes so as to conceal her figure entirely, are
almost unbearable in their ghoulish pathos. Like Golyadkin, Yefimov
continues to exculpate himself up to the very last (" 'You hear, *it's
not I; I am not guilty in this,*' " he tells Netotchka, pointing to the
corpse), and he completes his perfidy by abandoning the little girl
as they wander homeless through the snowy Petersburg streets in
the dead of night (2: 186-188). This first part of Dostoevsky's novel
contains one of the most bitter indictments of Romantic egoism, in
its "artistic" variety, that can be found in the literature of the time.
Only Dickens's Harold Skimpole in *Bleak House* (published four
years later) can compare with Yefimov as a moral condemnation of
the heartlessness of Romantic aestheticism.

4
———

The second sequence of *Netotchka Nezvanova*—called *A New Life*—
whisks the heroine, by a miracle of fate, into that very world she
had dreamed about under the influence of Yefimov's obsession. The
latter dies in madness two days after his disgraceful abandonment
of the terrified child; and she is taken in by Prince X., who has previously learned her strange history from B. The Prince is described
as "a well-known dilettante, a person who deeply understood and
loved art"; and Netotchka remarks how struck she was with his face,
"so serious, but so kindly, looking at me with such profound compassion" (2: 189). There is some mystery in the life of the Prince that
Dostoevsky reserves for later elucidation; his importance for the
moment is that he transfers Netotchka from a world dominated by
Yefimov to one in which a love of art is combined with the highest
moral and human qualities.

This second sequence of the novel must itself be divided into two
sections—one recounting Netotchka's meeting with another orphan

adopted by Prince X., Larya, and the next dealing with her relation to Princess Katya. The meeting with Larya is quite brief and foreshadows a later development: called "the future hero of my story" by Netotchka, the little boy vanishes rapidly with the assurance that he will be heard from again. Dostoevsky eliminated this scene when he decided to republish *Netotchka Nezvanova* as a fragment; but it must be considered in any analysis of his original plan. For Larya's importance is not only in his future role as "hero"; he also acts as a "reflector" for Netotchka, and helps her, even at this early stage, to understand the significance of her own twisted psychic history. As she listens to Larya's account of his life, "more and more I was illuminated by recognition," she says. "And it was Larya who was chosen to explain all my grief to me through his own story" (2: 442).

Larya is burdened with a terrible sense of guilt because of behavior whose psychological source is very similar to that of Yefimov. In spite of realizing how much his parents loved him, and how difficult their life was, he deliberately exaggerated all his childish distresses and complaints so as to enjoy their unhappiness. "I would be so stupid and thoughtless that when I'd come home from school I'd tell on purpose that the other boys pinched me," he says, "but I'd tell it because I already knew that Mama would start crying when I'd told everything." He deliberately tortured his parents in this fashion "because I liked it so much, I mean, that Mama was crying about *me*" (2: 443). However, he makes up his mind at last not to continue in this behavior because "I did feel sorry for Mama, Netotchka" (2: 444); but fate forestalls him from putting his resolution into practice. His father suffers a stroke on the very night Larya has decided inwardly to reform; and a few days later, his mother follows his father to the grave. Larya is thus left with an excruciating sense of guilt, unable to expiate his cruel ingratitude toward parents who had lavished upon him all their love.

Larya's story has a profound effect on Netotchka, clarifying her own feelings and revealing them to her in all their shamefulness. Dostoevsky only indicates this process of self-recognition, however, and does not portray it taking effect. Instead, the mature Netotchka generalizes about how children can be perverted by the wrong kind of early environment, and how easy it is to encourage them into cultivating "false sentimentality" and "fantasy" which causes them "to show off and idolize [themselves] and to develop egoism, self-love and sensuality" (2: 443). A child who develops in such a way will turn into another Yefimov so far as other people are concerned. "A child is by nature a despot, and who knows, perhaps Larya had already discovered the cowardly satisfaction of taking an insult on himself and then wreaking it on another, an innocent one, just as I later met many egoists who had driven their egoism to the point of the most refined, the most depraved sensualism, and would wreak on others the insults they had endured all their lives, not nursing in their outraged souls a hate for egoism, but maintaining one conviction—to be in principle the same egoists, so as to get on in life and torment others in the name of their own misfortunes, to enjoy the role of onlooker and observe from the side how others will bear up" (2: 443).

The moral condemnation of this form of "sensuality" is perfectly clear and explicit: those who have suffered because of the egoism of others should nurse "in their outraged souls a hate for egoism," and not seek revenge by becoming egoistic oppressors in their turn. Larya had been on the point of overcoming this type of "enjoyment" when his parents died; and in his role of future hero, he would probably have brought to bear the lessons learned in the course of his repentance. The next episode in this second sequence brings Netotchka into contact with another child—Princess Katya, the youngest daughter of Prince X—whose fineness of character conquers the temptation of egoistic resentment in a much more active and decisive fashion.*

5

Princess Katya has of course led a totally different kind of life than the poverty-stricken orphan Netotchka. The petted and coddled darling of the world in which she lives, Katya is proud and headstrong,

---

* Scholars have noted some striking resemblances between this part of the novel and Eugène Sue's *Mathilde*, a feuilleton-novel that Dostoevsky read, and probably began to translate, in 1844. (See p. 128.) "In Sue's novel, too," writes Victor Terras, "we meet two little girls, one blonde, the other brunette (although in *Mathilde* their roles are reversed: the blonde is in charge), whose experiences are pretty much the same as those of Netotchka and Katya in Dostoevsky's novel. Mme Leotard, Katya's governess, is much like Mme Blondeau in Sue's novel, while Prince X., Katya's father, has some common traits with M. de Mortagne. Even the dog-motif is there, as a white wolf-dog, Felix, plays much the same role in *Mathilde* as the bulldog Falstaff in *Netotchka Nezvanova*. The psychological details of the 'romance' [between the two girls] follow Sue quite closely." Victor Terras, *The Young Dostoevsky*, 1846-1849 (The Hague, 1969), 206-212.

Even more parallels could be cited; but these are enough to make the imputation of influence quite plausible. The schema of Sue's novel, which Dostoevsky had worked over only two years previously, was certainly in his mind. Dostoevsky, however, uses it for his own purposes, and with an incomparably deeper grasp of character and motivation, though he also takes over some of Sue's didactic moralism in presenting Netotchka's story.

overflowing with vitality and beauty, simply unable to understand
that life could not conform to her wishes in every respect. "The prin-
cipal defect of the Princess, or better, the chief trait of her character," writes Netotchka, ". . . was pride." The qualification implies
that "pride" is not always a "defect," and Netotchka stresses that
whatever faults Katya may have, "none . . . were born with her—all
were acquired, and she struggled with them all" (2: 207). Netotchka
notes that although Katya's mother exercised "a moral tyranny" over
her, and the little girl much preferred her father, she nonetheless
obeyed her mother without resentment because she understood all
"the immensity of her [mother's] love, sometimes going so far as to
seem an unhealthy frenzy" (2: 206). The contrast with Netotchka in
the same situation is obvious.

The relations between Katya and Netotchka develop into the type
of psychological duel that Dostoevsky would later use in so many
variations. The impressionable Netotchka, starved for affection,
falls passionately in love with the beautiful Katya in a fashion whose
erotic overtones are perfectly explicit. Katya is very well aware of
Netotchka's infatuation; but she refuses to respond to it because her
fierce pride resents Netotchka's intrusion into a world over which,
up to that point, Katya herself had reigned supreme. As compensation, she observes Netotchka's transports covertly, enjoying to the
full her sense of power over the emotions of the poor orphan. Princess Katya is thus the first of Dostoevsky's "infernal women," whose
wounded pride stands in the way of their acceptance of the gift of
love and generates, rather, hatred and persecution of the lover; but in
this early phase, where the drama is played out between children,
the wound is not yet so deep that it can no longer be healed.

Katya is driven to the most outrageous breaches of behavior because she knows that Netotchka is watching her with panic-stricken
adoration. And she finally commits the unforgivable sin: she allows
the ferocious bulldog, Sir John Falstaff, to invade the upstairs apartment of her pious and Pecksniffish aunt. Even Katya cannot escape unscathed from such an enormity; and Netotchka, spontaneously taking the blame on herself in the moment of crisis, is exiled to
a dark closet as punishment. It is this gesture of self-sacrifice that
wins Katya at last, and decides the struggle in her proud little breast
between resentment and love. The act of self-sacrifice dissolves
pride and is met with love in return; Katya does not allow pride to
trap her indefinitely into prolonging the sadistic "enjoyment" derived from the torments of Netotchka's unrequited love. This experi-

ence also helps Netotchka to understand something more about the sufferings of her poor mother, whose self-sacrifice for Yefimov never received any such recompense.

It is evident, from Dostoevsky's portrayal of Katya, that he was already a master of the love-hate dialectic which was to become so important a feature of his major works. Both Yefimov and Larya have been depicted in a way that reveals this dialectic in action; but in Katya for the first time it becomes completely self-conscious. When asked about her past behavior by Netotchka, she replies: " 'Well, I always loved you, always! But then, I was not able to bear it; I thought, I'll devour her with kisses, or I'll pinch her to death' " (2: 220). This is the naive form in which Katya explains her ambiguous feelings, which stem from the unwillingness of the prideful ego to surrender its own autonomy to the infringement represented by the temptation of love. In *Netotchka Nezvanova*, this conflict is still presented purely in moral-psychological terms; but one should not overlook that the self-sacrifice of Netotchka, and Katya's response, already contain the emotive-experiential basis of Dostoevsky's Christianity. Salvation for Dostoevsky would always depend on the capacity of the prideful ego (which later becomes identified with the prideful intellect) to surrender to the free self-sacrifice of love made on its behalf by Christ.

6

The third and last episode involves Alexandra Mikhailovna, Katya's older half-sister, the child of the previous marriage of Prince X.'s wife. Netotchka is sent to live with her after Katya and the family leave Petersburg, and her story thus becomes intertwined with that of her new guardian. This section has much stronger social overtones than the earlier ones, though not so much in the fashion of the Natural School as in that of "George Sandism." The intrigue of this part focuses on the human injustice of class barriers and the life-blighting prejudices to which they give rise, particularly in the relations between the sexes. This is illustrated both by what we learn of Alexandra Mikhailovna's life, and also by Netotchka's development. But, as we shall see, Dostoevsky does not lose sight of his theme of masocho-sadistic "sensuality," and blends it with "the woman question" in a manner anticipating the similar fusion of the moral-psychological and the social-ideological in his best novels.

From the strict point of view of aristocratic caste, Alexandra Mik-hailovna is herself of suspect social origin. Her father, a wealthy land speculator, had left her no great dowry, and it had been diffi-cult to marry her off satisfactorily. Without bothering about the young girl's wishes, her mother had succeeded in making a match with a satisfactory bridegroom who was "wealthy and of very high rank" in government service. Alexandra Mikhailovna is twenty-two years old, of a sweet, gentle, and loving disposition, and seems to have everything in the world necessary for happiness; but Netotchka notices that "some sort of hidden heartfelt sadness cast a severe shadow over her beautiful features." The life of Alexandra Mik-hailovna, who is herself the soul of generosity ("compassion always gained the upper hand in her soul over repugnance"), was haunted by some secret grief whose origin Netotchka could never fathom; and she lives side by side with her for eight years without unriddling the enigma of her ineradicable sorrow (2: 224-225).

Alexandra Mikhailovna's husband is an important bureaucrat, eternally preoccupied with the functions of his office, very ambitious and successful, "uncommunicative, cold, and even when in the company of his wife finding very little to say to her" (2: 226). Peter Alexandrovich is Dostoevsky's version of Goncharov's uncle in *An Ordinary Story*, and both are in the line of the self-complacent, self-assured Russian bureaucrats whose greatest incarnation is the knuckle-cracking husband of Anna Karenina. All the same, Alex-andra stands in terrified awe of his wishes, and courts his approval with trembling anxiety. Once or twice during the course of eight years, "a sort of hatred, a sort of indignation shone on her usually gentle visage, instead of the invariable self-abasement and venera-tion of her husband" (2: 228); but such moments led only to pro-longed crises of depression and prostration. The hold that Peter Alexandrovich exercises over his wife resembles that of Murin over Katerina; and it is, in fact, a transposition of much the same drama into the social terms of the late 1840s.

Netotchka discovers the clue to this baffling relationship one day when she is eighteen years old. Picking up a novel casually (Scott's *St. Ronan's Well*), she finds in it an old, faded letter spotted with tears and written to her beloved Alexandra Mikhailovna. Penned by a young man, its contents disclose that the two had had a deeply intimate (but presumably Platonic) friendship, which had caused a good deal of gossip, and made it necessary for the young man to exile himself forever from Alexandra's presence. What had caused the gossip was not so much the tenderness of their communion (though a corrupt world could not help misunderstanding its nature), but the fact that the young man was a nobody of low social rank. "If only I had had importance, some personal value as they understood it," he writes, and "had inspired more respect in their eyes, then they would have forgiven you!" (2: 252). Despite his grief, the writer tells Alexandra not to despair, and to remember that there is one person in the world who truly understands and trusts her—her husband Peter Alexandrovich.

This letter explains to Netotchka why Alexandra Mikhailovna lives in such chilling solitude despite her social position, and uncovers the source of the profound melancholy that has been causing her to waste slowly away. Even more, it helps Netotchka understand why she has always disliked Peter Alexandrovich in spite of his outward solicitude for his wife and his irreproachable external conduct. Netotchka now recalls one incident whose meaning she had never grasped before—a glimpse of Peter Alexandrovich standing before a mirror just before going in to visit his spouse. A moment earlier, she had seen him relaxed and smiling; but then, "the smile disappeared as if by command, and some sort of bitter feeling curled his lips . . . some sort of convulsive pain brought creases to his forehead and lowered his brows. His glance hid gloomily behind his glasses—in a word, in one instant, as if by order, he became a totally different person" (2: 251).

It now becomes clear to Netotchka that Peter Alexandrovich has been playing a consummately hypocritical role. He has, presumably, forgiven his wife her regrettable breach of the social proprieties; but he poisons her life by never letting her forget the "sin" she had committed in the past. His presence is always calculated to keep her guilt alive, and to fill her scruple-ridden heart with terror. Peter Alexandrovich thus embodies, in a more insidious form, the same masocho-sadistic "sensuality" previously analyzed in Yefimov, Larya, and Katya; and the state of mind to which he has reduced his wife is similar to that of the inwardly enslaved Katerina in *The Landlady*.

The revelation of Alexandra Mikhailovna's tragedy is interwoven with Netotchka's own emotional development, stimulated by the personal encounters we have already mentioned and also by her education under Alexandra Mikhailovna's guidance. This follows the precepts of freedom and informality laid down in Rousseau's *Émile* (there are a number of allusions to Rousseau in the novel); and one of the works they read together with the most enthusiasm is a French translation of Plutarch, which Alexandra Mikhailovna is

said to know by heart. Deleted in later editions, the reference probably is meant to imply that Netotchka's character is being steeled
by absorbing the precepts of this bible of republican virtue. Most important of all is that Netotchka, discovered to have a voice of great
power and promise, begins to take lessons at the Conservatory; and
her artistic gifts go hand-in-hand with a personality that has become
morally transformed. For once again she is confronted with the
trauma inflicted in her childhood by Yefimov's relation to her mother;
but now she aligns herself unhesitatingly with the victim against the
persecutor and oppressor.

The last few scenes add an additional complication to the intrigue
because Alexandra Mikhailovna suspects her husband of having designs on the now-nubile Netotchka. Indeed, she even accuses him,
with truly Freudian prescience, of being overly critical of Netotchka
because he is sexually attracted to her, and yet of so severe and
upright a character that he can only express his feelings by antagonism. But the major action involves the letter, which Peter Alexandrovich sees in Netotchka's hands and believes to be addressed to
her.

To spare her benefactress the crushing blow of having the letter
brought to light, Netotchka willingly takes on herself the onus of a
secret correspondence with a presumptive lover. But Alexandra does
not believe either her husband's charges or Netotchka's admission
of guilt; nor does the mere existence of a letter, in her eyes, prove
that Netotchka has done anything reprehensible. Indignant at her
husband's attempt to break the young girl's spirit, as he has broken
her own, she rallies to Netotchka's defense. " 'We are all sinners,'
she said in a tearful, quivering voice, looking at her husband with
humility, 'and which of us has the right to reject the hand of another? Give me your hand, Annette . . . you cannot offend me by
your presence because *I too am a sinner*' " (2: 246). To this paraphrase of St. John, the furious Peter Alexandrovich responds with
veiled and insulting insinuations that Netotchka now understands
for the first time.

In conclusion, Netotchka hands the letter over privately to Peter
Alexandrovich and bitterly denounces his moral tyranny over his
long-suffering wife. " 'You wanted to maintain a superiority over her,
and you did so. But why? Because you wanted to triumph over her
phantoms, over her sick and disordered imagination, in order to show
her that she had erred and that you were *more virtuous*' " (2: 266).
With these accusing words, Netotchka shows Peter Alexandrovich
that she is made of sterner stuff than his wife and will not allow her-

self to be trampled on. If the book had been continued, we should certainly have seen Netotchka displaying the same lofty independence and the same moral-social opposition to tyranny of any kind under other circumstances. But, alas, we shall never know what the important message is that Netotchka is about to receive when the fragment ends, nor how Katya will behave when the two girls (now young ladies) meet again, nor in what guise Larya will turn up to become "the hero" of the book. Too bad!

CHAPTER 24

Envoi

The last installment of *Netotchka Nezvanova* was published in the May issue of *Notes of the Fatherland* without the name of Dostoevsky as author. He had been arrested on April 23, and Kraevsky was forced to obtain special permission to use the manuscript he had already received from the political suspect now under lock and key. No more of the book was written, and Dostoevsky did not take it up again when he began to think of resuming his literary career six or seven years later. Whether the novel would have restored him to fame, if he had been able to complete it as planned, can only remain a matter for conjecture. The critical response to the individual sections had been mixed, but more favorable than to all the stories except *White Nights*. The power of the scenes involving Yefimov was recognized, the encounter between Netotchka and Larya was compared to Dickens (Paul and Florence in *Dombey and Son*), and the character of the Princess Katya was especially singled out for commendation. Such straws in the wind indicate that Dostoevsky had at last begun to make some headway against his detractors. But his name vanished from sight after his arrest, and what remained predominant until he returned was the negative verdict of Belinsky on everything he had written after *Poor Folk*.

For us, *Netotchka Nezvanova* is primarily of interest because it sheds so much light on Dostoevsky's internal evolution as a writer. There are, to begin with, a number of suggestions of future characters and motifs that may be added to those already noted in earlier chapters. Yefimov is evidently the prototype of all of Dostoevsky's later "dreamers" and intellectuals, whose frustrated idealism (whether in relation to themselves or to mankind as a whole) will be allied to delusions of grandeur and to a similar inhumanity. The relation between Netotchka and Katya is a paradigm for what Dostoevsky's greatest protagonists will later find so difficult to accomplish—the grateful surrender of pride to love and self-sacrifice. Peter Alexandrovich shows up again in the form of all the perfectly respectable and self-satisfied reprobates—Luzhin, Totsky, Velchaninov—who assume as their right the power to wreak havoc with female lives. Prince X. is the first of Dostoevsky's "perfectly good" men, who include Colonel Rostanev of *The Village of Stepanchikovo*, Prince Myshkin, and Alyosha Karamazov.

Much more important, however, is that Dostoevsky moves decisively beyond the limits of the Natural School and already stands at the threshold of the world of his major novels—a threshold he is usually considered to have reached only about fifteen years later. The setting of his action is no longer confined to the slums of Petersburg, or to the world of the bureaucratic chancelleries and their inhabitants; nor can his characters any longer be classified in the well-defined and, by this time, fairly conventional social-ideological categories of his earlier stories ("the downtrodden people" and the "dreamer"). For the first time Dostoevsky's horizon embraces the higher social sphere of the enlightened, cultivated aristocracy, and his people are now complex individuals grasped primarily in terms of their own quality of personality and in the light of Dostoevsky's fully elaborated and original psychology of masocho-sadism. The significance of *Netotchka Nezvanova*, which has so far not been sufficiently appreciated, is that it enables us to pinpoint this pivotal moment in Dostoevsky's literary career.

Starting out as a member of the Natural School and as a disciple of Gogol (though a very independent one, who was never merely an imitator), Dostoevsky distinguished himself immediately by his psychological handling of social themes in *Poor Folk*. More and more, though, he became concerned with the psychic distortions suffered in the struggle of personality to assert itself and to satisfy the natural human need for dignity and self-respect in a world of rigid class barriers and political despotism. But so long as Dostoevsky's stories continued to use the familiar iconography of the Natural School, a social causation was always at least implied for the psychic malformation of his characters—even if not stressed sufficiently to satisfy Belinsky. In *The Landlady*, however, Dostoevsky suggested strongly for the first time that such malformations can lead to a masochistic "enjoyment" of self-degradation which reinforces the bonds enslaving personality and makes its captivity partially self-imposed. Nonetheless, the symbolism of the story still attributes the "cause" of Katerina's emotional imprisonment to a malevolent external force.

It is only with *Netotchka Nezvanova* that we can see how Dostoevsky's explorations of personality have gradually led him, not only to reverse the hierarchy between the psychological and the social assumed by the Natural School, but entirely to disengage his psychology from its earlier direct dependence on social conditioning. For here Dostoevsky brings the theme of masocho-sadistic "sensuality" to the foreground as the major *source* of cruelty and oppression in human relations; and the conquest of such "sensuality" now becomes *the* overriding moral-social imperative. To be sure, this moral-psychological theme does not stand alone, and is interwoven with the social-ideological motifs of the status of art and "the woman question"; but such motifs remain subordinate to the inner struggle of the characters between good and evil. Even though the social position and relations of the characters serve to frame and motivate the action, Dostoevsky's focus is no longer on external social conditions and their reflection in consciousness and behavior (as with Devushkin, Golyadkin, or Polzunkov). It is, rather, on the personal qualities that the characters display in the battle against the instinctive tendency of the injured ego to hit back for whatever social-psychic lesions and traumas it has been forced to endure. The world of *Netotchka Nezvanova* is thus no longer exclusively social-psychological but has already become the moral-psychological universe of his later fiction. For the capacity to overcome the masocho-sadistic dialectic of a wounded egoism—the capacity to conquer hatred and replace it by love—has now emerged as the ideal center of Dostoevsky's moral-artistic cosmos.

But all this exists as yet only in germ, as yet contained within the limits of a world where the conflicts have not been driven to the extreme and where nothing (except death) is irreparable. The truly tragic dimension of the later Dostoevsky is still lacking, the sense of the immitigable and the irreconcilable, the clash of contending values each with its claim to absolute hegemony—love and justice, faith and reason, the God-man and the Man-god—which Dostoevsky alone of all the great novelists has known how to convey with such unrivaled force. Most of what the great Dostoevsky was to accomplish is already present schematically in his work of the 1840s; but the experiences he was soon to undergo would enable him to fill out and expand these schemas into the monumental forms we admire. And these experiences will include, not only his agonizing purgatory as an individual, but also the agitated upheaval of Russian social-cultural life that coincided with the resumption of his literary career. Dostoevsky returned to Russia at a time when the age-old moral-social norms of his society were being challenged more radically than ever before. What had been only implicit and covert in the 1840s now had become explicit, aggressive, and overtly threatening; and Dostoevsky reacted to these changes in terms of the lessons he believed he had learned about human life, and about the Russian people, in the house of the dead. His great novels will emerge as a product of the creative synthesis between the accidents of his personal fate, the tumultuous course of Russian social-historical experience in the 1860s and 1870s, and the literary evolution we have been tracing so far with its final focus on the conflict between egoism and love.

NOTES

CHAPTER 2

1. F. M. Dostoevsky, *Diary of a Writer* (Jan. 1877), trans. Boris Brasol (George Braziller, 1954), 6. I shall cite Dostoevsky's *Dnevnik Pisatelya* in this English version wherever possible as *DW*, though with numerous revisions of the translation; see also, for the self-comparison with Tolstoy, F. M. Dostoevsky, *The Notebooks for A Raw Youth*, ed. Edward Wasiolek, trans. Victor Terras (Chicago & London, 1969), 425, 544-545.

2. Leonid Grossman, *Zhizn i Trudy Dostoevskogo* (Moscow-Leningrad, 1935), 21. Cited hereafter as ZT.

3. A. M. Dostoevsky, *Vospominania* (Leningrad, 1930), 17-18.

4. *F. M. Dostoevsky v Vospominaniakh Sovremmenikov*, ed. A. Dolinin, 2 vols. (Moscow, 1964), 1: 44. For convenience I shall cite Andrey Dostoevsky's reminiscences in this collection wherever possible. Cited hereafter as DVS.

5. *DW* (1873, No. 1), 6.

6. A. M. Dostoevsky, 18-19.

7. *DVS*, 1: 49.

8. *Ibid.*, 51.

9. F. M. Dostoevsky, *Pisma*, ed. and annotated by A. S. Dolinin, 4 vols. (Moscow, 1928-1959), 2: 549; August 16, 1839. Cited hereafter as *Pisma*.

10. V. S. Nechaeva, *V Seme i Usadbe Dostoevskikh* (Moscow, 1939), 109.

11. *Ibid.*, 5.

12. Aimée Dostoevsky, *Feodor Dostoevsky* (London, 1921), 34-35.

13. *DVS*, 1: 76.

14. Nechaeva, 90.

15. *Ibid.*, 77.

16. *DVS*, 1: 87.

17. Nechaeva, 81.

18. *Ibid.*, 99.

19. *DW* (1873, No. 50), 152.

20. Nechaeva, 13.

21. *Ibid.*, 106.

22. *Ibid.*

23. *Ibid.*, 109.

24. *Ibid.*, 111.

CHAPTER 3

1. *DVS*, 1: 55.

2. Orest Miller and Nikolay Strakhov, *Biografia, Pisma i Zametki iz Zapisnoi Knizhi F. M. Dostoevskogo* (St. Petersburg, 1883), 6. Cited hereafter as *Biografia*.

3. *DVS*, 1: 57.

4. *Ibid.*, 157.

5. Miller, *Biografia*, 141.

6. *Letters of Sigmund Freud*, selected by Ernst L. Freud and trans. by Tania and James Stern (New York, 1960), 332.

7. Freud's essay has been widely reprinted. I cite a volume in the paperback edition of Freud's collected papers issued by Collier Books. Sigmund Freud, *Character and Culture*, ed. Philip Reiff (New York, 1963), 279.

8. *Ibid.*, 280-281.

9. *DVS*, 1: 191.

10. The relevant quotation from Andrey Dostoevsky is given in *Literaturnoe Nasledstvo*, No. 86 (Moscow, 1973), 550; see also the reference in the memoirs of K. A. Trutovsky, which refer to 1849, *DVS*, 1: 109 and the remark of Dostoevsky to Solovyev about his lethargic sleep, which speaks of it as part of the nervous disorders of his "youth" (*yunost*, which means late adolescence or early manhood). He does not say that it goes back to his "childhood" (*detstvo*). *Ibid.*, 2: 191.

11. Leonid Grossman, *Dostoevsky na Zhiznennom Puti* (Moscow, 1928), 33. Cited hereafter as *DZhP*.

12. *DVS*, 1: 64.

13. *Ibid.*, 66.

14. Nechaeva, *V Seme*, 37.

15. *DW* (January 1876), 208.

16. Nechaeva, 83.

17. *DVS*, 1: 209.

18. *Ibid.*, 70.

19. *DW* (July-August 1877), 752.

20. *DVS*, 1: 72.

21. *Ibid.*, 76.

22. *Ibid.*

23. *Ibid.*, 75.

24. Grossman, *DZhP*, 26.

25. *DVS*, 1: 82.

26. *Ibid.*, 75.

27. *Ibid.*, 81.

28. F. M. Dostoevsky, *The Notebooks for The Possessed*, ed. Edward Wasiolek, trans. Victor Terras (Chicago & London, 1968), 66.

29. *Ibid.*, 64.

30. *DVS*, 1: 83-84.

31. *Ibid.*, 84.

32. *Pisma*, 1: 52; October 31, 1838.

33. *Ibid.*, 215; March 9, 1857.

34. *DVS*, 1: 59.

CHAPTER 4

1. Alexander Herzen, *My Past and Thoughts*, trans. by Constance Garnett, revised by Humphrey Higgens, 4 vols. (New York, 1968), 1: 42. Cited hereafter as *MPT*.

2. *Ibid.*, 2: 412.

3. *Ibid.*, 1: 42.

4. "La foi enfantine de Léon Tolstoi est avant tout affective, impulsive presque, sans grand contenu intellectuel au départ. . . . De sa religion, il n'a qu'une caricature. Car il ne semble pas avoir reçu une instruction religieuse plus digne, il ne semble pas que le mystère du Christ lui ait été montré dans sa profondeur, ni qu'il ait entrevu l'Ancien Testament dans sa majesté formidable." Nicolas Weisbein, *L'Evolution religieuse de Tolstoi* (Paris, 1960), 27.

5. *DW* (1873, No. 50), 152.

6. Miller, *Biografia*, 5-6.

7. *DVS*, 1: 75.

8. *Ibid.*

9. A. P. Stanley, *Lectures on the History of the Eastern Church* (London, 1924), 303.

10. *DW* (1873, No. 50), 152.

11. *Voyage en Russie* (Paris, n.d.), 276.

12. *La Russie en 1839*, 4 vols. (Paris, 1843), 3: 243.

13. Stanley, *Lectures*, 279.

14. *Ibid.*, 319.

15. A. M. Dostoevsky, *Vospominania*, 48-49.

16. *Pisma*, 2: 264; March 25/April 6, 1870.

17. Gautier, 298-299.

18. *DW* (July-August 1877), 803.

19. See George P. Fedotov, *The Russian Religious Mind* (New York, 1960), Chapter 4.

20. A. Leroy-Beaulieu, *The Empire of the Tsars and the Russians*, 3 vols. (New York, 1902), 3: 48.

21. *DVS*, 1: 42-43.

22. *DW* (April 1876), 284-285.

23. *Ibid.* (February 1876), 208-209.

24. *DVS*, 1: 61.

25. *Ibid.*

26. Nechaeva, *V Seme*, 117-118; February 2, 1838.

27. *Ibid.*, 73; June 29, 1832.

28. *Ibid.*, 107; June 2, 1835.

29. *Pisma*, 3: 177; June 10/22, 1875.

30. Lev Shestov, "Dostoevsky and Nietzsche: The Philosophy of Tragedy," in *Essays in Russian Literature, The Conservative View: Leontiev, Rozanov, Shestov*, sel., ed., and trans. by Spencer E. Roberts (Athens, Ohio, 1968), 3-183.

CHAPTER 5

1. Ernest J. Simmons, *Dostoevsky* (London, 1950), 20.

2. *Pisma*, 2: 298; December 2/14, 1870.

3. William Wordsworth, *The Prelude*, Bk. 6, lines 339-340.

4. Marc Raeff, *Origins of the Russian Intelligentsia* (New York, 1966), 142.

5. *Pisma*, 4: 196; August 18, 1880.

6. For a useful summary of the material, see Edmund K. Kostka, *Schiller in Russian Literature* (Philadelphia, 1965); Chapter 7 is devoted to Dostoevsky. Also, D. Chizhevsky, "Schiller v Rossii," *Novy Zhurnal* 45 (1956), 109-135, and the spirited study by the

Soviet Germanist N. Vilmont, "Dostoevsky i Schiller" in his *Velikie Sputniki* (Moscow, 1966), 7-316.

7. *DW* (June 1876), 343.

8. *Pisma*, 4: 196; August 18, 1880.

9. Cited in Louis Pedrotti, *Jósef-Julian Sękowski* (Berkeley & Los Angeles, 1960), 116.

10. Leonid Grossman, *Biblioteka Dostoevskogo* (Odessa, 1919), 70; for more details, see A. L. Bem, *U Istokov Tvorchestva Dostoevskogo* (Prague, 1936), 37-123; a good recent treatment is D. D. Blagoy, "Dostoevsky i Pushkin," in *Dostoevsky—Khudoznik i Myslitel* (Moscow, 1972), 344-426.

CHAPTER 6

1. The prose translation I am quoting is by Edmund Wilson, and is included as an appendix to D. S. Mirsky, *Pushkin* (New York, 1963), 261-270.

2. *DW* (January 1876), 184.

3. *Ibid.*, 185.

4. *Ibid.*, 184.

5. *Ibid.*, 186.

6. Fyodor Dostoevsky, *The Notebooks for Crime and Punishment*, ed. and trans. Edward Wasiolek (Chicago, 1967), 64.

7. *DW* (January 1876), 186.

8. *Ibid.*

9. Benedetto Croce, *Storia d'Europa nel Secolo Decimonono* (Bari, 1953), 55.

10. Konstantin Mochulsky, *Dostoevsky*, trans. Michael Minihan (Princeton, N.J., 1967), 9.

11. *Pisma*, 4: 236; February 4, 1838.

12. Cited in Leonid Grossman, *Dostoevsky* (Moscow, 1962), 29. This work has now appeared in English: *Dostoevsky*, trans. by Mary Mackler (Indianapolis/N.Y., 1975), 28.

13. *Pisma*, 4: 235; February 4, 1838.

14. *Ibid.*, 267.

15. *DVS*, 1: 122.

16. *Pisma*, 1: 46; August 9, 1838.

17. *DVS*, 1: 106.

18. *Ibid.*, 127.

19. *Ibid.*, 97.

20. *Ibid.*

21. *Ibid.*, 99.

22. *Ibid.*, 97.

23. Sigmund Freud, *Character and Culture*, 282.

24. *Pisma*, 1: 57; January 1, 1840.

25. *Ibid.*, 4: 233; December 3, 1837.

26. *Ibid.*

27. *Ibid.*, 1: 49; October 31, 1838.

28. *Ibid.*, 4: 238; June 5, 1838.

29. *Ibid.*

30. *Ibid.*, 1: 52; May 10, 1839.

31. *DVS*, 1: 210.

32. Nechaeva, *V Seme*, 121.

33. E. H. Carr, "Was Dostoevsky an Epileptic?" *The Slavonic and East European Review* 9 (1930), 429.

34. *Pisma*, 2: 549; August 16, 1839.

35. *Ibid.*, 550.

36. *Ibid.*

CHAPTER 7

1. Cited in V. G. Belinsky, *Selected Philosophical Works* (Moscow, 1948), 410-411. Cited hereafter as *Works*.

2. *Pisma*, 4: 242; May 5, 1839.

3. *DVS*, 2: 191.

4. *Pisma*, 1: 56; January 1, 1840.

5. *Ibid.*

6. Cited in M. P. Alekseev, *Ranii Drug F. M. Dostoevskogo* (Odessa, 1921), 17.

7. *Pisma*, 1: 51; October 31, 1838.

8. Alekseev, 13.

9. Cited in G. Prochorov, "Die Brüder Dostojevski und Shidlovski," *Zeitschrift für Slavische Philologie* 7 (1930), 320.

10. *Ibid.*

11. *Ibid.*

12. Belinsky, *Works*, 14.

13. *Pisma*, 1: 56; January 1, 1840.

14. *Natural Supernaturalism* (New York, 1971), 65.

15. *Ibid.*, 66.

16. *Literaturnoe Nasledstvo*, No. 86 (Moscow, 1973), 398; Letter 52, note 1.

CHAPTER 8

1. *Pisma*, 1: 47; August 9, 1838.

2. P. V. Annenkov, *The Extraordinary Decade*, trans. Irwin R. Titunik (Ann Arbor, Mich., 1968), 13. Cited hereafter as *Decade*.

3. *Pisma*, 1: 47; August 9, 1838.

4. *Ibid.*

5. *Pisma*, 1: 46; August 9, 1838.

6. *Ibid.*, 50; October 31, 1838.

7. *Ibid.*

8. Erich Auerbach, *Mimesis*, trans. by Willard Trask (Princeton, N.J., 1968), 440.

9. Cited in Benno von Wiese, *Friedrich Schiller* (Stuttgart, 1959), 448.

10. See Prochorov, 323; Chapter 7, note 9.

11. *Pisma*, 1: 47; August 9, 1838.

12. *Ibid.*

13. The best discussion is still that of Leonid Grossman, "Balzak i Dostoevsky," in *Poetika Dostoevskogo* (Moscow, 1925), 64-115; this has recently appeared in English: Leonid Grossman, *Balzac and Dostoevsky*, trans. Lena Karpov (n.p., 1973), 11-51.

14. Cited in Peter Demetz, *Marx, Engels und die Dichter* (Frankfurt-Berlin, 1969), 171.

15. *The Gates of Horn* (New York, 1963), 191.

16. *Pisma*, 1: 51; October 31, 1838.

17. Cited in David Owen Evans, *Social Romanticism in France, 1830-1848* (Oxford, 1951), 81.

18. Victor Hugo, *Oeuvres complètes* (Paris, 1882), 6: 91.

19. Herzen, *MPT*, 3: 1056.

20. V. V. Vinogradov, *Evolutsia Russ-kogo Naturalizma* (Leningrad, 1929), 127-152.

21. *Pisma*, 1: 58; January 1, 1840.

22. See D. G. Charlton, *Social Religions in France, 1815-1870* (London, 1963), 84.

23. *Pisma*, 1: 55; January 1, 1840.

24. C. A. Sainte-Beuve, *Portraits Contemporains* (Paris, 1869), 2: 230.

25. P. N. Sakulin, *Russkaya Literatura i Sotsializm* (Moscow, 1922), 317-318. This is still the best work on the subject.

CHAPTER 9

1. *Pisma*, 1: 76; March (February) 24, 1845.

2. A. I. Riesenkampf, "Vospominania o F. M. Dostoevskom," *Literaturnoe Nasledstvo* (Moscow, 1973), No. 86, 325.

3. *Ibid.*, 330.

4. *Ibid.*, 331.

5. *Ibid.*

6. *DVS*, 1: 95.

7. *Pisma*, 1: 65; December 23, 1841.

8. *Ibid.*, 4: 450; September 5, 1844.

9. *DVS*, 1: 112-113.

10. Victor Brombert, *Stendhal: Fiction and the Themes of Freedom* (New York, 1968), 29.

11. *Pisma*, 1: 56-57; January 1, 1840.

12. *Ibid.*, 58.

13. *Ibid.*, 58-59.

14. *Ibid.*, 69; 2nd half of January 1844.

15. V. G. Belinsky, *Izbrannye Filosofskie Sochinenia*, 2 vols. (Moscow, 1948), 1: 215. Cited hereafter as *IFS*.

16. Cited by N. G. Chernyshevsky, *Izbrannye Filosofskie Sochinenia*, 3 vols. (Leningrad, 1950): 1: 441.

17. I. I. Panaev, *Sobranie Sochinenii*, 6 vols. (Moscow, 1912), 6: 212. Cited hereafter as *SS*.

18. Cited in Yu. Oksman, *Letopis Zhizn i Tvorchestvo V. G. Belinskogo* (Moscow, 1958), 194.

19. *Ibid.*, 195.

20. Panaev, *SS*, 6: 273.

21. Belinsky, *Works*, 159.

22. *Ibid.*, 164-165.

23. Annenkov, *Decade*, 112.

24. See N. V. *Gogol v Russkoi Kritike* (Moscow, 1953), 122.

25. Annenkov, *Decade*, 112.

26. Belinsky, *IFS*, 1: 432.

27. Belinsky, *Works*, 192-193.

28. *DVS*, 1: 129.

29. D. V. Grigorovich, *Polnoe Sobranie Sochinenii*, 12 vols. (St. Petersburg, 1896), 12: 266.

CHAPTER 10

1. *DVS*, 1: 114.

2. Grossman, *DZhP*, 92.

3. Belinsky, *Works*, 323.

4. *Pisma*, 1: 78; May 4, 1845.

5. Harold March, *Frédéric Soulié* (New Haven, 1931), 177.

6. George Sand, *The Last of the Aldinis*, trans. George Burnham Ives (Philadelphia, 1900), 359-360.

7. *DW* (June 1876), 346.

8. Cited in M. Polyakov, *Vissarion Belinsky* (Moscow, 1960), 325.

9. For more details, see Ivan Pouznya, "George Sand et Dostoievski," *Études*, 238-239 (1939), 345-360.

10. *DW* (June 1876), 349.

11. *DVS*, 1: 116-117.

12. *Pisma*, 1: 73; September 30, 1844.

13. *Ibid.*, 76; March (February) 24, 1845.

14. This view has been advanced by K. K. Istomin and A. L. Bem. For further discussion, see Bem's suggestive article, "Pervye Shagi Dostoevskogo," *Slavia*, 12 (1933-1934), 134-161.

15. Honoré de Balzac, "Eugénie Grandet," *La Comédie humaine*, ed. Marcel Bouteron (Paris, 1947), 3: 599.

16. Mochulsky, *Dostoevsky*, 27.

17. For the reference to Blagoy's article, see above, Chapter 5, note 10.

CHAPTER 11

1. *DW* (January 1877), 584.
2. *Pisma*, 1: 75; March (February) 24, 1845.
3. Annenkov, *Decade*, 150.
4. *Pisma*, 1: 82; October 8, 1845.
5. Victor Terras, *The Young Dostoevsky*, 1846-1849 (The Hague, 1969), 76-86.
6. Belinsky's article is reprinted in *F. M. Dostoevsky v Russkoi Kritike* (Moscow, 1956; hereafter cited as *DRK*), 16.
7. *Ibid.*, 15.
8. *Ibid.*, 24.
9. See the article on *Poor Folk* by G. M. Fridlender in *Istoria Russkogo Romana*, 2 vols. (Moscow-Leningrad, 1962), 1: 412; also V. Kirpotin, *F. M. Dostoevsky, Tvorcheskii Put, 1821-1859* (Moscow, 1960), 255.
10. Vinogradov, *Evolutsia*, 311-338. This is part 2 of Vinogradov's classic study of *Poor Folk*. I am greatly indebted to Vinogradov for section 4 of my own chapter.
11. *Ibid.*, 307.

12. N. V. Gogol, *Collected Tales and Plays*, trans. Constance Garnett, ed. Leonard J. Kent (New York, 1964), 566.
13. Terras, *The Young Dostoevsky*, 14-15; for discussions of parody, see Wido Hempel, "Parodie, Travestie und Pastiche," *Germanisch-Romanische Monatsschrift*, 46 (April 1965), 150-176, and Yu. Tynyanov, "Dostoevsky i Gogol (K teorii parodii)," in *Texte der Russischen Formalisten*, ed. Jurij Striedter (Munich, 1969): 1: 301-371. This volume reprints the original Russian texts, with a facing German translation.
14. Cited in V. I. Kuleshov, *Naturalnaya Shkola v Literature XIX Veka* (Moscow, 1965), 256. This is a very informative study devoted entirely to the Natural School of the 1840s.
15. *Evolutsia*, 390.
16. M. Bakhtin, *Problemy Poetiki Dostoevskogo* (2d ed., Moscow, 1963). The analysis of Dostoevsky's language is contained in Chapter 5.

CHAPTER 12

1. Cited in Grossman, *DZhP*, 121.
2. *Pisma*, 1: 82; October 8, 1845.
3. Ivan Turgenev, *Literary Reminiscences*, trans. David Magarschack (New York, 1958), 148.
4. *Pisma*, 1: 84; November 16, 1845.
5. *Ibid.*, 84-85.
6. *Ibid.*
7. *Ibid.*, 82-83; October 8, 1845.
8. *Ibid.*, 84; November 16, 1845.
9. *Ibid.*
10. *DVS*, 1: 140.
11. *Ibid.*, 141.
12. *Ibid.*
13. *Ibid.*, 142.
14. *Ibid.*, 142-143.
15. *Pisma*, 1: 102; November 26, 1846.
16. *DVS*, 1: 131-132.
17. *Pisma*, 1: 90; April 26, 1846.

18. For details, see *DVS*, 1: 154-157.
19. *Ibid.*, 2: 191.
20. *Pisma*, 4: 143; May 14, 1880; see also *DVS*, 1: 399 for the facts so far as they are known.
21. K. Chukovsky, "Dostoevsky i Pleyada Belinskogo," in *N. A. Nekrasov: Stati i Materialy* (Leningrad, 1926), 348.
22. *Pisma*, 1: 85; November 16, 1845.
23. *Ibid.*, 89; April 1, 1846.
24. *Ibid.*, 107-108; January-February 1847.
25. It is reprinted in Grossman, *DZhP*, 121-122.
26. Cited in Chukovsky, 348.
27. Reprinted by Chukovsky, 350-367; see also V. Evgenyev-Maksimov, *Zhizn i Deyatelnost N. A. Nekrasova*, 3 vols. (Leningrad, 1950), 2: 198-205.

CHAPTER 13

1. *DW* (January 1877), 587-588.
2. *Pisma*, 1: 81; October 8, 1845.
3. *Ibid.*, 85; November 16, 1845.
4. *Ibid.*, 86; February 1, 1846.
5. *Ibid.*, 86-87.
6. Cited in *DRK*, 30.

7. Grigorovich, *Polnoe Sobranie Sochinenii*, 12: 273.
8. Annenkov, *Decade*, 151.
9. *DRK*, 27.
10. *Ibid.*, 28.
11. *Pisma*, 1: 88; April 1, 1846.

12. *Ibid.*, 89.
13. *Ibid.*
14. *Ibid.*
15. *Ibid.*, 102; November 26, 1846.
16. *Ibid.*, 103.
17. Belinsky, *Works*, 384.
18. *Ibid.*, 385.
19. *Ibid.*
20. V. G. Belinsky, *Izbrannye Pisma*, 2 vols. (Moscow, 1955), 2: 296-297. Cited henceforth as *IP*.
21. *Pisma*, 1: 100; end of October, 1846.

22. *Ibid.*, 78; May 4, 1845.
23. Belinsky, *Works*, 478.
24. *Pisma*, 1: 103; November 26, 1846.
25. Belinsky, *IP*, 2: 369-370.
26. N. F. Belchikov, *Dostoevsky v Protsesse Petrashevtsev* (2d ed.: Moscow, 1971), 105.
27. Belinsky, *IP*, 2: 388.
28. *Ibid.*
29. Cited in Grossman, ZT, 52.

CHAPTER 14

1. *Pisma*, 2: 364; May 18/30, 1871.
2. V. L. Komarovich, "Yunost Dostoevskogo," reprinted in *O Dostoevskom*, intro. Donald Fanger (Providence, R.I., 1966), 78. Komarovich's article, originally published in 1924, is still one of the best studies of this period of Dostoevsky's life, though it needs correction in detail.
3. Victor Considérant, *La Destinée sociale*, 3 vols. (Paris, 1851), 2: 38.
4. Belinsky, *Works*, 165-166.
5. Maxime Leroy, *Histoire des idées sociales en France*, 3 vols. (Paris, 1946-1954), 2: 442.
6. Belinsky, *Works*, 328.
7. *Pisma*, 1: 83; October 8, 1845.
8. Annenkov, *Decade*, 35.
9. Turgenev, *Literary Reminiscences*, 123.
10. Belinsky, *IP*, 2: 259.
11. Karl Löwith, *From Hegel to Nietzsche* (New York, 1967), 336.
12. Annenkov, *Decade*, 211-213.
13. Belinsky, *IP*, 2: 286.
14. Belinsky, *Works*, 369.
15. V. Evgenyev-Maksimov, *Sovremmenik v 40-50 Godov* (Leningrad, 1934), 143-144.
16. Belinsky, *IP*, 2: 302.
17. Annenkov, *Decade*, 208.
18. Belinsky, *IP*, 2: 389.

19. A. Rammelmeyer, "Dostoevskij's Begegnung mit Belinskij," *Zeitschrift für Slavische Philologie*, 21 (1951-1952), 1-5.
20. *DW* (No. 1, 1873), 6-7.
21. *Ibid.*, 148.
22. *Ibid.*, 6.
23. Belinsky, *IP*, 2: 259.
24. *DW* (No. 1, 1873), 7.
25. *Ibid.*
26. *Ibid.*
27. *Pisma*, 2: 364; May 18/30, 1871.
28. *DW* (No. 1, 1873), 8.
29. *Ibid.*
30. *Ibid.*, 9.
31. See the "Zapiska o Dele Petrashevtsev," written by F. N. Lvov and found among the papers left by Herzen. *Literaturnoe Nasledstvo*, No. 63 (Moscow, 1956), 188.
32. *DVS*, 1: 169.
33. Konstantin Leontyev, *Sobranie Sochinenii*, 9 vols. (Moscow, 1912), 8: 199.
34. See Henri de Lubac, *Le Drame de l'humanisme athée* (Paris, 1950), esp. Part 3 and also the penetrating remarks, based on a wide knowledge of the sources, in Andrzej Walicki, *W Kręgu Konserwatywnej Utopii* (Warsaw, 1964), Chapter 14.
35. Löwith, 334-335.

CHAPTER 15

1. *Pisma*, 1: 95; September 17, 1846.
2. *Ibid.*; October 7, 1846.
3. *Ibid.*, 103; November 26, 1846.
4. Grigorovich, *Vospominania*, 277.
5. *Ibid.*
6. Cited from the memoirs of Flerovsky in *Sorokovie Gody XIX Veka* (Moscow, 1959), 191. This is a collection of texts illustrating the social-cultural situation in the 1840s.
7. Sakulin, *Russkaya Literatura*, 348.

8. Kuleshov, *Naturalnaya Shkola*, 145.
9. A. N. Pleshcheev, *Polnoe Sobranie Stikhotvorenii* (Leningrad, 1964), 83.
10. *Pisma*, 1: 95; September 17, 1846.
11. *Ibid.*; November 26, 1846.
12. F. M. Dostoevsky, *Dnevnik Pisatelya za 1873 God* (Paris, n.d.), 47.
13. Valerian Maikov, *Kriticheskoe Opyty* (St. Petersburg, 1891), 25-31.
14. See the useful brochure of T.

Usakina, *Petrashevtsy i Literaturno-Obschestvennoe Dvizhenie Sorokovykh Godov XIX Veka* (Saratov, 1965), 95 and *passim* in Chapter 1.

15. Maikov, 394.
16. *Ibid.*, 325.
17. *Ibid.*, 327.
18. *Ibid.*
19. *Ibid.*, 328.
20. *Ibid.*, 342.
21. *Ibid.*, 129.
22. *Ibid.*, 62.
23. *Ibid.*, 68.

24. *Ibid.*, 295.
25. *Ibid.*, 66.
26. *Ibid.*, 64.
27. See the article on "Nationality" in *Proizvedeniya Petrashevtsev*, 193-195.
28. Evgenyev-Maksimov, *Sovremmennik*, 117.
29. Annenkov, *Decade*, 218.
30. Belinsky, *Works*, 371.
31. *Ibid.*, 359-360.
32. *Ibid.*, 363.
33. *Ibid.*, 375.

CHAPTER 16

1. *Pisma*, 1: 84-85; November 16, 1845.
2. *Ibid.*, 87; February 1, 1846.
3. *Ibid.*, 97; October 7, 1845.
4. *Ibid.*, 104; December 17, 1846.
5. Cited in V. L. Komarovich, "Petersburgskie feletony Dostoevskogo," in *Feletony sorokovykh godov*, ed. Yu. Oksman (Moscow-Leningrad, 1930), 93.
6. Cited in V. S. Nechaeva, *V. G. Belinsky*, 4 vols. (Leningrad, 1949-1967), 4: 298.
7. This work has been identified as *Sboyev*, by A. Nestroyev. The name is a pseudonym for P. N. Kudryavtsev, a

friend of Belinsky, who later became Professor of History at the University of Moscow. Belinsky commented on the same character and scene that Dostoevsky had also singled out. Belinsky, *Works*, 477.
8. Herzen, *MPT*, 2: 549.
9. A. I. Herzen, *Sochinenia*, 10 vols. (Moscow, 1955), 2: 382-383.
10. Cited in A. G. Tseitlin, *I. A. Goncharov* (Moscow, 1950), 6.
11. *Ibid.*, 62.
12. *Pisma*, 1: 106; January-February 1847.
13. See Komarovich, note 5 above.

CHAPTER 17

1. *Pisma*, 1: 106; January-February, 1847.
2. Belchikov, *Protsesse*, 124. This volume, first published in 1936, reproduces all the official documents concerning Dostoevsky's involvement in the Petrashevsky affair along with excellent editorial comments and clarification. The second edition includes valuable new material and a new introduction. The introduction by the editor to the first edition is also highly recommended.
3. Cited in V. I. Semevsky, *M. V. Butashevich-Petrashevsky i Petrashevtsev* (Moscow, 1922), 71. This is still the best work on the subject.
4. *Proizvedenia Petrashevtsev*, ed. V. I. Evgrafova (Moscow, 1953), 184.
5. *Ibid.*, 370.
6. Semevsky, 153.
7. *Ibid.*, 85.
8. Belchikov, 96.
9. *Ibid.*
10. Semevsky, 108.
11. *Ibid.*

12. *Ibid.*
13. *DVS*, 1: 169.
14. Belchikov, 107.
15. *Ibid.*, 96.
16. Miller and Strakhov, *Biografia*, 91.
17. *Delo Petrashevtsev*, ed. V. R. Leikina, E. A. Korolchuk, and V. A. Desnitsky, 3 vols. (Moscow-Leningrad, 1937-1951), 3: 412.
18. Oksman, *LZT*, 501.
19. *DVS*, 1: 181.
20. Belchikov, 100.
21. *Petrashevtsy*, ed. P. S. Schegolev, 3 vols. (Moscow-Leningrad, 1926-1928), 1: 92.
22. *Delo Petrashevtsev*, 3: 3-4.
23. Belchikov, 99.
24. *Ibid.*, 106.
25. *Ibid.*
26. *Ibid.*, 107.
27. *Delo Petrashevtsev*, 3: 442.
28. *DVS*, 1: 209.
29. Belchikov, 111.
30. *Ibid.*, 146.

31. Evgenyev-Maksimov, *Sovremmenik*, 213.
32. Milyutin, *Izbrannye proizvedenia* (Moscow, 1946), 355.
33. Belchikov, 146; Sakulin, 174-175.
34. *DVS*, 1: 185.
35. *Ibid.*
36. Belchikov, 112, 226.
37. See A. S. Dolinin, "Dostoevsky sredi Petrashevtsev," *Zvenya*, No. 6 (Moscow-Leningrad, 1936), 528-529.
38. Franco Venturi, *Roots of Revolution*, trans. Frances Haskell (New York, 1960), 85.

39. August von Haxthausen, *Studies on the Interior of Russia*, trans. Eleonore L. M. Schmidt, ed. S. Frederick Starr (Chicago, 1972), 89.
40. Belchikov, 123.
41. *Delo Petrashevtsev*, 3: 225.
42. *Ibid.*, 250.
43. Belchikov, 112.
44. Miller and Strakhov, *Biografia*, 90-91.
45. *DVS*, 1: 211.
46. *Ibid.*, 186.

CHAPTER 18

1. *Petrashevtsy*, 1: 134.
2. *Ibid.*, 75.
3. *DVS*, 1: 206.
4. *Petrashevtsy*, 1: 135.
5. Karl Marx, *Frühe Schriften*, ed. Hans-Joachim Lieber and Peter Furth, 2 vols. (Darmstadt, 1971), 1: 828. This reference, if nothing else, has guaranteed Dézamy's immortality.
6. Semevsky, *Petrashevsky*, 192.
7. *Proizvedenia Petrashevtsev*, 489.
8. *Ibid.*
9. *Ibid.*, 492.
10. *Ibid.*, 496-497.
11. *Petrashevtsy*, 3: 60.
12. Semevsky, 194.
13. *Ibid.*, 124.
14. *Ibid.*, 125.
15. *Ibid.*, 130.

16. *Petrashevtsy*, 3: 63.
17. Belchikov, *Protsesse*, 265.
18. This account is now available in *ibid.*, 271-274.
19. *Petrashevtsy*, 1: 59.
20. *Ibid.*, 3: 69.
21. Miller and Strakhov, *Biografia*, 90.
22. *Proizvedenia Petrashevtsev*, 503-504.
23. *DW* (No. 50, 1873), 147.
24. *DVS*, 1: 172.
25. Miller and Strakhov, *Biografia*, 85.
26. *DVS*, 1: 184.
27. *Ibid.*, 1: 173.
28. *DW* (April 1876), 312.
29. Cited by Dolinin, *Zvenya*, No. 6 (1936), 533.

CHAPTER 19

1. *Delo Petrashevtsev*, 3: 272-273.
2. Belchikov, *Protsesse*, 139.
3. *Petrashevtsy*, 3: 59.
4. Auguste Barbier, *Iambes et poëmes* (Paris, 1871), 158.
5. *DVS*, 1: 184-185.
6. *Petrashevtsy*, 3: 124.
7. Belchikov, 141.
8. *Ibid.*
9. See, most recently, Jean Drouilly, *La Pensée politique et religieuse de Dostoievski* (Paris, 1971), 116. My interpretation of the facts differs totally from that of Drouilly, whose aim is to prove that Dostoevsky, as a Christian, could never have been a genuine radical.
10. *Petrashevtsy*, 3: 385.
11. *A Soldier's Conversation* is reprinted in *Delo Petrashevtsev*, 3: 233-237.
12. *Ibid.*, 250.
13. *Petrashevtsy*, 3: 200.

14. Cited in D. O. Evans, *Social Romanticism in France*, 39.
15. E. M. Feoktistov, *Vospominania* (Leningrad, 1929), 164; cited in V. R. Leikina - Svirskaya, "Revolutsionnaya Praktika Petrashevtsev," *Istoricheskie Zapiski* 47 (1954), 210-211. Feoktistov, later a powerful bureaucrat, was one of the students to whom Pleshcheev spoke.
16. *Delo Petrashevtsev*, 3: 295.
17. *Ibid.*, 226.
18. Belchikov, 144.
19. Miller and Strakhov, *Biografia*, 90.
20. *Delo Petrashevtsev*, 3: 419.
21. *Ibid.*, 424-425.
22. *Ibid.*, 426.
23. *Ibid.*, 427.
24. *Ibid.*, 435.
25. *Petrashevtsy*, 3: 201.
26. Both are cited in Belinsky, *Works*, 529.
27. *Ibid.*, 506.

28. *Ibid.*, 506-507.
29. *Ibid.*, 504.
30. *Delo Petrashevtsev*, 3: 435.

31. *Ibid.*, 436.
32. *DVS*, 1: 193.

CHAPTER 20

1. *Pisma*, 1: 78; May 8, 1845.
2. *Ibid.*, 81; October 8, 1845.
3. *Ibid.*, 108; January-February 1847.
4. *Ibid.*
5. The most recent study is Natalie Reber, *Studien zum Motiv des Doppelgängers bei Dostoevskij und E. T. A. Hoffmann* (Geissen, 1964); also Charles Passage, *Dostoevski the Adapter* (Chapel Hill, N.C., 1954). Passage's book is vitiated by the idea indicated in the title—that Dostoevsky did nothing else but "adapt" Hoffmann.
6. Vinogradov, *Evolutsiia*, 214.
7. *Pisma*, 1: 81; February 1, 1846.
8. G. M. Fridlender, *Realizm Dostoevskogo* (Moscow-Leningrad, 1964), 70.
9. F. Evnin, *"Ob Odnoi Istoriko-Literaturnoi Legenda," Russkaya Literatura* 2 (1965), 3-26.
10. See his influential article "Zabitie Liudi" in *DRK*, 58-94.
11. This is a point well brought out in Evnin's article (note 9 above), though he reads the work much too exclusively in the Dobrolyubov tradition for me to accept his view as a whole.
12. Bakhtin, *Problemy Poetiki Dostoevskogo*, 291-292; Vinogradov, 261-267.
13. See Terras, *The Young Dostoevsky*, 206-212; M. F. Lomagin, "K Vo-

prosu o Positsii Avtora v 'Dvoinike' Dostoevskogo," *Filologicheskie Nauki* 14 (1971), 3-13; most recently, Wolf Schmid, *Der Textaufbau in den Erzählungen Dostoevskijs* (Munich, 1973), 85-146.
14. Cited in A. L. Bem, *U Istokov*, 143.
15. V. G. Belinsky, "Petersburgskii Sbornik," in *DRK*, 27.
16. P. V. Annenkov, *Vospominania i Kriticheskie Ocherki*, 3 vols. (St. Petersburg, 1879), 2: 23.
17. These notes are now in 1: 432-435; they have been translated in *The Unpublished Dostoevsky*, ed. Carl R. Proffer (Ann Arbor, Mich., 1973), 1: 15.
18. A detailed study of these revisions can be found in the article by P. I. Avanesov, "Dostoevskii v rabote nad 'Dvoinikom,'" in *Tvorcheskaya Istoria*, ed. N. K. Piksanov (Moscow, 1927), 154-191.
19. *Pisma*, 1: 257; October 1, 1859.
20. *DW* (November 1877), 882-883.
21. This tendency is regrettably manifest in the otherwise classic study of Dimitri Chizhevsky, "The Theme of *The Double* in Dostoevsky," in *Dostoevsky*, ed. René Wellek (Englewood Cliffs, N.J., 1962), 112-129.

CHAPTER 21

1. *Pisma*, 1: 95; September 17, 1846.
2. Cited in the excellent article of Yu. Mann, "Filosofia i Poetika 'Naturalnoi Shkoli,'" in *Problemi Tipologii Russkogo Realizma*, ed. N. L. Stepanov and Yu. R. Fokht (Moscow, 1969), 282.
3. Maikov, *Opyty*, 291.
4. See, for example, Terras, *The Young Dostoevsky*, 26; but for the opposite view, see Schmid, *Der Textaufbau in den Erzählungen Dostoevskijs*, 148-171.
5. For a discussion of Mikhail Dosto-

evsky as a writer, see Kuleshov, *Naturalnaya Shkola*, 230-232 and *passim*.
6. *Pisma*, 1: 85; November 16, 1845.
7. A translation of this text into English, by Frederick K. Plous, is included as Appendix I in Terras, 291-298. My citations are taken from this version.
8. I should like to express my gratitude to my colleague, Professor Clarence Brown, for his help in translating this passage.
9. Terras, 47.
10. Bakhtin, *Problemy*, 337.

CHAPTER 22

1. There has been a rash of discussion about this formula recently in

Russian criticism. For a summary, which places a similar assertion in the mouth of Turgenev, see S. A. Reiser, "Iz Istorii Formuli 'Vse mi Vishli iz Gogolevskogo Shineli," in *Poetika i Stilistika Russkoi Literaturi* (Leningrad, 1971), 187-189.

2. Cited in *Istoria Russkogo Romana*, I: 272.

3. Vladimir Nabokov, *Nikolai Gogol* (Norfolk, Conn., 1964), 63-74.

4. *Pisma*, I: 108; January-February 1847.

5. See A. L. Bem, "Dramatizatsiya Breda (*Khozyaika* Dostoevskogo)," in his collection of studies, *Dostoevskii* (Prague, 1938), 77-141.

6. Belinsky, *Works*, 478.

7. See the interesting article by Rudolf Neuhäuser, "*The Landlady*: A New Interpretation," *Canadian Slavonic Papers* 10 (1968), 57.

8. Yu. M. Proskurina, "Povestvovatel-rasskazchik v romane F. M. Dostoevskogo *Belie Nochi*," *Filologicheski Nauki*, 9 (1966), 133.

CHAPTER 23

1. *Pisma*, I: 97; October 7, 1846.

2. *Ibid.*, 100; end of October 1846.

3. *Ibid.*, 104; December 17, 1846.

4. *Ibid.*, 108; January-February 1847.

5. *Ibid.*, 89; April 1, 1846.

6. *Ibid.*, 104; December 17, 1846.

7. *Ibid.*, 108; January-February 1847.

8. Miller and Strakhov, *Biografia*, 91.

9. For more information, see George Siegel, "The Fallen Woman in Nineteenth Century Russian Literature," *Harvard Slavic Studies* No. 5 (1970), 81-107.

Freud's Case-History of Dostoevsky*

It is well known that the discovery of the importance of Dostoevsky's work in Western Europe, and the acceptance of his novels as an astonishing harbinger of the crisis of values that has haunted Western culture for the past half-century, coincided with the development of psychoanalysis and the growth of its influence. Dostoevsky's novels—whose main characters so often wrestle with repressed aspects of their personality, and whose psychology, in most cases, is so emotionally ambivalent—could not but help attract the attention of Freud himself and the growing army of his disciples, who were only too happy to cull examples from the latest cultural idol with which to illustrate and garnish their speculations.

Dostoevsky's works proved to be a goldmine for psychoanalysts because, as Freud remarked, "he [Dostoevsky] cannot be understood without psychoanalysis–i.e., he isn't in need of it because he illustrates it himself in every character and every sentence." These words come from a letter that Freud wrote to Stefan Zweig in 1920;[1] and they show that even at this relatively early date, Freud had already become fascinated with the Russian novelist. This interaction between psychoanalysis and Dostoevsky scholarship in Germany was crowned by Freud's notable essay, "Dostoevsky and Parricide," first printed in 1928 as the preface to a volume in the famous German edition of Dostoevsky's works–the Piper edition–containing some of the material in Dostoevsky's notebooks and letters relating to The Brothers Karamazov.

Freud's article was translated into English the very next year and published in a journal called The Realist. Ever since then it has occupied a prominent place in much of the writing outside of Russia devoted to the study of Dostoevsky's character and its relation to his work. There was, to be sure, some expression of dissent in Freud's inner circle at the time his article appeared. Theodore Reik answered it in the second issue of Imago, protesting against what he considered the rather philistine view of Dostoevsky implicit in Freud's remarks.

---

*This Appendix first appeared in the T.L.S., July 18, 1975, and is included here by permission.

Freud criticizes Dostoevsky for the "compromise with morality" inherent in the belief that "a man who has gone through the depths of sin can reach the highest summits of morality"; and Reik countered that Freud seems to place a stamp of unconditional approval on the dullest conformist to the ethical code of society in preference to Dostoevsky. Freud parried in an exchange of private letters that indicated he did not wish to become seriously engaged in arguing the matter. On the one hand, he said that he accepted Reik's "subjective psychological view of ethics"; but, on the other, he maintained that "I should not wish to deny the excellent Philistine a certificate of good ethical conduct, even though it has cost him little self-discipline." He added that his paper on Dostoevsky was just a "triviality," which he did not think warranted any more extensive consideration.[2]

Reik's article did not arouse any public interest in debating Freud's point of view; and with the exception of another article by E. H. Carr in 1930, which raised questions about Freud's acceptance of one factual point[3]—we shall return to this matter later—there has been very little critical discussion of the text. Philip Rieff has remarked in passing on Freud's "facile identification" of the novelist's later support of Tsarism with his attitude towards his father.[4] Fritz Schmidl, in 1965, traced Freud's evident hostility towards Dostoevsky to the fact that, at the time he was analyzing the great defender of the need for religious faith, he was also at work on *The Future of an Illusion*. For the most part, however, Freud's article has been hailed as a classic work, the most extended psychoanalytic exploration of a major literary figure by the founder of psychoanalysis, and a canonical text for the psycho-historical investigations which have now become so much the vogue.

It so happens that my own work on Dostoevsky has led me, in the course of the past year or two, to review all the available source material concerning Dostoevsky's life, and particularly the material relating to his early years on which Freud naturally focuses. In the course of doing so, I became aware of disturbing discrepancies between this material and the account of Dostoevsky that Freud gives—an account which I had long accepted as being reliable in its data, even if, as is so often the case with psychoanalysis, the conclusions drawn from such data could only be highly conjectural. As a result my curiosity was aroused, and I decided to see if I could pin down my uneasiness about Freud's article with some precision. How reliable is Freud on the purely factual level, so far as this can be established? What are his sources, and how did he use them? These are questions it seemed to me worth trying to answer in the interest of historical truth.

Freud's knowledge of Dostoevsky is revealed in the letter to Stefan Zweig, already quoted (October 19, 1920), thanking his friend for having sent him a copy of his book, *Three Masters*. This work contains a biographical study of Dostoevsky along with two others on Balzac and Dickens (actually, Zweig's long essay is an expressionistic rhapsody very short on "facts" and information and very long on overheated lyricism). Declaring himself quite satisfied with Zweig's treatment of both the English and French author, Freud adds, however, that "the confounded Russian Dostoevsky" is another story. "Here," Freud remarks, "one feels gaps and unsolved riddles"; and he then proceeds "to produce some material" to solve these riddles "as it comes to my layman's mind." Freud means, of course, that he is a "layman" as a literary critic or historian; but far from disqualifying him from venturing an opinion about Dostoevsky, he thinks that in this instance quite the opposite is true. "It is also possible that here the psychopathologist, whose property Dostoevsky must inevitably remain, has some advantage." (One suspects that Freud may have felt piqued and challenged by Zweig's remark that "not the psychologists, men of science though they be, have laid bare the deep recesses of the modern soul, but the men of genius who overstepped all frontiers.")[5]

Zweig's portrait of Dostoevsky as a mad Russian genius—the Rasputin of literature, as it were—laid stress on epilepsy as a key to his enigmatic character; but Freud objects to the notion that Dostoevsky was a true epileptic. "Epilepsy is an organic brain disease independent of the psychic constitution," he writes, "and as a rule associated with the deterioration and retrogression of the mental performance." True epilepsy, in Freud's view, always leads to mental degeneration (or almost always; the great scientist Helmholtz is cited as the single known counter-example). What is generally considered epilepsy in men of genius, according to Freud—who is here polemicizing with the then influential theory of Cesare Lombroso—are always "straight cases of hysteria." So-called epileptic geniuses thus fall within the province of psychiatry rather than of medicine, since "hysteria springs from the *psychic constitution itself* [italics added] and is an expression of the same organic basic power which produces the genius of an artist." As a result, Freud says, "I feel that the whole case of D. could have been built on his hysteria."

However, Freud is not content with attributing Dostoevsky's genius solely to an innately hysterical psychic constitution. For he assures Zweig that, important though Dostoevsky's "constitution" may be as a cause of hysteria, "it is nevertheless interesting that the other factor to which our theory [psychoanalysis] attaches importance can also be demonstrated in this case." This "other factor" turns out to be a severe punishment for some childhood offense. "Somewhere in a biography of D.," Freud writes, "I was shown a passage which traced back the later affliction of the man to the boy's having been punished by his father under very serious circumstances—I vaguely remember the word 'tragic,' am I right? Out of 'discretion,' of course, the author didn't say what it was all about."

Freud, though, knows very well what it was "all about"—it was about the classic threat of punishment for masturbation which creates a castration complex. He does not, to be sure, say so explicitly; but he remarks that Zweig, as the author of *Erste Erlebnisse*—a volume of short stories dealing with the sexual awakening of children and adolescents—would certainly know what he was alluding to. "It was this childhood scene . . . which gave to the later scene before the execution the traumatic power to repeat itself as an attack, and D.'s whole life is dominated by his twofold attitude to the father-tsar-authority, by voluptuous masochistic submission on the one hand, and by outraged rebellion against it on the other. Masochism includes a sense of guilt which surges toward 'redemption.' "

This is Freud's original sketch of his analysis of Dostoevsky; and a number of points in it call for comment. First, the question of whether Dostoevsky's epilepsy was "organic" or "psychic" in character. I am not competent to utter a word about the rightness or wrongness of Freud's views from a scientific point of view; but there is one fact of Dostoevsky's biography that Freud does not mention either now or later, and which has some relevance to this question. In May 1878 Dostoevsky's three-year-old son Aleksey died suddenly because of a severe and unexpected epileptic attack lasting three hours and ten minutes. It would thus appear that epilepsy ran in Dostoevsky's family, and that the child had probably inherited it from his father. This creates a strong presumption that Dostoevsky's epilepsy was organic in origin and not primarily hysterical. But since Freud, as we know, was an unrepentant Lamarckian, who continued to believe in the inheritance of acquired characteristics long after this view was generally abandoned, he might well have argued that the epilepsy originated with the writer nonetheless.

Secondly, there is the reference to the passage that Freud once saw in a biography. This can only refer to a tantalizing footnote in the official biography (1883) by Orest Miller and Nikolay Strakhov.[6] In the section written by Miller, he remarks that, according to a well-informed source, there was "a very particular piece of evidence about the illness of Feodor Mikhailovich which relates to his earliest youth and connects it with a tragic event in their [the Dostoevskys] family life." Freud, as we have seen, immediately transforms this into a reference to a castrating incident by a tyrannical father, even though there is nothing about either "punishment" or "father" in the passage. Moreover, Dostoevsky scholars agree that the footnote, in all probability, contains an allusion to the murder of Dostoevsky's father in the spring of 1839, when Dostoevsky, a student at the Academy of Engineers, was eighteen years old and by no means the "child" Freud thinks him to have been. To be sure, Freud could not have known about the murder when he wrote his letter; the event became public knowledge only with the appearance in 1921 of the memoirs of Dostoevsky's daughter Lyubov.

Freud's ignorance of the murder is also important in interpreting the final sentence quoted from his letter. At this point, he could only have assumed that Dostoevsky's first epileptic attack occurred in the 1850s while he was in prison camp. By "the later scene before the execution," Freud is presumably referring to the mock execution ceremony arranged by Nicholas I. Dostoevsky was led to believe that he and his companions under arrest in 1849 were going to be shot by a firing squad; but a few moments later they learned their true sentences of exile and hard labor. Freud links Dostoevsky's previous punishment by his father as a boy with this later "scene," and seems to mean that the psychic pressure induced by this repetition of his childhood trauma finally brought on epilepsy shortly thereafter in Siberia. In this way, Dostoevsky's alternating pattern between masochistic submission and outraged rebellion became established for the remainder of his life.

Here we have Freud's first stab at working out a case-history for Dostoevsky; and one cannot help admiring the ingenuity with which he does so. Even without knowing anything about the murder of Dostoevsky's father, he manages to interpret his epilepsy as a symptom of an unresolved conflict between submission and revolt.

3

Eight years later, Freud has learned about the murder and the family story connected with it. "According to family traditions," Lyubov Dostoevsky wrote in her book, "it was on learning of the death of his father that Dostoevsky had his first attack of epilepsy."[7] This new information now becomes the center of Freud's interpretation; the "scene" before the firing-squad is mentioned tangentially, but it no longer plays any determining role in *causing* the epilepsy.

Freud's article is considerably expanded over the casual remarks he makes in his letter, and it contains a much fuller treatment of his point of view. This is not the place to discuss all the implications of that point of view—not only the implications pointed out by Reik, but such an excursion into ethnopsychology as the remark that Dostoevsky's "compromise with morality" was "a characteristically Russian trait" which can also be seen in Ivan the Terrible, as well as in the behavior "of the barbarians of the great migrations, who murdered and did penance for it, till penance became an actual technique for enabling murder to be done." I do not wish to quarrel with Freud's opinions or ideas, but to limit myself solely to the facts he adduces to support his argument. This argument begins, as it did in the letter, with a much lengthier discussion of whether Dostoevsky's epilepsy was "organic" or "affective." Freud is much more cautious in writing for publication, and admits that "we know too little in this instance to make any confident diagnosis." But he nonetheless concludes that it is "extremely probable" Dostoevsky's disease was of the second type.

Freud's analysis of Dostoevsky's psychic constitution is also much more detailed, but a good bit of it has nothing in particular to do with Dostoevsky at all—or only as much as with any other male member of the human race. For as background Freud outlines his theory of the Oedipus complex and the inevitable "ambivalence" of the relation of every boy to his father because of a desire for the mother; when this desire is repressed by the threat of castration, it leads to the creation of an unconscious sense of guilt.

Such a "normal process" of psychic development, however, is complicated when the constitution of the child in question contains a strong factor of bisexuality. In such instances, the boy wishes to *replace* the mother as an object of his father's love; but this also involves castration (for how otherwise become a woman?), and so this desire is repressed as well. According to Freud, this latter type of repression leads to a "pathogenic intensification" that is "one of the preconditions or reinforcements of neurosis." Freud finds such a strong feminine attitude of latent homosexuality in Dostoevsky, and cites as proof "the important part played by male friendships in his life . . . his strangely tender attitude towards rivals in love . . . his remarkable understanding of situations which are explicable only by repressed homosexuality, as many examples from his novels show."

These statements are so unspecific that it is difficult to know to what they refer; but they seem to me very questionable all the same.

Freud is probably thinking of the intense male friendships of Dostoevsky's late adolescence with Ivan Berezhetsky, a fellow student at the Academy of Engineers; with the slightly older Ivan Shidlovsky, both a friend and father-figure, at the same period of his life; and perhaps, a few years later, the strong but very short-lived attachment he felt for Turgenev. But all these friendships were very brief, and not at all typical. There are no male friendships in Dostoevsky's life comparable in length and emotional importance to Freud's own friendships with, for example, Wilhelm Fleiss and Josef Breuer. Dostoevsky's relations with women—his two wives, his mistress Apollinaria Suslova, and several others whom he courted or with whom he flirted—were of much greater significance all through his maturity. His later friendships with men, so far as one can judge from the evidence, did not involve any deep emotional ties (with the single exception of his friendship with his older brother, Mikhail), and were based rather on common intellectual interests or ideological convictions.

The same is true about Dostoevsky's attitude towards rivals in love. Presumably, Freud is referring here to Dostoevsky's efforts to obtain a promotion for a young man competing with him for the hand of the widow in Siberia who later became his first wife. His reason for doing so was that, if she did reject him and marry his rival, he did not wish her to live in misery. At the same time, it should be pointed out that he was doing everything in his power to dissuade Mme Isaev from entering on what he thought would be a disastrous marriage and to persuade her to choose him instead.

Also, there are numerous illustrations, both in his letters and in the memoirs of his (much younger) second wife, of his pathological jealousy towards possible rivals. Freud has thus taken the one incident in Siberia and blown it up out of all proportion in relation to other material. It is true that examples of this type of behavior can be found in Dostoevsky's novels, particularly in *The Insulted and Injured*; but such "tenderness" was a literary and cultural cliché of the period. It is far more important both in the life of the revolutionary Nikolay Chernyshevsky, and in his novel *What Is To Be Done?* (entirely based on the theme of the nobility of a self-sacrifice for a rival in love), than anything we can find in Dostoevsky.

4

Freud, in any event, sees Dostoevsky's character-pattern shaped by the combination of his Oedipal ambivalence and a strong bisexual disposition, later becoming transformed into a sadistic superego (the repressed hatred of the father) and a masochistic ego (the repressed wish to become the mother). The severity of a conflict between the two, Freud remarks, depends on "the accidental factor" of "whether the father, who is feared in any case, is also especially violent in reality. This was true in Dostoevsky's case, and we can trace back the fact of his extraordinary sense of guilt and of his masochistic conduct of life to a specially strong feminine component." What "violence" means in a Freudian context is not very clear; but if we take the word in the ordinary sense, as implying physical brutality, then Freud's statement is unsubstantiated. The only evidence we have, given in the memoirs of Dostoevsky's younger brother, Andrey, portrays the elder Dostoevsky as irritable, quick-tempered and despotic; but he disapproved of the corporal punishment of children and never struck his own. Indeed, he sent them all to private schools (though he could scarcely afford the luxury) to avoid the possibility of their being beaten for disciplinary purposes.

Freud's conviction that Dr. Dostoevsky was "especially violent in reality," however, unquestionably goes back to the notion expressed in his letter that Dostoevsky had undergone some "tragic" punishment as a child. This is no longer stated directly as a fact; but Freud cites, in a long footnote, the passage that first established it in his mind, as well as additional material seeming to confirm it. "Of special interest," he writes, "is the information that in the novelist's childhood 'something terrible, unforgettable and agonizing' happened to which the first signs of his illness were to be traced."

Freud's quotation is taken from an article by Aleksey Suvorin, written shortly after Dostoevsky's death and also assumed by Dostoevsky scholarship to allude to the murder of his father. This is followed by the quotation from Miller already given, which Freud has now succeeded in locating. And he remarks, using almost the wording of his letter, that "biographers and scientific research workers cannot feel grateful for [Miller's] discretion" in refusing to specify the "tragic event." This footnote is appended to an assertion that the first symptoms of Dostoevsky's illness appeared in childhood, long before the murder of his father; the references are evidently meant to document some "event" that brought on these first symptoms. Freud, in other words, persists in interpreting this material exactly as he had done before knowing anything about the murder of the father at all. Perhaps he simply did not make the connection, or was misled by the loose use of the word "childhood"; perhaps he stubbornly stuck to his own view despite the weight of opinion, as he did on so many other questions.

To be sure, to have given up his belief in the existence of a specially severe childhood "trauma" in Dostoevsky's life would have been fatal to his theory; he could not have abandoned it without seeing his entire case-history collapse. For he wished to show that the presumed coincidence between the murder of the father and the first epileptic attack was only the culmination of an inner process that had begun a long while before, and which had been triggered by the violence of the father acting on Dostoevsky's innately and strongly bisexual constitution. This had led to the appearance of symptoms in Dostoevsky's childhood foreshadowing the later disease, but not as yet in themselves epileptic. And Freud finds these symptoms confirmed in some other material.

"We have one *certain* starting point," he writes (italics added):

We know the meaning of the first attacks from which Dostoevsky suffered in his early years long before the incidence of the "epilepsy." These attacks had the significance of death; they were heralded by a fear of death and consisted of lethargic, somnolent states. The illness first came over him, while he was still a boy, in the form of a sudden, groundless melancholy, a feeling, as he later told his friend Solovyev, as though he were going to die on the spot. And there in fact followed a state exactly similar to real death. His brother Andrey tells us that even when he was quite young Feodor used to leave little notes about before he went to sleep, saying that he was afraid he might fall into this death-like sleep during the night and therefore begged that his burial should be postponed for five days.

Such symptoms, Freud says, show an identification with a person one wishes dead; and for a boy, "this other person is usually his father . . . and . . . the attack is thus a self-punishment for a death-wish against a hated father."

If such symptoms are really the only "certain" starting-point for Freud's diagnosis of Dostoevsky, then his conclusions can only be said to rest on very "uncertain" premises. For if we turn to the sources, we see that there is no evidence whatever relating such symptoms to Dostoevsky's childhood. He did speak to his friend Vsevolod Solovyev about a fear of death; but he dates it very precisely at a much later time. "My nerves have been unsettled since my youth," he told Solovyev in 1873. "Just about two years before Siberia, at the period of my various literary difficulties and quarrels, I was overcome by some sort of strange and unbearably torturing nervous illness . . . it often seemed to me that I was dying, and really—actual death came and then went away."[8] There is nothing else available that would place such nervous attacks any farther back in Dostoevsky's life than 1846-1847; and they coincide, as we know, with a severe nervous disorder documented in his letters of the time.

Freud's dating is equally mistaken with regard to Dostoevsky's fear of lethargic sleep. Andrey Dostoevsky does not refer to any such symptom in his memoirs dealing with his own childhood and that of his brother. He mentions it in an article he wrote in 1881 to the Russian newspaper *New Times*—an article whose aim was to *deny* that Dostoevsky suffered from anything resembling epilepsy as a child. In the course of doing so, he remarks that he had seen his brother "from 1843 to April 1849" almost every week, and that he had never heard about any such childhood illness even though they often talked about matters of health. "True," he writes, *"within this period of time* (I do not now recall the exact year) he [Feodor] was quite irritable and, it seemed, suffered from some sort of nervous illness [italics added]." The reference to lethargic sleep and the notes follows this sentence, and unmistakably places them *only* within this time-span; they also probably began in 1846-1847.[9]

It is quite likely that the second-hand German sources on which Freud relied only quoted snippets from the Russian material and did not date the information they gave very precisely; his mistakes about these "preliminary symptoms" were thus inadvertent. But there was one issue on which he knew that his own ideas were in conflict with most of the available evidence, and where he continues to maintain them all the same. The issue, quite simply, is whether, if Dostoevsky's epilepsy began in 1839, there is any reason to believe that it ceased or became less severe during his years in Siberia. This is a very important question for Freud because its answer provides a crucial test for his theory.

If it is true that Dostoevsky's first epileptic attack occurred on his hearing about the murder of his father, then this onset of the acute phase of the disease can be interpreted as the expression of a particularly harsh need for self-punishment. He had been repressing a hatred of his father presumably indicated by his earlier symptoms; and "it is a dangerous thing if reality fulfills such repressed wishes. The phantasy has become reality and all defensive measures are thereupon reinforced."

As a result, Dostoevsky's self-punishment "had become terrible, like his father's frightful death itself." When this internal punishment was replaced by the external punishment of a sentence to exile and hard labor for rebellion against the father-figure of the Tsar, the pressure of internal conflict should have been relieved. This is why Freud remarks, a little uneasily, that "it would be very much to the point if it could be established that they [his epileptic attacks] ceased completely during his exile in Siberia; but other accounts contradict this." A few pages later, he reiterates: "If it proved to be the case that Dostoevsky was free from his seizures in Siberia, that would merely substantiate the view that his seizures were his punishment."

Now, it is regrettably awkward for Freud's whole thesis that, according to *all* the evidence *except* the family tradition, Dostoevsky's epilepsy *began* in Siberia; the only possible proof of Freud's argument thus turns out to be a counter-proof. To circumvent this difficulty, he tries to undermine the embarrassing evidence without openly contradicting it. "Most of the accounts," he writes in a footnote, "including Dostoevsky's own . . . assert . . . that the illness only assumed its final, epileptic character during the Siberian exile. Unfortunately there is reason to distrust the autobiographical statements of neurotics. Experience shows that their memory introduces falsifications, which are designed to interrupt disagreeable causal connections."

Freud here clearly imagines Dostoevsky in the role of one of his own patients, asked to recount the past and naturally distorting it under the influence of repression. However, the evidence about Dostoevsky's illness in Siberia does not at all depend on the *memory of a remote past*, as Freud implies. It derives from Dostoevsky's *letters* of the early 1850s, immediately after his release from prison, which mention the outbreak of the disease just a year or two earlier and still indicate uncertainty about whether or not the attacks are genuinely epileptic.

It is scarcely credible to imagine that, in the feverish letters which he poured out to his family on being released from prison-camp—letters in which he tried to tell them everything important that had happened to him in the interim—Dostoevsky should have spoken about epileptic symptoms which had not occurred, or mentioned as a distressing novelty an illness with which he had long been familiar. Moreover, people who knew Dostoevsky well both before and after Siberia all speak of his epilepsy as a new development of these Siberian years. There is just not a single scrap of evidence of any kind to support Freud's position.

Nevertheless, even though his epilepsy probably began (or at least worsened) in Siberia, Dostoevsky's health did improve there in some respects. The symptoms of his "nervous illness" of the 1840s (fear of death, hallucinations, dizziness, hypochondria, etc.) were all alleviated, probably by the hard physical labor he was forced to perform at the camp. In later life, he often mentioned this general improvement of his physical condition; but such statements do not in any way contradict what he says about his epilepsy. Indeed, references to both are often made together—for example, in his letters on being released from prison.

Freud, we may assume, was probably aware of the distinction between the two kinds of illness; but he tends to confuse them for the purposes of his argument. For while in one place he admits that "it cannot be proved that Dostoevsky's epileptic attacks abated in Siberia" (a statement which implies, of course, that some evidence less than "proof" leads him to think this may have been so), elsewhere he remarks that "it appears certain that Dostoevsky's detention in the Siberian prison markedly altered his pathological condition." This last statement is true of Dostoevsky's "nervous illness"; but to a reader unfamiliar with all the details of Dostoevsky's biography, and warned by Freud not to trust the declaration of a neurotic, it certainly creates the presumption that Freud has some good reason besides theoretical necessity for believing Dostoevsky's *epilepsy* to have let up in Siberia.

5

There is still one other matter that needs discussion, though here I can be very brief because the question has been fully explored by E. H. Carr. Freud, as we have seen, accepts the family tradition that Dostoevsky's first attack of epilepsy was caused by hearing about his father's murder. How much credence should be given to this rumor?

Mr. Carr surveyed all the existing material in his 1930 article (nothing additional has come to light since), and found the rumor reflected in the three sources already mentioned: the article of Suvorin, the footnote of Miller, and the explicit assertion of Lyubov Dostoevsky. None of these people had any first-hand knowledge; nor did their presumed original source, Dostoevsky's second wife Anna Grigoryevna. There is no supporting evidence at all by anyone who knew Dostoevsky at the time (1839), even though a number of such people wrote reminiscences when Dostoevsky's epilepsy was known to all the world, and to have revealed the date of his first attack would not have been an indiscretion.

To supplement Mr. Carr's view, I may add that there is no mention of any such attack in the letter Dostoevsky wrote to his brother Mikhail in August 1839 expressing grief at his father's death. We should also remember that Dostoevsky was then sharing common quarters with a hundred other student-engineers, and could scarcely have concealed a severe epileptic attack even if he had wished to do so. It thus seems reasonable to accept Mr. Carr's summary and conclusion:

> The evidence is at best pure hearsay; it contradicts all our other information, written as well as verbal; and it is probable that a story so poorly attested would not have been taken seriously if it had not happened to fit in so well with the hypothesis of the psychoanalysts.[10]

There still remains the question of why such a story should have been spread about by Dostoevsky's second wife if it were not true. Mr. Carr supplies a complicated answer that I do not need to discuss; in my opinion it was probably just a mistake. A year before the murder of Dr. Dostoevsky, in the spring of 1838, Feodor learned that he was not to be promoted at the Academy of Engineers and wrote home to tell his father the bad news. The letter brought on an apoplectic stroke, and the stricken doctor had to be bled in order to relieve his condition. Feodor himself, as a result of all this, fell ill and spent some time in the academy hospital.

My own view is that Dostoevsky, reminiscing about these events with his wife, probably spoke of having fallen ill because of something that had happened to his father, and that this became intertwined with what he may have told her about the murder which occurred at approximately the same time. Obsessed as she was with his epilepsy, she naturally took the illness her husband mentioned to have been the onset of the disease that haunted her life as well as his; and the shocking horror of the murder overshadowed all the other surrounding events of that remote period. This innocent falsification was destined to have an astonishing career when it became the center of the case-history which Freud constructed, out of such fragmentary and questionable data, to deal with the enigma of Dostoevsky.

NOTES TO APPENDIX

[1] *Letters of Sigmund Freud*, selected and edited by Ernst L. Freud, translated by Tania and James Stern (New York, 1960), No. 191, 331-333.

[2] Reik's essay and Freud's reply are discussed in Fritz Schmidl, "Freud and Dostoevsky," *Journal of the American Psychoanalytic Association* 13 (July 1965), 518-532.

[3] E. H. Carr, "Was Dostoevsky an Epileptic?" *The Slavonic and East European Journal* 9 (December 1930), 424-431.

[4] Philip Rieff, *Freud: The Mind of the Moralist* (New York, 1961), 152.

[5] Stefan Zweig, *Master Builders* (New York, 1939), 202-203.

[6] Orest Miller and Nikolay Strakhov, *Biografia, Pisma i Zametki iz Zapisnoi Knizhi F. M. Dostoevskogo* (St. Petersburg, 1883), 141.

[7] Cited in E. H. Carr's article, 428.

[8] Solovyev's article is reprinted in *F. M. Dostoevsky v Vospominaniakh Sovremennikov*, edited by A. S. Dolinin (Moscow, 1964), 2: 191.

[9] The relevant citation from Andrey's article is given in *Literaturnoe Nasledstvo* 86 (Moscow, 1973), 550.

[10] E. H. Carr, 429.

INDEX

Library of Congress Cataloging in Publication Data

Frank, Joseph, 1918-
  Dostoevsky : the seeds of revolt, 1821-1849.

  Includes bibliographical references and index.
    1.   Dostoevskii, Fedor Mikhailovich, 1821-1881.
PG3328.F7   891.7'3'3 [B]   76-3704
ISBN 0-691-06260-9